Vong

The Professional School Counselor

An Advocate for Students

JEANNINE R. STUDER
The University of Tennessee, Knoxville

Australia • Canada • Mexico • Singapore • Spain
United Kingdom • United States

Executive Editor: *Lisa Gebo*
Helping Professions Editor: *Marquita Flemming*
Assistant Editor: *Shelley Gesicki*
Editorial Assistant: *Amy Lam*
Technology Project Manager: *Barry Connolly*
Marketing Manager: *Caroline Concilla*
Marketing Assistant: *Mary Ho*
Advertising Project Manager: *Tami Strang*
Project Manager, Editorial Production: *Trudy Brown*
Art Director: *Vernon Boes*
Print/Media Buyer: *Rebecca Cross*
Permissions Editor: *Stephanie Lee*
Production Service: *Shepherd, Inc.*
Copy Editor: *Jeanne Patterson*
Cover Designer: *Lisa Henry*
Cover Image: *Mary Kate Denny/PhotoEdit, Inc., Michael Newman/PhotoEdit, Inc.*
Compositor: *Shepherd, Inc.*
Text and Cover Printer: *Malloy Incorporated*

Printed in United States of America
1 2 3 4 5 6 7 08 07 06 05 04

Thomson Brooks/Cole
10 Davis Drive
Belmont, CA 94002
USA

Library of Congress Control Number:
2004110210

ISBN 0-534-60777-2

Asia
Thomson Learning
5 Shenton Way #01-01
UIC Building
Singapore 068808

Australia/New Zealand
Thomson Learning
102 Dodds Street
Southbank, Victoria 3006
Australia

Canada
Nelson
1120 Birchmount Road
Toronto, Ontario M1K 5G4
Canada

Europe/Middle East/Africa
Thomson Learning
High Holborn House
50/51 Bedford Row
London WC1R 4LR
United Kingdom

Latin America
Thomson Learning
Seneca, 53
Colonia Polanco
11560 Mexico D.F.
Mexico

Spain/Portugal
Paraninfo
Calle Magallanes, 25
28015 Madrid, Spain

This book is dedicated to

My parents, James and Margaret Steckel, who were my first advocates

My children, Sean and Erin, who taught me more about human growth and development than any text

My husband, Jim, for his love and support

Contents

Preface

- When violent acts occur in schools, school counselors provide assistance and succor.
- When parents need information on the academic and personal growth of their child, school counselors communicate essential information.
- When barriers to learning impair student progress, educators consult with school counselors for strategies to enhance instruction.
- When students need a caring adult, school counselors are available to listen and to advocate for youth.

There is no profession that is more vital to school-aged youth than that of the professional school counselor, who assists students with academic, career, and personal/social issues influencing their lives. The materials in this text present essential information, activities, and personal experiences written by practicing school counselors for individuals training for the role of the professional school counselor. The information provided in this text is intended as an introduction to the field of school counseling, but it also has a secondary purpose. Many of my students who have entered the school counseling profession have often commented that they lack the materials and activities that are often needed to assist students in the school. Therefore, this text has the dual purpose of serving to access information and activities that are needed by a practicing school counselor.

The materials in this text are divided into four parts as outlined in the core curricular and clinical areas identified by the Council for the Accreditation of Counselor and Related Educational Programs (CACREP):

- Part One: Foundations of School Counseling. This part includes history, legal and ethical issues, and procedures for working with students with diverse backgrounds including students with special needs. The specific chapters are
  - From Guidance Worker to Professional School Counselor
  - The Professional School Counselor and Legal and Ethical Issues
  - The Culturally Sensitive Professional School Counselor
  - Students with Special Needs
- Part Two: The Professional School Counselor: An Advocate for Students' Contextual Dimensions. This part includes an understanding of how the school counseling program relates to the entire school mission including accountability, career development, and prevention and intervention strategies. The specific chapters are
  - The Developmental, Comprehensive School Counselor Program
  - The Professional School Counselor and Accountability
  - The Professional School Counselor's Role in Career Development
- Part Three: Knowledge and Skill Requirements for School Counselors. This part is divided into two sections. The first section includes an understanding of program development including the use of tests and technology. The second section contains counseling and guidance information including the school counselor's role in crisis counseling, partnering with families, group work in the schools, and expressive arts in counseling school-aged youth. The specific sections and chapters are

  Section I: Program Development, Implementation, and Evaluation
  - The Professional School Counselor's Role in Testing and Assessment
  - The Internet's Influence on the School Counseling Profession

  Section II: Counseling and Guidance
  - Crisis Counseling and Critical Incident Management
  - The School Counselor and Family Partnership
  - Planning and Implementing Group Work in the Schools
  - Expressive Arts in Counseling Children and Adolescents
- Part Four: Clinical Instruction. School counseling students often express concern about the clinical experiences that are required in the counselor education program. This section includes information about supervision in clinical experiences and a section on consultation, a vital role of the school counselor that is often overlooked in training. The chapter included in this section combines not only consultation, considered as a knowledge and skill requirement, but also supervision, which is included in the clinical instruction for school counselors. The chapter is
  - The Supervision Process and the Professional School Counselor as a Consultant

FOR THE STUDENT

This text is intended to provide you with a foundation of the role of the school counselor. In addition to the materials in the text, a student workbook supplements the information in the text. The workbook includes a summary of the main concepts, additional activities for self-reflection, and strategies for implementation in a school counselor program. Additionally, resources including Web sites, books, tapes, and so on are listed for additional references and resources.

FOR THE PROFESSOR

An instructor's manual supplements the materials in this course. The manual includes test questions, resources, suggestions for lessons, and a syllabus that may be adapted to meet curricular needs.

ACKNOWLEDGMENTS

I would like to thank the many individuals who contributed their ideas, suggestions, and insights to this text. First, I would like to thank the anonymous reviewers for their thoughtful comments and suggestions. I also want to thank the individuals who contributed chapters to this text:

- Dr. Theresa A. Quigney, Associate Professor Special Education at Cleveland State University, Cleveland, Ohio. Dr. Quigney authored Chapter 4: Students with Special Needs.
- Dr. Judith A. Sommers, Adjunct Professor of School Counseling at Heidelberg College, Tiffin, Ohio, and former school counselor at Norwalk High School, Norwalk, Ohio. Dr. Sommers authored Chapter 6, The Professional School Counselor's Role in Career Development.
- Dr. Carole S. Robinson, Instructional Design. Dr. Robinson authored Chapter 10, The Internet's Influence on the School Counseling Profession.

I also want to acknowledge my former students and practicing school counselors, particularly William Karcher, Robert Douglas Ramsey, and Marlene Putnam; and, Vicki VanNess, counselor at Perkins High School.

My thanks to Dr. Marla Peterson, Professor, the University of Tennessee, for her insightful suggestions.

Finally, my deepest gratitude to Wadsworth Publishing Company for the opportunity to write this text. In particular I want to thank Shelley Gesicki and Marquita Flemming for their patience and encouragement.

PART I

Foundations of School Counseling

The chapters in the Foundations of School Counseling section provide information surrounding the history and current trends of the profession, and the school counselor's training and leadership as an integral component of the total school mission. Legal and ethical issues guiding the profession with respect to the many constituents who have a stake in the growth of students form the support structure of the program. Furthermore, as the face of society changes, school counselors have the unique opportunity to gain an understanding of diverse student populations and to develop tools to assist these students and their families.

The chapters in this section include: From Guidance Worker to Professional School Counselor, The Professional School Counselor and Legal and Ethical Issues, The Culturally Sensitive School Counselor, Students with Special Needs.

1

From Guidance Worker to Professional School Counselor

Recently, my nephew phoned me to share his excitement at being offered his first teaching position. He was quite ecstatic because he would not only work at the high school my father and his grandfather served as a former principal but he would also teach in the area for which he was trained and coach two sports. This news brought a smile to my face not only because of his enthusiasm but because I remembered the excitement I felt when I was hired for my first "real" job after graduating from college. But the rest of his news made me catch my breath, and I felt my heart pound as my thoughts rapidly spun around in my mind. The news that caught me so unprepared was his announcement that part of his job was serving as a school counselor for two periods each day.

It was difficult for me to genuinely congratulate him and to share in his joy as I thought back to the time and training (not to mention money) that I spent in pursuing a master's degree and credentialing as a school counselor for a position that was so casually handed over to my nephew without any training in counseling. Although coaches, teachers, advisors, and other adults can make positive changes with youth through listening skills, paraphrasing, questioning, confrontation, and other attending skills used by counselors, the fact remains that they are not counselors. Nor can the interpersonal involvement be considered as a counseling relationship, despite the growth-enhancing changes that often occur between the youth and the influential adult. What, then, is counseling?

The words *counseling* and *counselor* are perplexing terms defined differently by many individuals. Media implore us to see a *weight-loss counselor* if we wish to shed unwanted pounds. Or, if we are in the market for a new automobile and wish to discuss the best model within our budget, an *automobile counselor* can assist in providing the necessary information. Need financial advice? A *financial counselor* can provide assistance.

With the broad definition surrounding the word *counselor,* individuals have difficulty determining just what a counselor does, what the training and educational requirements are, and particularly how a school counselor differs from others in the counseling profession.

WHAT IS COUNSELING?

As in any profession, the individual receiving credentialing as a counselor must abide by the standards, expectations, and educational requirements outlined by the profession (Gibson & Mitchell, 2003). The professional organization that provides direction for the school counselor is the American School Counselor Association (ASCA). According to the position statement of the ASCA entitled *The Professional School Counselor and Credentialing and Licensure* (2003), ". . . ASCA supports the credentialing and employment of those who hold a master's degree in counseling related fields with training in all areas specified by the CACREP standards plus a one-year internship in a school under the supervision of a qualified school counselor and a university supervisor."

Professional school counselors provide the unique services of guidance and counseling, which focus on the academic, career, and personal/social concerns of school-aged youth. The process of counseling involves a professional relationship, is theory driven, and involves decision making and personal change (Gladding, 2004; Nugent, 1994).

The terms *guidance, counseling*, and *therapy* are often used as interchangeable words with similar connotations; in fact, there is some overlap, but there are also some differences. Guidance focuses on helping students make educational, personal, and career decisions based on personal values (Gladding, 2004). Counseling, on the other hand, is a relationship between a professionally-trained counselor that focuses on a student's academic, personal, or vocational needs (Gibson & Mitchell, 203). To further add to the confusion, the term *therapy* is often used with little understanding of how this term differs from counseling and guidance. Traditionally, therapy—or psychotherapy—was viewed as a focus on more serious concerns. Yet, the lines between the terms *counseling* and *psychotherapy* are blurred since counseling theories are often known as therapy with interchangeable skills (Gladding). School counselors do not have the time—nor, in many cases, the training—to deal with students with more serious psychological disorders, but they do provide counseling to individuals with academic, career, and personal/social developmental issues.

No professional is more vital to the lives of children and adolescents than the professional school counselor. No other professional has the opportunity to facilitate the growth of youth, advocate for students, assist parents and/or guardians, coordinate opportunities for educators in the school, and consult with community professionals, all with the purpose of creating a meaningful educational experience for children and adolescents.

In this chapter, a history of the school counseling profession and the progress and pitfalls the profession has faced is presented. The issues currently confronting the profession and a speculation of what the profession will look like in the future are provided. As you read through the historical, social, and economic events that have impacted the profession, think in terms of the activities in which today's school counselors are involved at every level, how you or others have been influenced by school counselors, and where you feel the profession is heading. You are also invited to self-reflect on the skills, experiences, values, attitudes, and knowledge that you bring to the profession that will impact student growth.

THE APPEARANCE OF SCHOOL GUIDANCE WORKERS THROUGHOUT HISTORY

Throughout the history of the world, people have sought assistance in understanding the meaning of life, self, and others. Historical accounts of developing and strengthening one's potential were found in writings from Grecian society, priests provided guidance to parishioners in the Middle Ages (Neukrug, 1999), and gurus were sought for their wisdom. The Industrial Revolution was instrumental in placing guidance workers in schools to guide individuals who sought information and advice.

The Industrial Revolution brought about a change from an agrarian society to an urban factory system. Factories depended upon women and young children as a cheap source of labor (Santrock, 1996). Poor urban children as young as age 6 were sent out to the city streets to scavenge cinders, rope, bottles, or any item that could be exchanged for money. Since these activities removed children from adult supervision, gambling, prostitution, and thievery were common behaviors among youth. Concerns that children were growing up without even a rudimentary education or moral guidance led to child labor and protection laws.

In 1916 child labor laws protected youth from deplorable working conditions and required youth to attend school at least through elementary school. Up until this time, schools were highly selective and only an elite group of wealthy males entered educational institutions to prepare for law, medicine, or the clergy (Schmidt, 1993). Students from diverse backgrounds were now entering schools with a host of issues that had never before been addressed. It was evident that the school structure now needed to be modified, but the question was, "how?"

Classroom teachers were assigned the responsibility of assisting these students. However, since these professionals had neither the time nor the training (Muro & Kottman, 1995; Schmidt, 1993), it was evident that school guidance workers were needed. Not only did career concerns need to be addressed but social and emotional direction was needed as well by this unique group of students.

Additionally, many believed that moral guidance was the answer to the unparalleled situations that were now evident within the educational system.

Proposals to infuse values into the curriculum were met with stiff resistance, particularly by the Roman Catholic Church due to the perception that these values had a Protestant focus (Herr, 2001). It is no surprise that recognition of moral education as a fundamental aspect of the school curriculum was also accompanied with a greater awareness of mental health.

The themes of vocational guidance, character education as a curricular component, and mental hygiene for school-aged youth had a continuing influence on guidance in the schools throughout the 20th century.

1900–1920

> Suddenly, and without the slightest warning, as a petulant child locked in a room for disobedience might treat a pillow, he seized me by an arm and jerked me from the bed. It was fortunate that the bones of my ankles and feet, not yet thoroughly knitted, were not again injured. And this was the performance of the very man who had locked my hands in the muff, that I might not injure myself. (Beers, 1908)

During the first part of the 20th century mental health concerns emerged largely through the work of Clifford Beers, the author of the preceding quote. Career and occupational decision making and using assessment and appraisal tools entered the guidance realm, and untrained guidance workers were given the responsibility of carrying out these tasks.

Mental Health Issues Clifford Beers brought attention to the plight of hospitalized mentally ill individuals due to his own experiences in a mental institution. In 1908 he authored *A Mind That Found Itself,* a publication that ushered in a greater awareness of the heartbreaking experiences of those confined to a mental hospital (Neukrug, 1999).

Other individuals contributing to mental health awareness during these decades included Sigmund Freud and John Dewey. Sigmund Freud's ideas about individual development and growth influenced guidance workers to think about the "whole" student. John Dewey believed that the educational system was responsible for the academic, personal, social, and moral growth of students (Nugent, 1994). Mental health as a concern of the guidance worker was a hotly contested issue, but few argued that vocational guidance was an essential responsibility of the guidance worker.

Vocational Guidance In 1900 Dr. Eli Weaver personalized and organized occupational/informational guidance services in New York City through the placement of city boys on farms for summer work. Although the superintendent of New York schools supported this approach to education, nothing developed partly because of the controversy surrounding the meaning of *guidance.* Some felt guidance was primarily job placement; others felt it was collecting occupational information for jobs; others defined this term as job training (Zeran, Lallas, & Wegner, 1964). Yet another group of individuals argued that guidance was assisting individuals to solve their own problems (Fitch, 1936).

Jesse B. Davis is believed to be the first person to have implemented systemwide guidance in the schools. From 1898 to 1907, Davis encouraged English teachers to incorporate guidance lessons into the curriculum with an emphasis on character development, interpersonal relationships, and vocational interests. Other pioneers promoting career guidance include Anna Y. Reed, who instituted a voluntary guidance effort in Seattle, Washington (Zeran et al., 1964); and Frank Goodwin, who developed a guidance delivery system in Cincinnati, Ohio (Muro & Kottman, 1995). However, the individual most widely recognized as the "father of [the] guidance" movement is Frank Parsons (Baker, 2000; Gladding, 2000; Herr, 2001; Muro & Kottman; Schmidt, 1993; Zeran et al.).

Although Frank Parsons earned an engineering degree from Cornell University in 1869, he never worked within this profession. He did, however, work as a laborer, teacher, lawyer, writer, lecturer, publicist, and adult education advocate—experiences that served as the catalyst for his growing concern with individuals entering the workforce without adequate training (Zeran et al., 1964).

As did others before him, Dr. Parsons attacked public schools for their strict emphasis on academics. Parsons believed that men would be better able to make the transition from school to the work setting through the marriage of academics and vocational education. It was his fervent belief that this could only be accomplished by placing trained professionals in the schools to assist students (Parsons, 1909).

Parsons organized the Vocation Bureau of Boston in 1908 to assist men seeking vocational advice, but what is particularly noteworthy is that the term *vocational guidance* was used for the first time in the minutes of the meeting. This action ushered in the charge to include vocational decision making in the schools (Zeran et al., 1964). Teachers were selected to serve as vocational counselors in what was called the *Boston Plan* in Boston's elementary and secondary schools (Nugent, 1994).

Parsons' posthumously published book *Choosing a Vocation* (1909) outlined his vocational decision-making model:

1. A greater self-understanding of aptitudes, skills, and interests
2. A better knowledge of requirements for different types of work
3. Job satisfaction is when there is congruence between the first two requirements (Zaccaria, 1969).

Controversy still surrounded the meaning of "guidance." Although there were concerted efforts to merge vocational guidance and education, many believed the two were separate entities. Some school administrators required counselors to discuss only academic and career issues and to refer students with personal issues. Other administrators recognized the delicate balance of personal issues influencing academic progress. Imagine how this controversy impacted the role of the counselor at this time!

A meeting was held in Boston in 1910 to resolve these differences; but, unfortunately, records of this meeting were not kept and the question remained unanswered. A second national conference was held in New York in 1913 with the goal of unifying various guidance organizations. The end result was the National Vocational Guidance Association (NVGA) (Zeran et al., 1964), a forerunner to today's American Counseling Association (ACA). The NVGA advocated and supported the integration of academic and vocational education and published this belief in its journal, the *Vocational Guidance Bulletin*, the prototype to the *Career Development Quarterly* journal (Zeran et al.). This publication is known today as the *Journal of Counseling and Development* (Gladding, 2000).

The passage of the Smith-Hughes Act in 1917 provided funds for vocational education and separated vocational from academic training (Gysbers, 2001; Nugent, 1994). Although the legislation was significant in recognizing the importance of careers, it confused guidance workers. Were guidance workers to devote their time to directing students in the occupational world? Or, did guidance mean guiding students in social and/or academic concerns?

Testing Movement The testing movement added another dimension to the guidance worker's role. As tests were developed, guidance workers—with little training—were assigned the responsibility for test administration and interpretation. Alfred Binet, the creator of the first intelligence test, served as the force behind the testing movement (Ferguson, 1963). The French government asked Binet to differentiate children who could not perform in school due to low ability from those students who would not perform due to other reasons, such as a lack of motivation. This test, developed in 1905, was the forerunner to intelligence tests used in schools today. As professional educators began to see the value of tests as a scientific method for assessing a person's interests, abilities, and deficiencies (Myrick, 1993; Schmidt, 1993), guidance workers took on the task of administering and interpreting tests.

1920s

> Vocational guidance for the few is as old as the schools themselves. Vocational guidance for the mass is of comparatively recent origin. (Ginn, 1924, p. 3)

Although the trends of the early 1900s set the groundwork for guidance workers in schools, the next 10 years were marked with the same issues with frustratingly little success in resolving these recurrent dilemmas. During this period of time, guidance program structure and training requirements for guidance specialists differed. Since larger numbers of guidance specialists emerged in schools, it is no surprise that the Vocation Bureau of Boston was the first to recommend requirements for vocational certification (Ginn, 1924). These requirements included

> [e]ither graduation from a college or university approved by the Board of Superintendents or from an institution of as high a grade, and evidence of three years' experience in teaching, a satisfactory portion of which shall have been in a vocational school or in such vocational work as the Board of Superintendents shall approve; or, graduation from a high school and a normal

Lawrence Hall, Harvard Graduate School of Education
Harvard University was the first college-based counselor education program in the country.

Special Collections. Gutman Library, Harvard Graduate School of Education. This permission is granted on behalf of the Harvard University Archives, who own the original print. Courtesy of the Harvard University Archives.

> school approved by the Board of Superintendents, and evidence of five years' experience in teaching, a satisfactory portion of which shall have been in a vocational school or in such vocational work as the Board of Superintendents shall approve. (p. 14)

The Vocation Bureau of Boston eventually changed its name to the Bureau of Vocational Guidance of the Division of Education. And, with the city of Boston serving as the model and advocate for the importance of guidance, it was natural that this organization eventually became the Graduate School of Education of Harvard University (Ginn, 1924). Harvard University took the lead in training guidance workers by becoming the first college-based counselor education program (Schmidt, 1993). The very first counselor certification program was adopted with requirements that a guidance worker have not only a teaching background but also vocational experiences.

Guidance services continued to be based on local discretion by teachers who "assumed the duties in addition to their teaching requirements. Vocational Instructors (men) and Vocational Assistants (women) are those who give full time to this work either in special schools or in the central department" (Ginn, 1924,

p. 14). These high-school-based guidance workers were sometimes called *deans of women,* for those women who worked exclusively with women, or *deans of men,* for those men who worked entirely with male students. Other service-oriented individuals appeared in schools and provided assistance to students that was often duplicated since no model existed for the coordination of services. In order to correct this dilemma, a college student personnel model was adopted as a model for secondary schools, but there was no consensus as to who needed to be included in this coordinated model. Generally, pupil personnel programs included information, appraisal, counseling, orientation, and research and evaluation services (Schmidt, 1993; Zaccaria, 1969).

Depending on the school and the district, guidance workers assisted with course selection and vocational guidance and facilitated personal decisions. Discipline, attendance, and administrative tasks (Muro & Kottman, 1995) were performed by some and not others. A crisis model in which a guidance worker would "put out fires" as problems occurred was the most commonly utilized approach (Muro & Kottman).

William Burnham, known as the "father of elementary school counseling" (Faust, 1968) affirmed the opinions of Freud and Dewey expressed in the early 1900s. Burnham perceived the role of the school-based guidance expert as one that promoted the total welfare of the individual, and he advocated for reaching youth in their early formative years. At that time only four states required any special training and certification, (Muro & Kottman, 1995) and elementary school counselors were virtually unknown.

1930s

> . . . Guidance work as it is being carried on in public schools, in placement offices, in adjustment services, and in social agencies is one of the tremendously important developments of the last quarter century. (Fitch, 1936, p. 760)

During the 1930s the Great Depression brought about a renewed need for career guidance. In addition, pupil personnel service coordination was revisited and the first systematic approach for delivering counseling was proposed by E. G. Williamson (1950).

The Great Depression Just as the Industrial Revolution introduced diversity into the schools, the scarcity of jobs at this time also brought a wide range of student characteristics into secondary schools. The large number of people who were unemployed forced the passage in 1933 of the Wagner-Peyser Act, which established the U.S. Employment Service; and the demand for career information prompted the first edition of the *Dictionary of Occupational Titles* to be published in 1939 (Gladding, 2000). This publication is now replaced by O*NET as a comprehensive resource for occupational information. The George-Deen Act of 1936 provided money for the expansion of existing vocational programs, yet people continued to be leery of the need for vocational education despite the growing need for career information.

The debate regarding guidance worker roles continued. As stated by Myers (1935), "probably no activity in the entire list suffers as much from lack of a coordinated program as does guidance, and especially the counseling aspect of it" (p. 807). One common expectation of the guidance expert was to change students' problematic behaviors; and although there were few successful results, school personnel still felt that there was a place and a need for this service in addition to the "dependable" and acceptable emphasis on vocational and educational decision making and psychometrics (Zeran et al., 1964).

Organization of Pupil Personnel Services School counselors comprised the most rapidly expanding group of specialists within the pupil personnel service model. Their primary task was assisting students in educational and vocational planning, but no model existed for guiding this process until Dr. E. G. Williamson, from the University of Minnesota, outlined his *directive approach* to counseling. This systematic approach, also known as the *Minnesota model,* was based on a medical model for assisting students with their problems. Williamson's model was published in 1939 in his book entitled *How to Counsel Students: A Manual of Techniques for Clinical Counselors* (Nugent, 1994).

> Counseling is . . . a point of view, a philosophy of education, emphasizing human values and human development. Counseling is likewise a body of techniques or ways of helping young people grow up normally through assisted or guided learning. . . . [I]t takes its place in a broadened scheme of education as an added method designed to achieve new goals on the one hand, and to help achieve more effectively those old goals. . . . (Williamson, 1950, p. 18)

Williamson's method, largely borrowed from Frank Parsons' philosophical approach, prescribed a six-step model (Muro & Kottman, 1995):

1. Analysis—gathering data about students
2. Synthesis—selecting and organizing information to understand the student
3. Diagnosis—forming a hypothesis regarding the student's concerns
4. Prognosis—predicting outcomes based on student problem solving
5. Treatment—selecting strategies to meet the goal
6. Follow-up—evaluating the counseling effectiveness (Schmidt, 1993)

Some individuals praised this scientific approach to assisting students, while others criticized it for being too narrow and problem-focused (Schmidt).

1940s

> Many of the present-day functions, activities, and whatnots that administrators feel called upon to include in a guidance or personnel service have no legitimate claim to inclusion therein. (Reed, 1947, p. 381)

The goals, purpose, and direction of school guidance in the 1940s were inconsistent (Landy & Kroll, 1966) and varied across school systems and among guidance

Dr. Williamson used a medical model for the development of the Directive Approach to counseling students

Courtesy of University of Minnesota Archives.

counselors themselves. To add to the confusion, Dr. Carl Rogers provided a non-directive approach to counseling that was in direct contrast to Dr. Williamson's directive approach. As stated by Rogers (1965) in his book *Counseling and Psychotherapy*,

> [Man] cannot simply rest comfortably upon the ways and traditions of his society, but finds many of the basic issues and conflicts of life centering in himself. Each man must resolve within himself issues for which his society previously took full responsibility. (p. 4)

The emphasis on careers was highlighted through the George-Barden Act of 1946, an amendment to the George-Deen Act of 1936. Local boards of education were more receptive to hiring additional school counselors since this act provided federal money for such things as reimbursement of guidance counselor salaries and research in guidance (Gysbers & Henderson, 2000).

1950s

> In one sense it is incorrect to apply the term "specialist" to the school counselor any more than one would apply the term to any other school staff member. The school counselor is a specialist in (1) understanding child and adolescent growth and development, (2) personality development and

Dr. Carl Rogers developed a nondirective approach to counseling, which was in direct contrast to Dr. Williamson's approach

Courtesy of Natalie Rogers.

> educational-vocational concerns and applicable information, and (3) guidance techniques, with emphasis on testing and the counseling interview. (Peters & Farwell, 1959, p. 23)

The significant events of the 1950s included reorganization of counseling organizations (see Box 1.1), a greater number of students entering school, and the landmark National Defense Education Act (NDEA).

Unification of Counseling Organizations The same issues the vocational guidance organizations had confronted in 1913 resurfaced in the 1950s. To solve these reoccurring concerns, hopefully permanently, a joint convention of "like-minded" guidance organizations was held in 1952 in Los Angeles (Newcombe, 1993). Four organizations formed the American Personnel and Guidance Association (APGA): the American College Personnel Association (ACPA); the National Vocational Guidance Association (NVGA); the Student Personnel Association for Teacher Education (SPATE), known later as the Humanistic Education and Development Association; and, the National Association of Guidance Supervisors and Counselor Trainers (NAGCT) (Simmons, 2002), now known as the Association of Counselor Educators and Supervisors (ACES).

In 1952 the American School Counselor Association (ASCA) was founded and became a division of APGA in 1953 (Simmons, 2002). While unification

BOX 1.1 The Organizations that Shaped the School Counseling Profession

1908 Vocation Bureau of Boston
Established as a result of Frank Parsons' work

1913 National Vocational Guidance Association (NVGA)
Published the *Vocational Guidance Bulletin,* now known as the *Journal of Counseling and Development*

1952 American Personnel and Guidance Association (APGA)
Formed from four similar organizations including:

American College Personnel Association (ACPA)

National Vocational Guidance Association (NVGA)

Student Personnel Association for Teacher Education (SPATE)
Later became known as Humanistic Education and Development Association

National Association of Guidance Supervisors and Counselor Trainers (NAGCT)
Now known as the Association of Counselor Educators and Supervisors (ACES)

1953 American School Counselor Association (ASCA) became a division of APGA

1983 American Association of Counseling and Development (AACD)
The APGA changed the organization's name to AACD

1992 American Counseling Association (ACA)
AACD changed the organization's name to ACA

Within ACA there are 18 divisions and one affiliate.

Association for Assessment in Counseling and Education (AACE)
Promotes assessment in counseling

Association for Adult Development and Aging (AADA)
Focuses on adult development and aging issues

American College Counseling Association (ACCA)
Focus is to foster student development in colleges and universities

Association for Counselors and Educators in Government (ACEG)
The purpose is to counsel clients and families in government or military-related agencies

Counseling Associations for Humanistic Education and Development (C-Head)
Promotes humanistic elements associated with human development

Association for Specialists in Group Work (ASGW)
Establishes standards for training and research in group work

Association for Spiritual, Ethical, and Religious Values in Counseling (ASERVIC)
Promotes spiritual, ethical, religious, and human values

American School Counselor Association (ASCA)
Promotes the school counseling profession and students

American Mental Health Counselors Association (AMHCA)
Assists mental health counselors advocate for client-access to quality health care services

Association for Multicultural Counseling and Development (AMCD)
Advocates for ethnic empathy and understanding

American Rehabilitation Counseling Association (ARCA)
Promotes the rehabilitation counseling profession and development of persons with disabilities

Association for Counselor Education and Supervision (ACES)
Emphasizes quality training and supervision of all counselors

Association for Gay, Lesbian and Bisexual Issues in Counseling (AGLBIC)
Focuses on reducing stereotypical thinking and homoprejudice

Counselors for Social Justice (CSJ)
Promotes and implements social action strategies

International Association of Addiction and Offender Counselors (IAAOC)
Advocates for the development of effective counseling and rehabilitation programs for addictive behaviors

BOX 1.1 The Organizations that Shaped the School Counseling Profession *(continued)*

International Association of Marriage and Family Counselors (IAMFC)
Helps develop healthy family systems through prevention, education, and therapy

National Career Development Association (NCDA)
Mission is to promote career development across the life span

National Employment Counseling Association (NECA)
Focus is to offer leadership to counselors in employment and career settings

Association for Creativity in Counseling (ACC)
Established as an affiliate of ACA for creativity in counseling

The American School Counselor Association (ASCA) membership is divided into four regions across the United States. These regions include: Midwest, Southern, North Atlantic, and Western. Each region is represented by a vice president who serves on the governing board.

ASCA grants a division charter to each of the 50 states. Individuals may join the state division without becoming a member of ASCA, although membership in both is encouraged.

did assist in giving members a greater foundation of support, individual divisions were concerned about losing their unique identity and autonomy (Gladding, 2000; Muro & Kottman, 1995; Simmons, 2002).

Greater Numbers During this decade, children were attending school in larger numbers than ever before. Correspondingly, greater numbers of school guidance counselors were placed in schools (Simmons, 2002), partly due to the funds available from the George-Barden Act.

The National Defense Education Act Perhaps the single most important event in the history of school counseling was the passage of the National Defense Education Act (NDEA) (Herr, 2001; Muro & Kottman, 1995; Myrick, 1993; Schmidt, 1993). In 1957 Russia launched the first space satellite, *Sputnik I,* which frightened Americans into believing that this signaled Soviet dominance in science (Herr, 2001). Concern abounded regarding the ability of the United States to compete with the Soviet Union for the race for space, and many believed that U.S. students were not adequately trained nor motivated to pursue careers in mathematics and science. In September 1958 Congress passed the NDEA to provide funding and incentives for individuals interested in a career as a middle- or high-school counselor. These individuals were given the charge of identifying and fostering students talented in mathematics and science (Herr; Muro & Kottman, 1995; Schmidt). As stated in Title V of the NDEA,

> The commissioner will contract with universities to operate institutes for training secondary school guidance counselors. During fiscal 1959, the institutions will receive $6.25 million. For each of the following three fiscal years, they will receive $7.25 million. Public school personnel who attend

> these institutes will receive stipends of $75 per week of attendance and $16 per week for each dependent. . . .

1960s

> Guidance . . . is like the fifth wheel of an automobile—the steering wheel. Guidance is the educative function which has a direct, synthesizing influence on the life of the student. It helps him organize his educational experiences and become a better functioning person. This service cannot be left to happenstance and incidental learning; neither can it be left only to designated guidance personnel. (Zeran et al., 1964, p. 3)

Certification standards were created in the 1960s to help define the role of the guidance counselor, and the greater needs of school-aged students propelled a discussion on the best counseling model to help these youth. Although legislators were willing to support school counselors, counselors themselves could not agree among themselves about the best educational training requirements needed to be fully prepared for this profession. To make matters worse, these professionals even disagreed about their role in the schools. As stated by Hill (1967),

> What might be called a "school of thought" regarding guidance in the elementary schools could be labeled the Chaos School. Members of this group decry what they assume to be variety of practice, lack of consistent theory, and seeming disorder in the ranks of the practitioner and the counselor educators of this new field of guidance service. (p. 188)

To clarify the school counselor's role, in 1964 the American School Counselor Association (ASCA) wrote a statement that specified the role and function of the school counselor (Gibson & Mitchell, 2003). For the most part, this effort was ignored because a strategy for implementing this role into the school system was missing.

Legislation Supporting School Counselors At this time school-aged youth brought unprecedented concerns into the school such as teenage pregnancy, drug and alcohol use, changing family structures, suicide, and aggression. These issues, in part, led to the passage of the Elementary and Secondary Education Act of 1965, which provided funds for the training of elementary school counselors (Paisley & Borders, 1995). Unfortunately, these professionals continued to be scarce in the schools.

Increased Educational Requirements Because school counselors were entering schools in larger numbers, school counselor certification and performance standards were upgraded. By 1960, 38 states had some type of certification for school counselors, with inconsistent preparation among training institutions (Nugent, 1994). In most states a teaching credential was required and a teacher only needed to take four or five graduate courses during the summer to qualify as a school counselor. The courses that were usually required included instruction in counseling theories, tests and measurement, occupational information, and an orientation to guidance services. Few programs required an internship. To assist in determining educational training for school counselors, the APGA published the first code of ethics for counselors in 1961 (Gladding, 2000) and in 1965 this association recommended that school counselors have a master's degree (Nugent).

Needs of School-Aged Youth The crisis approach formulated in the 1920s, the only known model known to assist students at risk, fell short in effectiveness. Dr. J. C. Gilbert Wrenn was instrumental in encouraging counselors to reject the remedial, crisis approach in favor of a preventive approach (Herr, 2001). As stated by Wrenn (1962),

> The school counselor's task can be seen only as the needs of children and young people are understood, for apart from these needs and the needs of the society of which they are a part, the counselor has no reason for existence. (p. 3)

Wrenn's vociferous beliefs led to a chair appointment on a committee investigating guidance in U.S. schools. *The Counselor in a Changing World* was the published report of this commission with the views that counselors should be involved with student group and individual counseling, consultation for parents and teachers, appraisal and assessment, educational/occupational planning, and curriculum development.

1970s

> A history of guidance and counseling also suggests that school administrators may be a major constraint to the development of a strong profession. This seems evident because school administrators largely control what school counselors do and how they spend their time. Also, history reveals that school administrators feel the major purpose of schools is that of teaching and learning. (Aubrey, 1975, as cited in Costar, 1978, p. 220)

Not only *affective* development was highlighted to assist with the needs of *all* students, but also *career* development was once again emphasized during the 1970s. Increased tasks assigned to school counselors led these professionals to ask the question, "How are we to respond to all these demands on our time?"

Assisting All Students Children with special needs gained major headway through the Education for All Handicapped Children Act (Pub. L. 94-142). Although this act did not specifically mention school counselors, these professionals were involved with curriculum planning, placement, and intervention with little to no training in understanding the educational needs of these students with special needs.

Career Focus Once again the importance of career development was underscored. In 1976 the National Occupational Information Coordinating Committee (NOICC) was created by the federal government to coordinate occupational information, to assist states in developing competency-based career programs, and to aid individuals with career decision making.

It was increasingly apparent that school counselors engaged in many useful activities, particularly as more and more tasks were added to the counselor's work setting. Yet, the public continued to ask the question, "Do counselors make a difference in the lives of students?"

To answer this question, the APGA conducted a project in 1977 to investigate the status of guidance and counseling. The findings were disturbing to school counselors who dedicated much time and energy to assisting students. The report indicated that there were vast differences in the organizational structure and counselor duties (Henderson & Gysbers, 1998) and little evidence that counseling services made a positive difference in the lives of students. This report, as well as a decline in student enrollment, led to the elimination of many school counseling positions (Myrick, 1993).

1980s

> The sad fact of the matter is that there exists a relative dearth of research specific to the school counseling profession, and most research that exists is not very good. Compared to other professions, school counseling has very little empirical data to show that its activities are helpful and successful. (Loesch, 1988, p. 170)

Educational deficiencies were made public, counseling standards were created for uniformity in counselor training, and the needs of elementary-aged children were highlighted in the 1980s. Serious deficiencies in the educational system were revealed in a publication entitled *A Nation at Risk* (Gardner, 1983, as cited in Schwallie-Giddis, ter Maat, & Pak, 2003; Herr, 2002). Although this report raised serious concerns about the quality of education and inspired debates on the best methods to "fix" U.S. schools, school counselors were noticeably absent as a solution to the problem. This omission intensified efforts to define the training that would standardize school counselor curriculum across the nation.

Upgrading Standards The Council for Accreditation of Counseling and Related Educational Programs (CACREP) was established in 1981 as an independent, affiliate organization to establish common goals and evaluate master and doctoral counselor training programs (Gladding, 2000; Nugent, 1994). The establishment of this council was a major step in standardizing education and training, and today CACREP has accredited 153 school counseling programs nationwide (CACREP, 2003).

Student Needs The 1980s were marked by a paradox. Many schools were eliminating counselor positions in the 1980s and 1990s because of financial difficulties, and at the same time there was growing recognition of the needs of elementary school children. Several states mandated elementary school counseling due to the renewal of Burnham's belief expressed in the 1920s that early intervention strategies could prevent problems from occurring in later years.

Although the needs of all students were part of the school counselor's role, secondary-level guidance counselors spent a large portion of their time assisting students who wished to matriculate to postsecondary education. The developmental needs of other students were virtually ignored. A growing awareness that all students merited assistance was partly responsible to a change in the name of the APGA in 1983 to the American Association of Counseling and Development (AACD) to more accurately reflect the mission, philosophy, and developmental needs of individuals (Gladding, 2000; Nugent, 1994).

1990s

> A number of role-related questions continue to be debated, such as "To what extent should school counselors be in the classroom?" and "What percentage of a school counselor's time should be devoted to direct services, and what percentage to administrative tasks?" (Paisley & Borders, 1995, p. 152)

The 1990s were filled with promise and progress for the school counseling profession. Passage of legislation and other initiatives, forceful endeavors to advocate for the profession of school counseling, and renovated attempts to emphasize career development marked this era. Furthermore, school counselors were lauded and recognized for their management of school crises brought to the front by the violence that devastated many schools throughout the nation.

Legislation and Initiatives In 1989 the National Governors' Association and President Bush adopted national education goals to raise the academic achievement of all students, a commitment that was renewed in 1994 when the Goals 2000: Educate America Act was signed into law. Although school counselors were implied in this legislation, they were not specifically mentioned, which once again underlined the belief that counselors were not integral to the academic growth of students.

However, school counselors were mentioned in an initiative that began in 1987 and continued to grow in this decade known as High Schools That Work (HSTW). One of the goals of HSTW is to partner schools with students, parents, and the community to improve academic and vocational concepts by connecting students and school counselors (SREB High Schools That Work, n.d.).

Tech Prep (sometimes known as a *2 + 2 program*), integrated into the Carl D. Perkins Vocational and Applied Technology Act Amendments of 1990, was designed to reach the "neglected majority" who leave high school without appropriate preparation to enter the technological workplace and to integrate programming between local educational institutions and postsecondary institutions. School counselors had an integral role to play in counseling and scheduling these students.

In 1991 the Secretary's Commission on Achieving Necessary Skills (SCANS) was formed by the U.S. Department of Labor to identify basic skills common to all jobs. Not surprisingly, drastic skill deficiencies were found at all levels by the commission. These findings resulted in the passage of the School-to-Work

Opportunities Act (STWOA) in May 1994. This act connected academic and work-related skills, and the school counselor once again focused attention and time on career development and training for work-related skills (*School-to-Work Transition,* 1996). In 1992 the American Association of Counseling and Development (AACD) changed its name to the American Counseling Association (ACA) to better clarify the counseling profession (Sheeley, 2002).

The importance of school counselors was highlighted in 1995 through the passage of the Elementary School Counseling Demonstration Act (ESCDA) (later renamed the Elementary and Secondary School Counseling Act) under Title X of Public Law 103-382. This act, reauthorized in 1999, funded $20 million for a competitive federal grant for school districts to provide greater access to counseling services, to improve school safety, and to enhance academic success (ACA, n.d.; Herr, 2003). On July 20, 1999, the passage of the "100,000 New School Counselors" legislation provided matching grants to schools to recruit, train, and hire 100,000 school counselors, school psychologists, and school social workers.

The DeWitt Wallace Readers Digest, in collaboration with The Education Trust, authorized monies to investigate the role school counselors play in assisting and advocating for disadvantaged youth. In 1996, 10 universities were chosen nationwide to design a theoretical model for changing graduate-level school counselor preparation programs. Common themes among all the programs included an emphasis on training school counselors who were (a) familiar with the educational process, (b) skilled in assisting students with educational and personal goals, and (c) advocates for decreasing barriers that impede academic success of poor and minority students. This initiative provided useful information about the need for counselor education transformation (Paisley & Hayes, 2003), and the ASCA National Standards document was designed to promote and redefine school counseling programs.

The National Standards In 1997 leaders in the ASCA aggressively renewed their commitment to implement and define the school counselor's role. Despite past efforts, what many felt was missing was a "national focus on a design or framework for program development and delivery" (Campbell & Dahir, 1997, p. 2).

The National Standards document is a national framework for program delivery and development that incorporates school counseling as a comprehensive, developmental program within the school system. In March 2001 the ASCA governing board agreed to create a National Model for School Counseling Programs that "maximizes the full potential of the National Standards document and reflects current education reform movements" (Bowers & Hatch, 2002, p. 10). Additional information on the National Standards Model and how counselors can transform existing school counseling programs is found in Chapter 5.

The School Counselor as a Critical Incident Manager Columbine, Paducah, and Springfield were ordinary towns with schools that faced extraordinary events. School violence painted a picture of the turmoil some students encounter and the resulting devastation left behind. School counselors were recognized for their leadership role in addressing individual risks and environmental conditions, improving the school climate, and intervening with peer groups responsible for spreading negative behaviors and attitudes.

Role ambiguity is in part a result of historical and social trends, lack of professional advocacy, and unrest among school counselors themselves. Even the professional title is used differently among school counselors as some refer to themselves as school guidance counselors and others call themselves professional school counselors. As a rule, ASCA encourages the title "professional school counselor" to identify the profession (J. Cook, personal communication, February 7, 2002). See Box 1.2 for a time line regarding the school counseling profession.

BOX 1.2 Historical Events Influencing the School Counseling Profession

1900	Industrial Revolution created a switch from a rural economy to an urban factory system.
1908	Clifford Beers authored *A Mind that Found Itself.* Publication brought attention to the need of individuals with mental illness. Individuals debated the need for moral education in the schools.
1900	Dr. Eli Weaver organized and personalized guidance services. Controversy surrounded the meaning of the word *guidance*.
1905	Alfred Binet developed the first intelligence test. Later named the Stanford-Binet after Stanford University who helped revise the test.
1908	Frank Parsons, "father of guidance," organized the Vocation Bureau of Boston and authored posthumously published book, *Choosing a Vocation*. Vocation Bureau of Boston later changed name to the Bureau of Vocational Guidance of the Division of Education and later became the Graduate School of Education of Harvard University.
1913	National Vocational Guidance Association founded. (NVGA)
1916	Child Labor Laws required youth to attend school. Educators were unprepared to deal with this influx of diverse students.
1917	Smith-Hughes Act of 1917 provided funds in agriculture, home economics, Technology and Industry (T & I) for the education of individuals over age 14 who have either entered or are planning to enter the workforce.
1929	Great Depression—Larger numbers of students from diverse backgrounds entered secondary schools.
1933	Wager-Peyser Act—Established the U.S. Employment Service.
1936	George-Deen Act—Legislation created 12 million per year for agriculture, home economics, T & I, and Distributive Education vocational programs.
1939	*Dictionary of Occupational Titles (DOT)* published and now replaced by O*NET.
1939	E. G. Williamson outlined his directive approach to counseling (also known as the Minnesota model).
1942	Carl Rogers designed his nondirective approach to counseling. This client-centered model outlined in his book, *Counseling & Psychotherapy*, deviated from Williamson's model.
1946	George-Barden Act (amended the George-Deen Act)—Funds were available to support guidance activities and guidance salaries.
1952	Formation of the American Personnel and Guidance Association (APGA).
1953	American School Counselor Association became fifth division of APGA.
1957	Russia launched *Sputnik I.*
1958	National Defense Education Act (NDEA)—Created funding for the training of counselors to identify gifted students in mathematics and science.

continued

BOX 1.2 Historical Events Influencing the School Counseling Profession *(continued)*

Year	Event
1962	Dr. J. C. Gilbert Wrenn published *The Counselor in a Changing World,* which advocated for a preventive counseling model.
1965	Elementary and Secondary Education Act—Provided funds for the training of elementary school counselors.
1974	Education for All Handicapped Children Act (Pub. L. 94-142) specified a nonrestrictive learning environment for students with special needs.
1976	National Occupational Information Coordinating Committee (NOICC)—Provided competency-based career programs.
1977	APGA investigated the status of guidance and counseling and revealed negative results.
1981	Council for Accreditation of Counseling and Related Educational Programs (CACREP) established to standardize counselor education programs.
1983	*A Nation at Risk* publication brought about serious concerns of the American educational system.
1983	APGA became the American Association of Counseling and Development (AACD).
1987	High Schools That Work (HSTW) initiative to connect school, parents, and community members to improve academic and vocational achievement.
1989	Goals 2000 created to raise achievement standards.
1990	Carl D. Perkins Vocational and Applied Technology Act integrated Tech Prep concepts.
1991	Secretary's Commission on Achieving Necessary Skills (SCANS) reported drastic skill deficiencies in the workforce.
1992	AACD changed its name to the American Counseling Association (ACA).
1994	School-to-Work Opportunities Act (STWOA)—Connected academic with work skills.
1994	Goals 2000: Educate America Act—Renewed commitment to upgrade academic standards.
1995	Elementary and Secondary School Counseling Act—Provided funds for school districts to provide greater access to counseling services.
1996	Dewitt Wallace Readers Digest offered a competitive grant to universities to change counselor preparation programs.
1997	ASCA implemented the National Standards.
1999	100,000 New School Counselors legislation provided money to recruit, train, and hire school counselors, school psychologists, and school social workers.
2001	ASCA created the National Model for school counselors.
2004	The Association for Creativity in Counseling (ACC) was established as an affiliate of ACA

THE PROFESSIONAL SCHOOL COUNSELOR TODAY

Addressing the personal, social, career, and academic development of students is critical to school guidance and counseling programs. School counselors must be at the forefront advocating for students and working to facilitate student learning and development. As a result of professional school counselors' work, students will benefit. (Hughey, 2001, iii)

With the 20th century having come to an end and the new millennium now here, many ask, "How are school counselors different today than yesterday?" Nearly a century after school guidance workers entered schools, counselors are still performing many administrative/clerical functions, completing duties for which they have not been trained, receiving inconsistent training, persisting in the struggle to define their role, and continuing to convince stakeholders that the services they provide do make a positive difference in the lives of students. School counselors trained today are now better prepared and organized to address the challenges confronting the profession. Today's school counselors are given the opportunity to assist students from diverse backgrounds and to provide evidence that school youth benefit from involvement in a school counseling program. From the lessons learned in the past, school counselors are now in a pivotal position to communicate their education, skills, and training.

Diversity and multicultural issues, vital considerations due to the changing demographics of society, have challenged the traditional counseling approaches. These conventional approaches are based on Western philosophy, a method that is often incompatible with individuals from other cultures. Preparation for cultural awareness is a relatively recent requirement, and counselors who have practiced in schools for some time may not have had formal training in multicultural issues. Additionally, most programs only offer one course on multicultural awareness with little opportunity to apply these concepts across the counselor preparation curriculum (Paisley & McMahon, 2001).

Proving positive student outcomes is a challenge for school counselors. A lack of understanding of adequate methods for accountability, limited time, minimal financial resources, and lack of confidence in research methods have led to counselor hesitancy in conducting a comprehensive evaluation (Paisley & McMahon, 2001). This serious omission has led to much criticism of school counselors and their programs. School counselors training today are better versed in accountability practices.

Although ASCA passionately supports the National Standards and has invested much time and training into this effort, a great deal of work still remains in delivering reliable, consistent services. For example, ASCA strongly encourages school counselors to have a master's degree, yet nine states still allow individuals to work as school counselors without this degree (Office of Public Policy and Legislation, 2001). Additionally, demands on time and programming place counselors in unrealistic positions to please all people at all times. The ideal counselor-to-student ratio suggested by ASCA is 1:100, with 1:300 considered as the maximum recommended ratio; but in reality the ratio sometimes exceeds 1:1,115 (ACA, 2001), an impossible caseload that produces negligible results.

School counselors must learn skills to vigorously and vociferously advocate for their profession so that time can be more effectively spent (Paisley & McMahon, 2001). The stage is now set for a new chapter to be written on the essential contributions of school counselors.

THE FUTURE OF THE SCHOOL COUNSELOR

With the multiple challenges facing school counselors, what does the future hold for this profession? Just as the Industrial Revolution ushered in a need for school reform, a similar reformation in education is now occurring. There is no time better than now for school counselors to take a leadership role (Paisley & Hayes, 2003) by speaking with one voice on how counselors benefit school-aged youth. Counselor education programs will take a lead in teaching future professional school counselors to aggressively campaign for a shared philosophy, program development, accountability, greater awareness of diversity issues, technology skills, professional skill development, a systems approach to school counseling, career development, prevention and intervention strategies for at-risk students, group work, collaboration, and advocacy.

A Common Philosophy

With school counseling as a part of the education revolution, it stands to reason that the traditional crisis-based service model would shift to one that is student-focused and results-based (Johnson & Johnson, 2003). Many practicing school counselors trained under this traditional model continue "business as usual" and are reluctant to embrace a comprehensive, developmental approach to counseling. Although these counselors are well-guided in their belief that what they are currently doing is working—and in many cases *is* working, they have rarely taken the time to evaluate their effectiveness. The future school counselor will receive training and support in organizational skills, knowledge of the new model, and confidence to advocate for this approach to counseling program delivery.

If counselors do not take the lead in serving as leaders of change, others will take the lead in the change process for them. For instance, school counselors have a rich understanding of curricular needs but few schools include counselors on curriculum review committees (Hart & Jacobi, 1992). Future school counselors will receive advocacy skills to assist them in communicating their role.

Program Development

Previous attempts to implement a developmental approach to school counseling did not produce the desired results, partly because the organizational structure was one that was more counselor-focused with no evidence of success (Gysbers, 2001). Education and prevention serve as the primary purposes behind comprehensive programs with services and activities designed to facilitate student achievement (Green & Keys, 2001) and procedures to document effectiveness.

There are compelling reasons to initiate comprehensive guidance programs (Gysbers, 2001). For example, students in Utah high schools with fully delivered comprehensive counseling programs rated their education more positively, took more advanced mathematics and science courses, and scored higher on the ACT (Lapan, Gysbers, & Petroski, 2003). In order to fully embrace these programs, future school counselors will be better prepared to document how youth benefit

(Whiston, 2002) through participation in a fully implemented, developmental school counseling program.

Accountability

There is increasing pressure on all educators to prove effectiveness for themselves and for the programs of which they are a part. Traditional counselors were evaluated based on such things as the number of students seen, quantity of programs conducted, and/or timeliness of reports, with the value of these activities based on counselor "intuition," testimonials, or personal impressions (Myrick, 1993). The future school counselor will have the continued responsibility of actively documenting contributions to students and effectiveness of interventions (Hart & Jacobi, 1992). Tomorrow's school counselors will be better trained in data-collection procedures, methods of interpreting data, and assessment of program performance (Green & Keys, 2001). Counselors who can confidently interpret data into readily understood information will reinforce the belief that counseling programs are important to the academic process (Hart & Jacobi).

Diversity

School counselors are responsible for the growth of *all* students. Examining personal beliefs, developing a greater understanding of diverse populations, addressing culture within the counseling program, and utilizing theories and techniques better suited to diverse populations (Green & Keys, 2001; Paisley & McMahon, 2001) are essential for increasing tolerance and understanding. Too often counselors unknowingly contribute to the continuation of educational inequities as a result of their unfamiliarity with minority and low-income students, personal stereotypes, and the excessively high ratio of students to counselors, as is commonly found in the inner-city schools (Hart & Jacobi, 1992). Moreover, future counselors will broaden their understanding of diversity by expanding their definition to include sexual orientation, disability, family structures, socioeconomic status, and learning styles (Gysbers, 2001; Paisley & McMahon).

Technology

Technology provides enhanced opportunities to reduce the "paper chase" and expand program development and accountability (Adelman, 2002). Additionally, computers can readily access information for students, provide a means to collaborate with other individuals, assist in obtaining professional resources, and allow individuals to communicate without the barriers of time or space (Bowers, 2002). Unfortunately, many counselors do not have the training or funds to access technology (Sabella & Booker, 2003). Financial concerns may prevent schools from updating software and prohibit school counselors from providing the most efficient service for the students. Tomorrow's school counselors will have greater capabilities and resources for grant writing to secure funding for improved technology.

Professionalism

Professional development is an ethical obligation that is specifically mentioned in the *Ethical Standards for School Counselors* (ASCA, 1998). In order to transform the "traditional" approach to school counseling, specific leadership training is necessary to assist counselors in creating change and to have them not be satisfied with the "status quo" (Hart & Jacobi, 1992).

Professional associations such as ASCA and the state and local counseling affiliates are influential in policy development and contribute much to the professionalism of counselors. Future professional school counselors will be much more active in their professional organizations; and these organizations, in turn, will be more active and aggressive in lobbying efforts for essential membership services.

Systems Approach in the School

The traditional counseling approach has consisted of a focus on individual change without regard to the systems (peer group, family, neighborhood) that surround and impact the individual (Green & Keys, 2001). This is a shortsighted attitude since events that affect the student also influence the school and impact the community. It has long been recognized that building a relationship between the family, school, and community positively influences student growth and family interaction. The future school counselor will have a greater understanding of counseling and collaboration from a systems perspective.

Career

Just as the Industrial Revolution brought about jobs that had never been imagined, today's societal advances are also ushering in careers that have never been considered. The 21st century will continue to challenge the future school counselor to connect career development with other aspects of life such as family, leisure, racial/sexual discrimination, and workplace environment. Due to the increasing emergence of multiple job changes in a person's life, the worldwide societal changes that influence careers, and future occupations that are unknown today, career development will continue to be a responsibility of the school counselor. This vision does not define the counselor's role as one of a career specialist, as many visualized the counselor's role in the past; rather, it defines the counselor's role as an opportunity to increase the linkage of careers to academics, decision making, and personal concerns.

At-Risk Students

At the beginning of this chapter I reflected on the fact that my nephew, formally prepared as a teacher and not as a counselor, is being asked to perform school counseling functions two periods each day. How appropriately will he be able to deal with factors such as poverty, nonattendance, pregnancy, drug and alcohol use, crime, inconsistent parenting, and unprotected sexual activity? These are just a few of the difficulties experienced by youth today. At-risk youth often acquire dysfunctional behaviors and inadequate coping skills early in life, and without appropriate intervention these individuals may develop multiple problems in adulthood (McWhirter, McWhirter, McWhirter, & McWhirter, 1998). This is where the school counselor enters. Schools are responsible for educating our youth. School counselors are charged with protecting our students and assisting them to become more resilient by teaching prevention and intervention strategies (Carlisle & Frare, 2003); and skills for working with at-risk youth will continue to be enhanced.

Group Work

Group intervention is an effective means of developing better social competencies, providing insights that may not be realized through individual counseling, and enhancing social skills. Moreover, groups are often more time-effective in that more students can be reached (Roland & Neitzschman, 1996). Tomorrow's school counselors will be engaged in more group work than counselors of today and yesterday and will be provided with better tools to build social and personal efficacy skills associated with academic achievement.

Collaboration

It is the rare school that has enough resources to respond to the increased concerns school-aged youth bring into the school building. School counselors are the ideal professionals to take a leadership role in weaving together the existing community and school resources (Adelman, 2002; House & Hayes, 2002). Counselors can work collaboratively with teachers to develop new innovative methods for working with students, teach support staff to complete routine paperwork, meet with administrators to discuss issues that may hinder learning, and utilize the expertise of community resources to provide additional assistance to the student (Hart & Jacobi, 1992).

A collaborative partnership between school and community will be more inviting and accessible to parents and families wishing to connect with these opportunities. With the school counselor serving as the coordinator and broker of these services, team members will likely serve as ambassadors for school counseling programs by publicizing the good things school counselors do (Paisley & McMahon, 2001).

Student Advocate

School counselors are capable of promoting schoolwide success for all students. Removing barriers to learning will be a central function of school counselors as they assist students in identifying values, beliefs, and behaviors that lead to personal growth (Herr, 2002), as well as those that are distractions. School counselors are in key positions for understanding the entire educational climate. Counselors have access to data, are aware of teachers who work in the best interests of their students, influence administrators' decisions, communicate with parents, and access community resources. As advocates for student achievement, school counselors will become more widely acknowledged and accepted as leaders of systemwide changes for all youth (House & Hayes, 2002).

SUMMARY

My nephew's news provided me with an opportunity to reflect on the noble history of the school counseling profession. Since the appearance of guidance workers in the school, the same questions, concerns, and performance confusion continue to resurface without resolution. Guidance and vocational organizations have met, debated, compromised, and lobbied for the profession with seemingly inconsequential results. Why, then, would anyone want to enter a profession that is tumultuous, undefined, and wrought with more questions than answers? The answer is clear: students benefit.

Today marks the beginning for the future of school counselors. The history of the profession has provided us with important lessons; and, by recognizing the struggles that have been previously confronted, we are able to see the future with a clearer lens. Just as the counselors of yesterday have taken the challenges confronting the profession, so will the counselor of tomorrow.

Future school counselors will have the training to demonstrate how counseling programs assist in student success. Counselor education programs will have the responsibility for better educating students in persuasion, advocacy, and collaboration skills. Training institutions will also work with site supervisors to better prepare novice school counselors. Facilitating activities that provide a greater understanding of the school milieu, implementing a transformed school counselor model into a traditional program, and advocating for students are just a few of the experiences in which counselors in training will be more actively engaged.

As the student body becomes more diversified and as new technology and software are developed, counselors of the future will need to keep current on technological advances. Membership in professional organizations is a key resource for counselors to learn new ideas, to gain support for advocating for change within the school system, and to become knowledgeable about professional trends.

A collaborative partnership between the school and community facilitated by the school counselor will aid in enhancing student development and achievement. Furthermore, career development will continue to be an important component within the school counselor's role—particularly as economic conditions change and technology advances.

I am encouraged and hopeful for future school counselors. The American School Counselor Association has made great strides in developing and voicing the promise the ASCA National Standards and Model hold for future school counselors and the students with whom they work. Many university preparation and continuing education programs for school administrators are now including the National Standards and Model as a part of their curricula. This information will enlighten future administrators on the essential skills of school counselors to support academic success. Through continued education, energy, and enthusiasm, the school counselors of the future will have the opportunity to perform the tasks and duties for which they have been trained and to advocate for all students today and those who will enter in the future.

REFERENCES

Adelman, S. H. (2002). School counselors and school reform: New directions. *Professional School Counseling, 5,* 235–248.

American Counseling Association. (n.d.). *Counseling Proposals for the Elementary and Secondary Education Act (ESEA).* Alexandria, VA: Author.

American Counseling Association. (2001). *U.S. student to counselor ratios* (Briefing Paper). Alexandria, VA: Author.

American School Counselor Association. (1998). *Ethical standards for school counselors.* Alexandria, VA: Author.

American School Counselor Association. (2003). *The professional school counselor and credentialing and licensure.* Alexandria, VA: Author.

Baker, S. B. (2000). *School counseling for the twenty-first century* (3rd ed.). Upper Saddle River, NJ: Merrill.

Beers, C. W. (1908). *A mind that found itself.* Garden City, NY: Doubleday, Doran & Company.

Bowers, J. L. (2002). Using technology to support comprehensive guidance program operations. In N. C. Gybers & P. Henderson (Eds.), *Implementing comprehensive school guidance programs: Critical leadership issues and successful responses* (pp. 115–120). Greensboro, NC: ERIC/CASS.

Bowers, J. L., & Hatch, P. A. (2002). *The national model for school counseling programs* (Draft). Alexandria, VA: American School Counselor Association.

CACREP. (2003). Council for the Accreditation of Counseling and Related Educational Programs. 5999 Stevenson Avenue, Alexandria, VA: Author.

Campbell, S., & Dahir, C. A. (1997). *Sharing the vision: The national standards for school counseling programs.* Alexandria, VA: American School Counselor Association.

Carlisle, C., & Frare, S. (2003, December). Resiliency in the wake of crisis. *ASCA School Counselor, 41,* 28–33.

Costar, J. W. (1978). The relationship of counselors to school principals. In American Personnel and Guidance Association, *The status of guidance and counseling in the nations' schools: A series of issue reports* (pp. 211–221). Washington, DC: Author.

Faust, V. (1968). *History of elementary school counseling: Overview and critique.* Boston: Houghton Mifflin.

Ferguson, D. G. (1963). *Pupil personnel services.* Washington, DC: The Center for Applied Education.

Fitch, J. A. (1936). Professional standards in guidance. *Occupations, 14,* 760–765.

Gibson, R. L., & Mitchell, M. H. (1999). *Introduction to counseling and guidance* (5th ed.). Upper Saddle River, NJ: Merrill.

Gibson, R. L., & Mitchell, M. H. (2003). *Introduction to counseling and guidance* (6th ed.). Upper Saddle River, NJ: Merrill.

Ginn, S. J. (1924). Duties of a vocational counselor in Boston public schools. *The Vocational Guidance Magazine, 3,* 3–7.

Gladding, S. T. (2000). *Counseling: A comprehensive profession* (4th ed.). Upper Saddle River, NJ: Prentice-Hall.

Gladding, S. T. (2004). *Counseling: A comprehensive profession* (5th ed.). Upper Saddle River, NJ: Prentice-Hall.

Green, A., & Keys, S. (2001). Expanding the developmental school counseling paradigm: Meeting the needs of the 21st century student. *Professional School Counseling, 5,* 84–95.

Gysbers, N. C. (2001). School guidance and counseling in the 21st century: Remember the past into the future. *Professional School Counseling, 5,* 96–105.

Gysbers, N. C., & Henderson, P. (2000). *Developing and managing your school guidance program* (3rd ed.). Alexandria, VA: American Counseling Association.

Hart, P. J., & Jacobi, M. (1992). *From gatekeeper to advocate: Transforming the role of the school counselor.* New York: College Board Publications.

Henderson, P., & Gysbers, N. (1998). *Leading and managing your school guidance program staff.* Alexandria, VA: American Counseling Association.

Herr, E. L. (2001). The impact of national policies, economics, and school reform on comprehensive guidance programs. *Professional School Counseling, 4,* 236–245.

Herr, E. L. (2002). School reform and perspectives on the role of school counselors: A century of proposals for change. *Professional School Counseling, 5,* 220–234.

Herr, E. L. (2003). Historical roots and future issues. In B. T. Erford (Ed.), *Transforming the school counseling profession* (pp. 21–38). Upper Saddle River, NJ: Merrill.

Hill, G. E. (1967). Agreements in the practice of guidance in the elementary schools. *Elementary School Guidance and Counseling, 1,* 171–188.

House, R. M., & Hayes, R. L. (2002). School counselors: Becoming key players in reform. *Professional School Counseling, 5,* 249–256.

Hughey, K. (2001). The complex, changing environment: A relative perspective. *Professional School Counseling, 5,* iii.

Johnson, S., & Johnson, C. D. (2003). Results-based guidance: A systems approach to student support programs. *Professional School Counseling, 6,* 180–184.

Landy, E., & Kroll, A. M. (Eds.). (1966). *Guidance in American Education 111: Needs and influencing forces* (Selected papers from the 1965 Summer Institute for Administrators of Pupil Personnel Services). Boston: Harvard Graduate School of Education.

Lapan, R. T., Gysbers, N., & Petroski, G. F. (2003). Helping seventh graders be safe and successful: A statewide study of the impact of comprehensive guidance and counseling programs. *Professional School Counseling, 6,* 186–197.

Loesch, L. C. (1988). Is "school counseling research" an oxymoron? In G. R. Walz (Ed.), *Building strong school counseling programs.* Alexandria, VA: American Association for Counseling and Development.

McWhirter, J. J., McWhirter, B. T., McWhirter, A. M., & McWhirter, E. H. (1998*). At-risk youth: A comprehensive response* (2nd ed.). Pacific Grove, CA: Brooks/Cole.

Muro, J. J., & Kottman, T. (1995). *Guidance and counseling in the elementary and middle schools: A practical approach.* Madison, WI: Brown & Benchmark.

Myers, G. E. (1935). Coordinated guidance: Some suggestions for a program of pupil personnel work. *Occupations, 13,* 804–807.

Myrick, R. D. (1993). *Developmental guidance and counseling: A practical approach* (2nd ed.). Minneapolis: Educational Media Corp.

Neukrug, E. (1999). *The world of the counselor: An introduction to the counseling profession.* Pacific Grove, CA: Brooks/Cole.

Newcombe, B. H. (1993). A historical descriptive study of the American Personnel and Guidance Association from April 1963 through July 1983 (Doctoral dissertation, Virginia Polytechnic Institute and State University, 1993).

Nugent, F. A. (1994). *An introduction to the profession of counseling* (2nd ed.). Upper Saddle River, NJ: Prentice-Hall.

Office of Public Policy and Legislation. (2001, March). *A guide to state law and regulations on professional school counselors.* Alexandria, VA: Author.

Paisley, P. O., & Borders, L. D. (1995). School counseling: An evolving specialty. *Journal of Counseling & Development, 74,* 150–153.

Paisley, P. O., & Hayes, R. L. (2003). School counseling in the academic domain: Transformations in preparation and practice. *Professional School Counseling, 6,* 198–203.

Paisley, P. O., & McMahon, G. (2001). School counseling for the 21st century: Challenges and opportunities. *Professional School Counseling, 5,* 106–115.

Parsons, F. (1909). *Choosing a vocation.* New York: Agathon Press.

Peters, H. J., & Farwell, G. F. (1959). *Guidance: A developmental approach.* Chicago: Rand McNally.

Reed, A. Y. (1947). *Guidance and personnel services in education.* Ithaca, NY: Cornell University Press.

Rogers, C. R. (1965). *Client-centered therapy.* Boston: Houghton Mifflin.

Roland, C. B., & Neitzschman, L. (1996). Groups in schools: A model for training middle school teachers. *Journal for Specialists in Group Work, 21,* 18–25.

Sabella, R. A., & Booker, B. L. (2003). Using technology to promote your guidance and counseling program among stake holders. *Professional School Counseling, 6,* 206–213.

Santrock, J. W. (1996). *Adolescence: An introduction* (6th ed.). Madison, WI: Brown & Benchmark.

Schmidt, J. J. (1993). *Counseling in schools: Essential services and comprehensive programs.* Boston: Allyn and Bacon.

School-to-Work Transition. (1996). Educational Resources Information Center, National Library of Education, Office of Educational Research and Improvement, U.S. Department of Education.

Schwallie-Giddis, P., ter Maat, M., & Pak, M. (2003). Initiating leadership by introducing and implementing the ASCA national model. *Professional School Counseling, 6,* 170–179.

Sheeley, V. L. (2002). American Counseling Association: the 50th year celebration of excellence. *Journal of Counseling and Development, 80,* 387–393.

Simmons, J. (2002, January). A golden opportunity. *Counseling Today,* 45.

SREB High Schools That Work. (n.d.). *New partnerships and national network to improve high school education.* Retrieved November 19, 2001, from http://www.sreb.org./programs/hstw/background/brochure.asp

Whiston, S. C. (2002). Response to the past, present and future of school counseling: Raising some issues. *Professional School Counseling, 5,* 148–155.

Williamson, E. G. (1950). *Counseling adolescents.* New York: McGraw-Hill.

Wrenn, C. G. (1962). *The counselor in a changing world.* Washington, DC: American Personnel and Guidance Association.

Zaccaria, J. S. (1969). *Approaches to guidance in contemporary education.* Scranton, PA: International Textbook Company.

Zeran, F. N., Lallas, J. E., & Wegner, K. W. (1964). *Guidance: Theory and practice.* New York: American Book Company.

2

The Professional School Counselor and Legal and Ethical Issues

I work in an elementary school with approximately 950 students. One of the principals who was employed in the district was reassigned to my school to help me by serving as a counselor. She does not have the credentials to perform as a school counselor, yet she is involved with "counseling" students, leading small counseling groups, consults with teachers, and provides "family counseling." I am concerned about the legal and ethical implications of her performing these duties. What advice can you give me?

The preceding statement is a communication I recently received from one of my former colleagues and is just one example of some of the concerns school counselors face. This chapter addresses the legal/ethical issues surrounding professional school counselors and includes situations that school counselors commonly confront.

School counselors are placed in positions of trust and required to act in ways that maintain this expectation. The American Counseling Association (ACA), the parent organization for all counselors, is comprised of 18 chartered divisions, each with an interest in enhancing human development. The American School Counselor Association (ASCA), one division of the ACA, has ethical standards based on the ACA ethical guidelines that specifically relate to professional school counselors (Linde, 2003). These ethical guidelines will serve as the source for this chapter.

Legal mandates are based on ethical standards and also regulate school counselors' performance with greater penalties for noncompliance. Federal and state legislative bodies enact laws and regulations that influence the behavior of counselors. State boards of education and local school districts create policies and procedures that reflect their own state and community needs (Linde, 2003), but boards do not have the authority to create policies beyond the limits expressed in the law (Schmidt, 1993). The difficulty is that ethical guidelines and legal mandates are not always compatible, and at times even conflict with each other.

ETHICAL GUIDELINES

The ASCA outlines standards of practice for school counselors; they are found in Appendix A. Because standards do not give specific guidelines for every situation, the counselor is faced with the responsibility of interpreting the situation according to his or her own beliefs (Huey, 1986) within the limits of the law. Each of the elements of the ethical guidelines is discussed with a case illustration.

Responsibilities to Students

Counselors should refrain from imposing personal beliefs on minors and, instead, should challenge and assist students to make decisions based on their own belief system (Huey, 1986). Through self-examination counselors can be aware of their own values and beliefs and how these attitudes influence students and other individuals with whom they have established a counseling relationship. Certain situations may arise in which a counselor may choose to express personal values. If these values interfere with the student's autonomy, the counselor should refer the student to another professional with whom an effective relationship can be established. Staying current on laws, regulations, and policies is also an ethical obligation the school counselor owes to the student and other stakeholders (Cottone & Tarvydas, 1998).

> Mrs. Murdoch has a student assigned to her caseload for whom she experiences many uncomfortable, negative feelings. As much as she has tried to figure out the cause of these feelings, she simply feels overwhelmed by her intense, unpleasant emotions. There are only two counselors in the school, and she does not want to inconvenience her colleague by assigning an additional student to her colleague's already overwhelming caseload. Mrs. Murdoch finally decides to ignore her feelings and continue to work with the student. How do you feel about Mrs. Murdoch's decision?

Confidentiality *Confidentiality*, an ethical mandate within the counseling profession, assures clients that what is said to the counselor will not be shared outside of the counseling relationship (Baker, 2000; Nederson & Fall, 1998). Confidentiality is based on the premise that the client has privacy rights that should be protected (Baker, 2000; Cottone & Tarvydas, 1998), since this right is a cornerstone for a successful counseling relationship (Jagim, Wittman, & Noll, 1978, as cited in Strein & Hershenson, 1991). Without the assurance that communication will remain confidential, students will not seek help, will not be totally honest, or may intentionally omit disclosing essential information.

Courts have not always recognized the right of minors to understand and consent to the counseling process, making confidentiality the most difficult ethical dilemma school counselors experience (Isaacs & Stone, 1999). Even when the counselor informs the student of the meaning and limits of confidentiality, there are exceptions, which include suspected child abuse or neglect and indications of intent to do harm to self or others (Baker, 2000; Cottone & Tarvydas, 1998; McCarthy & Sorenson, 1993). Since confidential sessions cannot be guaranteed (McCarthy & Sorenson), students need to be advised about this limitation before counseling begins and not after the student discloses something that is reportable by legal mandates.

Tyrone told his counselor that he and his friends stole the final examination from the science teacher's file cabinet. Discuss whether or not the counselor is obligated to maintain confidentiality and not disclose this information to the teacher.

Counseling Plans Goals need to be clear with attainable outcomes. When the counselor views a situation from the student's perspective, realistic expectations and workable solutions can be identified. One of the challenges encountered by the counselor is to assess each student in terms of the motivation to change and to assist that individual in reaching the chosen goals.

Tyla has been working with her counselor on several personal issues. For one, her mother is dating a man Tyla dislikes intensely. Additionally, Tyla is having difficulties with her own boyfriend, and her grades are dropping. Tyla has decided that she wants to find ways that she can confront her mother's boyfriend. The counselor feels that connecting with her mother is the more important goal. How should the counselor handle this situation?

Dual Relationships Whenever a counselor interacts with a client in more than one role, a dual relationship occurs that could negatively influence the counseling process (Cottone & Tarvydas, 1998). Examples of this dual relationship include friendships between the counselor and the student, counseling the child of a close personal friend, or counseling teachers or other educational personnel. A commonly occurring situation is when there is only one counselor in the educational setting responsible for all the students within the school. It would probably not be in the best interests of the student if the counselor refused counseling services due to a relationship with the family, yet the counselor needs to consider how the counseling session could be impacted. Additionally, it is not unusual for counselors to play a dual role in serving as administrators that deliver punishment for breaking school regulations and then performing as a counselor for that same individual. This creates not only an ethical concern but also a legal ramification in that the counselor may be performing out of his or her scope of practice.

Susan, a 14-year-old student, was seeing her counselor on a regular basis due to personal issues resulting from her parents' divorce 2 months earlier. The school counselor was the mother of a 6-year-old son and a 3-year-old daughter. She asked Susan if she would be able to babysit for her on Saturday night. Is this a request that could be considered as a dual relationship? Why or why not?

Appropriate Referrals It is not unusual for situations to arise that are beyond the knowledge and training level of the school counselor. In these situations, students are often better served through the expertise of other professionals either within the school setting or in the community. Counselors are expected to establish a network of outside experts for students who need help; and, if a referral is needed, three sources are recommended to be given to the student and/or parent (Muro & Kottman, 1995). The importance of providing at least three referrals was emphasized at one point in my career. I felt that a student who was engaged in self-mutilating behaviors would be better served through the counseling services of a mental health professional in the community. I gave the counselor's name to the parents of the student, and a few days later the student's mother called to let me know that she felt the community counselor was extremely unprofessional and she felt that I was a poor judge of character. Providing a list of professionals empowers the student and parents to make a decision, and then the consequences of that decision belong to the family. Furthermore, there may be legal ramifications if a referral is made. For instance, if a referral is given in certain circumstances, not unlike an IEP meeting, the school district may be held liable for paying the referral source.

Mrs. Scherger, a school counselor, was working with Marianne, a sixth-grader who revealed that she was binging and purging after eating and was unable to stop this behavior. She also revealed that she was secretly seeing a boy of a different race that her parents had forbidden her to see and she was concerned about her 16-year-old sister who was drinking on a regular basis. Mrs. Scherger contacted Marianne's mother about the eating disorder and provided her with the name of an individual in a neighboring community who specialized in eating disorders. Marianne's mother followed through on this recommendation, and the community counselor called Mrs. Scherger to discuss this case. What are your thoughts/feelings regarding Mrs. Scherger's behavior?

Group Work Both the ASCA and the Association for Specialists in Group Work (ASGW) outline ethical standards in regard to working with groups, and both organizations emphasize that school counselors only provide services for which they are qualified and trained (Linde, 2003). For example, students with substance abuse issues require a counselor who has been trained in issues of chemical dependency, including knowledge of the unique dynamics (e.g., anger, denial, etc.) that are specific to addicted youth. Counselors also have an ethical responsibility to provide information about the group process to the participants, and in a school setting this guideline includes providing information to parents and/or guardians (Terres & Larrabee, 1985) as well as the students.

Groups, within the constraints of the school, should be considered in design and implementation. The group purposes, number of sessions, meeting times, evaluation, and leader qualifications are to be shared with the teachers, student participants, and parents or guardians. Counselors need to recognize that they cannot guarantee confidentiality since not all members will honor the confidentiality agreement at all times (Terres & Larrabee, 1985). This concept is a topic of discussion at the beginning of each group session (McCarthy & Sorenson, 1993; Strein & Hershenson, 1991) and includes a plan for the consequences of breaking confidences.

A student who has been a self-esteem group participant arrives in the counselor's office in tears because one of the group members was telling other students what was discussed in the group. How should the counselor handle this?

Danger to Self or Others When counselors have a reasonable expectation that a student's behavior may lead to harm of self or others, counselors are to inform authorities. Since standards within each of the states are not consistent, the counselor needs to be aware of state guidelines and school district policies (Strein & Hershenson, 1991).

Mike and Susan, sixth-graders in a small middle school, barged into their counselor's office with news that they overheard one of their peers announce that she was going to "get back" at another class member. The counselor was aware that this student had a few minor incidents in which she had punched and kicked other classmates. Discuss whether or not the counselor has an ethical responsibility to report this information.

Student Records The professional school counselor often maintains personal notes to assist with the counseling process; and, because they are kept separate from educational records, they are considered the property of the counselor. Once this information is shared it is no longer considered confidential. Therefore the notes should be kept in a location unknown to anyone other than the counselor, and discretion is to be maintained in keeping personal student records on the computer or any compact disc that may be accessed by others (Linde, 2003).

In order to provide quality assistance to students, the school counselor keeps her own individual notes that she personally uses to remember the issues discussed in individual counseling sessions. She locks the notes up in her cabinet at the end of each day so that no one else can access these records. The principal is aware of these private records and wishes to see them. How should the counselor handle this situation?

Evaluation, Assessment, and Interpretation School counselors are trained in testing concepts and are obligated to apply pertinent standards in test selection, orientation, administration, and interpretation (Cottone & Tarvydas, 1998; Muro & Kottman, 1995). ASCA ethical guidelines specify that certain types of computer-based tests may require specific training that must be obtained prior to using the computer-based instrument. The counselor should use extra caution in ensuring that the student's confidentiality is maintained when computers are used for testing purposes.

The professional school counselor of a local high school was responsible for 600+ students and felt as if she couldn't possibly work with all of them. To help solve this problem, she had student aides administer some of the tests. Explain your thoughts and feelings about this behavior.

Computer Technology Privacy deals not only with the confidences revealed to the counselor but also with record disposal, tape recordings, and computer use for recording notes (Cottone & Tarvydas, 1998). Computer applications may enhance services to students, and counselors have an obligation to explain the benefits and limitations of computer use. Many computer programs are designed for counselors to quickly and effortlessly document counseling concerns, but in using this technology counselors need to safeguard computer data and preserve student anonymity (Nederson & Fall, 1998). Specific ethical concerns regarding online counseling are addressed by the National Board for Certified Counselors (NBCC) (Dollarhide & Saginak, 2003).

Mrs. Santos is the only counselor in a middle school of 600 students and has difficulty seeing students on an individual basis. To better assist her students with working through personal and career issues, she provides many Web sites for them to search the information that they need. Discuss Mrs. Santos' behavior.

Peer Helper Programs Students often bring about positive changes with their peers and serve as the powerful agents behind peer facilitation programs in schools. Peer facilitators in schools are used to assist in such areas as tutoring, conflict mediation, orienting students to new schools, and leadership of groups. Selected students receive training in listening, confidentiality, and communication. Peer facilitators are informed of the limits of their training with the understanding that they are not counselors but are trained in interpersonal skills. This distinction should be clear. Peers need to be carefully selected and monitored and not be placed in the position of conducting a group without the presence of a trained counselor (Dollarhide & Saginak, 2003).

Mr. Hinton is a high-school counselor who believes in the power of peer helper programs. He selected students for this program and provided them with training at the beginning of the school year. He advised the peer helpers to see him whenever they have an issue to discuss. Discuss whether Mr. Hinton's behavior was appropriate or not.

Responsibilities to Parents

The ASCA specifies the obligation school counselors have to parents (Cottone & Tarvydas, 1998). Since courts have granted the rights of minors to their parents or guardians (Isaacs & Stone, 1999), serious concerns arise when counselors who advocate for the students they assist make an effort to keep the students' disclosures confidential.

The ASCA recognizes that school counselors have multiple constituents to whom they are responsible and that making decisions in the best interests of all concerned parties is sometimes difficult (Isaacs & Stone, 1999). Noncustodial parents are specifically mentioned in the ASCA standards, and school counselors are often confronted with specific dilemmas concerning information sharing with these parents. In all states, birth parents or guardians are equally accorded legal parental rights and responsibilities unless a court decision explicitly states differently. The school counselor is responsible for making efforts to involve the noncustodial parent based upon knowledge of the legal status of the family unit and parents or guardian (Wilcoxon & Magnuson, 1999).

The Jeffersons have gone through a bitter divorce ending in the mother receiving custody of the children. Because of this arrangement, Mrs. Jefferson does not allow her ex-husband's parents to have contact with their grandchildren. The grandparents are well known and respected in the community. They arrive in the counselor's office concerned about the welfare of their grandchildren and want to know how they are performing academically. How should this situation be handled?

The professional school counselor has an obligation to inform parents of the confidential nature of the counseling process through written and verbal information. Counselors develop brochures that inform parents of the role and responsibilities of the school counselor. Yet, even with guidelines outlined, parents often request information their child has communicated to the counselor. The counselor is faced with an ethical challenge in that, by revealing the child's confidences, the rights of the child are jeopardized. To make matters worse, there are no clear answers among professionals in the field.

Huey and Remley (1988b, as cited in Strein & Hershenson, 1991) contend that parents act in the best interests of their children and have a parental right to know the information, even in cases where the student requests that information not be shared. Other researchers (Fisher & Sorenson, 1996, as cited in Isaacs &

Stone, 1999) believe that student information does not need to be shared with parents unless specifically written in school policy. Some school counselors reveal only essential general information without disclosure of specific details (Glosoff & Pate, 2002). Still others believe that educating parents as to how they can support their child without revealing the child's confidences is the most prudent course of action. Other practitioners believe that the younger the child, the greater the allegiance to the parents/guardians (Wagner, 1981, as cited in Huey, 1986).

Mr. and Mrs. Wilson referred their son Ryan to the counselor because he has been spending too much time with his friends and not enough time with them. In addition, he has recently adopted a "disrespectful attitude" toward them when they try to talk with him. Mr. and Mrs. Wilson are hoping that the counselor can "straighten out" Ryan. When the counselor talked to their son, Ryan revealed that he feels his parents are too strict, use harsh language to him, and are too demanding. After several weeks, the Wilsons want to know what the counselor and Ryan discussed. How should the counselor handle this?

Responsibilities to Colleagues and Professional Associates

Professional Relationships Every school counselor is to have a job description that outlines the specific duties and tasks to be performed. School counselors deal with sensitive issues; and when the job description specifies that the counselor is to work only with academic concerns, role confusion may result (Isaacs, 1997) due to the difficulty in separating educational issues from social/personal concerns.

Aaron saw his school counselor about his chances for a scholarship. When he discussed his goals with his counselor, it was obvious that he was clearly conflicted about his desire to go to art school and his father's wish that he become a medical doctor. At what point can the counselor separate the academic concerns from Aaron's personal issue?

The job description should be one that is jointly designed by the building administrator and the counselor, reflects the education and training of the school counselor, and is approved by the school board.

Sharing Information with Other Professionals Counselors are members of multidisciplinary teams and are sometimes the only individuals on these teams bound by confidentiality (Strein & Hershenson, 1991). Therefore, school counselors are faced with the dilemma of balancing the student's right for confidentiality and the concerns of others who act in the student's best interest (Isaacs &

Stone, 1999). Since teachers and administrators are not constrained by confidentiality, these professionals sometimes have difficulty understanding why school counselors are unable to divulge significant information (Nederson & Fall, 1998). Counselors have responded in several ways. At one end of the continuum, the practitioner will not share any information revealed by the student with the team members. At the other end of the spectrum, if the team is considered as a group of professionals who make decisions that positively impact the student, the counselor will feel an ethical responsibility to share information without restrictions. Most counselors take a position somewhere in the middle of these two extremes by informing the multidisciplinary team members of the ethical guidelines surrounding confidentiality and revealing only essential information. To assist in making the decision to disclose, the following questions serve as guidelines: "Will the information I am ready to disclose substantively facilitate that individual's work with the student?" and, "Do the others need to know this information?" (Glosoff & Pate, 2002).

Arturo was referred to the school multidisciplinary team for failure to turn in homework assignments, erratic attendance, and general inattentiveness in class. Prior to the referral he was an average student and attended classes on a regular basis. The school counselor, Mr. McLaughlin, had been counseling with Arturo who revealed that he was unable to sleep at night because of his parents' constant fighting. Apparently, Arturo's father was having an affair with one of the teachers in the school. How much should the counselor reveal to the team?

Responsibilities to the School

Local school boards develop and adopt policies and procedures based on state regulations and law (Linde, 2003). Counselors have the responsibility to advocate for students who are harmed by school board policies and to find a solution that protects the student. The student is to be the counselor's first allegiance and the school the second (Huey, 1986). If the counselor feels that the institutional policies conflict with his or her own values, philosophy, and ethical guidelines, then the counselor has an obligation to correct the situation or terminate employment (Cottone & Tarvydas, 1998).

Raymond worked as a high-school counselor in a school in which there was an increase in the number of students becoming pregnant. The school board collaborated with parents and community members and investigated how other schools handled this problem. The decision was made to make condoms available to students as a preventive measure. Raymond was given the responsibility of distributing the condoms that were provided by a local community agency—a task with which he vehemently disagreed. He resigned from this position at the end of the academic year. Discuss your feelings about his decision.

Responsibilities to the Community

Professional school counselors have an ethical obligation to be aware of the services that are available in the community and to form a collaborative relationship with the agencies involved. At the same time, school counselors need to communicate their training, education, and role. Without this information, the role and function of the school counselor will be based on assumptions and misconceptions resulting in an undesirable partnership. Through an awareness of the school community, the counselor may recognize factions that may be in opposition to school counselor programs (Linde, 2003), as well as those whose philosophy corresponds with the counseling program. The ASCA proposes a student counseling ratio of 100 to 1 as an ideal, and up to 300 to 1 as a maximum. The ratios in many schools far exceed this recommendation. In many schools the ratio of students to counselor is so extreme that counselors are not able to provide adequate services, and referring students to other professionals provides students with services that are desperately needed (Nederson & Fall, 1998).

The school counselor visited the various social agencies in her community to obtain a list of the individuals who work at each of the agencies and their education and training levels. At the same time, the school counselor shared her training and education with the various agencies she visited. What are your thoughts and feelings regarding this behavior?

Responsibilities to Self

Professional Competence Professional competence relates to the quality of services provided within the boundaries of training and education. Both ethical and legal standards exist to ensure that professionals provide appropriate services that are in the best interests of their client (student) (Linde, 2003) and the profession (Cottone & Tarvydas, 1998). Counselors who hold several credentials need to be aware of and follow the policies within the institution in which they are employed. For instance, if a professional school counselor also holds a credential as a clinical counselor, this professional needs to operate in the capacity defined by the school policies (Linde). Credentials that accurately reflect training and education are to be displayed and conveyed to consumers, and counselors should not in any way imply that their credentials allow them to work in areas for which they are not trained (Cottone & Tarvydas). Furthermore, counselors who hold doctorates in areas outside of the counseling profession are not to use the title of doctor in their work as a counselor (Linde).

School counselors have an obligation to self-reflect, monitor their own psychological health, and keep updated on professional information through conference and workshop attendance. Self-awareness provides counselors with an understanding of how their own personal issues may serve as motivators for their behaviors (Varhely & Cowles, 1991). For instance, a counselor may be uncomfortable counseling with a student who discloses he is gay, and the counselor's personal motives may be to disclose this information to parents, without regard to the student.

> Mr. Garcia is a seventh-grade counselor who is very involved with the lives of his students. It is not uncommon for him to stay at the school until 7:00 or 8:00 at night developing programs that will help his students. Students who have more serious concerns are given his home phone number and told to call him if they ever need to talk with him. Students often remark that he is one of the few people who really care about them. Discuss how you feel about Mr. Garcia's behavior.

Multicultural Skills Counseling theory evolved from a Western perspective, upon which some counselors base the counseling process without considering the worldviews of their students (Cohen & Cohen, 1999). Counselors have a professional obligation to perform in ways that are in the best interests of their stakeholders, including having personal awareness of biases and prejudices that may negatively impact the counseling relationship. School counselors have an obligation to assess their own multicultural competence, remain unbiased to provide for client autonomy (Cohen & Cohen), and seek training in areas in which improvement is needed (Nederson & Fall, 1998)

> Mr. Nishimura was asked to lead a group for Hispanic students who recently immigrated to the country. Although Mr. Nishimura has not had any experience with individuals from this ethnic group, he said that he could "read up on these people" and lead the group. Explain whether or not this behavior is ethical.

Responsibilities to the Profession

Professionalism Professionalism includes working within the policies established by the federal, state, and local governments; conducting him or herself in a manner established by the ASCA; not using his or her professional capacity to recruit clients for a private practice; and not seeking favors for personal gain (McCarthy & Sorenson, 1993). Students' privacy must be guarded in connection with research activities, and participants must be protected from harm. Informed consent is mandatory before students can participate in data collection for research purposes.

> Mrs. Taylor has multiple credentials, both as a school counselor and as a private clinical counselor. She works in a small, rural town in which agencies are scarce. She started her own private practice to help meet the mental health needs of the community, and she often refers students to her practice when she feels they require more attention than she can provide in the school setting. Discuss Mrs. Taylor's decision.

Contribution to the Profession The school counselor has an obligation to advocate for the school counseling profession and to contribute to the profession through conference and workshop attendance and sharing expertise with colleagues.

The high-school counselor, Mr. Smythe, wants to attend the state counselors' conference that is to be held for 2 days during the school week. The school principal, approached for permission to attend the conference, stated that the school district did not have the money to send him and that he was needed more at the school than at the conference. How should Mr. Smythe handle this situation?

Maintenance of Standards

The ASCA and many state school counselor associations have ethics committees that handle ethical complaints and serve in a consulting role for individuals dealing with ethical dilemmas. School counselors should consult with colleagues if an ethical violation of another professional member is perceived; and, when appropriate, the counselor should approach and communicate with the colleague whose behavior is in question before making a formal complaint.

Mr. Perez, a high-school counselor, has been counseling with Alena, an 18-year-old female senior. Alena reveals to him that she has been having a relationship with Mr. Alpine, a counselor employed at a neighboring school. She is having doubts about the relationship and wants to discuss how she can terminate the relationship with Mr. Alpine. Alena does not know that Mr. Perez personally knows Mr. Alpine from professional meetings. What should Mr. Perez do?

Resources

Ethical guidelines and resources are available to the professional school counselor. In particular, the ASCA has published position statements on various issues that are valuable to the counselor. In addition to the resource listing contained in the ASCA Ethical Standards, memberships in national, state, and local associations also provide additional resources. List Serves are also an expedient source for obtaining information, and confidentiality is to be respected when accessing these sites (Dollarhide & Saginak, 2003).

The principal of a local elementary school assigned administrative duties to the school counselor. As the principal stated, "There really isn't any documentation out there that shows counseling is effective anyway." How should this situation be handled?

Both ethical standards and legal mandates exist to ensure appropriate behavior for the benefit of all individuals involved. As mentioned previously, these two issues are often in conflict, particularly in regard to children's rights. There is continual debate as to whether children have the ability to make rational choices or whether parents own this right exclusively (Muro & Kottman, 1995). If the counselor is irresponsible in fulfilling his or her professional obligations, he or she can be found guilty of malpractice or negligence (Baker, 2000; Linde, 2003). *Malpractice* concerns professional conduct and occurs when the school counselor performs an action outside of his or her training leading to harmful results. For example, if a counselor not trained in hypnotism uses this approach with a student who is experiencing test anxiety (Baker; Linde), this is considered malpractice.

Negligence is the *failure* of the counselor to perform a duty that is part of the professional's obligation, for instance, the failure to report suicidal intent (Baker, 2000; Linde, 2000). In a study conducted by Hermann (2002), school counselors were asked which legal issue they encountered most frequently. The three most common responses included: determining whether a client was suicidal (90% of the respondents), ascertaining whether to report suspicions of child abuse (89% of the respondents), and assessing whether a client posed a danger to others (73% of the respondents).

LEGAL ISSUES INFLUENCING THE SCHOOL COUNSELOR

A discussion of all the legal issues influencing the school counselor is beyond the scope of this chapter. Issues including privileged communication, minor consent laws, child abuse, suicide, educational records and policies, placement in programs, Title IX, and academic advising are discussed in the following sections.

Privileged Communication

As discussed earlier in the chapter, confidentiality is an ethical standard, not a legal mandate. The legal status that pertains to confidentiality is known as *privileged communication* (Nederson & Fall, 1998; Stanard & Hazler, 1995). Privileged communication is the right of the client (student), which means that a student is protected from confidential communications being disclosed in court (Baker, 2000; Nederson & Fall). A problem arises for school counselors when the client is the student who is dependent upon parents or guardians since the question becomes, "Who owns confidentiality, the child or the parent?" (Isaacs, 1997).

Counselors have an ethical responsibility to maintain each individual's "right to privacy," yet youth under the age of 18 are not always given this right (Glosoff & Pate, 2002). In some states children's rights to privileged communication depend on how parents, guardians, or the courts interpret this benefit (Nederson & Fall, 1998). Privileged communication is limited through federal, state, and local laws that define its limits; and in certain areas a counselor in an agency setting may be covered, but a school counselor may not (Linde, 2003; Stanard & Hazler, 1995). In some states, student/counselor relationships are designated as privileged communication, and in other states this privilege is not extended to students (Baker, 2000). Because of the law variance among states, school counselors are to be aware of the limits that exist within their state and are to consider the positive and negative impact on the relationship when information is disclosed in court (Morse, 1990, as cited in McCarthy & Sorenson, 1993).

Despite privileged communication laws, exceptions occur when (a) the client gives permission for the counselor to release information; (b) the counselor is court ordered to disclose information, and there is no statute in that state regarding privileged communication; and (c) the client reveals harm to self or others (Remley & Sparkman, 1993). When a student reveals an indication of "clear and imminent danger" to self or others, the counselor is obligated to inform authorities and parents or guardians; this is known as the *duty to warn* (Nederson & Fall, 1998).

The duty to warn was a result of the 1974 *Tarasoff* case in California. In this situation, a graduate student at the University of California, Berkeley, told his psychologist about his intention to kill his girlfriend when she returned from Brazil because she had previously rejected him. The therapist consulted with two colleagues, and the decision was made to detain the student for questioning. The campus police detained him after being notified by the psychologist and later released him after being convinced that he would stay away from the girl. The victim and her family were not warned, and 2 months later the student killed the girl. The California Supreme Court ruled that the psychologist had a duty to warn a known victim (Henderson, 1987; Isaacs, 1997; Linde, 2003). Although this decision occurred in California, other state courts have used it as a prototype for similar legislation (Baker, 2000). In the *Tarasoff* case, the duty to warn superceded confidentiality (Cottone & Tarvydas, 1998). Other considerations regarding confidentiality include the following:

1. Clerical assistants who file or handle records or personal information. School personnel who work with the school counselor have legitimate reasons for having access to student records. School counselors have an obligation to discuss confidentiality issues with office personnel in relation to records, disclosure of information to other parties, and keeping counselor appointments in a concealed location (Cohen & Cohen, 1999).
2. Consultation with others. The school counselor is often in situations such as team meetings or with parents, where shared information is in the best interest of the student. The school counselor needs to determine whether sharing the information will actually benefit the student (Newman, 1993) or jeopardize the counseling relationship.
3. Group sessions. When there is more than one individual in a group, confidentiality cannot be guaranteed (Linde, 2003). The school counselor may seek the guidance of other professionals to find ways to maintain confidentiality in group settings (Strein & Hershenson, 1991).

4. Informed consent. This is both a legal and ethical principle (Glosoff & Pate, 2002). It is the right of the student to participate in counseling or other services after understanding information on the type of assistance that will be provided (Baker, 2000; Isaacs & Stone, 1999). Students seeking counseling should be informed about the counseling process; the meaning of confidentiality, including limitations; and the possibility that the counselor may wish to consult with others (Cottone & Tarvydas, 1998; Nederson & Fall, 1998). Since most students are not yet of legal age to provide consent, some counselors inform the student's parents or guardians about the counseling process. This information includes ethical issues and limits to confidentiality. Other school districts have specified that because the counseling program is part of the educational program of the school, parental consent is not necessary (Remley & Herlihy, 2001, as cited in Glasoff & Pate). Other school policies state that the school counselor may see a student without parental permission for two or three sessions but subsequent sessions will require parental permission (Glosoff & Pate). Other schools have adopted a policy in which the school counselor is to inform all parents in writing of the benefits of the counseling program and, if parents or guardians do not want their child to participate in counseling, they are to notify the counselor of that decision in writing.
5. Mandated counseling. At times students are ordered to receive personal counseling. For example, an officer of the court may mandate counseling for a student on probation and, if mental health counselors are scarce in the community, this task may be given to the school counselor. In cases such as this, confidentiality cannot be guaranteed. To resolve this issue, the counselor can define the limits of confidentiality to the person mandating the counseling and discuss with the student what information will be released (Strein & Hershenson, 1991). Or, the counselor may establish that only information that satisfies the purpose of the referral will be revealed (Strein & Hershenson). In all cases, the counselor should inform the client at the initial session about the information that will be shared and the consequences of not cooperating during counseling.
6. Supervision. The purpose of supervision is to enhance the skills of the supervisee. As the supervisee counsels students, information needs to be revealed to the supervisor to maintain quality services.

Minor Consent Laws

As previously discussed, informed consent involves obtaining permission for counseling services with full knowledge and understanding of the counseling process and services. Although the law does not specify parental permission, the legal ability of the student to receive counseling is an issue (Remley & Herman, 2000, as cited in Dollarhide & Saginak, 2003). When students reach the age of 18, they are considered as autonomous with rights accorded adults (Dollarhide & Saginak).

All states have conditions under which minors may seek treatment without parental consent, usually in cases involving substance abuse, mental health issues, and sexually transmitted diseases (STDs). The Drug Abuse Office and Treatment Act of 1976 protects the identity and confidentiality of any individual receiving treatment for drug and alcohol use, including students under the age of 18, as long as the program is subsidized by the federal government (Sealander, Schwiebert, Oren, & Weekley, 1999). This law also prohibits the release of records without the client's consent even if the client is a minor. Additional precautions should be made in maintaining the confidentiality of these records (Dollarhide & Saginak, 2003), since it is possible that students may go from referral to treatment completion without parent or guardian awareness (Linde, 2003). Furthermore, the school counselor should recognize state modifications of this statute (Dollarhide & Saginak). School policies also vary. Some consent statutes cover medical personnel under certain conditions. For instance, a school nurse may be covered but not a school counselor.

Counselors often utilize a developmentally based rather than chronological age assessment when considering confidentiality issues with minors (Glosoff & Pate, 2002). For instance, the age of 14 has been considered by many states as the age at which a student may self-refer without parental knowledge. However, the developmental capacity of 14-year-olds varies from individual to individual. School counselors are to determine the maturity level of the student and whether or not that student has the ability to make life-altering decisions without the guidance of parents (Isaacs & Stone, 1999).

Child Abuse

All states have procedures for reporting suspected child abuse (Dollarhide & Saginak, 2003; Muro & Kottman, 1995; Nederson & Fall, 1998). Every individual who works in a human services capacity is considered a *mandated reporter,* meaning that these reporters are responsible for reporting suspicions of abuse or neglect. Many states vary in their definition of what constitutes abuse and the required amount of time to report the abuse once it is suspected (Baker, 2000). In all states the reporter is immune from prosecution regardless of the outcome of the investigation (Baker).

School officials establish policies as to when to report, to whom, how, and what to report. In cases of abuse by school employees, even if the abuse occurred off the school property, this information must be reported (Newman, 1993). For example, a middle-school counselor at a large, urban middle school was counseling a freshman whose step-father taught in the same school building. The student revealed that the step-father was physically and verbally abusive. Upon hearing this complaint the counselor had conflicting feelings as to the best method of handling this concern. As a mandated reporter she felt an obligation to the student and the law. Even though she was aware that her name would not be revealed for making the report, she was afraid that the parents would be able to figure out the source of the information. At the same time, she felt compelled to discuss the situation with the step-father prior to making the report since she had to maintain a professional relationship with the step-father and colleague.

Some educators have reported having little information regarding child abuse and symptoms and plead a lack of understanding as to what constitutes abuse; however, ignorance of the law will not excuse the individual from reporting (Newman, 1993). Many schools set a policy that if a teacher or counselor suspects child abuse they must report this suspicion to the principal who, in turn, will report the suspicion. If the report is not made by the mandated individual, the person who originally suspected the abuse may be held liable (Dollarhide & Saginak, 2003; Linde, 2003). Failure to report involves a serious penalty that could include a loss of professional license, disciplinary action, or employment termination (Linde).

Suicide

School counselors have an obligation to identify warning signs of suicide and use professional judgment in determining appropriate actions to take (Remley & Sparkman, 1993). Based on *Eisel v. Board of Education,* a Maryland high court ruled that school counselors had an obligation to share student suicidal ideation and intentions with the child's parents, a duty that does not extend to counselors who are unaware of or could not be expected to know about a student's suicidal intentions (Newman, 1993). In the *Eisel* case, Nicole Eisel's friends informed the school counselor that Nicole was contemplating suicide. The counselor spoke to Nicole, who denied this claim. Later, one of Nicole's friends, who attended another school, shot Nicole and killed herself in the park behind the school during school vacation. As a result of this incident, all school counselors in Maryland must report the child's suicidal intentions to parents, a standard that has served as a guideline for school counselors in other states (Linde, 2003).

Although the school counselor has a duty to warn, appropriate judgment should be exercised in determining whether these steps are warranted and will not result in serious damage to the student and their families. For instance, consider the example of a well-adjusted student who sees a counselor about failing grades in mathematics class and states to the counselor, "I am going to kill myself if I fail another test." The counselor may disclose this information to the parents, who in turn may convey alarm and stress and subsequently claim that the counselor caused undue anxiety and apprehension over an unfounded statement. When the counselor reveals to parents or guardians that a student is at risk for self-harm, legal responsibility ends, yet the trust of the student may be irreparably damaged (Remley & Sparkman, 1993).

Educational Records and Procedures

In November 1974 the Family Educational Rights and Privacy Act (FERPA), also known as the Buckley Amendment, became law. With the passage of this law, parents and eligible students were given the right to inspect school records and to give permission for the release of educational records. As a result of this mandate, each school district must implement procedures for record accessibility and release to parents (Cottone & Tarvydas, 1998; McCarthy & Sorenson, 1993). If parents wish to examine their child's educational record and are denied access or information is provided to third parties without parental permission, federal funds may be withheld (McCarthy & Sorenson). When students reach the age of 18, they are granted the same rights as parents. School counselors need to pay particular attention to the issue of parents' refusal of their child's participation in school activities, including counseling programs (Sealander et al., 1999; Schmidt, 1993). Courts have stated that parents do not have the right to deprive their children of an education, but the law does not specifically address children's rights to participate in counseling services based on parental objections to these services (Muro & Kottman, 1995).

The FERPA provides exceptions to the release mandates in certain cases. For instance, a counselor's personal records pertaining to progress in counseling sessions are not required to be released if they are the counselor's personal notes (Dollarhide & Saginak, 2003). Yet, if any of the personal notes are shared with other professionals, the materials do fall under legal stipulations (McCarthy & Sorenson, 1993).

Public directory information, such as names and addresses, telephone number, date and place of birth, and so on, may also be released without parental permission. In order to release this information the school policies must identify what is considered as directory information, communicate this decision, and allow a reasonable period of time for the parents to respond if they do not want their child's records released. For instance, if a student is transferring to a new school, the student's records can be released to the new school without permission if the parents were notified in advance and the institution routinely operates in this manner (McCarthy & Sorenson, 1993). Personal notes should be regularly destroyed based on a calendar that is consistent with the destruction for records mandated by the school district (Dollarhide & Saginak, 2003). Under federal guidelines, materials used in federally assisted research or experimental projects must be made available to parents, and if parents object in writing the child may not participate (McCarthy & Sorenson).

Placement in Programs

Controversy often arises when children are placed in special education courses. School personnel are required to observe the laws surrounding students with special needs. The year 1975 marked the passage of the Education for All Handicapped Children Act (Pub. L. 94-142) and the 1990 amendment to this act, the Individuals with Disabilities Education Act (IDEA) (101-476). These acts provide free and appropriate education for all youth with special needs (Sealander, et al., 1999) and require a full evaluation based on multiple criteria before placing a student with disabilities. One of the central tenets of the IDEA is an Individual Education Plan (IEP) that clearly identifies goals, needs, objectives, accommodations, and evaluative criteria (McCarthy & Sorenson, 1993). This plan is considered a legal contract.

Title IX of the 1972 Educational Amendments

Title IX protects students from discrimination as a result of sex, marital status, or pregnancy (Baker, 2000; Schmidt, 1999, as cited in Dollarhide & Saginak, 2003). Equal access to educational programs, extracurricular activities, and occupational training is mandated in this law. Furthermore, this law forbids the use of assessment instruments that are gender-biased and requires guidelines for school officials to follow in the event of a sexual harassment charge (Dollarhide & Saginak).

Negligence in Academic Advising

Historically, school counselors have not been held responsible for providing inaccurate academic advice to students—until the year 2001. In the case *of Sain v. Cedar Rapids Community School District,* Bruce Sain, a senior at Jefferson High School in Cedar Rapids, Iowa, received a scholarship to Northern Illinois University for basketball. Prior to his matriculating to the university, he received a letter from the National Collegiate Athletic Association (NCAA) stating that he was deficient in the number of English credits needed to qualify for the scholarship. Because his high school failed to submit one of his English classes for NCAA approval, he was no longer eligible for the scholarship. Sain's parents filed suit against his school counselor for this omission. Although the court dismissed the case against the school district, the findings are noteworthy in that school counselors need to be aware of the importance of information they provide and that "the claim of negligent misrepresentation is akin to claims filed against lawyers and accountants when they give erroneous advice" (Stone, 2002, p. 31).

SPECIAL CONSIDERATIONS IN COUNSELING MINORS

School counselors' legal obligations vary from state to state and even between schools within a community (Baker, as cited in Linde, 2003). Counselors may take different courses of action in protecting the rights of a student, depending upon their work situation. Controversial issues surrounding sexuality, birth control, abortion, and AIDS sometimes create dilemmas for the school counselor. Some states allow minors to discuss these issues with the school counselor without parental notification (Sadler, 1989, as cited in Nederson & Fall, 1998), and other states mandate notification. Some school systems, particularly those with a religious affiliation, strictly forbid counselors to discuss birth control with their students. Counselors need to be aware of school and state policy regarding controversial issues; and if these policies do not exist, the counselor should take the lead in designing a board-approved policy.

What Constitutes Harm to Self?

School counselors often have difficulty determining what behaviors constitute harm to self and others. For instance, does a 16-year-old female who is 4 months pregnant and abusing drugs constitute harm to self and others? The counselor needs to examine personal values since smoking, body tattoos and piercings, drug use, cult membership, criminal activity, eating disorders, and pregnancy will be considered differently among counselors. Different courses of action will be tried to persuade the student to discontinue the destructive actions. If this request does not produce the desired results, the counselor should tell the student that authorities (principal or teacher) will be contacted without releasing the name of the student. And, if this still does not produce the desired results, the counselor needs to determine how to handle the situation (Stude & McKelvey, 1979). Some counselors will notify parents about some or all of the preceding concerns, and other counselors will not (Isaacs & Stone, 1999). Vernon (as cited in Isaacs & Stone) states that student age and maturity, consequences of disclosure on the counseling relationship, and the ethical standards and laws of the state or school should be considered before determining whether or not to reveal personal information the counselor determines to be harmful (Isaacs & Stone).

Oftentimes the counselor's decision of when to breach confidentiality is in part due to the perceived dangerousness of the behavior. Drug use, abortion, robbery, and sex with multiple partners are often considered as behaviors in which confidentiality is broken. Counselors working in different settings handle confidentiality differently. Elementary counselors were less strict in applying confidentiality and more likely to involve parents in decision making, followed by middle-school counselors. High-school counselors are least likely to involve parents. Inversely, elementary counselors were more reluctant to inform students about counseling records, while secondary counselors were more likely to discuss these records with their students (Wagner, 1981). Yet, both the chronological age and maturity level of the child seem to have serious weight in determining the child's right to maintain confidence (Isaacs & Stone, 1999). If the counselor determines that parents need to be contacted, an alternative to revealing all the information the child has disclosed would be to provide guidance on how they, as parents, can assist the child (Zingaro, as cited in Nederson & Fall, 1998). Nevertheless, counselors sometimes must involve adults (Sheeley & Herlihy, 1987).

Release of Information

Counselors often wonder about liability in writing unfavorable letters of recommendation for a student or providing information regarding disruptive behavior that may possibly have a negative influence on others. America's School Act of 1994, an amendment to the FERPA, has ruled that school personnel have a responsibility to release relevant data, including disciplinary action that was taken against a student who posed a threat to self or others (Sealander et al., 1999), as long as the information is factual. For instance, school personnel have an obligation to communicate the history of disruptive behavior committed by secondary students to an institution of higher learning, as long as this information is documented (McCarthy & Sorenson, 1993). For example, a graduate from a suburban high school entered a small liberal arts college to begin his college career. His first semester was marked by incidents of vandalism and theft that finally led to charges of arson when he started a fire in the dorm. Upon further investigation the college representatives learned that this individual had a history of this behavior while in high school. Just because a student's information is unfavorable does not mean that the material cannot be shared. Good practice recommends providing information that is factual and supported by data since personal opinion alone could lead to issues of liability (McCarthy & Sorenson).

GUIDELINES FOR ETHICAL DECISION-MAKING

1. Use disclosure/informed consent statements. These statements should be written in an understandable format and include the issues of confidentiality and privileged communication. In addition, the purposes, goals, and individual responsibilities need to be outlined.
2. Use discretion in determining whether or not to break confidentiality. Consultation with a counseling professional, administrator, state and/or national professional school counselor association and/or seeking the advice of the school attorney is advisable.
3. Document a rationalization for the course of action to serve as a basis for the steps that were taken.
4. Provide only pertinent information. Information that is relevant only to the concern, and how the third party can assist the client helps protect the client from having too much personal information revealed (Glosoff, Herlihy, & Spence, 2000).
5. Limit statements to facts. The counselor that is mandated to appear in court to testify should limit statements to factual information only, rather than expressing personal opinions (Remley & Herman, 2000, as cited in Dollarhide & Saginak, 2003).
6. Stay informed. The school counselor should stay current on professional standards of care and conduct and should assist in writing a job description that reflects district policy (Isaacs, 1997). Failure to perform duties outside of the job description may result in litigation (Muro & Kottman, 1995).
7. Know the law. The counselor should keep informed on law changes at the federal, state, and district levels; advocate for laws that protect the best interests of students, and work with personnel at the district level who are primary recipients of law and code changes.
8. Utilize a preventive approach to informing stakeholders about the counseling process on a regular basis, with the understanding that different individuals will request information about students and other stakeholders at some point (Glosoff & Pate, 2002).

9. Talk with the student about the amount of information that he or she is willing to disclose rather than making the assumption that the child does not want information to be shared (Glosoff & Pate, 2002).
10. In regard to providing vital information, collaborate with others in taking responsibility for providing accurate facts (Stone, 2002).
11. In supplying critical information regarding courses for future plans, or graduation credits that could influence future plans, have the student and parents acknowledge, in writing, that they have received the information (Stone, 2002).

THE COUNSELOR AND THE COURT SYSTEM

> Well, I went to court on Monday—it wasn't too bad, but I sure worried about the confidentiality aspect. I was surprised and pleased that each lawyer started his/her questioning with "with respect to confidentiality, can you tell me. . . ." It eased my mind knowing I wasn't going to have to make that decision.

The preceding statement was a communication I received from an elementary school counselor who was subpoenaed to appear in court on behalf of an elementary student. In this litigious society, counselors are finding themselves in the courtroom as witnesses involving such incidents as child custody, divorce, child abuse, and vocational issues (LaForge & Henderson, 1990). Although this is often an intimidating situation, there are certain procedures that are followed that make this event less threatening. Common procedures include preparing case information, attending the pretrial conference, qualifying the witness, and attending the deposition. When a school counselor receives a subpoena it is wise to discuss it with the student, and/or the parents, and the school attorney (Linde, 2003). When testifying in court, careful record keeping is critical. The case records the counselor keeps usually include such information as when the student was seen, the plan implemented, and the time spent. A review of these case notes prior to the court appearance helps refresh the memory.

To prepare for the upcoming trial, the counselor should request a meeting with the retaining attorney to learn more about what to expect in the courtroom. A deposition for the purpose of "fact finding" may also be held prior to the court date in which legally binding information is collected in the presence of an attorney. The counselor will be asked to testify as either an expert witness or a fact witness. An expert witness is selected based on education and experiences and provides clear, accurate facts based on that witness's expertise. A fact witness testifies what he or she knows or has observed (LaForge & Henderson, 1990). The communication of the role of the counselor became evident when I was subpoenaed into court as an expert witness.

In this situation my credentials were under question. The prosecuting attorney stated that since I was a counselor and not a psychologist, that my testimony was not valid. Although the retaining attorney tried to describe my credentials and experience, it was evident that he also was not quite sure of how a counselor fits into the mental health hierarchy. At this point I was asked to explain how my position is different from a psychologist, and after much debate (and a brief recess) I was allowed to testify. This incident once again clarified for me how important it is to communicate regarding our profession of counseling.

When the counselor is asked to reveal confidential information, two courses of action can be considered. Either the counselor can inform the judge that the release of information would violate confidentiality and request a ruling, or the counselor can request that the information be heard without spectators present (Sheeley & Herlihy, 1987). If the judge requires the counselor to reveal information, the court—not the counselor—can be sued by the client for violating confidentiality.

If the counselor is subpoenaed to court due to malpractice or neglect, the standard of practice will be established through the testimony of peers who are considered experts based on their education and experience. The more training and education the subpoenaed counselor has received, the higher the standard to which he or she will be held in court (Linde, 2003).

SUMMARY

Professional school counselors are often in situations in which there are no clear-cut answers. The American School Counselor Association (ASCA), a division of the American Counseling Association (ACA), developed ethical guidelines based upon the ethical standards established by ACA. Although ethical standards direct the profession, they are sometimes in conflict with legal statutes. To add even more confusion, school counselors work with minor students who do not have the rights accorded to adults, which confounds the counseling relationship. This chapter summarizes the ASCA ethical guidelines and provides ethical dilemmas to consider. Furthermore, this chapter contains information regarding legal issues, special considerations for working with children, and preparation for court appearances.

REFERENCES

Baker, S. (2000). *School counseling for the 21st century* (3rd ed.). Upper Saddle River, NJ: Prentice-Hall.

Cohen, E. D., & Cohen, G. S. (1999). *The virtuous therapist: Ethical practice of counseling & psychotherapy*. Pacific Grove, CA: Thomson.

Cottone, R. R., & Tarvydas, V. M. (1998). *Ethical and professional issues in counseling*. Upper Saddle River, NJ: Prentice-Hall.

Dollarhide, C. T., & Saginak, K. A. (2003). *School counseling in the secondary school: A comprehensive process and program*. Boston: Allyn and Bacon.

Glosoff, H. L., Herlihy, B., & Spence, E. B. (2000). Privileged communication in the counselor-client relationship. *Journal of Counseling & Development, 78,* 454–461.

Glosoff, H. L., & Pate, R. H. (2002). Privacy and counseling in school counseling. *Professional School Counseling, 6,* 20–27.

Henderson, D. H. (1987). Negligent liability and the foreseeability factor: A critical issue for school counselors. *Journal of Counseling and Development, 66,* 86–89.

Hermann, M. A. (2002). A study of legal issues encountered by school counselors and perceptions of their preparedness to respond to legal challenges. *Professional School Counseling, 6,* 12–27.

Huey, W. C. (1986). Ethical concerns in school counseling. *Journal of Counseling and Development, 64,* 321–322.

Isaacs, M. L. (1997). The duty to warn and protect: Tarasoff and the elementary school counselor. *Elementary School Guidance & Counseling, 31,* 326–342.

Isaacs, M. L., & Stone, C. (1999). School counselors and confidentiality: Factors affecting professional choices. *Professional School Counseling, 2,* 158–166.

LaForge, J., & Henderson, P. (1990). Counselor competency in the courtroom. *Journal of Counseling & Development, 68,* 456–459.

Linde, L. (2003). Ethical, legal, and professional issues in school counseling. In B. T. Erford (Ed.), *Transforming the school counseling profession* (pp. 263–292). Upper Saddle River, NJ: Prentice-Hall.

McCarthy, M. M., & Sorenson, G. P. (1993). School counselors and consultants: Legal duties and liabilities. *Journal of Counseling & Development, 72,* 159–167.

Muro, J. J., & Kottman, L. (1995). *Guidance and counseling in the elementary and middle schools: A practical approach.* Madison, WI: Brown & Benchmark.

Nederson, D. A., & Fall, M. (1998). School counseling. In R. R. Cottone & V. M. Tarvydas (Eds.), *Ethical and professional issues in counseling* (pp. 263–292). Upper Saddle River, NJ: Prentice-Hall.

Newman, J. L. (1993). Ethical issues in consultation. *Journal of Counseling & Development, 72,* 148–156.

Remley, T. P. (1985). The law and ethical practices in elementary and middle schools. *Elementary School Guidance and Counseling, 19,* 181–189.

Remley, T. P., & Sparkman, L. B. (1993). Student suicides: The counselor's limited legal liability. *The School Counselor, 40,* 164–169.

Schmidt, J. J. (1993). *Counseling in schools: Essential services and comprehensive programs.* Boston: Allyn and Bacon.

Sealander, K. A., Schwiebert, V. L., Oren, T. A., & Weekley, J. L. (1999). Confidentiality and the law. *Professional School Counseling, 3,* 122–127.

Sheeley, V. L., & Herlihy, B. (1987). Privileged communication in school counseling: Status update. *The School Counselor, 34,* 268–272.

Stanard, R., & Hazler, R. (1995). Legal and ethical implications of HIV and duty to warn for counselors: Does Tarasoff apply? *Journal of Counseling & Development, 73,* 397–406.

Stone, C. (2002). Negligence in academic advising and aborting counseling: Courts rulings and implications. *Professional School Counseling, 6,* 28–35.

Strein, W., & Hershenson, D. B. (1991). Confidentiality in nondyadic counseling situations. *Journal of Counseling & Development, 69,* 312–320.

Stude, E. W., & McKelvey, J. C. (1979). Ethics and the law: Friends or foe? *Personnel and Guidance Journal,* 453–456.

Terres, C. K., & Larrabee, M. J. (1985). Ethical issues and group work with children. *Elementary School Guidance and Counseling, 19,* 190–197.

Varhely, S. C., & Cowles, J. (1991). Counselor self-awareness and client confidentiality: A relationship revisited. *Elementary School Guidance & Counseling, 25,* 269–276.

Wagner, C. A. (1981). Confidentiality and the school counselor. *Personnel and Guidance Journal, 59,* 305–310.

Wilcoxon, S. A., & Magnuson, S. (1999). Considerations for counselors serving noncustodial parents: Premises and suggestions. *Professional School Counseling, 2,* 275–279.

Zingaro, J. C. (1983). Confidentiality: To tell or not to tell. *Elementary School Guidance and Counseling, 17,* 261–267.

3

The Culturally Sensitive Professional School Counselor

We all have been placed in new situations that are uncomfortable because of the unfamiliar surroundings, the people we encounter, and the expectations placed upon us. Imagine what this experience must be like for a new student entering an unfamiliar country and encountering that customs are strange and a language that is foreign. When I first met Yung Ling he was entering the United States from China. His parents were given a visa that permitted the family to work in a local restaurant under the sponsorship of a relative who had arrived several years earlier. The parents spoke no English, Yung Ling spoke very little of the language, and his sponsor was unable to come to the school to assist in registering her nephew. As a counselor in a rural school district I did not have many of the resources he needed. With his limited English and the help of a mathematics instructor who provided him with sample problems to complete, I was able to come up with a skeleton schedule that would at least allow me time to investigate resources to assist this adolescent. Interestingly, as I attempted to communicate with him I found myself speaking not only very slowly but also very loudly, as if the very volume would help him understand me better.

Schools in the United States are in a pivotal position to foster acceptance and cultural sensitivity by providing opportunities to develop self-awareness and to learn about others from a culturally different environment (Johnson, 1995). Counselors need to develop self-awareness, knowledge, and skills so that they can advocate for all students from diverse backgrounds.

Most counselor education programs offer a separate course that deals with cultural diversity themes in counseling. This chapter is meant not to replace this course but, rather, to supplement the information surrounding the cultural development of youth.

Never before has our society seen such vast demographic changes (Sue, 1991, cited in Holcomb-McCoy, 2003) with such a wide range of multiethnic and multilingual individuals. According to projections from the U.S. Census Bureau (2001), by the year 2005 Caucasian Americans will have had the lowest increase in population, with the largest projected increase among Hispanics, African Americans, and Asian Americans. For many years the "melting pot" concept, coined from a 1908 play by Israel Zangwill, assumed that the increasing numbers of individuals with diverse backgrounds arriving in the United States would discard their own cultural values and adopt the customs and values of the dominant culture (Pedersen, 1994). Yet, for numerous reasons, individuals opted to hold on to their own beliefs, traditions, and heritage (Baruth & Manning, 2003), and this projection never came to fruition. Counselors can no longer hold onto traditional approaches to assist individuals who are seeking counseling services; they need to be ready to adapt their skills to effectively work with students and their families from diverse backgrounds.

Because the field of multicultural counseling is relatively new, too many counselors have learned theoretical approaches and intervention strategies that are a reflection of the White Western worldview, a perspective that is neither appropriate nor helpful for individuals from culturally diverse populations (Baruth & Manning, 2003; Sue, Ivey, & Pedersen, 1996, as cited in Baker, 2000). Further complicating the issue is that multicultural counseling is difficult to define (Holcomb-McCoy, 2003). The Association for Multicultural Counseling and Development (AMCD), a division of the American Counseling Association (ACA), defines multiculturalism narrowly and as relating to five major cultural groups within the United States and its territories: African, Asian, Caucasian, Hispanic, and Native American (Holcomb-McCoy, 2003). The Council for the Accreditation of Counseling and Related Educational Programs (CACREP) views multiculturalism in broader terms that include not only characteristics of race but also "age, gender, sexual orientation, ethnicity, language, disability, culture, spirituality, and other factors related to the assessment and evaluation of individuals, groups, and specific populations" (CACREP, 2001, p. 5). Since many authors argue for a broader range of characteristics to consider, the term *diversity-sensitive counseling* has been coined to reflect the wide range of diverse groups, (Sue, 1992, and Weinrach & Thomas, 1998, as cited in Baker, 2000) and is the term used throughout this chapter. Counseling diverse student populations, characteristics of the populations that are greatly increasing in numbers within the United States, and adolescent gender orientation issues are the focus of this chapter.

DEFINITION OF TERMS

Race is sometimes viewed as a product of human invention (Armelagos, Carlson, & Van Gerven, 1982, as cited in Cameron & Wycoff, 1998). The construct originated to explain human differences and later served as a justification for the exploitation of "inferior" people (Cameron & Wycoff). Although race is typically viewed through specific physical attributes, it is impossible to classify individuals through identifiable characteristics. Although the term *race* has been discredited as a scientific construct, it does still play a significant role politically as well as psychologically. Schools and other institutions need this information to track students' progress, enrollment, graduation rate, college matriculation, scholarships, and so on (Baruth & Manning, 2003; Freitag, Ottens, & Gross, 1999).

Culture is defined through physical and subjective features that are transmitted from generation to generation (Cameron & Wycoff, 1998). *Physical culture* refers to such things as tools used and types of roads, buildings, eating utensils, and so on, while *subjective culture* includes beliefs, values, and norms. Members of a racial group have their own culture, while ethnic groups within a race have different cultures (Root, 1993). Culture has been not only defined narrowly as an individual's ethnicity or nationality but also in a broader perspective that includes demographics such as socioeconomic status, gender, religion, values, sexual orientations, and disabilities (Baruth & Manning, 2003; Freitag et al., 1999; Holcomb-McCoy, 2003).

The second definition is not without its critics. Some researchers argue that this definition sullies its pure meaning since there is disagreement as to whether age, lifestyle, and other affiliations are really culturally different. However, advocates for the broader, more inclusive definition assert that not only do different ethnic groups in a single population have different cultures but individuals within the same ethnic group may also have a different culture (Pederson, 1994). Culture is fluid and evolves as people interact and change.

Intragroup and intergroup differences of individuals need to be understood as well as their subcultures and intraculture. For example, a counselor cannot assume that all Asian Americans share the same beliefs or that all Hispanic American women worship in the same way. Individuals who belong to gangs, members of the gay population, or the community of people who are disabled share characteristic ways of behaving that are different from the dominant society. Likewise, each individual has a *personal culture* based on such things as experiences, education, socioeconomic background, geographic location, and so on (Baruth & Manning, 2003). The diversity-sensitive counselor recognizes the dynamics within individuals and groups as well as between individuals and groups (Yagi, 1998).

Ethnicity is "embedded within the culture" (Cameron & Wycoff, 1998, p. 278). An *ethnic group* is a culturally distinct population whose members share a collective distinctiveness and common heritage viewed as separate and distinct from the cultural majority (Diller, 1999). Ethnic characteristics include a shared sense of identity due to common values, behaviors, beliefs, communication, and historical perspectives (Holcomb-McCoy, 2003). A larger cultural group is composed of several ethnic groups. Although ethnicity and culture share similarities, they are different (Cameron & Wycoff). The United States has a national culture with concepts accepted and shared by the majority of the people within the nation. For instance, there is an acceptance of monetary values; driving cars on the right side of the road; stopping at a stop sign; and eating with knives, spoons, and forks.

Within the national culture are many ethnic groups that share attitudes, beliefs, and behaviors that are unique to each group (Cameron & Wycoff). For example, a Jewish American female is a member of the national culture and a member of an ethnic group within this culture and retains her own culture due to her personal attitudes, experiences, and beliefs.

BECOMING SKILLED IN DIVERSITY-SENSITIVE COUNSELING

The challenge for counselors is in obtaining the awareness, knowledge, and skills to work effectively with individuals from other backgrounds without creating new stereotypes (Baker, 2000; Carney & Kahn, 1984; Freitag et al., 1999, as cited in Holcomb-McCoy, 2003). The following competencies are reflected throughout this chapter:

1. An awareness of one's own personal worldviews and how these views are a result of cultural socialization
2. Knowledge of the worldview of individuals from a different cultural background
3. Skills that are needed to work with individuals from a different background (Corvin & Wiggins, 1989, as cited in Holcomb-McCoy & Myers, 1999)

Awareness

Counselors often underestimate the impact of their own socialization (Pederson, 1994; Yagi, 1998) since there is little thought as to what it means to be a member of a different racial/ethnic group (Parker, Moore, & Neimeyer, 1998). Self-understanding can be accomplished by determining areas in which one needs greater competence. The following exercise can be used for developing greater self-awareness.

Exercise

Complete the following sentences with the first adjective or group of words that comes to mind upon reading the statements. Do not censor your thoughts; simply write the first thing that comes to mind.

Amish are generally . . . .

It is well known that African Americans are . . . .

When I meet someone who is an Islamic individual I feel . . . .

One thing I would like to say to a Mexican American is . . . .

The trouble with gays and lesbians is . . . .

Native Americans are generally . . . .

One word I would use to describe someone from an Asian culture is . . . .

Italians are . . . .

Females are . . . .

Males are different from females in that they are . . . .

In looking over your responses, do you note any patterns? Discrepancies? Surprises? Areas in which you need more training? Sharing answers with other class members may provide the opportunity to look at other perceptions.

Knowledge

Two different models are used for understanding and respecting the worldviews of culturally different clients (Holcomb-McCoy, 2003). The *Emic model* emphasizes a culturally specific approach in that the counselor learns as much as possible about a culture and applies this information when working with an individual from that particular culture. For instance, without awareness that an individual from an Asian culture may be reluctant to self-disclose, the counselor may be quick to label this individual as "resistant." Another Emic approach is recognizing that Native Americans respect traditional healers and may accept the wisdom of these individuals before seeking a counselor. Or, a counselor raised in a Western society that values promptness may have difficulty accepting the "lateness" of individuals from cultures who view time as flexible (Diller, 1999). The *Etic model* is a culture-general concept in which the counselor uses a common frame of reference to view similar traits and characteristics shared across cultures rather than a focus on differences between groups (Baruth & Manning, 2003; Freitag, et al., 1999; Santrock, 1996). This approach emphasizes that counseling methodologies and techniques have relevance for all individuals, regardless of their culture (Diller). For instance, data collected from a study by Ekman and Frusen (1975, as cited in Simmons, 1998) revealed that ethnically diverse individuals were highly consistent in identifying facial expression and the corresponding emotions—concluding universal recognition of facial expressions and emotions.

Some professionals believe that both models lead to cultural insensitivity since the Emic approach highlights group differences while the Etic model ignores these differences (Baruth & Manning, 2003). The following exercise is designed to develop a greater knowledge base of other cultures or ethnic/racial groups.

Exercise

Imagine you are from a culture different from your own. How do you think your life would be different? Think in terms of gender differences, family interactions, economic considerations, educational inconsistency, values, beliefs, and so on.

Skills

Although knowledge is important in understanding culturally different students and their parents, it is not enough. Skills are also needed (Holcomb-McCoy, 2003) for proficiency with a particular cultural group. *Skill training* assists the counselor in developing and practicing appropriate intervention techniques (Holcomb-McCoy). *Microskill training,* in which skill areas are subdivided into smaller units, is effective because appropriate skills are selected to assist individuals from different backgrounds and concerns (Pederson, 1994). Counseling with any individual can be regarded as diversity-sensitive counseling because everyone belongs to multiple groups that impact perceptions, beliefs, feelings, thoughts, and behaviors (Patterson, 1996).

Counseling jargon alone may unconsciously reveal bias. For example, the terms *self-esteem* and *self-understanding* are common counseling terms based on a Western perspective but inappropriate for individuals from collectivist cultures such as Japan. In these cultures the welfare of the family or the group is more important than the welfare of the individual; promoting an individual's self-concept above the family would be considered neglectful and even harmful (Pederson, 1994).

In addition, Western ideology may unconsciously promote discrimination when counselors adhere to the belief that formal individual counseling is more helpful than the individual's natural support system. Counselors need to recognize, endorse, and promote the effectiveness of family and friends and other members of the community (Pederson, 1994) in creating change. These significant people provide resiliency and encouragement; and it is possible that some individuals prefer to discuss personal concerns with parents, friends, and other family members rather than professional counselors (Baruth & Manning, 2003).

One midwestern high school made the effort to make all foreign exchange students and students from other countries feel welcome by hanging the flags of the countries from which these students came. If the student was from a family whose parents were from another country, that flag was also displayed in the cafeteria for all to view.

Understanding the student's worldview is part of the counselor's task (Baruth & Manning, 2003). Several factors influential to one's worldview include cultural group, racial or ethnic group, family, state or country, social class, gender, sexual orientation, and/or disability (Baruth & Manning) as well as sociopolitical factors (Merchant & Dupuy, 1996) and developmental characteristics. The intersection of these factors with the developmental life span and tasks associated with each developmental stage are significant. Children and adolescents have unique developmental characteristics that differ significantly from other life span cultures.

DEVELOPMENTAL ISSUES OF CHILDREN AND ADOLESCENTS

Understanding the developmental concerns of children and adolescents is a challenging task for counselors, particularly as development overlaps with cultural issues (Baruth & Manning, 2003). For instance, adolescent development emerged as a Western concept in that social support, life stressors, and individual responses to stress have been explained according to White middle-class populations.

The United States and other industrialized countries socialize individuals for achievement and independence, whereas adolescents socialized in nonindustrialized countries place more merit on obedience and family loyalty (Santrock, 1996). Even various adolescents in U.S. society are socialized differently. Mexican American adolescents are socialized to be less competitive and achievement-oriented, but more cooperative than Caucasian American adolescents (Santrock). Moreover, Asian American adolescents are more achievement-oriented than Caucasian American students (Sue & Okazaki, 1990, as cited in Santrock).

Differences in sexuality are also found among adolescents from different cultures. Sexual activity among adolescents in some cultures is considered normal but is forbidden in other countries. The Ines Beag live on a small island off the coast of Ireland. The individuals in this culture believe that sexual intercourse is unhealthy and reduces their energy level. Tongue kissing and stimulating the penis by hand is despised. In contrast, boys from the South Pacific Mangaian culture learn about masturbation at the early age of 6 or 7 and undergo a surgical procedure in which a small incision is made in their penis at the age of 13. Following this procedure the boys engage in intercourse and are provided with instruction in orgasm and pleasing sexual partners with a woman experienced in sexual matters. Sexual intercourse is a frequent activity of these adolescent males. American adolescents engage in sexual behavior somewhere in the middle of this continuum (Santrock, 1996).

Because American minorities are overrepresented in the lower socioeconomic groups, differences are often explained away as ethnic attitudes and behaviors rather than a result of socioeconomic status. Little research is available on the interaction of ethnicity and social class. For example, child-rearing practices differ within American families. Working-class, lower-socioeconomic-class parents, regardless of ethnic/racial background, place emphasis on obedience and neatness; and discipline is administered through criticism and spankings. In contrast, middle-class parents place value on self-control and engage in discipline through such authoritative means as assertion and negotiation (Santrock, 1996).

Most individuals from a diverse cultural group confront their ethnicity for the first time in adolescence and become more aware of the negative appraisals accorded their group (Baruth & Manning, 2003). One major task faced by adolescents is developing an identity that also includes a cultural identity. Too many adolescents develop an identity under difficult circumstances including such issues as poverty, prejudice, and negativism, with few role models represented within their ethnic/cultural group (Baruth & Manning, 2003). These adolescents are conflicted as to how to negotiate the values, beliefs, and behaviors of their own group and those of the majority culture. In addition, goal setting is difficult if they perceive that opportunities are limited. School counselors have a professional and ethical obligation to promote and advocate for activities designed to endorse human respect and discourage discrimination (Johnson, 1995).

The remainder of the chapter focuses on the competencies advocated by the AMCD and the largest growing populations within our schools: African Americans, Asian Americans, and Hispanics. Counseling concerns of males and females, including individuals with gender identity concerns, are also discussed. A separate chapter will be devoted to counseling students with special needs, including gifted and talented students, a unique population with significant needs.

COUNSELING AFRICAN AMERICAN STUDENTS AND THEIR FAMILIES

The school principal in a suburban high school was having difficulty with one of the African American 11th-graders. This adolescent was continually tardy to class and seemed to have difficulty completing his homework assignments. When the principal called the young man's home for a conference, he was surprised when the mother, grandmother, and aunt arrived for the conference.

Poverty, limited employment, fewer educational opportunities, and acts of discrimination are issues influencing persons of African ancestry (Young, 1993). African Americans often do not take advantage of counseling services because of the perceived insensitivity of counselors, few available African American counselors, and the perception that counselors have little understanding of the African American culture (Baruth & Manning, 2003). Interventions that target kinship, family roles, and religion are useful strategies for school counselors who work with African American students and their families (Diller, 1999).

Awareness

School counselors need to understand an African American's personal history and family experiences. Most African American families have complex family networks that include both biological relations and nonbiological connections, vital supports for personal and emotional survival. This collective identity, referred to as "fictive kinship" by Fordham and Ogbu (as cited in Howard-Hamilton & Behar-Horenstein, 1995), is one of the greatest sources of satisfaction and self-concept (Gary et al., as cited in Wilson & Stith, 1993). Many African American students live in single-parent, female-headed homes with the father figure often absent and with grandparents accepting the responsibility for raising their grandchildren (McDavis & Parker, 1993).

The strong spirituality evident among African American individuals is a powerful resource. The church is often the only place where African Americans feel a sense of belonging and acceptance. Church members are often assigned roles within the church that contribute to positive self-concept (McDavis & Parker, 1993); and during times of stress the school counselor may consider asking the family to bring their minister in to assist in providing direction to a problematic situation.

Knowledge

Some of the most common concerns African American adolescents bring to the counseling session include identity issues, academics, interpersonal relationships, aggressiveness, and goal setting (Baruth & Manning, 2003). The culturally aware counselor recognizes the difference between African American and White American values. White Americans place a greater value on independence, achievement, materialism, goals, and power; while many African Americans place a greater emphasis on sharing, obedience to authority, spirituality, and personal heritage (Wilson & Stith, 1993). Counselors are aware that children and adolescents often encounter language problems and conflict in schools. African American dialect is accepted in the home and community (McDavis & Parker, 1993), while Standard English is used in the schools.

Skills

The culturally competent counselor should be cognizant of the verbal and nonverbal communication patterns of the African American student. African Americans are attentive to nonverbal language because it is considered as being more honest than verbal communication. Sue (1981, as cited in Exum & Moore, 1993) pointed out that African Americans prefer a closer spatial arena than other cultural groups when conversing. Moreover, because African Americans tend to avoid eye contact when listening to another person, many educators mistakenly believe that this behavior is a sign of disinterest (Young, 1993).

One of the most serious issues facing African Americans is the decline in educational status. African American students are disproportionately represented in special education classes and as underachievers in reading and mathematics. When African American youth are identified with learning disabilities, mental retardation, or slow learning traits, they are at a greater risk of not achieving academically, socially, and emotionally and of developing a poor self-identity (Campbell-Whatley, Algozzine, & Oblakor, 1997). In a study by Faribaldi (1992, as cited in Exum & Moore, 1993), 95% of African American males reported that they expected to graduate from high school but felt that their teachers did not motivate them to continue past high-school education. Instructional materials such as tutoring, role playing, and self-help books have been effective in enhancing self-esteem and promoting positive attitudes among African American youth (Washington, 1989, as cited in Holcomb-McCoy & Myers, 1999).

Exercise

The following questions are designed to develop an awareness of self and others from different backgrounds.

1. What was your earliest awareness of your racial or ethnic group membership?
2. Go back into your youth and think of times that you felt "different" from others. What are your feelings? Thoughts? What did you do?

3. What events in your life defined your "distinctness" from others? What events underlined your "sameness"?
4. Were there times when you wished you had been different? What precipitated these events? What did you do about these times?
5. Think about people you encountered in your youth who were different. How did you treat them? What have you experienced that has made you think differently about this group of people?

COUNSELING ASIAN AMERICAN STUDENTS AND THEIR FAMILIES

As an American teaching a graduate course in Hokkaido, Japan, I was intrigued with the deep respect and value placed on learning and education. After each class at least one student would inevitably thank me for teaching him or her. The importance of group harmony was also apparent when one of the graduate students, a local junior-high-school teacher, apologized profusely for coming late to class. He explained that one of his students had been picked up by the police for shoplifting and, since he was the student's homeroom teacher, it was his responsibility to go to the police station. Only after it was resolved were the parents called.

Asian American students, one of the fastest growing cultural groups in the schools, are not a homogeneous group but consist of many cultural subgroups, each with its own unique culture and history (Baruth & Manning, 2003; Morrissey, 1997). These groups include East Asian (Chinese, Korean, Japanese), Pacific Islander (Hawaiian and Samoan), Southeast Asian (Cambodian and Vietnamese), and South Asian (Indian and Pakistani). Although there are strong cultural commonalities of family, gender, role, religion, tradition, custom, language, and identity among Asian Americans (Morrissey; Yagi, 1998), there is tremendous diversity between and among these groups (Root, 1993).

Many people of Asian descent adhere to the beliefs of Confucius in which moral worth is accorded to one's allegiance to his or her group, misconduct is controlled by public humiliation, and compliance is conferred to authorities (Pederson, 1994). Because of the time spent doing homework, performing education-related activities, and participating in tutoring, many label this group as the "model minority." This label leads to the belief that Asian Americans have few problems, when in fact this group has been found to be more anxious and apprehensive than their Caucasian peers and suffer from the same issues confronting other adolescents (Morrissey, 1997; Sue & Sue, 1993).

Awareness

The family unit is viewed with respect and reverence, and undesirable behavior is handled within the family unit. Adolescents and children express extreme stress in reconciling loyalties between the traditional Asian beliefs and the majority culture.

Asian students are more likely to show interest in fields such as engineering, science, and mathematics partly due to the structured, unambiguous settings inherent within these occupations. Counselors may unintentionally confine these students to these proscribed occupations due to the large numbers of Asians in these fields (Sue & Sue, 1993).

Knowledge

Asian American adolescents and children are faced with the challenge of fulfilling the expected role of the "model minority." Studies report that Asian Americans do spend more time on homework, take more advanced courses, and have a higher rate of completing high school and college than their peers from other racial and ethnic groups (Baruth & Manning, 2003). Conversely, individuals from Southeast Asia such as the Hmong may have additional difficulty in school due to their lack of previous familiarity to any writing system. This disadvantage may be exacerbated by learning disabilities, hearing difficulties, or speech disorders (Schwartz, n.d.).

Asian Americans tend to be more socially inhibited and reluctant to engage in social activities (Sue & Sue, 1993). This social isolation is attributed to working parents, evenings at *juku* (an after-school tutoring class), and the trend toward smaller families (Woronoff, 1980). Individuals of Asian descent are dependent on parental and authority figures with clearly defined expectations. Asian American students often feel conflicted between Western values of individualism, independence, and self-reliance and Asian values of family obligation and deference (Sue & Sue).

Skills

The Asian student often comes to counseling with a socially acceptable concern in the form of either a somatic complaint or an educational/occupational concern (Diller, 1999; Morrissey, 1997; Sue & Sue, 1993). Due to the hierarchical communication pattern, children are taught to be respectful of authority figures and avoid questioning adults and tend to be more comfortable in structured situations in which the authority figure provides advice or practical solutions (Sue & Sue). Therefore, the school counselor facilitates counseling by offering direct, specific counseling interventions with individuals of Asian descent.

Counselors may wish to engage the parents due to the strong family-centered values of Asian Americans. Or, the use of solution-focused strategies that deal with issues in a positive, problem-solving, present focus with homework tasks is also successful with individuals from an Asian background (Morrissey, 1997).

Revealing personal details is considered as dishonoring the family (Diller, 1999; Sue & Sue, 1993). Restraint and silence are considered a sign of strength and respect (Root, 1993), whereas emotional expression is construed as a sign of immaturity (Sue & Sue) and personal weakness (Root). Moreover, Asian Americans are sensitive to nonverbal language and pay attention to nonverbal signals such as body position and facial expressions (Schwartz, n.d.)

Group interventions with Asian students may be difficult since harmony and orderliness are valued and any disagreement tends to smolder rather than disappear (Woronoff, 1980). When conflicts do emerge, mediation is difficult because of the hierarchical social "rule" in which personal beliefs and attitudes different from those of their peers are not to be expressed. Yet, peer groups can be influential in changing negative behaviors (Kim, Omizo, & Salvador, 1996).

Sociodrama, a method that has been used for attending to diversity issues, addresses community and group issues in much the same way that psychodrama addresses specific situations of individuals. This drama/action was used successfully in a college community that was surrounded by prejudice and diversity concerns and is easily adapted for different age groups. The following sociodrama exercise is designed for the school counselor to use with school-aged youth.

Exercise

Ask participants to think of a time when they felt different from other people. One volunteer will act out this memory, another person will play the role of the counselor, and other participants will be selected to serve as significant individuals who are part of this memory. Props as well as individuals may be used to make the sociodrama more realistic.

Following this reenactment the counselor may ask the following questions.

1. What insights did you develop?
2. How did it feel to be part of this scene?
3. (To the volunteer whose memory was reenacted) What new thoughts do you now have as a result of reliving this experience?

COUNSELING HISPANIC AMERICAN STUDENTS AND THEIR FAMILIES

Esperanza is a first-generation Mexican American graduate student studying to be a school counselor. "We need more counselors in the schools who are conversant in Spanish," Esperanza explains. "When I was a student and my parents were summoned to the school for parent conferences, I would interpret what the counselor or teacher was saying because my parents did not understand English very well. Naturally, I would interpret in a manner that was beneficial for me. My parents rarely realized that I was often reprimanded for things I did in school because I would tell them differently."

Hispanic Americans comprise one of the fastest growing cultural groups in the United States; and, like Asian Americans, several national, cultural, and ethnic groups exist within this population. Hispanics are from such countries as Mexico, Central and South America, Puerto Rico, Cuba, and Guatemala.

Awareness

Masculine pride is a strong value that clearly distinguishes male expectations and behaviors from those of females (Baruth & Manning, 2003). The belief that males are more valuable than females and women are submissive and dependent is inconsistent with Western ideology that emphasizes equality between the sexes (Hayes, 1997). Conflict arises when a female is in an authoritative position (e.g., teacher) and a male (e.g., student) must follow the directives of this female (Hayes). Similar to African Americans, language may present a challenge as there is a tendency for Hispanics to speak Spanish in the home and English in the schools.

Knowledge

Many Hispanic American youth live in poverty with disadvantaged educational backgrounds or experiences. In a study by Baruth and Manning (2003), one out of every six Hispanic American high-school students has not acquired adequate achievement in English language arts and is associated with a higher dropout rate, more disruptive behaviors, and lower academic aspirations in comparison with peers from other cultural groups. These characteristics often negatively influence self-concept.

Strong family ties serve as a foundation for decision making. The needs of the family are more important than the needs of the individual. Religion is also an important part of many Hispanics' culture; and although counselors skirt the issue of religious beliefs, religion is often an essential component to consider in the assessment of the Hispanic individual (Hayes, 1997).

Skills

Since relatively little information exists on the mental health needs of Hispanic adolescents, school counselors have difficulty effectively choosing intervention methodologies (Baruth & Manning, 2003). Hispanics prefer relationships that are on a personal, familiar level, and culturally skilled counselors note the importance of "small talk" in connecting to their clients (Hayes, 1997). Group intervention may be appropriate with students of Hispanic descent due to their orientation to group cohesiveness.

Although it is advisable to engage the family in children's career planning as early as possible (Baruth & Manning, 2003), postsecondary decision making and goal setting are difficult (Avila & Avila, 1993) due to the focus on the present rather than the future. Sadly, a disproportionate number of Hispanic children are removed from their family and placed in foster care because of the differences in the value system—such as in the area of folk treatment and faith healing—among Caucasian counselors and Hispanic families. For instance, some Hispanics believe colic is caused by foods that are wedged to the stomach and is treated by pulling on the child's skin, rubbing oil on its body, or administering foul herbs (Beal & Beal, 1993).

The following exercise is designed to investigate personal perceptions regarding individuals from other groups. After completing the exercise, share and discuss your personal responses and insights with a partner.

Exercise

In the following table, check the group(s) that best fits each item listed. Go with your first impressions and do not spend a lot of time thinking about each item. Your first response is generally the most accurate. After completing the worksheet go back over the items and decide whether or not there are any items that surprise you. What are your thoughts? Feelings?

	Hispanic	Asian	African American	Muslim	Gifted	Amish	Gay	Lesbian	Bisexual	Jewish	Homeless	Biracial
Individuals you knew as a child?												
Individuals with whom you went to high school												
Individuals with whom you have worked												
Individuals you would like to get to know better												
Individuals who intimidate you the most												
Individuals you avoid the most												
People you know the least about												

GENDER ISSUES IN COUNSELING

Most counseling and human development models are based on a male orientation with the male as the standard (Wastell, 1996). Inappropriate counseling occurs when females are compared to this standard without consideration of different gender development issues. Counselors may negatively influence the counseling process if their own attitudes and beliefs about gender differences are not examined (Wastell). In a study by Simon, Gaul, Friedlander, and Hetherington (1992), a significant relationship existed among gender, sex-role orientation, and the impressions and expectations of counselors. In fact, the very labeling of traits and characteristics as being either masculine or feminine leads to stereotyping and referrals to counseling.

The perception that girls are less competent than boys negatively influences the self-concept of females (Santrock, 1996) and is associated with lower academic and vocational aspirations than boys. Carol Gilligan discovered that girls reach a pivotal point in their development in early adolescence (11–12 years of age) at which time they realize that they are not as highly valued as males (Santrock). The stereotype of females as emotional and males as rational beings (Shields, as cited in Santrock) creates perceptions in differences among male and female communication and relational styles (Tannen, 1990, as cited in Santrock). However, gender differences have been drastically exaggerated. For example, both genders use the same facial expressions, report similar emotional experiences, and use the same terms to describe emotions (Santrock).

Other researchers point out that males have needs that are often overlooked. Men often feel as if they cannot properly express themselves, creating defensiveness; are distanced from others; and prioritize work over family (Santrock, 1996). The effective counselor must believe in the potential of women and how their potential is blocked by stereotypes and must encourage students to question traditional gender roles and make life decisions (Thomas, 1977, as cited in DeVoe, 1990).

Awareness

There is a paucity of information regarding the adolescent's gender, the gender of the school counselor, and the effects of these similarities and differences on the counseling relationship. Researchers reveal that qualities associated with women such as expressiveness, connectedness, and intimacy are more desirable in the counseling process than qualities attributed to men, such as reluctance to seek counseling and to self-disclose (Heatherington & Clinchot, 1988, as cited in Simon et al., 1992). Conversely, even though these feminine characteristics are perceived as more desirable for the success of the counseling process, they are also seen as more pathological if the female is perceived as dependent and lacking in decision making. The following exercise may assist in developing a greater awareness of gender attitudes.

Exercise

Complete the following sentences with the first thought that comes to your mind.

1. As a child I was taught that girls should . . . .
2. As I child I was taught that boys should . . . .
3. One of my beliefs about females is . . . .
4. One of my beliefs about males is . . . .
5. One of the things that my mom taught me about females is . . . .
6. One of the things that my dad taught me about females is . . . .
7. One of the things that my mom taught me about males is . . . .
8. One of the things that my dad taught me about males is . . . .
9. Teachers were always telling girls that . . . .
10. Teachers were always telling boys that . . . .

Knowledge

Erik Erikson defined identity versus role confusion as the task that needs to be accomplished in the adolescent years (Wastell, 1996). This theory has been criticized in that his focus and research were based on males rather than females (Peck, 1986, as cited in McBride, 1990). In a national study of adolescents, identity formation was very different between males and females. Boys were able to describe future identity in work-related skills and competencies, whereas girls discussed their future self in terms of romance and interpersonal relationships (Douvan & Adelson, 1966, as cited in Horst, 1996).

Autonomy issues have also received attention (McBride, 1990) in the field of counseling. Women were traditionally dependent on others for financial resources and livelihood and socialized to meet the needs of others rather than attending to their own desires (McBride). The following exercise can assist in obtaining greater understanding of gender issues.

Exercise

On a piece of paper make two lists as shown in the following table. On one side of the paper list the expectations society has of women. On the other side list the expectations society has of men.

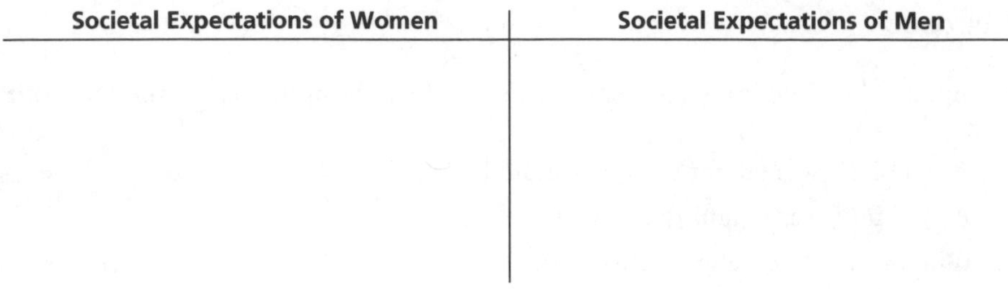

Societal Expectations of Women	Societal Expectations of Men

1. How have these expectations influenced you? Others?
2. If you were a member of the opposite sex how would these expectations be different?

Skills

New possibilities are revealed by vicariously experiencing how others have adapted to gender-related situations through autobiographical and biographical narratives. Students can be encouraged to describe role models encountered through actual interaction, in the media, or in biographies. The student can identify strengths and limitations of their favorite characters or how these people deal with difficulty and success.

Other activities include describing or drawing themselves as they would like to be in the future and identifying characters from books, television, or fairy tales that exhibit similar qualities to their own. Through storytelling, individuals begin to recognize their own life stories and how personal choices influence change.

Many women conform to others' expectations and often develop a set of irrational beliefs that inhibit personal growth and assertiveness (e.g., "I must be competent in all areas to be a success"). Male counselors need to pay attention to certain issues when counseling with women. The issues of anger, autonomy, power, and stereotypical roles have great impact on females and are important issues in counseling. Women are socialized to believe that anger is unacceptable. Therefore, counselors can provide a safe environment for the appropriate expression of anger and for teaching assertiveness skills (DeVoe, 1990).

Assertiveness training includes skill acquisition, modification of cognitive processes, and changes in underlying beliefs about the world. The following exercise may assist in understanding one's view of anger.

Exercise

Complete the following phrases and discuss your responses with a partner.

1. When I am upset I usually . . . .
2. When someone is angry with me, I . . . .

3. I feel angry when others . . . .
4. When a woman gets angry, I usually . . . .
5. When a man gets angry, I usually . . . .

Gay and lesbian youth make up approximately 10% of the school population (Schneider, 1988, as cited in Marinoble, 1998). Since school personnel often show biased treatment toward males and females, imagine the type of treatment that is received by students with gender orientation issues. Identity issues are difficult enough for adolescents to figure out without having to make sense of gender orientation associated with negative attitudes and behaviors.

> Mrs. Alvarez, a high-school counselor in a rural school in a conservative southern town, recalled one of her dilemmas with Ella, a sophomore female student who revealed to her that she was sexually involved with Mary. Mary was an older female student who had dropped out of school the previous year but was frequently seen hanging out around the school.
>
> Ella was a low-functioning student with poor socialization skills and few friends. Mary took an interest in Ella, befriended her, and provided her with the care and attention that Ella craved. Eventually this attention became more serious as kisses turned into fondling and caresses turned into sexual activity. "I never realized I was a lesbian," Ella declared to Mrs. Alvarez, "and I want your help in telling my parents."
>
> Mrs. Alvarez struggled with this issue because she was aware that adolescents often freely experiment with same-sex peers as a part of their search for identity, and at the same time she was not certain whether or not she should confirm Ella's self-label of lesbian. Mrs. Alvarez sighed as she recalled this situation and added, "I am still not certain as to how this should have been handled."

Schools are among the most homophobic institutions in the United States with high episodes of violence and harassment. Little is known about homosexual youth, particularly lesbian youth, since the body of knowledge is scant (Center for Population Options, 1992; Robinson, 1994). For a variety of reasons, gay and lesbian student needs go virtually unnoticed and their identity as a minority group is ignored.

GAY AND LESBIAN YOUTH

Lesbian, gay, and bisexual youth face tremendous challenges growing up in a culture that is widely homophobic (Gonsforek, 1988, as cited in Marinoble, 1998). Homophobia is expressed through hate crimes, from overt harassment and abuse to being ignored through omission in school policies and procedures (Herek, 1989, as cited in Fontaine, 1998).

Studies regarding school counselor involvement with homosexual youth are mixed. In a study by Price and Telljohann (as cited in Fontaine, 1998), school counselors reported working with students with sexual identity issues. More than half of the junior/senior school counselors reported assisting at least one student who was confused about sexual identity issues. At least 21% of responding elementary counselors knew of students in their schools who were identifying as gay or lesbian and/or questioned their identity. Conversely, other studies reveal that one in six secondary school counselors believed there were no gay students in the school (Center for Population Options, 1992).

Some individuals argue that the issue of gay, lesbian, and bisexual youth has no place in our schools. However, the reality is that these individuals are already in our schools. Recent legal rulings have made schools accountable for failing to intervene in anti-gay abuse.

A jury decided that Jamie Nabozny, a gay student in Ashland, Wisconsin, schools, was not protected from harassment and violence. When other students assaulted him because of his sexual orientation, his high-school and middle-school administrators were held responsible for not protecting him (Pflag, n.d). In March 1997 the Office for Civil Rights of the U.S. Dept. of Education created new guidelines that make any type of harassment illegal, thus making schools legally responsible for adopting sexual harassment guidelines.

One of the school counselor's roles is to serve as an advocate for ending homophobia. Gay students and those who are perceived to be gay are at risk of abuse, as are their friends and family members. A safe school environment is essential for all students; however, unfortunately, teachers, counselors, and administrators exhibit distressingly high levels of homophobic attitudes and feelings (Fontaine, 1998).

Awareness

Deficient counseling occurs when many counselors mistakenly assume that all clients are heterosexual. Moreover, some mental health professionals still feel that homosexuality is a developmental issue or mental illness (McFarland, 1998) and some counselors tend to believe that the problems presented by homosexual students are a result of their sexual orientation. In fact, homosexuals seek counseling services at the same rate and for many of the same issues as their heterosexual peers (Robinson, 1994). Counselors who have assisted homosexual youth report that the most prominent group of problems presented by gay and lesbian students include developmental and social identity issues such as poor self-esteem, depression, and self-doubt. Attempts to avoid exposure create a social distance from peers and family and require a tremendous amount of energy and effort (Cooley, 1998; Fontaine, 1998).

Gay and lesbian adolescents feel that they are alone in the world and that they have no one in whom they can confide. Counselors need to be available to these adolescents (Cooley, 1998).

The *Rainbow flag* first appeared in 1978 in the San Francisco Gay and Lesbian Freedom Parade. The flag was designed with symbols borrowed from the hippie and civil rights movements with the various colors representing values important to the community (e.g., red for life, orange for healing, green for nature, etc.). The Pink Triangle originates from World War II when Hitler rose to power. Homosexual relations were forbidden during this regime, and if convicted offenders were sent to prison and then to a concentration camp. The penalty was sterilization, most often in the form of castration, and then death. In the concentration camp these prisoners were required to wear an inverted pink triangle to designate the individuals as homosexual (TeenCentre.net, n.d.).

The following exercise may be used to develop a greater awareness of your own personal feelings and thoughts regarding gay and lesbian youth.

Exercise

Respond with your first, honest thoughts without censoring any of these thoughts. Discuss your answers with a partner.

1. When I hear someone is gay or lesbian, I . . . .
2. Homosexuality is a result of . . . .
3. If a student told me he or she was gay or lesbian, I would . . . .
4. If I overheard another teacher making a homophobic comment or joke, I . . . .
5. If a student was being harassed because of gender orientation, I would . . . .

Knowledge

Marino (1995, as cited in Fontaine, 1998) stated that no part of the homosexual community suffers more than gay, lesbian, and bisexual adolescents. Feelings of isolation, peer relationship issues, family acceptance, and substance abuse are some of the many concerns faced by these youth.

Feelings of Isolation and Stigmatization Isolation is a concern for all minority group members but is particularly serious for the homosexual adolescent (Robinson, 1994). The school environment often intensifies the isolation and stigmatization experienced by gay and lesbian youth. Declining academic performance, running away behaviors, and other school-related problems (Black & Underwood, 1998; Fontaine, 1998) are associated behaviors of gay and lesbian youth. The U.S. Dept. of Health and Human Services estimates that of the 5,000 suicides completed annually by adolescents between the ages of 15 and 24, more than 30% may be directly related to sexual identity issues. Among adolescents, homosexual youth are 2 to 3 times more likely than other adolescents to attempt suicide (Black & Underwood; McFarland, 1998) and usually use more lethal means than do heterosexual youth.

Students who do express their sexual orientation encounter homophobic teachers, counselors, or administrators who either refuse to address the issue or make inappropriate remarks. To counter the effects of isolation, these individuals sometimes perfect the art of "passing." For example, some may wear gender-appropriate clothing and act in accordance with society's image of how they should act. Others become model students through involvement in extracurricular activities, leadership positions, or academic success while keeping a deep secret that many find repugnant (Black & Underwood, 1998).

Some students make the choice to "come out" or disclose their homosexuality to others (Black & Underwood, 1998). For some, peers force the coming out process and take away personal choice. In either case this process presents the possibility of rejection or verbal and physical abuse.

Peer Relationship Problems Gay and lesbian students sometimes exhibit difficulties and a lack of confidence in their interactions with peers. They often believe that they do not belong to a group of supportive peers (Gumaer, 1987) and engage in heterosexual relationships to hide their orientation. Sometimes these students display academic success but at the same time are afraid of participating in extracurricular or social activities for fear of being discovered by their peers (Marinoble, 1998) and losing their friendships.

Family Disruptions "Should I come out to my parents? and, if so, "How?" are commonly asked questions (Cooley, 1998). Family attitudes toward homosexuality vary. Some families are supportive, while others are rejecting (Gibson, as cited in McFarland, 1998; Hunter & Schaecher, 1987). Violence against gay and lesbian adolescents often takes place in the home and is perpetuated by family members. In a study by Gonsiorek (1988, as cited in Cooley), gay and lesbian youth revealed that they fear retribution more from fathers than mothers and that 22% had been sexually abused by a family member following the discovery of their sexual orientation.

Parents often go through a grieving process much like those who have lost a child through death when they learn of their child's homosexual orientation (Gumaer, 1987). Parents may also force their child to receive counseling or to leave home if the child's sexual orientation is seen as a sin within their religion (Gibson, as cited in McFarland, 1998). Twenty-six percent of gay youth are forced to leave home, and many engage in prostitution to survive (Center for Population Options, 1992).

Substance Abuse Many gay and lesbian adolescents abuse drugs and alcohol to decrease or alleviate their emotional pain (Dempsey, 1994, as cited in Cooley, 1998), and this behavior is associated with suicidal ideation.

The following exercise may provide some insight into some of the issues experienced by youth with sexual orientation issues.

Exercise

Answer the following questions as honestly as you can. Discuss your responses with a class member.

1. Think about a time in your life where you just did not "fit in." What was this experience like for you?
2. What messages were you given in your family about gender differences?
3. What traits do you think characterize women? Men? Gay/Lesbian?

Skills

Negative attitudes toward homosexuals are revealed through omission of gay and lesbian students from curricula, nonexistent or antidiscrimination policies that are not enforced, few available resources, and a small number of gay and lesbian role models (Fontaine, 1998). At all grade levels counselors can play an important role in promoting a supportive environment for gay, lesbian, and bisexual students through formulating policies and procedures, providing information, using appropriate attending skills, and providing in-service training.

Policies and Procedures School district personnel are often concerned about opening discussion about policies regarding sexual orientation and refuse to even address the issue. School personnel are concerned about parental reaction or the belief that open communication will encourage the development of a homosexual orientation (Robinson, 1994). There is no evidence to support this belief (Black & Underwood, 1998; Robinson).

Information and Curriculum In a survey by Tellojohann and Price (1993, as cited in Black & Underwood, 1998), lesbian students repeatedly stated how discussion about homosexuality would make their lives at school easier. Gay and lesbian literature and posters acknowledging homosexuals need to be in the counselor, nurse, and school psychologists' offices (Marinoble, 1998). Additionally, parental informational meetings that address homosexuality and identify supportive agencies assist in dispelling inaccurate information (see Box 3.1).

BOX 3.1

Resources for Support

PFLAG	Project 10
P.O. Box 27605	Fairfax High School
Washington, DC 20038	7850 Melrose Ave.
	Los Angeles, CA 90046

BOX 3.2

Gay and Lesbian Role Models

Martina Navratilova, tennis player	Tchaikovsky, composer
Bruce Hayes, 1984 Olympic gold medal winner	Walt Whitman, poet
Janis Ian, lyricist and pop singer	Thornton Wilder, author
K.D. Lang, lyricist and pop star	Roman Emperor Hadrian
May Sarton, novelist and poet	Barney Frank, U.S. representative (D–Mass).

Homosexuality issues need to be included in library books and textbooks, and teachers should be encouraged to include a discussion of famous individuals with a homosexual orientation in their subject areas (Anderson, 1994). (See Box 3.2.)

Attending Skills The counselor can show additional support and sensitivity by simply using non-gender-specific language in discussing relationships rather than making a reference to an opposite sex partner (Marinoble, 1998). Examples include open-ended questions such as, "Are you involved with anyone?" or "Can you tell me about your special, close friends?" (Dillon, 1980, as cited in Robinson, 1994).

In-Service Training A panel of gay, lesbian, and bisexual community leaders may serve as informational resources to educators and parents to improve awareness of issues surrounding homosexual youth (Robinson, 1994). Teachers rarely challenge even seemingly innocent name-calling; but if adults criticize other forms of harassment, including name-calling, but ignore antigay remarks, the end result is children believing that this type of language is acceptable (Gordon, n.d.).

Counselors can take the time to teach the meaning of certain words since terms are often used without an understanding of their implication. For example, the word *faggot* is a derogatory term used to describe a gay individual. The term originated when gays served as the kindling wood for fires to burn witches at the stake. These individuals were forced to wear a bundle (or *faggot*) of sticks on their shirts indicating that they were the kindling for the fire (Gordon, n.d.).

Counselors have the professional obligation of serving all students. Gay and lesbian youth are in our schools with developmental issues more complex and difficult than their heterosexual peers because of harassment, isolation, and negative sense of self that often accompanies these individuals. School counselors are in a pivotal position to assist in the personal sense of well-being of all individuals regardless of their sexual orientation.

SUMMARY

This chapter is organized around the issues of diversity-sensitivity counseling and the competencies of awareness, knowledge, and skills, as identified by the Association for Multicultural Counseling and Development (AMCD). African Americans, Asian Americans, and Hispanics, the fastest-growing groups in American society, are summarized and discussed. Moreover, the developmental needs of males and females are highlighted along with a forgotten group of minority students—gay and lesbian youth. Exercises that enhance awareness, knowledge, and skills of these various groups are provided in this chapter for school counselors who advocate for all students in schools.

REFERENCES

Anderson, J. D. (1994). School climate for gay and lesbian students and staff members. *Phi Delta Kappan, 6,* 151–154.

Avila, D. L., & Avila, A. (1993). Mexican-Americans. In N. A. Vacc, J. W. Wittmer, & S. B. Devaney (Eds.), *Experiencing and counseling multicultural and diverse populations* (2nd ed.), (pp. 289–315). Muncie, IN: Accelerated Development.

Baker, S. B. (2000). *School counseling for the 21st century* (3rd ed.). Upper Saddle River, NJ: Prentice-Hall.

Baruth, L. G., & Manning, M. L. (2003). *Multicultural counseling and psychotherapy: A lifespan perspective* (3rd ed.). Upper Saddle River, NJ: Merrill Prentice-Hall.

Beal, M. J., & Beal, K. L. (1993). Transcultural counseling and the Hispanic community. In J. McFadden (Ed.), *Transcultural counseling: Bilateral and international perspectives* (pp. 213–238). Alexandria, VA. American Counseling Association.

Black, J., & Underwood, J. (1998). Young, female, and gay: Lesbian students and the school environment. *Professional School Counseling, 1,* 15–20.

CACREP. (2001). Council for the Accreditation of Counseling and Related Educational Programs. Alexandria, VA: Author.

Cameron, S. C., & Wycoff, S. M. (1998). The destructive nature of the term race: Growing beyond a false paradigm. *Journal of Counseling & Development, 76,* 277–285.

Campbell-Whatley, G. D., Algozzine, B., & Oblakor, F. (1997). Using mentoring to improve academic programming for African American male youths with mild disabilities. *The School Counselor, 44,* 362–367.

Center for Population Options. (1992). *Lesbian, gay and bisexual youth: At risk and underserved*. 1025 Vermont Ave. NW, Suite 210, Washington, DC 20005.

Cooley, J. J. (1998). Gay and lesbian adolescents: Presenting problems and the counselor's role. *Professional School Counseling, 1*, 31–34.

DeVoe, D. (1990). Feminist and nonsexist counseling: Implications for the male counselor. *Journal of Counseling & Development, 69*, 33–36.

Diller, J. V. (1999). *Cultural diversity: A primer for the human services*. Albany, NY: Brooks/Cole.

Exum, H. A., & Moore, Q. L. (1993). Transcultural counseling from African American perspectives. In J. McFadden (Ed.), *Transcultural counseling: Bilateral and international perspectives* (pp. 193–12). Alexandria, VA: American Counseling Association.

Fontaine, J. H. (1998). Evidencing a need: School counselors' experiences with gay and lesbian students. *Professional School Counseling, 1*, 8–14.

Freitag, R., Ottens, A., & Gross, C. (1999). Multicultural themes from bibliotherapeutic literature: A neglected resource. *Counselor Education and Supervision, 39*, 120–133.

Gordon, L. (n.d.). What do we say when we hear "faggot"? *Interracial Books for Children Bulletin, 14*, 25–28.

Gumaer, J. (1987). Understanding and counseling gay men: A developmental perspective. *Journal of Counseling & Development, 66*, 144–146.

Hayes, L. L. (1997, August). The unique counseling needs of Latino clients. *Counseling Today*. Alexandria, VA: American Counseling Association.

Holcomb-McCoy, C. (2003). Multicultural competence. In B. T. Erford (Ed.), *Transforming the school counseling profession* (pp. 317–330). Upper Saddle River, NJ: Merrill Prentice-Hall.

Holcomb-McCoy, C. C., & Myers, J. E. (1999). Multicultural competence and counselor training: A national survey. *Journal of Counseling & Development, 77*, 394–302.

Horst, E. A. (1996). Reexamining gender issues in Erikson's stages of identity and intimacy. *Journal of Counseling & Development, 73*, 271–278.

Howard-Hamilton, M. F., & Behar-Horenstein, L. S. (1995). Counseling the African American male adolescent. *Elementary School Guidance & Counseling, 29*, 198–205.

Hunter, J., & Schaecher, R. (1987). Stresses on lesbian and gay adolescents in schools. *Social Workers in Schools, 9*, 180–189.

Johnson, L. S. (1995). Enhancing multicultural relations: Intervention strategies for the school counselor. *The School Counselor, 43*, 103–113.

Kim, B. S., Omizo, M. M., & Salvador, D. S. (1996). Culturally relevant counseling services for Korean American children: A systematic approach. *Elementary School Guidance & Counseling, 31*, 64–74.

Marinoble, R. M. (1998). Homosexuality: A blind spot in the school mirror. *Professional School Counseling, 1*, 4–7.

McBride, M. C. (1990). Autonomy and the struggle for female identity: Implications for counseling women. *Journal of Counseling & Development, 69*, 22–26.

McDavis, R. J., & Parker, W. M. (1993). Counseling Black people. In N. A. Vacc, J. W. Wittmer, & S. B. Devaney (Eds), *Experiencing and counseling multicultural and diverse populations* (2nd ed.), (pp. 127–150). Muncie, IN: Accelerated Development.

McFarland, W. P. (1998). Gay, lesbian, and bisexual student suicide. *Professional School Counseling, 1*, 26–34.

Merchant, N., & Dupuy, P. (1996). Multicultural counseling and qualitative research: Shared worldview and skills. *Journal of Counseling & Development, 74*, 537–541.

Morrissey, M. (1997, October). The invisible minority: Counseling Asian Americans. *Counseling Today*. Alexandria, VA: American Counseling Association.

Parker, W. M., Moore, M. A., & Neimeyer, G. J. (1998). Altering White racial identity and interracial comfort through multicultural training. *Journal of Counseling & Development, 76,* 302–310.

Patterson, C. H. (1996). Multicultural counseling: From diversity to universality. *Journal of Counseling and Development, 74,* 227–231.

Pederson, P. (1994). *A handbook for developing multicultural awareness* (2nd ed.). Alexandria, VA: American Counseling Association.

Pflag. (n.d.). *A brochure for educators. From our house to the schoolhouse. Families & educators partnering for safe schools.* 1726 M St. NW, Suite 400, Washington, DC 20036.

Robinson, K. E. (1994). Addressing the needs of gay and lesbian students: The school counselor's role. *The School Counselor, 41,* 326–331.

Root, M. P. P. (1993). Guidelines for facilitating therapy with Asian American clients. In Atkinson, Morten, & Sue (Eds.), *Counseling American minorities* (4th ed.), (pp. 211–223). Madison, WI: Brown & Benchmark.

Santrock, J. W. (1996). *Adolescence.* Dubuque, IA: Brown & Benchmark.

Schwartz, W. (n.d.). *A guide to communicating with Asian American Families.* ERIC Clearinghouse on Urban Education. (Digest No. 94). Columbia University, NY.

Simmons, C. (1998). Are emotional expressions universal or cultural specific? In T. M. Singelis (Ed.), Teaching about culture, ethnicity, and diversity (231–235). Thousand Oaks, CA: Sage Publications.

Simon, L., Gaul, R., Friedlander, J. L., & Heatherington, L. (1992). Client gender and sex role: Predictors of counselors' impressions and expectations. *Journal of Counseling & Development, 71,* 48–52.

Sue, D. M., & Sue, D. (1993). Asian Americans. In N. A. Vacc, J. W. Wittmer, & S. B. Devaney (Eds.), *Experiencing and counseling multicultural and diverse populations* (2nd ed.), (pp. 239–262). Muncie, IN: Accelerated Development.

TeenCentre.net. (n.d.). *Flags and symbols: What they mean.* Retrieved September 2, 2003, from http://www.enqueue .com/na

U.S. Census Bureau. (2001). *Resident population by race, 1980 to 2000, and projections* (No. 14). Statistical Abstract of the United States: Author.

Wastell, C. A. (1996). Feminist developmental theory: Implications for counseling. *Journal of Counseling & Development, 74,* 575–581.

Wilson, L. L., & Stith, S. M. (1993). Culturally sensitive therapy with Black clients. In D. R. Atkinson, G. Morten, & D. W. Sue (Eds.), *Counseling American minorities* (4th ed.), (pp. 101–111). Madison, WI: Brown & Benchmark.

Woronoff, J. (1980). *Japan: The coming social crisis.* Tokyo, Japan: Yohan Publications.

Yagi, D. T. (1998). Multicultural counseling and the school counselor. In J. M. Allen (Ed.), *School counseling: New perspectives and practices* (pp. 29–34). Greensboro, NC: ERIC.

Young, C. (1993). Psychodynamics of coping and survival of the African American female in a changing world. In D. R. Atkinson, G. Morten, & D. W. Sue (Eds.), *Counseling American minorities* (4th ed.), (pp. 75–87). Madison, WI: Brown & Benchmark.

4

Students with Special Needs

THERESA A. QUIGNEY, PH.D.

Cleveland State University, Cleveland, Ohio

In its description of the role of a professional school counselor, the delegate assembly of the American School Counselor Association (ASCA) noted that "school counselors work with all students, including those who are considered at-risk and those with special needs" (Delegate Assembly, American School Counselor Association, 1999, p. 1). This organization further elaborated upon this point in its position statement entitled "The Professional School Counselor and the Special Needs Student," noting that a major goal of school counselors is to assist all students to succeed despite their disabilities (American School Counselor Association, 1999).

School counselors may achieve this goal in a number of ways. They may be involved with individual and group counseling activities, participate in multidisciplinary teams for the identification of disabilities, collaborate with personnel and parents on relevant issues, or assist in career planning and transitional programming (American School Counselor Association, 1999; Bowen & Glenn, 1998; Erk, 1995; Quigney & Studer, 1998; Quigney & Studer, 1999). The importance of their role has been acknowledged by the U.S. Department of Education, which stated that school counseling and guidance were the top services needed by youth with special needs (cited in Bowen & Glenn).

Historically, however, preparation programs for school counselors have been inadequate in their exposure to content related to special education and students with disabilities (Bowen & Glenn, 1998; Frantz & Prillaman, 1993; Greer, Greer &

Woody, 1995; Korinek & Prillaman, 1992; Scarborough & Deck, 1998; Studer & Quigney, 2004). This chapter provides a starting point from which to build a strong and practical foundation in special education issues for professional school counselors. To this end, the chapter provides an overview of the legal background of special education, as well as information on key concepts and practices.

SPECIAL EDUCATION AND THE LAW

Individuals with Disabilities Education Act (IDEA)

While special education has a rich history of both litigation and legislation from which to draw, there is little doubt which of the laws has had the greatest impact on the provision of specialized services to students with disabilities. The Individuals with Disabilities Education Act, often referred to as IDEA, was a landmark piece of legislation, originally passed in 1975. At that time, the law was referred to as the Education for All Handicapped Children Act, Public Law (Pub. L.) 94-142. In 1990 one of the amendments to the law changed its name to the Individuals with Disabilities Education Act. To fully appreciate the importance of this law to the field of special education, one must briefly review its historical evolution and significant components, highlighted with major revisions or reauthorizations.

Education for All Handicapped Children Act, Public Law 94-142 (1975)
While this historical legislation generally addressed the need for providing appropriate education and related services to children with disabilities, six key principles typify its intention (Friend & Bursuck, 2002; Heward, 2003; Katsiyannis, Yell, & Bradley, 2001; Kirk, Gallagher, & Anastasiow, 2003; Smith, Polloway, Patton, & Dowdy, 2001; Turnbull, Wilcox, Turnbull, Sailor, & Wickham, 2001):

- *Zero reject:* No child with a disability may be excluded from receiving a free appropriate public education. States are required to implement a system of finding and assessing children suspected of having disabilities.
- *Nondiscriminatory evaluation:* To determine whether a child has a disability, schools must utilize nonbiased, multifactored assessment methods. The evaluation procedures must not be discriminatory based on a child's racial, linguistic, and cultural background. Every 3 years, a reevaluation assessment must be completed (Kirk et al., 2003).
- *Free, appropriate public education:* All children with disabilities are to be provided an education at public expense and at no cost to the parents. The education provided must also be individualized for the child, based on his/her particular needs. To assist in accomplishing this, an individualized education program (IEP) must be developed and implemented. The IEP includes items such as a statement of the child's present levels of performance, goals and short-term objectives, specification of responsible parties for service delivery, location and length of services, and methods for assessment of progress (Friend & Bursuck, 2002).
- *Least restrictive environment:* To the maximum extent appropriate, students with disabilities must be educated with nondisabled students. They should only be

removed to separate environments when the disabilities are so severe that they are unable to receive an appropriate education in the general education setting, even with supplemental aids and services. In other words, the intent is that students with disabilities be involved in the general education environment as much as is appropriate and feasible. However, for those students for whom general education is not the least restrictive environment, a full continuum of placements must be available. This continuum includes special classes and schools, and instruction in a home or hospital.

- *Due process:* Schools are required to provide a set of procedural safeguards to ensure that the rights of the children with disabilities and their parents are protected. For example, parents have the right to request a hearing when they disagree with the school in regard to issues such as the child's identification, assessment, placement, or education. In addition, a school district may initiate due process procedures if it disagrees with parental requests in regard to the special education of the child with a disability.
- *Parental participation:* Parents have the right to access the educational records of their child. They are also to be included in decisions concerning their child's placement, IEP, and related services.

The Education for All Handicapped Children Act (1975) also described categories of disabilities that would fall under the regulations of this law and enable children to receive special education services. Table 4.1 lists all of the disability categories and descriptions for all the disabilities covered under the 1975 law, as well as those added in later revisions.

This law further denoted related services for which eligible students may qualify. A related service is that which allows an individual with a disability to benefit from receiving special education services. Many of the related services had been designated in the 1975 law, and others were added thereafter. Related services include audiology services, medical services, counseling services, occupational therapy, psychological services, early identification and assessment of disabilities in children, school health services, orientation and mobility services, rehabilitation counseling services, physical therapy, speech-language pathology, parent counseling and training, recreation, social work services in schools, and transportation (U.S. Department of Education, Office of Special Education and Rehabilitative Services, n.d., 34 C.F.R., S300.24).

Education of the Handicapped Amendments, Public Law 99-457 (1986)
These amendments lowered the age of eligibility for special education services to the age of 3 for children with disabilities, and established an early intervention infants and toddlers program (Culatta, Tompkins, & Werts, 2003). An individualized family services plan (IFSP) is written by a multidisciplinary team, including the parents, to denote the particular services required for early intervention.

Education of the Handicapped Amendments, Public Law 101-476 (1990)
One of the major results from these amendments was the change in the name of the law to Individuals with Disabilities Education Act (IDEA). A second major

Table 4.1 Disability Areas Covered Under the Individuals with Disabilities Education Act (IDEA)

Disability	Description
Autism	A developmental disability significantly affecting verbal and nonverbal communication and social interaction, generally evident before age 3, that adversely affects a child's educational performance. Other characteristics often associated with autism are engagement in repetitive activities and stereotyped movements, resistance to environmental change or change in daily routines, and unusual responses to sensory experiences.
Deaf-blindness	Concomitant hearing and visual impairments, the combination of which causes severe communication and other developmental and educational needs that cannot be accommodated in special education programs solely for children with deafness or children with blindness.
Deafness	A hearing impairment that is so severe that the child is impaired in processing linguistic information through hearing, with or without amplification, that adversely affects a child's educational performance.
Emotional disturbance	A condition exhibiting one or more of the following characteristics over a long period of time and to a marked degree that adversely affects a child's educational performance: 1. An inability to learn that cannot be explained by intellectual, sensory, or health factors; 2. An inability to build or maintain satisfactory interpersonal relationships with peers and teachers; 3. Inappropriate types of behaviors or feelings under normal circumstances; 4. A general pervasive mood of unhappiness or depression; 5. A tendency to develop physical symptoms or fears associated with personal or school problems. The term includes schizophrenia. The term does not apply to children who are socially maladjusted, unless it is determined that they have an emotional disturbance.
Hearing impairment	An impairment in hearing, whether permanent or fluctuating, that adversely affects a child's educational performance but that is not included under the definition of deafness.
Mental retardation	Significantly subaverage general intellectual functioning, existing concurrently with deficits in adaptive behavior and manifested during the developmental period, that adversely affects the child's educational performance.
Multiple disabilities	Concomitant impairments (such as mental retardation–blindness, mental retardation–orthopedic impairment, etc.), the combination of which causes such severe educational needs that cannot be accommodated in special education programs solely for one of the impairments. The term does not include deaf-blindness.

Continued

Table 4.1 Continued

Orthopedic impairment	A severe orthopedic impairment that adversely affects a child's educational performance. The term includes impairments caused by congenital anomaly (e.g., clubfoot, absence of some member, etc.), impairments caused by disease (e.g., poliomyelitis, bone tuberculosis, etc.), and impairments from other causes (e.g., cerebral palsy, amputations, and fractures or burns that cause contractures).
Other health impairment	Having limited strength, vitality or alertness, including a heightened alertness to environmental stimuli, that results in limited alertness with respect to educational environment, that 1. is due to chronic or acute health problems such as asthma, attention-deficit/hyperactivity disorder, diabetes, epilepsy, a heart condition, hemophilia, lead poisoning, leukemia, nephritis, rheumatic fever, and sickle cell anemia; and 2. adversely affects a child's educational performance.
Specific learning disabilities	A disorder in one or more of the basic psychological processes involved in understanding or in using language, spoken or written, that may manifest itself in an imperfect ability to listen, think, speak, read, write, spell, or do mathematical calculations, including conditions such as perceptual disabilities, brain injury, minimal brain dysfunction, dyslexia, and developmental aphasia. The term does not include learning problems that are primarily the result of visual, hearing, or motor disabilities; of mental retardation; of emotional disturbance; or of environmental, cultural, or economic disadvantage.
Speech or language impairment	A communication disorder, such as stuttering, impaired articulation, a language impairment, or a voice impairment, that adversely affects a child's educational performance.
Traumatic brain injury	An acquired injury to the brain caused by an external physical force, resulting in total or partial functional disability or psychosocial impairment, or both, that adversely affects a child's educational performance. The term applies to open or closed head injuries resulting in impairments in one or more areas, such as cognition, language, memory, attention, reasoning, abstract thinking, judgment, problem solving; sensory, perceptual, and motor abilities; psychosocial behavior; physical functions; information processing; and speech. The term does not apply to brain injuries that are congenital or degenerative or to brain injuries induced by birth trauma.
Visual impairment including blindness	An impairment in vision that, even with correction, adversely affects a child's educational performance. The term includes both partial sight and blindness.

Note: Adapted from U.S. Department of Education, Office of Special Education and Rehabilitative Services, (n.d.), *IDEA '97 Final Regulations*, 34 C.F.R., Part 300, S30.7.

revision related to the expansion of the list of disabilities covered under IDEA to include children with autism and traumatic brain injury.

In addition, *transition services* and *assistive technology services* were added as special education services available for IEP consideration. Transition services refer to activities that will assist the student to successfully move from school to post-school life. Assistive technology includes devices such as computers with enlarged keyboards, touch screens, and voice activation, as well as communication boards, and magnification or amplification aids. Two other services were also added as related service options: social work services and rehabilitation counseling (Culatta et al., 2003).

Individuals with Disabilities Education Act (IDEA) Amendments of 1997, Public Law 105-17 This reauthorization of the law continued to support the mandates from the earlier versions of the legislation and examined other important concepts. These amendments "provided the most substantial revision of the law relating to the education of children with disabilities since P. L. 94-142 was passed in 1975" (Hunt & Marshall, 2002, p. 19).

The following is a summary of some of the major issues addressed in Public Law 105-17:

- *Individual education programs (IEPs) and access to general education curriculum:* Prior to the amendments in 1997, IDEA did not specifically regulate the extent of involvement in general education curriculum by students with disabilities. The assurance that students with disabilities would have access to the general curriculum was a principal issue of IDEA's 1997 reauthorization (Wehmeyer, Lance, & Bashinski, 2002). There was a particular emphasis on the utilization of the IEP to strengthen the student's experience in the general education curriculum. There are now provisions in the IEP focusing on the student's ability to access and participate in general education curriculum, as well as keeping track of progress made. Specifically, the IEP addresses: (a) how the student's disability impacts his or her participation and progress in the general education curriculum, (b) goals that will assist the child to participate and progress in general education to the maximum extent appropriate, and (c) a statement of program accommodations or modifications to assist the child with his or her involvement and progress in the general education curriculum (U.S. Department of Education, Office of Special Education Programs, n.d.). It is obvious that the intent of the law was to provide students with disabilities the supplementary assistance needed to participate and advance in the general education curriculum, not simply be present in the classroom (Pugach & Warger, 2001).
- *Involvement of the general education teacher:* IDEA 1997 required that a regular education teacher be a member of the IEP team for a child with a disability, if that child is participating currently or may be participating later in the general education environment (U.S. Department of Education, Office of Special Education and Rehabilitative Services, n.d., 34 C.F.R., S300.344). The regular education teacher's involvement can include activities related to the development of the IEP, as well as to its reviews and revisions.

- *Parental participation:* Parental participation in the IEP process and decision making about the child's placement and educational program were clarified and strengthened with IDEA 1997. In addition to participating in educational and placement decisions, parents are to be part of the team that determines the child's eligibility for special education services. In addition, the progress of students with disabilities must be reported to the parents at least as often as it is reported for children without disabilities (Friend & Bursuck, 2002).
- *Eligibility and evaluation:* If eligibility for special education services is based on limited proficiency in the English language, or a lack of instruction in math or reading, the student should not be identified as having a disability. Further, for the purposes of a 3-year reevaluation of eligibility for special education services, existing assessment information may be used in the decision-making process (Salend, 2001).
- *Attention-deficit/hyperactivity disorder (AD/HD):* AD/HD has not been listed as a separate category of disability under IDEA, like those listed in Table 4.1. However, it is viewed as a disorder that might enable a child to be eligible for specialized services under the category of *other health impaired (OHI)*. The rationale for the possibility of including AD/HD under this category of disability seems to be based on the reference to issues with alertness in the definition of *other health impaired* (U.S. Department of Education, Office of Special Education Programs, n.d.).
- *Transition:* Lewis and Doorlag (2003) define *transition* as the "process of preparing students to meet the challenges of adulthood including those involved in postsecondary education, vocational pursuits, and home and community" (p. 446). The process of addressing transitional issues for a student with a disability begins at age 14. At this age, a student's IEP must address transition service needs focusing on the student's courses of study (Mastropieri & Scruggs, 2000). As part of the IEP, transition issues are continually updated, and at age 16 and older (or younger, if appropriate), the plan includes services that the student may acquire outside of the school environment, in the community in which he or she lives.
- *General state and districtwide assessments:* A deadline of July 2000 was mandated to states to include *all* students in state and districtwide systems of accountability (Ford, Davern, & Schnorr, 2001). Students with disabilities must be included in these types of assessment programs with appropriate accommodations and adaptations being made available to them (e.g., extended time, the test format in Braille, oral testing, etc.). For those students unable to participate in these types of evaluations, alternate assessments must be made available. Decision making is done on an individual basis and is conducted by the IEP team.

  The Individuals with Disabilities Education Act (IDEA) Amendments of 1997 (Pub. L. No. 105-17) give the individualized education program (IEP) team the authority to select individual accommodations and modifications in administration needed for a child with a disability to participate in state and districtwide assessments of student achievement. If the IEP determines that the child will not participate in a particular state or districtwide assessment of student achievement (or part of an assessment), the IEP team states how the child will be assessed (Cohen & Heumann, 2001, p. 1).

The law also requires that states make public a report of the performance of the students with disabilities on both regular and alternate assessments. The confidentiality of the students must be maintained, but the reports must occur with the same frequency and detailed information as those associated with students without disabilities (Heumann & Warlick, 2001).

- *Graduation with a regular diploma:* The increased emphasis on the involvement of students with disabilities in state and districtwide assessments naturally leads to the issue of graduation requirements. The document, *IDEA '97 Final Regulations, Major Issues* (U.S. Department of Education, Office of Special Education Programs, n.d.), noted the following:

    - Graduation from high school with a regular diploma is considered a change in placement requiring written prior notice;
    - A student's right to FAPE [free, appropriate, public education] is terminated upon graduation with a regular high-school diploma (the statutory requirement for reevaluation before a change in a student's eligibility does not apply); and
    - A student's right to FAPE is not terminated by any other kind of graduation certificate or diploma (U.S. Department of Education, Office of Special Education Programs, n.d., p. 3).

- *Discipline:* In regard to the issues of suspension and expulsion, IDEA 1997 mandated the following procedures:

    - Schools could remove a child for up to 10 school days at a time for any violation of school rules as long as there was not a pattern of removals;
    - A child with a disability could not be long-term suspended or expelled from school for behavior that was a manifestation of his or her disability; and
    - Services must continue for children with disabilities who are suspended or expelled from school (U.S. Department of Education, Office of Special Education Programs, 1999, p. 1).

School authorities may also remove a student to an interim alternative educational placement for up to a period of 45 days, if the student brings a dangerous weapon to school, or knowingly possesses illegal drugs, or is involved in the solicitation of the sale or sale of controlled substances. Schools may also request a hearing officer to remove a student for up to a period of 45 days if maintaining the student in his or her current placement would likely result in injurious behavior to others or himself or herself. The student must continue to receive educational services during this time period, which will enable him or her to make progress in the general education curriculum as well as progress in the IEP goals and objectives. Further, once a student with a disability has first been moved from his or her current placement in excess of 10 school days in a school year, the IEP team needs to be involved with the development and/or review of behavioral assessment and behavioral intervention plans (U.S. Department of Education, Office of Special Education Programs, 1999).

- *Mediation:* When there is a disagreement between the school and the parents regarding issues such as a child's assessment, identification, or placement, mediation offers an opportunity to resolve the dispute before initiating a formal due process hearing. Under IDEA 1997, states must extend the offer of mediation services to school districts and parents to resolve the issues in question. Mediation is strictly a voluntary process. There is no obligation for parents to participate in mediation, and mediation must not be used to delay or deny a parent's right to request a due process hearing (Friend & Bursuck, 2002; Katsiyannis et al., 2001; Salend, 2001; Smith et al., 2001).

The Rehabilitation Act of 1973, Section 504, Public Law 93-112

A second important piece of legislation to the field of special education is Section 504 of the Rehabilitation Act of 1973 (Pub. L. 93-112), which functions essentially as a civil rights law for individuals with disabilities. This law protects them from discrimination based on disability in any activity or program receiving federal financial assistance. Section 504 requires that

> No otherwise qualified individual with a disability in the United States . . . shall, solely by reason of her or his disability, be excluded from the participation in, be denied the benefits of, or be subjected to discrimination under any program or activity receiving Federal financial assistance. . . . (Section 504 of the Rehabilitation Act of 1973, as amended, 29 U.S.C. 794, as cited in U.S. Department of Education, Office for Civil Rights, 1999, p. 1).

Because of the stipulation of the receipt of federal financial assistance, this law applies to any school or agency receiving this type of funding, including public school districts, some universities and institutions of higher education, and local and state educational agencies (U.S. Department of Education, Office for Civil Rights, 1999).

Definition of Disability Under Section 504 of the law, a person with a disability is described as "any individual who (i) has a physical or mental impairment which substantially limits one or more of such person's major life activities, (ii) has a record of such impairment, or (iii) is regarded as having such an impairment" (29 U.S.C. Sec. 706 (8), as cited in Council of Administrators of Special Education, Inc., 1999, p. 18). The terms of physical or mental impairment from the aforementioned description are further defined as

> (A) any physiological disorder or condition, cosmetic disfigurement, or anatomical loss affecting one or more of the following body systems:

neurological; musculoskeletal; special sense organs; respiratory; including speech organs; cardiovascular; reproductive; digestive; genito-urinary; hermic and lymphatic; skin; and endocrine; or

(B) any mental or psychological disorder, such as mental retardation, organic brain syndrome, emotional or mental illness, and specific learning disabilities. (34 Code of Federal Regulations Part 104.3, as cited in Council of Administrators of Special Education, Inc., 1999, p. 18)

The previous description of an individual with a disability also mentioned that the impairment substantially limited one or more of the major life activities. These activities include "functions such as caring for one's self; performing manual tasks, walking, seeing, hearing, speaking, breathing, learning and working" (34 Code of Federal Regulations Part 104.3, cited in Council of Administrators of Special Education, Inc., 1999, p. 18). Obviously, the major life activity that is of particular significance to school personnel is *learning*.

Eligible Students Because the definition of disability in Section 504 is broader than that used in IDEA, students who may not be eligible for services under IDEA may be covered under 504. Some groups of individuals who may fall under the protections of Section 504 are students with attention-deficit/hyperactivity disorder (AD/HD), and students with health or medical issues, for example, epilepsy, asthma, AIDS, or hepatitis (Friend & Bursuck, 2002; Smith, 2002). For access to services under Section 504 for these individuals, as well as other groups of individuals with disabilities, it must be determined if the impairment limits the individual's ability to learn or be involved in another major life activity (U.S. Department of Education, Office for Civil Rights, 2002).

The Americans with Disabilities Act (ADA), Public Law 101-336

The Americans with Disabilities Act (ADA) was signed into law in 1990. Although this law was based on the Rehabilitation Act of 1973, it extended the provisions in its intention to provide civil rights and protection to individuals with disabilities. It addressed equal opportunity for people with disabilities in such areas as public services (e.g., transportation, public facilities, etc.), employment, public accommodations (e.g., stores, restaurants, parks, theaters, etc.), and telecommunications (Culatta et al., 2003; Hunt & Marshall, 2002).

Although the Americans with Disabilities Act does not address the instructional needs and educational programs of students with disabilities as does IDEA, the ADA does influence special educational services. Title II of this law prohibits discrimination against individuals with disabilities by local and state government programs, including public elementary and secondary school systems, vocational education, and public higher education institutions (Culatta et al., 2003). Title III of this law ensures that the facilities of the schools are accessible to individuals with disabilities (Salend, 2001).

No Child Left Behind Act of 2001, Public Law 107-110

In January 2002 President Bush signed into law the No Child Left Behind Act of 2001. This law is the newly reauthorized rendering of the Elementary and Secondary Education Act, first enacted in 1965. Some of the major provisions of the law include

> increased accountability for States, school districts, and schools; greater choice for parents and students, particularly those attending low-performing schools; more flexibility for States and local educational agencies (LEAs) in the use of Federal education dollars; and a stronger emphasis on reading, especially for our youngest children. (U.S. Department of Education, 2002, p. 1)

Although this law is not specifically a special education law, the Council for Exceptional Children (CEC), the learned society in special education in the United States, notes that it has important implications for policy and practice in the field of special education. One of the major areas of note is that of accountability. Schools are required to demonstrate adequate yearly progress (AYP) toward the goal of proficiency in reading and math for *all* students in grades 3 through 8, within 12 years. Assessment results will be broken down into particular groups, including disability.

> If children with disabilities (grades 3 through 8) within a school fail to make adequate yearly progress toward reaching 100% proficiency in reading and math by 2012, the school will face a host of accountability measures intended to improve performance of students failing to make AYP. (Council for Exceptional Children, 2002, p. 7)

A second area where the No Child Left Behind Act will affect special education is in regard to personnel licensure. To ensure the aforementioned AYP goal for all students, including those with disabilities, by 2012, states must have a plan developed to require that every teacher will be highly qualified by the conclusion of the 2005–2006 academic year. While this is certainly a preferred goal, with the current personnel shorage in special education, the acquisition of this goal by the required date may be a challenge (Council for Exceptional Children, 2002).

IDENTIFICATION OF DISABILITIES AND PROGRAM SERVICES

With a foundation in the basic tenets of the preceding laws, one is able to progress to a discussion of more specific types of activities with students with disabilities in which school counselors may be involved. It is certainly reasonable to expect that a school counselor may participate in activities relating to the assessment of students' eligibility for special education or specialized services, as well as participate in the development of eligible students' IEPs or 504 plans. Consequently, the next section addresses information pertinent to the school counselor's understanding of how disabilities are identified and programs are developed for appropriate students. The discussion focuses first on disability definitions, followed by identification and placement information according to the Individuals with Disabilities Education Act (IDEA), and concludes with the mandates of Section 504 of the Rehabilitation Act.

Definition of Disabilities

As with the discussion of the law, the reader is again requested to review Table 4.1. This table denotes and defines the 13 specific areas of disability currently covered under IDEA. Based on the previous discussion of Section 504 of the Rehabilitation Act of 1973, it is also apparent that not all areas of disability specifically fall under IDEA. While defining all the areas of disability not listed in Table 4.1 is beyond the scope of this chapter, one area of disability requires further attention, as it is one that school counselors may frequently encounter.

Attention-deficit/hyperactivity disorder (AD/HD) is not specifically listed in Table 4.1 as falling under the protections of IDEA. However, as previously noted, it may be perceived as a disorder that enables a child to receive services under the label of *other health impaired* (OHI). In the previous discussion, it was also reported that students with AD/HD may be eligible for services under Section 504. Consequently, it may be possible for students with AD/HD to receive special education services under either IDEA or Section 504, assuming that the requirements of the laws and regulations are met. To understand how AD/HD is defined, one must be familiar with the criteria listed in the *Diagnostic and Statistical Manual of Mental Disorders,* fourth edition (American Psychiatric Association, 1994), shown in Box 4.1.

School counselors also need to be aware of the possibility of students having dual diagnoses, such as students with disabilities who are also gifted. Students with disabilities and giftedness are often neglected when considering the gifted population as a whole (Grimm, 1998). This may be due to the challenges one faces in attempting to identify children with dual areas of exceptionality, for example, students who are gifted and identified as having specific learning disabilities (SLD) or attention-deficit/hyperactivity disorder (AD/HD) (Fetzer, 2000; Leroux & Levitt-Perlman, 2000).

Through the discussion thus far, the reader has been exposed to many areas of disability, which may be dually diagnosed with being gifted. However, to truly understand how children with disabilities may also be gifted, it is necessary to address the definition of the term *gifted*. This may appear to be a relatively easy task, but there has been a great deal of discussion surrounding this topic for some time. This may be due to the fact that intelligence, often considered a factor of giftedness, has been such a controversial concept to explain.

Various definitions of giftedness have been posed throughout the years, with various implications for identification. Since a detailed discussion of this topic is not possible in this chapter, the following definition will hopefully serve as a representative of educational thought in this area. This definition was cited in the document entitled *National Excellence: A Case for Developing America's Talent,* by

BOX 4.1 Attention-Deficit/Hyperactivity Disorder Diagnostic Criteria

A. Either (1) or (2):

1. six (or more) of the following symptoms of **inattention** have persisted for at least 6 months to a degree that is maladaptive and inconsistent with developmental level:
   a. often fails to give close attention to details or makes careless mistakes in schoolwork, work, or other activities
   b. often has difficulty sustaining attention in tasks or play activities
   c. often does not seem to listen when spoken to directly
   d. often does not follow through on instructions and fails to finish schoolwork, chores, or duties in the workplace (not due to oppositional behavior or failure to understand instructions)
   e. often has difficulty organizing tasks and activities
   f. often avoids, dislikes, or is reluctant to engage in tasks that require sustained mental effort (such as schoolwork or homework)
   g. often loses things necessary for tasks or activities (e.g., toys, school assignments, pencils, books, or tools)
   h. is often easily distracted by extraneous stimuli
   i. is often forgetful in daily activities

2. six (or more) of the following symptoms of **hyperactivity-impulsivity** have persisted for at least 6 months to a degree that is maladaptive and inconsistent with developmental level:

Hyperactivity

   a. often fidgets with hands or feet or squirms in seat
   b. often leaves seat in classroom or in other situations in which remaining seated is expected
   c. often runs about or climbs excessively in situations in which it is inappropriate (in adolescents or adults, may be limited to subjective feelings of restlessness)
   d. often has difficulty playing or engaging in leisure activities quietly
   e. is often "on the go" or often acts as if "driven by a motor"
   f. often talks excessively

Impulsivity

   g. often blurts out answers before questions have been completed
   h. often has difficulty awaiting turn
   i. often interrupts or intrudes on others (e.g., butts into conversations or games)

B. Some hyperactive-impulsive or inattentive symptoms that caused impairment were present before age 7 years.

C. Some impairment from the symptoms is present in two or more settings (e.g., at school [or work] and at home).

D. There must be clear evidence of clinically significant impairment in social, academic, or occupational functioning.

E. The symptoms do not occur exclusively during the course of a Pervasive Developmental Disorder, Schizophrenia, or other Psychotic Disorder and are not better accounted for by another mental disorder (e.g., Mood Disorder, Anxiety Disorder, Dissociative Disorder, or a Personality Disorder).

Specify Type:

- **Attention-Deficit/Hyperactivity Disorder, Combined Type:** if both Criteria Al and A2 are met for the past 6 months
- **Attention-Deficit/Hyperactivity Disorder, Predominantly Inattentive Type:** if Criterion Al is met but Criterion A2 is not met for the past 6 months
- **Attention-Deficit/Hyperactivity Disorder, Predominantly Hyperactive-Impulsive Type:** if Criterion A2 is met but Criterion Al is not met for the past 6 months

Note: For individuals (especially adolescents and adults) who currently have symptoms that no longer meet full criteria, "In Partial Remission" should be specified.

Note: From the American Psychiatric Association. (1994). *Diagnostic and Statistical Manual of Mental Disorders,* 4th ed. Washington, DC: Author.

the United States Department of Education, Office of Educational Research and Improvement, in October 1993:

> Children and youth with outstanding talent perform or show the potential for performing at remarkably high levels of accomplishment when compared with others of their age, experience or environment.
>
> These children and youth exhibit high performance capability in intellectual, creative, and/or artistic areas, possess an unusual leadership capacity, or excel in specific academic fields. They require services or activities not ordinarily provided by the schools. Outstanding talents are present in children and youth from all cultural groups, across all economic strata, and in all areas of human endeavor. (p. 4)

Having a basic understanding of giftedness may enable the reader to recognize it in students with and without disabilities. However, since the focus of this chapter is specifically on students with disabilities, our discussion now moves from defining disabilities to the identification and placement processes under the requirements of IDEA and Section 504.

Individuals with Disabilities Education Act (IDEA): Identification and Placement

Identification of Disabilities According to the *Twenty-Second Annual Report to Congress on the Implementation of the Individuals with Disabilities Education Act,* in excess of 11% of students from ages 6 through 17 had received special education and related services during the 1998–1999 academic year (U.S. Department of Education, Office of Special Education Programs, 2000). The *Twenty Third Annual Report to Congress on the Implementation of the Individuals with Disabilities Education Act* noted a 2.6% increase from the 1998–1999 school year for students with disabilities, ages 6 through 21 (U.S. Department of Education, Office of Special Education Programs, 2002). For these students to have been eligible for services under IDEA, specific requirements and criteria needed to be followed.

Often the first step in the process of determining the existence of a disability is a system of prereferral interventions. At this point, usually the general education teacher has identified issues of concern with a particular student and has collaborated with other school personnel to ascertain strategies that could be undertaken with the student in the general education classroom. This step precedes a formal referral for assessment for special education. There are various names for the prereferral intervention teams that assist the general education teacher, such as *intervention assistance teams* or *building level teams.*

Assuming that the prereferral interventions did not attain the desired result, often the next step in the process is that of a formal referral for the assessment of a suspected disability. Parental consent for the assessment process must be obtained. This assessment must be comprehensive, nondiscriminatory, and multifactored, in that multiple areas of a child's abilities and functioning are evaluated, including all areas of the suspected disability. If appropriate, these areas may include vision, hearing, health, general intelligence, communicative status, social emotional status, motor abilities, and academic performance (U.S. Department of Education, Office of Special Education and Rehabilitative Services, n.d., 34 C.F.R., S300.532).

Upon completion of the multifactored evaluation (MFE), the evaluation team, including the parents, determines if the child has a disability. If it is determined that the child has a disability and is in need of special education, an IEP must be developed and placement issues addressed. The IEP must be monitored and reviewed on an annual basis; and, at least every 3 years, a reevaluation must be completed to determine continued need for specialized services.

IDEA 1997 regulations also particularly address the area of *specific learning disability* by noting additional procedures for assessment consideration. The evaluation team needs to consider whether a student is achieving commensurate with his or her ability and age level in one or more of the following areas, as well as whether there is a severe discrepancy between intellectual ability and achievement in one or more of these areas:

- Oral expression
- Listening comprehension
- Written expression
- Basic reading skill
- Reading comprehension
- Mathematics calculation
- Mathematics reasoning

To determine the existence of a specific learning disability, the team must also examine exclusionary criteria. In other words, the team must not identify a student as having a specific learning disability if the severe discrepancy between achievement and ability is primarily due to (a) a visual, hearing, or motor impairment; (b) mental retardation; (c) emotional disturbance; or (d) environmental, cultural, or economic disadvantage. Further, at least one member of the team, excluding the child's regular teacher, must observe the child's educational performance in the general education classroom, or an environment appropriate for a younger-than-school-age child (U.S. Department of Education, Office of Special Education and Rehabilitative Services, n.d., 34 C.F.R., S 300.540).

Individual Education Plan (IEP) and Placement As stated previously, if a student is determined to be eligible for special education services, an IEP must be developed to address the areas of need. This plan must be developed by a team of individuals, and school districts must ensure that particular individuals are participants of this team. According to IDEA 1997, the IEP team must include the following individuals:

- *The student's parents.* The parents of the student are essential partners in this process and must be included whenever the IEP is developed or amended.
- *A regular education teacher.* If a child is currently or may be participating later in regular education, a regular education teacher must be part of the IEP team.

- *A special education teacher.* The special education teacher's expertise is needed for the development of the IEP, and this individual will undoubtedly be a major factor in the coordination and provision of specialized services to the student.
- *An individual who can interpret the results of the evaluation.* A school psychologist or someone who is able to interpret and explain the assessment results must be in attendance.
- *An individual representing the local educational agency.* This must be an individual who has the authority to commit resources for the implementation of the IEP.
- *Additional individuals who may have knowledge or a particular expertise about the child.* This could include individuals like a tutor or physician, invited either by the parents or the school.
- *The student, if appropriate.* If the student can contribute to the IEP development, his or her attendance would most likely be appropriate. If transition planning is an issue, the secondary student needs to be a participant. Further, if transition planning is a part of the IEP process, a representative from service agencies would be appropriate (Gibb & Dyches, 2000).

The IEP is the document that guides the educational services and specialized instruction for the student. Based on assessment results and other pertinent information, the IEP team writes annual goals and short-term objectives and makes decisions about assessment of progress and location of educational services. As noted previously, the IEP must be reviewed at least on an annual basis. Table 4.2 summarizes some of the major points to be included in the content of the IEP.

In regard to the issue of service delivery, the aforementioned principle of least restrictive environment is key. To review, this principle requires that all students with disabilities be included with nondisabled children to the maximum extent appropriate and only be removed from the regular education setting if the severity or nature of the disability is such that, even with supplementary aids and services, education in that environment cannot be achieved satisfactorily (U.S. Department of Education, Office of Special Education and Rehabilitative Services, n.d., 34 C.F.R., S300.550). The cited document, *IDEA '97 Final Regulations,* goes on to say that a continuum of alternative placements must also be made available, including instruction in regular education classes, special classes, home instruction, special schools, and instruction in institutions and hospitals, as well as the option of supplementary services, such as a resource room, in partnership with the regular class setting (S300.551).

School counselors play a vital role in facilitating the process of IEP development, as they are familiar not only with the student's academic and/or behavioral issues but also with a variety of approaches, resources, and opportunities available to accommodate the particular needs of the student. Their input at IEP meetings in regard to student goals, objectives, and service provision is a beneficial and practical addition to the program planning. Moreover, their training in counseling techniques and expertise in group dynamics lend themselves not only to being an information resource and service provider to the student but also to

Table 4.2 Major Components of the IEP

Component	Description
Current performance	The IEP must state how the child is currently doing in school (known as present levels of educational performance). This information usually comes from the evaluation results such as classroom tests and assignments; individual tests given to decide eligibility for services or during reevaluation; and observations made by parents, teachers, related service providers, and other school staff. The statement about "current performance" includes how the child's disability affects his or her involvement and progress in the general curriculum.
Annual goals	These are goals that the child can reasonably accomplish in a year. The goals are broken down into short-term objectives or benchmarks. Goals may be academic, address social or behavioral needs, relate to physical needs, or address other educational needs. The goals must be measurable—meaning that it must be possible to measure whether the student has achieved the goals.
Special education and related services	The IEP must list the special education and related services to be provided to the child or on behalf of the child. This includes supplementary aids and services that the child needs. It also includes modifications (changes) to the program or supports for school personnel—such as training or professional development that will be provided to assist the child.
Participation with nondisabled children	The IEP must explain the extent (if any) to which the child will not participate with nondisabled children in the regular class and other school activities.
Participation in state and districtwide tests	Most states and districts give achievement tests to children in certain grades or age groups. The IEP must state what modifications in the administration of these tests the child will need. If a test is not appropriate for the child, the IEP must state why the test is not appropriate and how the child will be tested instead.
Dates and places	The IEP must state when services will begin, how often they will be provided, where they will be provided, and how long they will last.
Transition service needs	Beginning when the child is age 14 (or younger, if appropriate), the IEP must address (within the applicable parts of the IEP) the courses he or she needs to take to reach his or her post-school goals. A statement of transition services needs must also be included in each of the child's subsequent IEPs.
Needed transition services	Beginning when the child is age 16 (or younger, if appropriate), the IEP must state what transition services are needed to help the child prepare for leaving school.
Age of majority	Beginning at least 1 year before the child reaches the age of majority, the IEP must include a statement that the student has been told of any rights that will transfer to him or her at the age of majority. (This statement would be needed only in states that transfer rights at the age of majority.)
Measuring progress	The IEP must state how the child's progress will be measured and how parents will be informed of that progress.

Note: Adapted from U.S. Department of Education, Office of Special Education and Rehabilitative Services. (2000). *Guide to the Individualized Education Program*. Washington DC: Author.

acting as a liaison between the parents of the student and other educational and community professionals.

Parents of students with disabilities may at times be overwhelmed by the inundation of information they receive about their child at IEP or related meetings. Often these meetings involve numerous educational professionals providing advice and ideas. The school counselor, acting as an advocate and supportive resource for the parents, may assist in diffusing a potentially intimidating situation for the parents (Quigney & Studer, 1998). For example, they can ensure that the other school participants at the IEP meeting are not conversing in educational terminology unfamiliar to most laypeople but are explicitly clarifying the identified issues and potential solutions. School counselors can also work to keep the discussion at IEP meetings focused, positive, comfortable, and conducive to an open exchange between the parents and other team members. Parents need to be welcomed as equal partners in the IEP process and not be hesitant to provide their input, pose questions, or ask for detailed explanations.

In addition to acting as an advocate and resource for parents at the IEP and related meetings, the school counselor needs to be available to the parents outside of the formal meeting environment. Parents may have additional questions and concerns after the meetings, and the school counselor may act as their contact for information and/or services or as a liaison to the personnel appropriate to the request.

Section 504 of the Rehabilitation Act of 1973: Identification and Placement

Identification of Disabilities While the requirements for eligibility under IDEA are considered more circumscribed than those used for Section 504, the latter does mandate that particular evaluation conditions be met. Eligibility under Section 504 is not related to particular classifications of disability, as in IDEA; rather, it is rooted in the practical implications of a mental or physical impairment on a major life activity (Smith, 2002).

Under Section 504, the evaluation process must draw from a variety of sources of information, considering all significant components of the learning process. The sources may include achievement and aptitude assessments, adaptive behavior, and teacher recommendations. The information must be documented and decisions made by a group of individuals knowledgeable about the data and placement options. Periodic reevaluations are required (U.S. Department of Education, Office for Civil Rights, 1999).

504 Plan and Placement As with IDEA, students eligible for services under Section 504 must be provided with a free appropriate public education. Under 504, eligible students can receive accommodations within the regular education classroom, specialized instruction, or related services. The services must include a plan that specifies the needed accommodations and ensures accessibility to the educational environment's programs and services (deBettencourt, 2002; Mastropieri & Scruggs, 2000).

The format of the 504 plan is not as formally prescribed as that of an IEP. Box 4.2 provides an example of a format for a Section 504 Accommodation Plan, as proposed by the Council of Administrators of Special Education, Inc. (1999).

The plan will address the accommodations needed by the student, which may include modifications in testing and homework assignments, use of the tape recorder (Smith, 2002), alternative options for displaying mastery of the material, extended time for assignments, oral presentations instead of written term papers, and so on. For additional ideas of possible accommodations, refer to Box 4.3, which lists accommodations proposed by the Council of Administrators of Special Education, Inc. (1999).

TRANSITIONAL PLANNING

From the aforementioned discussion, it is apparent that there are many legal and regulatory standards concerned with the provision of special education and related services. It is also no doubt apparent that school counselors are needed as active participants in various facets of the educational careers of students with disabilities, from the identification process to service delivery, to assisting the students to prepare for a successful life once they leave the confines of the school environment. Many of the activities that are generally defined within the realm of the school counselor are directly applicable to the role they should play with students with disabilities. In a study of the amount of time school counselors spent with students with special needs, among the most frequently occurring activities were the provision of individual and career counseling, collaboration with personnel about student needs, providing consultation and support to families, scheduling needed classes and services, and participating in IEP meetings (Studer & Quigney, 2003).

However, one issue related to the role functions of a school counselor that may require additional discussion is transitional planning. This is the process and plan that are to assist the student with disabilities to make a smooth and productive transition from school to post-school life. Effective transitional planning may require school counselors to exceed the conventional expectations of their function, in that a formalized plan is required to be completed. Certainly, school counselors are often very involved in assisting students plan for their futures, but in the case of students identified as disabled under IDEA, there is a legal mandate requiring that a written plan be developed by a team of individuals as part of the IEP process. According to the document, *IDEA '97 Final Regulations* (U.S. Department of Education, Office of Special Education and Rehabilitative Services, n.d.), transition services are defined as a coordinated array of activities, which

(1) Is designed within an outcome-oriented process that promotes movement from school to post-school activities, including postsecondary education, vocational training, integrated employment (including supported employment), continuing and adult education, adult services, independent living, or community participation;

BOX 4.2 Example of Section 504 Accommodation Plan

SECTION 504 ACCOMMODATION PLAN

Student Name ______________________ Birthdate __________ Grade _________

School ______________ Initial Referral Date__________ Reevaluation Due ____________

Beginning Date of This Plan ______________ Annual Review Date ______________

Describe how the identified disability substantially limits a major life activity: ______________

____

____

Accommodation/Action to Be Taken	Person(s) Responsible

Participation in assessment: ___ no modifications

___ modifications as defined in accommodations

Team Signatures	Position	Date
____________	School 504 Team Chairperson	________
____________	Parent/Guardian	________
____________	Teacher	________
____________	Other(s)	________

cc: Student's Cumulative Folder
District 504 Coordinator
Parent

Note: Adapted with permission from Council of Administrators of Special Education, Inc. (1999). *Section 504 and the ADA, promoting student access: A resource guide for educators.* Albuquerque, NM: Author.

BOX 4.3 Examples of Accommodations within the General Education Environment

CLASSROOM AND FACILITY ACCOMMODATIONS

The intent of Section 504 is to "accommodate" for differences within the general education environment. For this to be accomplished, all staff must be provided with awareness activities and given specific information concerning the district's procedures for dealing with Section 504 referrals.

As individual students are identified, the classroom teacher may need specific training in the area of the identified disability (e.g., training from the school nurse on danger signs of an impending asthma attack, training from a physical therapist on correct positioning of a wheelchair-bound student at his/her desk, etc.). The following classroom/facility accommodations are presented as examples of ways in which Section 504 disabilities may be successfully accommodated within the regular education environment.

I. Communication

A. There may be a need to modify parent/student/teacher communications. For example:
—develop a daily/weekly journal
—develop parent/student/school contacts
—schedule periodic parent/teacher meetings
—provide duplicate sets of textbooks for the home
—utilize a modified grading system

B. There may be a need to modify staff communications. For example:
—identify resource staff
—network with other staff
—schedule building team meetings
—maintain on-going communication with building principal

C. There may be a need to modify school/community agency communication. For example, with parent consent:
—identify and communicate with appropriate agency personnel working with student
—assist in agency referrals
—provide appropriate carryover in the school environment

II. Organizational and Environmental Management

A. There may be a need to modify the instructional day. For example:
—allow student more time to pass in hallways
—modify class schedule
—modify the length of the instructional day

B. There may be a need to modify the classroom organization/structure. For example:
—adjust placement of student within classroom (e.g., study carrel, proximity to teacher, etc.)
—increase/decrease opportunity for movement
—determine appropriate classroom assignment (e.g., open versus structured)
—reduce external stimuli

C. There may be a need to modify the district's policies/procedures. For example:
—allow increase in number of excused absences for health reasons
—adjust transportation/parking arrangements
—approve early dismissal for service agency appointments

III. Alternative Teaching Strategies

A. There may be a need to modify teaching methods. For example:
—adjust testing procedures (e.g., length of time, administer orally, tape record answers)
—individualize classroom/homework assignments
—utilize technology (computers, tape recorders, calculators, etc.)

B. There may be a need to modify materials. For example:
—utilize legible materials
—utilize materials that address the student's learning style (e.g., visual, tactile, auditory, etc.)
—adjust reading level of materials

IV. Student Precautions

A. There may be a need to modify the classroom/building climate for health purposes. For example:
—use an air purifier in classroom
—control temperature
—accommodate specific allergic reactions

B. There may be a need to modify classroom/building to accommodate equipment needs. For example:
—plan for evacuation for wheelchair-bound students
—schedule classes in accessible areas

C. There may be a need to modify building health/safety procedures. For example:
—administer medication
—apply universal precautions
—accommodate special diets

CASE, Student Access/Section 504
1999 Edition, Copyright CASE, Inc.

Note: Adapted with permission from Council of Administrators of Special Education, Inc. (1999). *Section 504 and the ADA, promoting student access: A resource guide for educators.* Albuquerque, NM: Author.

(2) Is based on the individual student's needs, taking into account the student's preferences and interests; and
(3) Includes
   (i) Instruction;
   (ii) Related services;
   (iii) Community experiences;
   (iv) The development of employment and other post-school adult living objectives;
   and
   (v) If appropriate, acquisition of daily living skills and functional vocational evaluation. (U.S. Department of Education, Office of Special Education and Rehabilitative Services, n.d., 34 C.F.R., S300.29)

The cited document, *IDEA '97 Final Regulations,* also notes that by age 14, a statement of the transition service needs of the student will be included as part of the IEP, focusing on the student's courses of study, such as vocational education or advanced placement courses. Beginning at age 16, or younger if determined to be appropriate by the IEP team, the IEP must include a statement of the needed transition services for the student and any needed collaborations or interagency responsibilities (U.S. Department of Education, Office of Special Education and Rehabilitative Services, n.d.).

Assisting in the formalization of a transition plan for a student with a disability seems like a natural match for the training and expertise of school counselors. With their knowledgeable input and participation, students with disabilities will receive an appropriate and relevant education while in school and leave their secondary educations with a plan for the future. As reported in the *Twenty-Third Annual Report to Congress on the Implementation of the Individuals With Disabilities Education Act,* the graduation rates of students with disabilities age 14 and older have steadily increased since 1993–1994, while the dropout rate of this population has declined (U.S. Department of Education, Office of Special Education Programs, 2002). Transition planning will hopefully assist in continuing that trend of success into life after high school.

SUMMARY

Professional school counselors need to play an integral role in the lives of students with disabilities. Because of the importance of their role to these students and the nature of special education programming, school counselors must know about the legal and practical aspects of special education and related services. Many facets of special education programming respond to the tenets of the law, particularly IDEA and Section 504 of the Rehabilitation Act of 1973 and their regulatory interpretations. Consequently, school counselors must continually be aware of these mandates not only to be in legal compliance but also to more effectively function in the various aspects of providing effective counseling services to students with special needs.

REFERENCES

American Psychiatric Association. (1994). *Diagnostic and statistical manual of mental disorders* (4th ed.). Washington, DC: Author.

American School Counselor Association. (1999). *Position statement: Special needs students, the professional school counselor, and the special needs student*. Retrieved January 10, 2003, from http://www.schoolcounselor.org/content.cfm?L1=1000&L2=32

Bowen, M. L., & Glenn, E. E. (1998). Counseling interventions for students who have mild disabilities. *Professional School Counseling, 2*(1), 16–25.

Cohen, M., & Heumann, J. E. (2001). *Memorandum: Clarification of the role of the IEP team in selecting individual accommodations, modifications in administration, and alternate assessments for state and districtwide assessments of student achievement*. Retrieved January 2003 from http://www.dssc.org/frc/fed/JointAssessmentMemo.final.doc

Council for Exceptional Children. (2002). *No Child Left Behind Act of 2001: Reauthorization of the Elementary and Secondary Education Act, a technical assistance resource*. Retrieved January 2003 from http://www.cec.sped.org/pp/OverviewNCLB.pdf

Council of Administrators of Special Education, Inc. (1999). *Section 504 and the ADA, promoting student access: A resource guide for educators* (2nd ed.). Albuquerque, NM: Author.

Culatta, R. A., Tompkins, J. R., & Werts, M. G. (2003). *Fundamentals of special education: What every teacher needs to know* (2nd ed.). Upper Saddle River, NJ: Merrill Prentice-Hall.

deBettencourt, L. U. (2002). Understanding the difference between IDEA and Section 504. *Teaching Exceptional Children, 34*(3), 16–23.

Delegate Assembly, American School Counselor Association. (1999). *The role of the professional school counselor*. Retrieved January 10, 2003, from http://www.schoolcounselor.org/content.cfm?L1=1000&L2=69

Erk, R. R. (1995). A diagnosis of attention deficit disorder: What does it mean for school counselors? *School Counselor, 42*(4), 292–299.

Fetzer, E. A. (2000). The gifted/learning disabled child: A guide for teachers and parents. *Gifted Child Today Magazine, 23*(4), 44–50.

Ford, A., Davern, L., & Schnorr, R. (2001). Learners with significant disabilities: Curricular relevance in an era of standards-based reform. *Remedial and Special Education, 22*(4), 214–222.

Frantz, C. S., & Prillaman, D. (1993). State certification endorsement for school counselors: Special education requirements. *School Counselor, 40*(5), 375–379.

Friend, M., & Bursuck, W. D. (2002). *Including students with special needs: A practical guide for classroom teachers* (3rd ed.). Boston: Allyn & Bacon.

Gibb, G. S., & Dyches, T. T. (2000). *Guide to writing quality individualized education programs: What's best for students with disabilities*. Needham Heights, MA: Allyn & Bacon.

Greer, B. B., Greer, J. G., & Woody, D. E. (1995). The inclusion movement and its impact on counselors. *School Counselor, 43,* 124–132.

Grimm, J. (1998). The participation of gifted students with disabilities in gifted programs. *Roeper Review, 20*(4), 285–286.

Heumann, J. E., & Warlick, K. R. (2001). Memorandum: Guidance on including students with disabilities in assessment programs. Retrieved January 2002 from http://www.dssc.org/frc/fed/OSEP01-06.FFAssessment.doc

Heward, W. L. (2003). *Exceptional children: An introduction to special education* (7th ed.). Upper Saddle River, NJ: Merrill Prentice-Hall.

Hunt, N., & Marshall, K. (2002). *Exceptional children and youth: An introduction to special education* (3rd ed.). Boston: Houghton Mifflin.

IDEA '97 Final Regulations, 34 C.F.R. S300.24 (1999).

IDEA '97 Final Regulations, 34 C.F.R. S300.29 (1999).

IDEA '97 Final Regulations, 34 C.F.R. S300.344 (1999).

IDEA '97 Final Regulations, 34 C.F.R. S300.532 (1999).

IDEA '97 Final Regulations, 34 C.F.R S300. 540 (1999).

IDEA '97 Final Regulations, 34 C.F.R S300.550 (1999).

IDEA '97 Final Regulations, 34 C.F.R S300.551(1999).

Katsiyannis, A., Yell, M. L., & Bradley, R. (2001). Reflections on the 25th anniversary of the Individuals with Disabilities Education Act. *Remedial and Special Education, 22*(6), 324–334.

Kirk, S. A., Gallagher, J. J., & Anastasiow, N. J. (2003). *Educating exceptional children* (10th ed.). Boston: Houghton Mifflin.

Korinek, L., & Prillaman, D. (1992). Counselors and exceptional students: Preparation versus practice. *Counselor Education and Supervision, 32*(1), 3–11.

Leroux, J. A., & Levitt-Perlman, M. (2000). The gifted child with attention deficit disorder: An identification and intervention challenge. *Roeper Review, 22*(3), 171–176.

Lewis, R. B., & Doorlag, D. H. (2003). *Teaching special students in general education classrooms* (6th ed.). Upper Saddle River, NJ: Merrill Prentice-Hall.

Mastropieri, M. A., & Scruggs, T. E. (2000). *The inclusive classroom: Strategies for effective instruction.* Upper Saddle River, NJ: Merrill Prentice-Hall.

Pugach, M. C., & Warger, C. L. (2001). Curriculum matters: Raising expectations for students with disabilities. *Remedial and Special Education, 22*(4), 194–196, 213.

Quigney, T. A., & Studer, J. R. (1998). Touching strands of the educational web: The professional school counselor's role in inclusion. *Professional School Counseling, 2*(1), 77–81.

Quigney, T., & Studer, J. (1999). Transition, students with special needs, and the professional school counselor. *Guidance and Counseling, 15*(1), 8–12.

Salend, S. J. (2001). *Creating inclusive classrooms: Effective and reflective practices* (4th ed.). Upper Saddle River, NJ: Merrill Prentice-Hall.

Scarborough, J. L., & Deck, M. D. (1998). The challenges of working for students with disabilities: A view from the front lines. *Professional School Counseling, 2*(1), 10–15.

Smith, T. E. C. (2002). Section 504: What teachers need to know. *Intervention in School and Clinic, 37*(5), 259–266.

Smith, T. E. C., Polloway, E. A., Patton, J. R., & Dowdy, C. A. (2001). *Teaching students with special needs in inclusive settings* (3rd ed.). Needham Heights, MA: Allyn & Bacon.

Studer, J. R., & Quigney, T. A. (2003). An analysis of the time spent with students with special needs by professional school counselors. *American Secondary Education, 31*(2), 71–83.

Studer, J. R., & Quigney, T. A. (2004). *The need to integrate more special education content into preservice preparation programs for school counselors.* Manuscript submitted for publication.

Turnbull, H. R., III, Wilcox, B., Turnbull, A., Sailor, W., & Wickham, D. (2001). IDEA, positive behavioral supports, and school safety. *Journal of Law and Education, 30*(3), 445–503.

U.S. Department of Education. (2002). *The No Child Left Behind Act of 2001, executive summary.* Retrieved January 2003 from http://www.ed.gov/offices/OESE/esea/execsumm.html

U.S. Department of Education, Office for Civil Rights. (1999). *Free appropriate public education for students with disabilities: Requirements under Section 504 of the*

Rehabilitation Act of 1973. Retrieved January 21, 2003, from http://www.ed.gov/offices/OCR/docs/FAPE504.html

U.S. Department of Education, Office for Civil Rights. (2002). *Protecting students with disabilities: Frequently asked questions about Section 504 and the education of children with disabilities*. Retrieved January 21, 2003, from http://www.ed.gov/offices/OCR/504faq.html

U.S. Department of Education, Office of Educational Research and Improvement. (1993). *National excellence: A case for developing America's talent*. Retrieved January 28, 2003, from http://www.ed.gov/pubs/DevTalent/intro.html

U.S. Department of Education, Office of Special Education and Rehabilitative Services. (n.d.). *IDEA '97 final regulations*. Retrieved January 15, 2002, from http://www.ideapractices.org/law/regulations/index.php

U.S. Department of Education, Office of Special Education and Rehabilitative Services. (2000). *Guide to the individualized education program*. Retrieved January 26, 2003, from http://www.ed.gov/offices/OSERS/OSEP/Products/IEP_Guide

U.S. Department of Education, Office of Special Education Programs. (n.d.). *IDEA '97: Final regulations, major issues*. Retrieved January 15, 2003, from http://www.ideapractices.org/law/addl_material/majorissues.php

U.S. Department of Education, Office of Special Education Programs. (1999). *Discipline procedures—changes from proposed Rules—topic brief*. Retrieved January 20, 2003, from http://www.ed.gov/offices/OSERS/policy/IDEA/brief5.html

U.S. Department of Education, Office of Special Education Programs. (2000). *Twenty-second annual report to Congress on the implementation of the Individuals With Disabilities Education Act*. Retrieved January 11, 2003, from http://www.ed.gov/offices/OSERS/OSEP/Products/OSEP2000AnlRpt/ExecSumm.html

U.S. Department of Education, Office of Special Education Programs. (2002). *Twenty-third annual report to Congress on the implementation of the Individuals With Disabilities Education Act: Executive summary*. Retrieved January 20, 2003, from http://www.ed.gov/offices/OSERS/OSEP/Products/OSEP2001AnlRpt/ExecSumm.html

Wehmeyer, M. L., Lance, G. D., & Bashinski, S. (2002). Promoting access to the general curriculum for students with mental retardation: A multilevel model. *Education and Training in Mental Retardation and Developmental Disabilities, 37*(3), 223–234.

PART II

The Professional School Counselor: An Advocate for Students' Contextual Dimensions

The chapters included in the Contextual Dimensions of School Counseling section provide information on advocacy, systemic change, leadership, and program development. An understanding of the components of a school counseling program as they are integrated into the educational mission provide a vital direction for the school counselor of today and tomorrow.

The chapters in this section include: The Developmental, Comprehensive School Counselor Program, The Professional School Counselor and Accountability, and The Professional School Counselor's Role in Career Development.

5

The Developmental, Comprehensive School Counselor Program

Esperanza was clearly excited about being hired as a middle-school counselor in a suburban area only about 20 minutes from where she lived. Esperanza had been trained in the ASCA National Standards and National Model and was quite excited to share her expertise in the implementation of a developmental, comprehensive school counselor program. Esperanza's enthusiasm about her new profession was temporarily subdued when she discovered that the counseling program utilized a service-centered, crisis-oriented approach to working with the students. When she inquired about this outmoded model, the Director of Guidance Services replied, "Our system works just fine. Our students consistently score high on graduation exams, and we place them in top colleges and universities. Why change something that is obviously helping our students?"

Esperanza was aware that many schools were reluctant to discard the traditional counseling model. Yet, at the same time she was aware that she would need to take an active leadership role to transform the school counseling program. Esperanza felt comfortable with her training and skills, and she was certain that she could take on the tasks before her, but she worried about the time it would take her to convince people that this change was in the best interests of her students.

According to McWhirter, McWhirter, McWhirter, and McWhirter (1998), minority students are at greater risk of dropping out of school, with 14% of African Americans and 28% of Hispanics and an even higher percentage of Native Americans leaving school without graduating. Increasing numbers of children under the age of 15 report engaging in sexual activities, and approximately 30% of youth under this age report having had sexual intercourse. More adolescents under the age of 15 are experimenting with drugs and alcohol.

With statistics such as these, school counselors are needed more today than ever before, with the primary goal of assisting students by enhancing academic, career, and personal/social growth. Despite the need, school counselors and programs are easily misinterpreted and used inappropriately. The traditional pupil personnel model is no longer a viable format for school counselors to utilize, and a transformed school counseling model is a challenge for many resisting change, despite its benefits. However, a comprehensive, developmental model keeps the growth of students at the forefront of the educational movement and creates the needed bridge between school counseling and education.

WHY A SHIFT TO A DEVELOPMENTAL, COMPREHENSIVE SCHOOL COUNSELING PROGRAM?

Although the American School Counselor Association (ASCA) has taken an active role in defining the role of the professional school counselor, external influences continue to define the role and function of the school counselor. Counselors are marginalized through the performance of quasi-administrative duties, clerical responsibilities (Gysbers, Lapan, & Jones, 2000; Ripley, Erford, Dahir, & Eschback, 2003), and other non-counseling-related tasks. Historically, school counseling has suffered from the lack of a consistent system of program delivery (Ryan & Zeran, 1972, as cited in Dahir, 2001), making it difficult for stakeholders to know what assistance these professionals are able to provide. For instance, as a school counselor trained under the pupil personnel model, I was actively involved with different activities and I mistakenly believed there was no question that I was doing my job. I realized how mistaken I was when one of the parents of an outstanding football senior angrily notified me that her son was ineligible to play football for the rest of the season. According to her, I did not regularly check her son's grades to determine eligibility and, therefore, his chances for a football scholarship vanished because of my negligence. Although I tried to explain that checking athletic eligibility was not one of my tasks, she "knew that this was one of my tasks, because no one else would have access to this information." Based on this experience, it became clear that I needed to do a better job publicizing my role.

The traditional pupil personnel service model utilized a service-centered, crisis-oriented approach that did not adequately address the needs of all students (Bowers & Hatch, 2003). Furthermore, because counselors have been remiss in documenting activities and proving the effectiveness of these strategies, power factions began to question how school counselors benefit the academic mission (Hart & Jacobi, 1992). School counseling programs viewed as existing outside of the K-12 curriculum are expendable during financial crises (Gysbers et al., 2000).

Added to these concerns, educational reform initiatives noted a lack of preparation and low achievement among U.S. students in comparison with students in other industrialized nations. Goals 2000: Educate America Act was enacted in 1994 to provide a national framework for education reform in continued response to the 1983 *Nation at Risk* report in which evidence suggested that,

> (1) compared to other nations, American students spend much less time on school work; (2) time spent in the classroom and on homework is often used ineffectively; and (3) schools are not doing enough to help students develop either the study skills required to use time well or the willingness to spend more time on school work. (National Commission on Excellence in Education, 1983)

The Secretary's Commission on Achieving Necessary Skills (SCANS) in the early 1990s was formed to advise the U.S. Secretary of Labor on the skills needed for the future workforce. The commission reported the disturbing news that half of our youth leave school without the knowledge and skills to perform adequately in the workforce (SCANS, 2000). Unfortunately, although the reports mentioned the need for students to be productive citizens with the ability to "work on teams" (SCANS) and to "provide equitable educational opportunities and high levels of educational achievement for all students" (Goals 2000), none of the reports mentioned school counselors as a vital component in improving student success. These distressing reports served as a catalyst for schools to demonstrate greater evidence of accountability, substantiation of achievement, implementation of standards, and benchmarks to ensure that U.S. students can compete in tomorrow's world (Dahir, 2001; Johnson, 2000; Ripley et al., 2003; Schmidt & Ciechalski, 2001).

It became essential for school counselors to respond by demonstrating how their program assists students to achieve a higher level of competency for survival in the 21st century (Ripley et al., 2003). The governing board of the ASCA recognized that the language of educational reform needed to be applied to systematize and align school counseling programs within current school board policies and curriculum.

As reported in the first chapter, the movement to transform school counseling from a service-reactive program to a student-oriented developmental schema was first initiated in the 1960s and 1970s with limited success. The state of Missouri took the leadership in demonstrating how students benefit from participation in a comprehensive school counseling program—evidence based on the research of Norman Gysbers in the late 1970s (Gysbers, Lapan, Blair, & Starr, 1999). The Missouri Comprehensive Guidance Program (MCGP) was developed as a result of a state initiative to develop and train school counselors in the MCGP model. One difference between the MCGP model and earlier comprehensive, developmental program attempts was the evaluative component that provided evidence that this transformed school counseling worked (Lapan, Gysbers, & Petroski, 2003).

Research conducted on Gysbers' MCGP revealed positive effects, greater interaction with program stakeholders, and more visibility and understanding of the school counselor's role (Burnham & Jackson, 2000). In another study, students who participated in a fully implemented K-12 comprehensive program earned higher grades, were better prepared for the future, and rated their education more positively than students who were not part of a comprehensive program (Gysbers et al., 1999). Additional evidence reveals that counselors in transformed school counseling programs had a more positive influence than counselors operating under a traditional approach (Lapan et al., 2003). Yet, these programs did not have the national support and advocacy that were needed for the change process until ASCA took an enthusiastic role in designing and advocating for developmental, comprehensive school counseling programs. The National Standards and the ASCA National Model, based largely on Gysbers' model, serve as a template for school counseling programs (VanZandt & Hayslip, 2001).

THE AMERICAN SCHOOL COUNSELOR ASSOCIATION NATIONAL STANDARDS

The ASCA introduced the National Standards in July 1997 to communicate the role and function of the school counselor program within the total school mission. The National Standards (see Box 5.1) identified school counseling programs as an integral component to the education purpose; created a framework for a K-12 comprehensive, developmental program; and offered a format to systematically assist *all* students (Dahir, Sheldon, & Valiga, 1998).

The National Standards assist student growth in three broad domains: academic, career, and personal/social. Three standards within each of these domains provide guidance and direction for school counseling programs. Each of the nine standards contains student competencies and indicators that define the knowledge, attitudes, and skills students should have as a result of participating in a school counseling program. In order to achieve these competencies, strategies are selected, individuals identified to lead the activities, and a time frame for accomplishing these competencies is chosen. In addition, methods for program assessment are selected to determine program success.

Academic Domain

The program standards for academic development guide the school counseling program to implement strategies and activities to support and maximize each student's ability to learn (Campbell & Dahir, 1997, p. 18). See Box 5.2 for an example of an identified competency, activity, indicator and evaluation to meet Academic Standard A; See Box 5.3 for an example of an identified competency, activity, indicator and evaluation to meet Academic Standard B; and see Box 5.4 for an example of an identified competency, indicatory activity, and evaluation to meet Academic Standard C.

Career Domain

The program standards for career development guide the school counseling program to provide the foundation for the acquisition of skills, attitudes, and knowledge that enable students to make a successful transition from school to the world of work, and from job to job

BOX 5.1 National Standards for School Counseling Programs

I. Academic Development

Standard A: Students will acquire the attitudes, knowledge, and skills that contribute to effective learning in school and across the life span.

Standard B: Students will complete school with the academic preparation essential to choose from a wide range of substantial postsecondary options, including college.

Standard C: Students will understand the relationship of academics to the world of work and to life at home and in the community.

II. Career Development

Standard A: Students will acquire the skills to investigate the world of work in relation to knowledge of self and to make informed career decisions.

Standard B: Students will employ strategies to achieve future career success and satisfaction.

Standard C: Students will understand the relationship among personal qualities, education and training, and the world of work.

III. Personal/Social Development

Standard A: Students will acquire the attitudes, knowledge, and interpersonal skills to help them understand and respect self and others.

Standard B: Students will make decisions, set goals, and take necessary action to achieve goals.

Standard C: Students will understand safety and survival skills.

across the life span (Campbell & Dahir, 1997, p. 19). See Box 5.5 for an example of an identified competency, indicator activity, and evaluation to meet Career Standard A; see Box 5.6 for an identified competency, indicator activity, and evaluation to meet Career Standard B; and see Box 5.7 for an identified competency indicator, activity, and evaluation to meet Career Standard C.

Personal/Social Domain

The program standards for personal/social development guide the school counseling program to provide the foundation for personal and social growth as students progress through school and into adulthood (Campbell & Dahir, 1997, p. 19). See Box 5.8 for an identified competency, activity, and evaluation to meet Personal/Social Standard A; see Box 5.9 for an identified competency, indicator activity, and evaluation to meet Personal/Social Standard B; and see Box 5.10 for an identified competency, indicator activity, and evaluation to meet Personal/Social Standard C.

THE AMERICAN SCHOOL COUNSELOR ASSOCIATION NATIONAL MODEL

In March 2001 the governing board of the ASCA determined that even more work was needed to assist counselors with this shift in program development and voted to create a National Model (Schwallie-Giddis, ter Maat, & Pak, 2003). This model capitalizes on the strategies outlined in the National Standards document (Bowers & Hatch, 2003) and reflects the societal demand for greater accountability.

BOX 5.2 Academic Standard A

Students will acquire the attitudes, knowledge, and skills that contribute to effective learning in school and across the life span.

Competency: A:A2	Acquire skills for improved learning
Indicator: A:A2.1	Students will apply time-management and task-management skills.
Name of Activity:	Where Does the Time Go?
Age:	Grade 7
Evaluation:	Student will adjust personal schedule to meet personal needs.
Materials Needed:	Worksheet and pen or pencil

Directions

The lesson will begin with a discussion of the number of hours in a week and of how people do not make good use of their time. Students should be guided to determine their "must do" activities and those activities they choose to do that may be interfering with accomplishing goals. Students will be asked to look at a typical week and the activities that take place in the week to determine how time is spent. The activities are to be placed on the wheel that represents a typical day. A discussion will follow as to how time is spent and how time could be used differently.

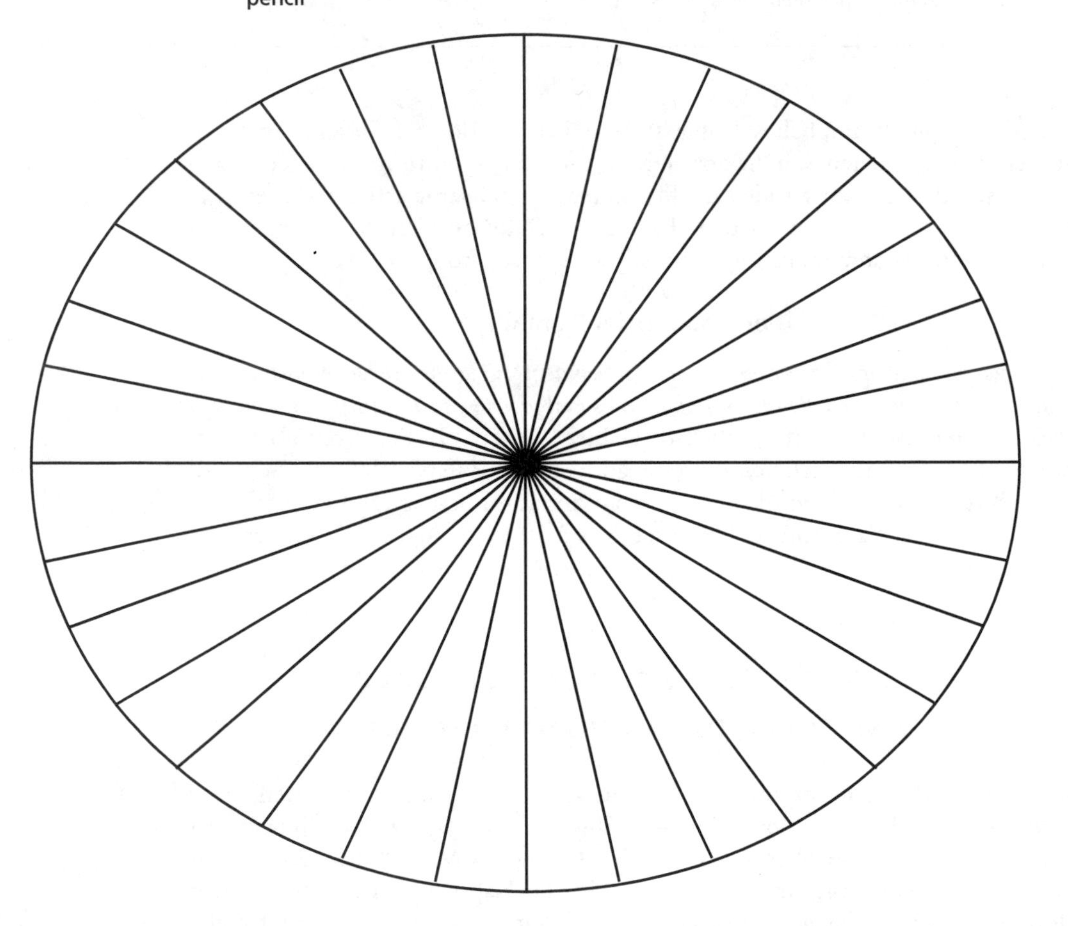

BOX 5.3 Academic Standard B

Students will complete school with the academic preparation essential to choose from a wide range of substantial postsecondary options, including college.

Competency: A:B1 Improve learning.

Indicator: A:B1.2 Students will learn and apply critical thinking skills.

Name of Activity: Get Unpuzzled

Age: Grade 10

Evaluation: Students will discuss how they solved the puzzles.

Materials: Worksheets and pencil or pen.

Directions

In groups of two or three, try to solve the following puzzles.

1 MOTH CRY CRY CRY	2 ME QUIT	3 ——O—— B.S. M.A. PH.D.	4 **DEAL**
5 HE'S/HIMSELF	6 CYCLE CYCLE CYCLE	7 S T O M A C H	8 PAS
9 R ROAD A D	10 STAND ——— I	11 K C E H C	12 KNEE LIGHT

Answers

1. Moth balls
2. Quit following me
3. Three degrees below zero
4. Big deal
5. He is beside himself
6. Tricycle
7. Upset stomach
8. Incomplete pass
9. Cross roads
10. I understand
11. Check up
12. Neon light

BOX 5.4 Academic Standard C

Students will understand the relationship of academics to the world of work and to life at home and in the community.

Competency: A:C1 — Relate school to life experiences.

Indicator: A:C1.4 — Students will demonstrate an understanding of the value of lifelong learning as essential to seeking, obtaining, and maintaining life goals.

Name of Activity: It's Academic

Age: Grade 5

Evaluation: Students will identify occupations, skills, and subjects that relate to each career cluster.

Materials: Career Cluster occupations sheet and pen or pencil

Directions

Students will list five occupations of interest. In groups of three the students are to place the identified occupations in the appropriate career cluster. Then the students are to list the skills that are needed for each occupation. Finally, the students are to list the academic subjects that are used in these occupations.

Career Cluster	Occupations of Interest	Skills Needed	Subjects That Relate to Career
Engineering/Technical			
Arts/Humanities			
Science			
Human services/Social sciences			
Business/People-oriented			
Business/Data-oriented			

BOX 5.5 Career Standard A

Students will acquire the skills to investigate the world of work in relation to knowledge of self and to make informed decisions.

Competency C:A1	Develop career awareness
Indicator: C:A1.4	Students will learn how to interact and work cooperatively in teams.
Name of Activity:	Hidden Triangles
Age:	Grade 10
Evaluation:	Students will discuss how working as a team achieved greater results.
Materials Needed:	Worksheet and pen or pencil

Directions
Give each student the worksheet with triangles. Ask the students to look at the picture and to count the number of triangles portrayed. After 5 minutes, have students get into groups of three or four and compare answers.

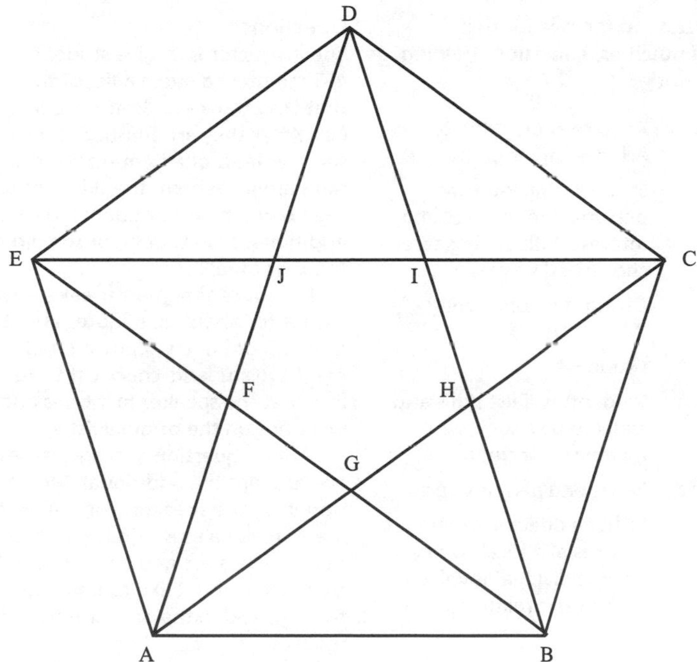

Answer
The correct answer is 35 triangles.

BOX 5.6 Career Standard B

Students will employ strategies to achieve future career goals with success and satisfaction.

Competency: C:B1	Acquire career information.
Indicator: C:B1.6	Students will learn to use the Internet to access career planning information.
Name of Activity:	Getting Technical Through Careers
Age:	Grade 9, career class
Evaluation:	Students will share one career Web site.
Materials:	Computer Internet access

Directions

Students will be shown how to access career Web sites through the computer. After the explanation by the career counselor, the students will be asked to locate one career Web site and share the information with the class.

BOX 5.7 Career Standard C

Students will understand the relationship between personal qualities, education, training, and the world of work.

Competency: C:C1	Acquire knowledge to achieve career goals.
Indicator: C:C1.3	Students will identify personal preferences and interests influencing career choice and success.
Name of Activity:	Giving the Community What It Needs
Age:	Grade 6
Evaluation:	Students will list skills and traits to be a successful member in society.
Materials Needed:	Paper and pen or pencil
Guest Speaker:	Either a director of human services at a local company or an individual involved with public relations

Directions

The instructor is to give students approximately 4–5 minutes to make a list of the skills or traits that they think employers are seeking in employees. After they are finished, each student will share at least one item from his or her list. As the skills are presented, the skills are to be written on the board. Instruct students to write down the additional skills that he or she did not include on the individual list.

Introduce the guest speaker. After he or she speaks for about 20 minutes about the skills and traits his or her company is looking for in employees, have students check off those items on their lists that the speaker mentions and add any that were not on the original list.

After a question and answer session, students are to share the additional items that were mentioned by the speaker. For the next step students are to make a plus sign (+) next to the skills they feel they possess and a minus sign (–) next to the traits they would like to improve. There traits are to be placed in the appropriate columns in the following chart.

+	–

Ask students to select one trait he or she wishes to improve and the strategies for improving this skill or trait.

BOX 5.8 Personal/Social Standard A

Students will acquire the knowledge, attitudes, and interpersonal skills to help them understand and respect self and others.

Competency: PS:A1	Acquire self-knowledge.
Indicator: PS:A1.5	Identify and express feelings.
Name of Activity:	M&Ms and Naming Feelings
Materials:	Bag of M&Ms
Age:	Elementary through high school
Evaluation:	Each person will recognize a feeling based on an event in his or her life.

Directions

The counselor will bring a bag of M&Ms to the group, and each participant will have an opportunity to select an M&M from the bag. The participant is to tell of a time he or she experienced a particular feeling based on the following chart.

Red = Angry

Yellow = Scared

Blue = Content

Brown = Frustrated

Orange = Excited

Purple = Embarrassed

Green = Friendly

BOX 5.9 Personal/Social Standard B

Students will make decisions, set goals, and take necessary action to achieve goals.

Name of Activity:	Life Circles
Competency: PS:B1	Self-knowledge application
Indicator: PS:B1.7	Students will demonstrate a respect and appreciation for individuals and cultural differences.
Age:	Grade 9
Evaluation:	Students will be able to name life experiences that are similar to those of other students.
Materials:	Life Circles Worksheet/pen or pencil

Directions

Break students into groups of three. Each member will put his or her name on one of the circles in the worksheet. Where the circles intersect with each other, students will write in similarities. Where circles do not intersect, students list experiences/facts that are unique to him or her.

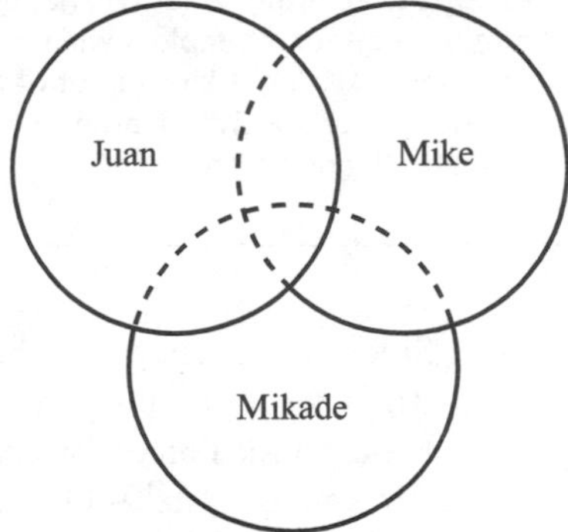

BOX 5.10 Personal/Social Standard C

Students will understand safety and survival skills.

Name of Activity:	Skills for Saying "No"
Competency: PS:C1	Acquire Personal Safety Skills
Indicator: PS:C1.9	Students will learn how to cope with peer pressure
Age:	Grade 7
Evaluation:	Students will be able to use skills for a given situation.
Materials Needed:	Sheet with skills listed

Directions

Students will be taught the following skills to use when confronted with a situation that could lead to trouble:

Step 1: **Ask questions.** When a person asks you to do something, rather than assuming what you think will happen, you need to ask questions such as, What are we doing? Who will be with us? When are we going to do this?

Step 2: **Name the trouble.** If the situation is against rules or laws, the most legal term for the behavior is to be named, for example, vandalism, theft, trespassing, and so on.

Step 3: **Name the consequences.** The student is to state *specifically* what will happen to him or her—for example, I will be grounded, I will get kicked out of the honor society, I won't be able to play basketball, and so on.

Step 4: **Suggest something else.** Suggest something that is fun and will not get you into trouble. For example, suggest watching a video instead, or watching TV, or playing basketball.

Step 5: **Leave.** If the other person puts pressure on you, get up and leave and let the person know that you will be available if he or she changes his or her mind.

The following script can assist in helping students understand how the process works. After practicing the steps, students can make up their own situations and practice the skills.

Esperanza: Gloria, do you want to go Nancy's house?

Gloria: What are we going to do there? (Step 1, ask questions.)

Esperanza: I want to prank her by ringing the doorbell and running away.

Gloria: That would be trespassing. (Step 2, name the trouble.)

Esperanza: No one will know it is us. We will hide quickly behind the front porch.

Gloria: If I get caught, my mom will ground me over the weekend and I won't be able to talk to you on the phone. (Step 3, name the consequences.)

Esperanza: No one will find out. Think of how funny it will be.

Gloria: How about if we go to my house and we will watch that new video. (Step 4, suggest something else.)

Esperanza: No, I will just find someone else to go with me to Nancy's house.

Gloria: I am going to go home to watch the video. If you change your mind, give me a call. (Step 5, leave.)

Since the inception of the standards, many were confused as to whether the standards were for programs or students. In November 2002 the ASCA National Model Task Force clarified that the standards are for K-12 students, not programs (Bowers & Hatch). The standards are defined as providing guidance and direction within each of the domains, the competencies are expectations of student achievement, and indicators more specifically define student achievement in the identified domains (Bowers & Hatch). With this program renewal the traditional question, *What* do school counselors actually do? is replaced with the question, *How* are students different as a result of participating in a school counseling program?

WHAT IS A DEVELOPMENTAL, COMPREHENSIVE SCHOOL COUNSELING PROGRAM?

Systematic planning, proven strategies, a team approach utilizing the skills of the program constituents (Ripley et al., 2003), and knowledge of human development guide program design (Baker, 2000). Additional program considerations include the students' developmental tasks, cultural and ethnic influences, and interpersonal relationships. This "results-based" guidance model is led by the school counselor who takes active responsibility for delivering sequential programming to *all* students. Conversely, the traditional approach was based on providing services for *some* of the students. The four interrelated components in the ASCA National Model include the foundation, the delivery system, the management system, and accountability. Themes of advocacy, collaboration, leadership, and systemic change are identified counselor roles incorporated throughout the program. The ASCA model is shown in Figure 5.1, and each component is discussed separately so that the various program elements can be better understood for implementation.

To assist with program development, a checklist is shown in Box 5.11 as a step-by-step worksheet for program planning, implementation, and evaluation. In viewing the National Model, note that the advisory council is identified under the management component. However, in my mind, because this team is the catalyst of program direction, change, and advocacy, it is presented at the beginning of the discussion on a comprehensive, developmental program.

Advisory Team

People with a vested interest in the school counseling program assist in the transition from a service program focus to one that is a student-oriented developmental curricular structure. The school-board-appointed advisory team serves as a link to the school and community (Rye & Sparks, 1999) throughout the change process. The size of the team should be large enough to represent the different interests of the school and community but small enough to work as a unit. Bowers and Hatch (2003) recommend a minimum of 8 and a maximum of 20 members. This team forms the foundation for policy, reviewing needs, providing direction, devising a time line, analyzing and releasing program evaluation, and making recommendations. Other considerations include the inclusion of individuals representing the various diverse community groups (Ripley et al., 2003; Rye & Sparks, 1999) and appointing individuals to this committee who have been vocal opponents to the program. This range of individuals assists in looking at situations from a different perspective and compromising for decision making.

Suggested advisory team personnel include an administrator from each building and grade level, parents representing different interests, teachers, students, business and community members, school resource people, and a school board member. A functional team will meet on a regular basis as the program is revised

FIGURE 5.1 The ASCA National Model

Reprinted by permission of the American School Counselor Association.

and at least twice annually once the program has been implemented (Bowers & Hatch, 2003; Ripley et al., 2003). The advisory members serve staggered appointments from 1 to 3 years for committee continuity. Members need to have prior knowledge of the purposes of the committee, length of meetings, and agenda items. One of the first tasks of this committee is to design, administer, analyze, and make recommendations for student competencies based on the results of a needs assessment.

BOX 5.11 Checklist for Program Development

I. Initial Stages
- _____ Gather data on effectiveness of developmental, comprehensive school counseling programs.
- _____ Discuss the research and advocate for program change with district administrators.
- _____ Present information to school board members and receive approval for initial steps.

II. Organizational Stage
- _____ Appoint board-approved members to advisory team.
- _____ Present data on developmental, comprehensive school counseling programs to team.
- _____ Provide workshops to educational community to generate support and knowledge of the program plan.

III. Planning Stage
- _____ Design needs assessment.
- _____ Analyze results of assessment and determine priority needs (content).
- _____ Create mission statement.
- _____ Establish rationale.
- _____ Develop program definition.
- _____ Diagram time line.
- _____ Scan current academic curriculum to determine program integration.
- _____ Specify delivery system.
  - Guidance curriculum
  - Individual planning
  - Support system
  - Responsive services
- _____ Determine accountability strategies.

IV. Implementation
- _____ Present plan for board approval.
- _____ Impart plan to teachers and other educational personnel.
- _____ Orient parents and students to plan.
- _____ Initiate delivery system while transitioning from old program.

V. Evaluation
- _____ Assess student competencies and delivery systems.
- _____ Crosswalk with state, national, and local reform initiatives.
- _____ Document changes while implementing plan.
- _____ Evaluate benchmark competencies.
- _____ Report progress to Board of Education.
- _____ Provide educators and parents with program progress.

Needs Assessment

The development of a needs assessment is an essential task for the advisory committee to establish the priorities and needs of the program stakeholders (Johnson, 2000). All individuals with an interest in the school counseling program (students, parents, community members, school board members, teachers, and other individuals influential to the success of the program) are to be assessed to determine program direction (VanZandt & Hayslip, 2001). Personal contacts, focus groups, or interviews are a few methods that can be used to obtain the necessary information.

The questions that may be asked for these face-to-face contacts may include the following:

1. What are some of the concerns you feel school-aged children face today?
2. What would you like students to be able to do upon graduating from high school?

3. What programs do you feel would assist school-aged youth in improving academic self-concept?
4. What resource personnel would be good consultants in assisting students to meet their needs?
5. What strategies can the school personnel implement to help K–12 students achieve academic success?
6. What are the best methods for helping students choose postsecondary options?
7. What can the school curriculum do to assist students in understanding the relationship of academics to future goals?
8. What skills do you feel are necessary in order to understand self and the world of work?
9. What strategies can school personnel implement to teach strategies for achieving goals?
10. What are some of the attitudes, knowledge, and interpersonal skills that are necessary for individuals to understand and respect self and others?
11. How can students learn to make decisions and set goals?
12. What are the best strategies to help students understand and apply safety and survival skills?

A questionnaire is another source of information to determine the needs of students. If a questionnaire is used, a one-page, easy-to-complete format is recommended (Johnson, 2000; Ripley et al., 2003). The questionnaire includes a cover letter explaining purposes, importance, and instructions for completion, in addition to the grade level and other information that will assist in tallying the results. Subject-related content (teen pregnancy, alcoholism, divorced parental homes, etc.) rather than service-related (consultant, referral service, group counseling, etc.) is suggested to identify areas of concern (Ripley et al., 2003). For compatibility and comparison purposes, parallel forms of the needs assessment to distribute to the various constituent groups are recommended. The scoring system should be easy, time efficient, and easy to interpret (Johnson, 2000) for the needs to be established and prioritized for competency and indicator identification (Baker, 2000). See Box 5.12 for a sample cover letter; see Box 5.13 for a sample needs assessment.

A comprehensive, developmental school program includes four interrelated components as identified in the ASCA National Model: (a) The *Foundation* provides the answer to the question *What* will students be able to know and do from school counseling program participation?; (b) the *Delivery System* answers the question, *How* will the activities and strategies be put into practice?; (c) *Accountability* answers the question, *How* have students benefited from the school counseling program?; and (d) the *Management System* answers the questions, *When* will activities occur? *Why* do students benefit from school counseling programs? and *Who* determines the program focus? (Bowers & Hatch, 2003).

BOX 5.12 Cover Letter for Needs Assessment

Today's school-aged youth have many more academic, career, and personal/social pressures than ever before in our society. The school counselor, trained in developmental growth, provides services to enhance growth in *all* students. In order to be certain that K–12 students in our school district are successful at all grade levels, we need your help.

Please complete the enclosed questionnaire and return it to the school counseling department by _____. Your answers will provide valuable information for determining the skills and knowledge that are important to achieving student growth. All answers will be confidential and will be compiled by the school counselor advisory committee. This is a valuable opportunity to provide us with your views on how students can be successful in the future. The results will be released at the PTA meeting and the school board in the month of January.

Thank you in advance for your help.

Sincerely,

The School Counselor Advisory Committee

BOX 5.13 Sample Needs Assessment

South High School
1234 Education Blvd.
Accountability, Indiana

To ______________________________
(parent, teacher, administrator, school board member, community person)

Your help is needed in assisting us to identify the goals that are most important to you in educating our K–12 students.

Write a "1" next to the items that you feel are very important, a "2" next to the items that you feel are moderately important, and a "3" next to the items that you feel are of least importance.

1 = Important
2 = Moderately important
3 = Least important

Academic Domain
Students should

_____ 1. Improve study habits.
_____ 2. Improve test-taking skills.
_____ 3. Improve reading literacy.
_____ 4. Increase mathematical skills.
_____ 5. Enhance goal setting for academic success.
_____ 6. Learn decision-making skills.
_____ 7. Acquire interpersonal communication skills.
_____ 8. Understand relationship of academics to career goals.
_____ 9. Complete school with ability to choose postsecondary options.
_____ 10. Learn how to access information for academic achievement.
_____ 11. Other skills not mentioned above _____
____
____

Career Domain
Students should

_____ 1. Understand career opportunities.
_____ 2. Understand effect work has on one's life.
_____ 3. Learn about leisure activities.
_____ 4. Learn skills needed for jobs.
_____ 5. Choose courses to prepare for a chosen career.
_____ 6. Be knowledgeable about employability skills.
_____ 7. Understand personal qualities compatible with a chosen career.
_____ 8. Acquire an understanding of skills needed for the future.

continued

BOX 5.13 Sample Needs Assessment (*continued*)

_____ 9. Understand requirements for specific jobs.

_____ 10. Be aware of societal factors influencing careers.

_____ 11. Other skills/knowledge not mentioned above ________________________________

____

____

Social/Personal Domain

Students should

_____ 1. Acquire skills, attitudes, and knowledge to understand self and others.

_____ 2. Make personal goals and take the appropriate steps to achieve these goals.

_____ 3. Understand personal survival skills.

_____ 4. Develop empathy and perspective taking.

_____ 5. Acquire skills to solve problems.

_____ 6. Develop an understanding of personal values and beliefs.

_____ 7. Identify alternative strategies for problem solving.

_____ 8. Appreciate individual differences.

_____ 9. Identify and express feelings.

_____ 10. Demonstrate cooperative behaviors.

_____ 11. Other skills/knowledge not mentioned above ________________________________

____

____

Other Information

1. Circle your role in relationship to the school: (Circle all that apply)

   Parent Community Member

   Board Member

   School Administrator

   Teacher Student

2. If you are a parent, in what grade(s) is (are) your child (children)? __________
3. If you are a teacher, what grade(s) do you teach? ____________________
4. If you are an administrator, indicate the grade(s) to which you are assigned. ________ ________________________________
5. If you are a student, indicate the grade in which you are currently enrolled. __________ ________________________________

Thank you for your help with this survey. If you have any questions or would like to serve on our school counselor advisory board, please contact any of the following counselors.

Mrs. Mary Smith

Mr. Takomoto Nishimura

Ms. Linda Adams

The Foundation

The Foundation component includes the mission statement, rationale, and program definition. Beliefs and philosophy are based on personal experiences reflected in the school mission statement and are unique enough to reflect the distinctness of the program (VanZandt & Hayslip, 2001). The program rationale answers the question, *Why* do students need the services of a school counseling program?; and the program definition answers the question, *What* is a comprehensive, developmental school program?

Mission Statement The advisory group helps in formulating the impressions of the guidance program, identifying the discrepancies between what is currently being done, what others think is being done, and the impressions of what should be done (Johnson, 2000; VanZandt & Hayslip, 2001). A mission statement based on the results of the needs assessment explains the philosophical purpose of the program, the integral role school counseling programs play in the school and community, the individuals involved in program delivery, the organization of the program, and the core values of the school counseling profession. Unless there is a consensus on the core values guiding the school counseling profession, it will be a difficult task to create a vision statement (Rye & Sparks, 1999). A common vision can be created by picturing the school counselor program 5 years into the future (Johnson) through the use of the following exercise.

Exercise

1. Ask each member of the advisory team to think of the ideal counseling program. "If you were a counselor working in this program, what would you be doing, with whom would you be working, what would you be thinking, and what does the environment look like?"
2. As a group, share the visions while the counselor writes down common themes.
3. Form small groups (three or four people). Based on the shared ideas, each group is to write a vision statement that includes no more than five or six sentences.
4. In a large group, the vision statements from each of the small groups are shared and a vision statement is generated and approved.

The preceding exercise can facilitate the development of a *mission statement* similar to the following:

> School counselors are human development experts who assist K-12 youth achieve and succeed academically, vocationally, and socially through participation in a comprehensive, developmental program. School counselors facilitate student potential through direct services in consultation with the school district constituents.

Rationale The program rationale identifies: (a) the program contributions that facilitate the developmental issues of children and adolescents and (b) the skills counselors possess in assisting pupil growth (Rye & Sparks, 1999). The rationale answers the question *Why? Why* do counselors perform program services such as responsive services, individual planning, guidance curriculum, and system support (Gysbers &

Henderson, 1994)? *Why* do students need these services? *Why* are counselors an integral part of the educational mission (Johnson, 2000)? A sample *rationale* follows:

> In order to develop the competencies that are needed to be a productive citizen in our society, K-12 students need to be provided with the knowledge, attitudes, and skills to achieve personal and career goals. The school counseling program is founded on developmental theory that promotes student growth and is integrated into the academic mission of the school district. The sequential, developmental program is proactive in focus, clearly defined, and led by a professional school counselor skilled in aspects of human development.

Definition The program definition is answered through the question, *What* is a comprehensive, developmental school program? The definition identifies

1. Clientele
2. Program components
3. Identified competencies individuals will possess
4. The program leaders and their training
5. Accountability (Gysbers & Henderson, 1994)

In other words, the definition will answer the questions, *What* is the counselor in relationship to whom? *What* is the purpose? and *What* is the result (Campbell & Dahir, 1997)? A sample *definition* follows:

> The professional school counselor is trained in human development and has a background in educational psychology, counseling theory and techniques, educational structure, and interpersonal relationships. As a leader of a sequential, systematic K-12 program that is integrated within and accountable to the educational mission of the school, *all* students are assisted in personal growth within the academic, career, and personal/social domains.

The National Standards form the program content based on the academic, career, and personal/social domains. Each of the standards contains identified competencies and indicators for student success as a result of participating in a school counseling program.

ASCA National Standards and Competencies The National Standards identify the essential elements of a comprehensive, developmental school counseling program and guide the school counseling vision into a reality. Competencies are expectations of attitudes, knowledge, and behavior; and indicators more specifically define these expectations (Bowers & Hatch, 2003). The transformed school counselor program is aligned with the local, state, and national competencies and indicators for greater compatibility and acceptance.

The Delivery System

In selecting prioritized needs, a view of the current school curriculum assists in the planning and implementation of services to avoid service duplication and redundancy. Evaluating the effectiveness of the existing curricular strategies provides an opportunity for the school counselor to integrate program competencies and to partner with others to enhance the educational benefits to students.

Guidance Curriculum Although the guidance curriculum has historical roots, the range of strategies, evaluative methods, and the foundational structure are relatively recent adaptations (Gysbers & Henderson, 1994). These additions have strengthened the power and effectiveness of the guidance curriculum, often considered as the "heart and soul" of the program because of its relationship within the total school curriculum. The program is delivered in structured groups and/or classroom presentations to students, educational sessions to parents/guardians, in-service training to teachers, and through other collaborative strategies. As the advisory committee assesses priority needs and curricular competencies, it may find that the needs are already being addressed within identified academic classroom units. Counselors may determine that a particular competency may be strengthened within a social studies unit and wish to team-teach with the teacher. Feelings of territorialism and philosophical differences may occur when professionals feel that others are invading their domain; but open communication, collaboration, and problem solving helps (Johnson & Johnson, 2003; Porter, Epp, & Bryant, 2000) to resolve any issues that arise. Furthermore, counselors may support the teacher with additional structured groups and/or classroom presentations (Gysbers & Henderson, 1994; VanZandt & Hayslip, 2001) to create even more positive opportunities to facilitate student growth. According to the ASCA (Dahir, Sheldon, & Valiga, 1998), the suggested time distribution for counselors to spend on the guidance curriculum is

- 35–45% Elementary school
- 25–35% Middle/junior high school
- 15–25% High school

Individual Student Planning Assisting students with academic, career, and personal/social growth is the cornerstone of a school counseling program—a task that is increasingly more complex due to the insurmountable pressures experienced by students in the present day. Students can be assisted individually, in small groups, or with other interested individuals such as parents or community members for maximum support. Advisement, assessment, and placement and follow-up also assist individuals:

- *Advisement* assists students with appropriate choices in the academic, career, and personal/social domains through information provided by the counselor.
- *Assessment* provides students with results of personal surveys, inventories, test results, and so on, for making individual decisions.
- *Placement and follow-up* aid in problem solving as students make the transition from school to school, or school to career, to monitor curriculum effectiveness and as a means to determine whether or not students are

adequately trained to meet changing societal demands (Gysbers & Henderson, 1994; VanZandt & Hayslip, 2001).

The suggested percentage of counselor time to focus on individual student planning according to the ASCA (Dahir, Sheldon, & Valiga, 1998) is

- 5–10% Elementary school
- 15–25% Middle/junior high school
- 25–35% High school

Responsive Services Individual counseling, small group counseling, consultation, referral, and peer facilitation are included in responsive services (Bowers & Hatch, 2003). Individual counseling is provided when an individual needs immediate help with personal problem resolution, while small group counseling is a time-effective method for assisting a number of students who are experiencing similar problems. Through consultation, students are more effectively assisted through the shared expertise and skills of professionals. Knowledge of community, national, state, and school-based resources is necessary, particularly when the issues of the student are beyond the training level and knowledge of the school counselor (Gysbers & Henderson, 1994; VanZandt & Hayslip, 2001). Peer facilitation is another effective strategy in which students help their peers with personal issues through closely monitored procedures. Through peer facilitation the students are trained in peer mediation to assist peers resolve conflict. The ASCA (Dahir, Sheldon, & Valiga, 1998) recommends the following percentage of counselor time to be spent in responsive services:

- 30–40% Elementary school
- 30–40% Middle/junior high school
- 25–35% High school

System Support This is the area in which time is spent

- Acquiring adequate facilities and equipment
- Renewing and upgrading training through professional development
- Communicating philosophy and competencies to stakeholders (Gysbers & Henderson, 1994; VanZandt & Hayslip, 2001)
- Consulting and collaborating with others

Management includes the activities in which events are scheduled, personnel are identified, and activities are outlined. Consultation activities, although included under the responsive services, are also shared with the support system because of the importance of collaboration with other professionals. Community outreach is the ability of the school counselor to be knowledgeable about community services and about the expertise of the individuals within these agencies. Finally, public relations provide the means for communicating the role and function of the school counselor program. Brochures, pamphlets, and Web site messages are

BOX 5.14 Sample Public Relations Brochure (Reduced)

IN OUR CHANGING WORLD:

- By age 21, today's young people have faced more decisions than their grandparents faced in a lifetime.
- One out of five families move each year.
- Everyone faces career decisions.

Young people face greater risks than previous generations:

- Young people face critical decisions about sexuality.
- Young people face increasing violence in our society and in their schools.
- Some young people face hopelessness that can lead to self-destructive behavior.

Young adolescents affected by these and other problems are not able to achieve at their full academic potential. The counselor's primary task is to help them become better learners by providing a comprehensive program that includes responsive services, individual planning, systems support, and a guidance curriculum.

The Professional School Counselor is a certified teacher with a master's degree in school counseling, including coursework in career development, human growth and behavior, guidance and information services, and a supervised internship.

(This space provided for your name, credentials, phone number, and other information about your counseling program that you wish to provide to the reader.)

Format for this brochure was provided courtesy Michigan School Counselor Association. MSCA is a state branch of the American School Counselor Association and a division of the Michigan Counseling Association http://www.mich-sca.org

Growing Through Counseling

SCHOOL LOGO

NAME YOUR MIDDLE SCHOOL

other sources of information to constituents regarding the role and mission of the program. An example of a public relations brochure developed by the Michigan School Counselor Association is shown in Box 5.14. The recommended amount of counselor time spent in system support according to the ASCA (Dahir, Sheldon, & Valiga, 1998) is

- 10–15% Elementary school
- 10–15% Middle/junior high school
- 15–20% High school

The Management System

An effective, efficiently managed school counseling program in which clear expectations are systematically delivered facilitates greater student growth. This component answers the questions, *Why* will the services be delivered? *Who* will conduct the activities? and *When* will the activities be conducted? (Bowers & Hatch, 2003).

Resources Human, financial, and political resources are vital elements for the success of a school counselor program:

- *Human resources* are individuals chosen because of their unique qualifications to assist the school counselor as a program partner.
- *Financial resources* are funds available for the counseling program to operate effectively.
- *Political resources* govern program direction and beliefs.

Educational personnel crucial to the program include teachers, administrators, resource personnel, school nurses, school media specialists, and clerical staff.

• *Teachers.* In this age of accountability, teachers are reluctant to dismiss students from class due to the risk of the student missing valuable information. Teachers serve as valuable allies to the school counselor as they are often initiators and facilitators of lessons designed to meet priority competencies. Furthermore, teachers serve as excellent referral and informational sources for children and adolescents experiencing difficulties.

• *Administrators.* Unfortunately, most administrators are no longer required to take courses in school counseling. As a result, administrators assign duties to counselors based on their own perception of how counselors should function in a school and often assign duties that are incompatible with the training and experiences of the school counselor. For example, as a new school counselor, my building principal called me into his office to tell me that one of my new tasks would be to take urine samples into the family planning clinic for any of the female students who thought they could possibly be pregnant. I explained to my supervisor that this was a task I did not feel comfortable doing, nor did I feel as if this was an ethical task for me to perform. My principal explained to me that if I wanted to continue working at "his" school, I would need to fulfill his request.

Administrators and other policy makers need information regarding a proactive, student-oriented approach to counseling, as well as data that reveal the positive influences of comprehensive, developmental programming. Today's school counselors are trained in communication and assertiveness skills to educate administrators—skills that would have helped me advocate for my position.

• *Resource personnel.* A clear identification of tasks and responsibilities of all educational personnel provides a picture in which expectations, roles, and duties are understood by all. Resource educators are valuable sources of information due to their special training and skills. Staffing patterns and job descriptions can assist in revealing the clear relationship among educational personnel and the counselors (Lukach, 1998). For instance, speech pathologists, special education teachers, librarians, nurses, reading specialists, and school psychologists all have specific strengths and skills that assist student growth and provide vital information to the school counselor through collaboration.

- *School nurse.* The physical health of students is an important assessment component, and the school nurse is a key person in providing health-related information to the counselor. For example, kids in crisis often express their discomfort through physical symptoms (stomachache, headache, etc.), and these complaints are often reported to the school nurse. The school nurse can also be helpful in partnering with the counselor on educational issues. At one large, public high school several students contracted HIV/AIDS. Students expressed great concern about becoming infected with this disease; and, with the alliance of the counselor and school nurse, educational sessions were held for students and parents in which information about the disease was provided and questions were answered to alleviate some of the concerns.

- *School media specialist.* A partnership between school counselors and media specialists can be formed through such means as publishing lists of current library materials and resources, making bibliocounseling possible through the acquisition of suitable materials, providing library space for career materials, supplying professional materials, assisting with technology, and making library space available for consultation and workshops. Additionally, school media specialists and counselors can work together by improving outcomes through information literacy and technology (Kasowitz-Scheer & Pasqualoni, 2002; Todd, 1999) and providing literature that addresses personal concerns of school aged youth, professional literature for educators and parents, materials for test preparation, and career information including job-seeking skills.

- *School clerical staff.* Secretaries are often the first individuals with whom parents have contact when their children enter the school. This initial meeting often sets the stage for first impressions. Therefore, secretaries need training in constructive, positive behaviors for meeting the public, responding to student needs, and supporting individuals who are distressed. Due to the sensitive, confidential nature of student records, clerical assistants also require training in record management, the types of information that may or may not be released, and guidelines for scheduling students who wish to contact the counselors.

> The importance of training became especially significant when one of the school secretaries left a counselor's appointment book on her desk and it was visible to anyone entering the office. When a student noticed the name of one of her classmates scheduled to see a counselor, she quickly spread the news around the school, thus compromising the confidential relationship between the counselor and student. In another case, a parent called the school requesting her daughter's recent ACT results. Since the counselor was unavailable, the secretary felt that she would be helpful in providing this information to the parents, an obvious ethical and legal violation.

- *Financial and political support.* In order to promote, advocate for, and publicize the school counseling program, the approval of significant stakeholders and financial support are essential. An adequate budget serves as a foundation for a properly implemented program. Program monies to be used for program implementation and management are to be a separate line item distinct from the testing budget. Too often monies set aside for the counseling program are often unfairly allocated for testing materials (Gysbers et al., 2000; Lukach, 1998) with no funding available for essential materials and supplies.

In an age in which serious decisions are made due to financial crises, valuable programs are often eliminated. When programs demonstrate success and contributions to student growth, it is unlikely that these programs will be viewed as unessential, fringe programs to be terminated when financial predicaments arise. The advisory board members are powerful allies in defending the program and its importance to the academic curriculum by guiding and advocating for the school counseling program, developing a time frame, and assessing program effectiveness.

Time Analysis A time analysis should be conducted at two levels: (a) to analyze services offered, frequency of services, and where time is spent appropriately or inappropriately; and (b) to analyze time through the use of a calendar for when events are to occur, benchmarks for evaluation, and when revisions are to occur. While needs are assessed, a time and task analysis can be conducted concurrently to analyze how time and tasks are presently performed and to determine whether time and tasks could more effectively and economically be performed by others (VanZandt & Hayslip, 2001). In analyzing time allocation and full program implementation, advisory board members can be grateful that a program does not have to be accomplished all at once. In fact, a time frame of approximately 6 years is recommended (VanZandt & Hayslip) with identified competencies, grades, and activities to be determined at specified times and school years. These activities are documented in an action plan.

Action Plan The action plan notes the National Standard to be addressed, the competency that will be met, the indicators, a description of the activity to reach the identified competency, the individual responsible for the activity, when the standard is to be addressed, and how the competency will be assessed. Through the evaluation process, it may be determined that the strategy used to address the competency may need to be revised or eliminated; either the competency did not match the developmental level of the identified students or the individual responsible for the competency had difficulty teaching the lesson. This is valuable information that requires careful attention to determine more appropriate strategies.

A sample action plan that encompasses the three standards, competencies, and indicators within the academic development domain is found in Table 5.1. This plan builds on the activities that were previously identified as strategies for meeting the identified domain and competency.

Table 5.1 **Academic Domain Action Plan**

Standard	Competency	Indicator	Activity	Who Will Lead?	When?	Evaluation Method
A:A Standard A Students will acquire the attitudes, knowledge, and skills that contribute to effective learning in school and across the life span.	A:A2 Acquire skills for improving, learning.	A:A2.1 Students will apply time-management and task-management skills.	Where Does the Time Go?	7th-grade English teacher and counselor	During unit on study skills	Students will complete the worksheet and adjust weekly time schedule.
A:B Standard B Students will complete school with the academic preparation essential to choose from a wide range of substantial postsecondary options, including college.	A:B1 Improve learning.	A:B1.2 Students will learn and apply critical thinking skills.	Get Unpuzzled	Counselor-led discussion in social studies class	During unit on critical thinking in grade 10	Students will discuss how they solved the puzzles.
A:C Standard C Students will understand the relationship of academics to the world of work and to life at home and in the community.	A:C1 Relate school to life experiences.	A:C1.4 Students will demonstrate an understanding of the value of lifelong learning as essential to seeking, obtaining, and maintaining life goals.	It's Academic	5th-grade teacher and counselor team teach	During 5th-grade homeroom class during scheduling for 6th grade	Students will identify occupations, skills, and subjects that relate to each career cluster.

An example of an action plan for the career development domain is found in Table 5.2. As in the academic domain, the activities that were identified to meet the standard, competency, and indicators are used as examples.

The personal/social development domain action plan is found in Table 5.3; and, as in the previous domains, the action plan utilizes the activities previously identified. As noted in the action plans, it is essential to identify when the activity is to occur and the evaluative method that will be used to measure success and to link the school counseling program to the academic mission.

Accountability

Previously, counselors were remiss in demonstrating and documenting how their interventions made a difference in the lives of students. Counselors were not adequately trained in appropriate ways to conduct assessment procedures; nor were they trained in appropriate methods to determine intervention effectiveness—partly because of the nature of the counseling process, in which results are not always immediately apparent (Ripley et al., 2003). Today's school counselors collect and use data that concretely show how students are different due to their participation in a school counseling program. Data collected and communicated to stakeholders

- Ensure that the program is implemented as designed
- Document program impact and effectiveness
- Communicate program success
- Improve the program
- Provide information on numbers of students involved in the program
- Provides documentation of stakeholders assisted

Evaluation takes place on both the program and counselor performance levels (Rye & Sparks, 1999).

Program Assessment Program assessment, in the form of both formative and summative evaluation, provides information on strategy effectiveness in reaching competencies:

- *Formative evaluation* considers the success of a particular activity during implementation to determine whether or not the means for meeting the competency is effectual. If a particular strategy proves ineffective, revisions are made, documented, and included in reports.
- *Summative evaluation* is a compilation of feedback collected at an identified time (benchmark) to determine whether or not specified activities are meeting the desired competencies (Ripley et al., 2003).

There are numerous assessment strategies that can be conducted that take minimum effort but produce enormous gain. They are discussed in more detail in Chapter 6, "The Professional School Counselor and Accountability." A discussion of how evaluation can be incorporated into each of the four program delivery components follows:

Table 5.2 Career Development Domain Action Plan

Standard	Competency	Indicator	Activity	Who Will Lead?	When?	Evaluation Method
C:A Students will acquire the skills to investigate the world of work in relation to knowledge of self and to make informed career decisions.	C:A1 Develop career awareness.	C:A1.4 Students will learn how to interact and work cooperatively in teams.	Hidden Triangles	Teacher-led activity	During 10th-grade career class	Students will discuss how working as a team achieved greater results.
C:B Students will employ strategies to achieve future career goals with success and satisfaction.	C:B1 Acquire career information.	C:B1.6 Students will learn to use the Internet to access career planning information.	Getting Technical Through Careers	Career specialist will team-teach with counselor.	9th-grade career class	Students will share one career Web site.
C:C Students will understand the relationship among personal qualities, education and training, and the world of work.	C:C1 Acquire knowledge to achieve career goals.	C:C1.3 Students will identify personal preferences and interests in influencing career choice and success.	Giving the Community What It Needs	6th-grade teacher and counselor-led discussion	6th-grade class unit on society and others	Students will list skills and traits to be a successful member in society.

Table 5.3 Personal/Social Development Domain Action Plan

Standard	Competency	Indicator	Activity	Who Will Lead?	When?	Evaluation Method
PS:A Students will acquire the attitudes, knowledge, and interpersonal skills to help them understand and respect self and others.	PS:A1 Acquire self-knowledge.	PS:A1.5 Students will identify and express feelings.	M&Ms and Naming Feelings	Teacher and counselor	During 3rd-grade unit on "understanding self"	Each person will recognize a feeling based on an event in his or her life
PS:B Students will make decisions, set goals, and take necessary action to achieve goals.	PS:B1 Self-knowledge application.	PS:B1.7 Students will demonstrate a respect and appreciation for individual and cultural differences.	Life Circles	Community member from agency	Students in 9th grade during Diversity Week in February	Students will be able to name life experiences that are similar to those of other students.
PS:C Students will understand safety and survival skills.	PS:C1 Acquire personal safety skills.	PS:C1.9 Students will learn how to cope with peer pressure.	Skills for saying "No"	Counselor and 7th-grade health teacher	Students in 7th grade during health unit on safety	Students will be able to use skills for a given situation.

BOX 5.15 Guidance Curriculum Evaluation

Domain ____________________
Standard ____________________
Competency ____________________
Indicator ____________________
Activity ____________________

1. What was one thing you learned from this activity?
2. How are you planning to use this information?
3. What is one thing that you liked best about the presentation?
4. What is one suggestion you would have for improvement?

- *The guidance curriculum.* A student evaluation is easily incorporated into the last few minutes of a classroom period for formative evaluation from teachers and students. Summative evaluation may include evidence of competency attainment, numbers of classrooms visited, or numbers of parent workshops conducted. The information in Box 5.15 can be adapted as an evaluation tool.

- *Individual student planning.* Quantitative and qualitative data can be used to document individual student planning activities and effectiveness. For instance, data can be presented using a chart with numbers of students seen for curriculum planning, college selection, job shadowing, and so on.

One high-school counselor in northern Ohio met individually with all incoming students to introduce herself, to explain her role, and to become acquainted with each of her assigned students. During this session each student was asked to identify one long-term goal (something to be accomplished that school year) and one short-term goal (to be accomplished during that grading term). Students were then asked to identify strategies to reach each of the goals. At the end of the academic year, the counselor met once again with each student to report on his or her progress in meeting the goals. Students summarized goals that were accomplished and barriers that prevented goal attainment, and they identified new goals for the following year. Data were collected on the content of the goals, strategies that facilitated goal achievement, and barriers to goal attainment. This data provided valuable information for concerns that needed to be addressed by the counseling department, as well as strategies that assisted students.

- *Responsive services.* Counselors can accumulate data addressing the number of issues students encounter, as well as maintain a current list of community resources. Additionally, data on the number of consultations provided, small groups led, and reports from peer facilitators provide documentation of program maintenance. As a crisis team leader the school counselor may also evaluate how well the crisis plan worked and arrange for continual training.

- *System support.* Counselors have an ethical obligation to maintain professional development. The numbers of conferences or workshops attended or in-service activities presented, types of consultation, partnering, and participation on advisory councils and committees provide useful data.

Counselor Performance Evidence is necessary to document the contributions of the school counselor and performance effectiveness. Counselor performance evaluations provide another type of data. For accurate appraisal, school counselor job descriptions should be in accordance with various tasks identified. Enumerative data are the tools most often used by counselors and are helpful in that they provide a record of the number of times an individual is contacted or provided with a service. This information can be very effective when the school board notes that throughout the year the counseling department had 1,345 individual counseling contacts. However, a disadvantage is that it does not reveal the effectiveness of the interventions—only that time was spent on certain activities.

School counselors are shortchanged when an appropriate evaluation tool is not utilized. An effective evaluative tool highlights job responsibilities and ensures that administrators understand the program. Too often the school counselor is evaluated according to an evaluation form designed for teachers. Therefore, the school counseling professional needs to actively advocate for a performance evaluation tool that accurately reflects his or her duties. There are several considerations in the design and implementation of an effective counselor evaluation form:

1. A well-defined job description provides the foundation for an effective evaluation tool.
2. In the design of an evaluation, begin with a straightforward process using evaluation tools that are compatible with the needs of the system.
3. The evaluation process is ongoing in that needs and tasks change (Synatschk, 2002). Administrators should evaluate school counselors annually with a rating scale determined in advance. Additionally, a mechanism in place for school counselors to self-evaluate assists in determining areas of self-improvement for annual goal setting.

More information on program and counselor accountability is found in Chapter 6.

The ASCA National Standards and Model serve only as a template and are not meant to serve as a cookie-cutter model for all schools. School counselors are encouraged to use this model as a reference when developing their own school counseling program, rather than "reinventing a new program." It is essential that the school board has a thorough understanding of the program, offers support, and, most importantly, endorses the model. Without school board approval, the shift to a comprehensive, developmental program stands little chance of succeeding. Evaluative strategies must be continuous throughout program implementation as well as after the program has been put into practice. Furthermore, the curricular model adopted by the school board should be compatible with the board-adopted curricular action plans.

SUMMARY

The school counselor is not the school counseling program. Historically, the school counselor has been viewed as part of a fringe, ancillary program with little contribution to the total school academic mission. With educational reform and the increased demand for effectiveness, school counselors are under greater pressure to show how their program has made a contribution to student growth. In 1997 the American School Counselor Association took an active role in the development and implementation of the National Standards; the ASCA later built upon these standards by creating a National Model based on the previous success of the Missouri Comprehensive Guidance Program introduced by Norman Gysbers and associates. Fervent promotion of this model has been undertaken by ASCA, and successful change is becoming evident. In contrast to counselors in the past, today's professional school counselors are more actively advocating for educational reform and communicating how a developmental, comprehensive school counseling program makes a difference in the lives of students. Yesterday's counselors assumed a passive stance and presumed that others were aware of the depth and breadth of their tasks and duties without documenting program success.

This chapter outlines the steps counselors can take to implement a developmental, comprehensive approach in today's schools. In making this transformation, school counselors will no longer need to be on the defensive when asked the question, What do school counselors do? Instead, as the leader of the program, the school counselor will be able to document results, share data, and communicate how students benefit from participation in a comprehensive, developmental school counseling program.

Novice school counselors—such as Esperanza, who was introduced at the beginning of the chapter—will no longer climb an uphill battle in convincing stakeholders that school counselors are important. Interaction with stakeholders, program visibility, careful documentation, and data will provide the needed evidence that students benefit when participating in a comprehensive, developmental school counseling program.

REFERENCES

Baker, S. (2000). *School counseling for the twenty-first century* (3rd ed.). Upper Saddle River, NJ: Prentice-Hall.

Bowers, J., & Hatch, T. (2003). *The ASCA National Model: A framework for school counseling programs*. Alexandria, VA: American School Counselor Association.

Burnham, J. J., & Jackson, C. M. (2000). School counselor roles: Discrepancies between actual practice and existing models. *Professional School Counseling, 4,* 41–49.

Campbell, S., & Dahir, C. (1997). *Sharing the vision: The National Standards for school counseling programs*. Alexandria, VA: American School Counseling Association.

Dahir, C. A. (2001). The National Standards for school counseling programs: Development and implementation for school counseling standards: A summary and comparison with other student services' standards. *Professional School Counseling, 4,* 328–333.

Dahir, C. A., Sheldon, C. B., & Valiga, M. J. (1998). *Vision into action: Implementing the National Standards for school counseling programs*. Fairfax, VA: American School Counseling Association.

Goals 2000. (1994). *Goals 2000: Educate America Act*. Retrieved June 18, 2002, from http://www.ed.gov/legislation/GOALS2000/TheAct

Gysbers, N. C., & Henderson, P. (1994). *Developing and managing your school counseling program* (2nd ed.). Alexandria, VA: American Counseling Association.

Gysbers, N. C., Lapan, R. T., Blair, M., & Starr, M. (1999). Closing in on the statewide implementation of a comprehensive guidance program model. *Professional School Counseling, 2,* 357–366.

Gysbers, N. C., Lapan, R. T., & Jones, B. A. (2000). School board policies for guidance and counseling: A call to action. *Professional School Counseling, 3,* 349–355.

Hart, P. J., & Jacobi, M. (1992). *From gatekeeper to advocate: Transforming the role of the school counselor*. New York: The College Board.

Johnson, L. S. (2000). Promoting professional identity in an era of educational reform. *Professional School Counseling, 4,* 31–40.

Johnson, S., & Johnson, C. D. (2003). Results-based guidance: A systems approach to student support systems. *Professional School Counseling, 6,* 180–184.

Kasowitz-Scheer, A., & Pasqualoni, M. (2002). *Information literacy instruction in higher education: Trends and issues*. Syracuse, NY: ERIC Clearinghouse on Information and Technology. (ERIC Document Reproduction Service No. ED465375)

Lapan, R. T., Gysbers, N. C., & Petroski, G. F. (2003). Helping seventh graders be safe and successful: A statewide study of the impact of comprehensive guidance and counseling programs. *Professional School Counseling, 6,* 186–197.

Lukach, J. (1998). Implementing the developmental comprehensive school counselor program model. In J. Allen (Ed.), *School counseling: New perspectives and practices* (pp. 99–104). Greensboro, NC: ERIC/CASS.

McWhirter, J. J., McWhirter, B. T., McWhirter, A. M., & McWhirter, E. H. (1998). *At-risk youth: A comprehensive response* (2nd ed.). Pacific Grove, CA: Brooks/Cole.

National Commission on Excellence in Education (1983, April 26). A nation at risk. Retrieved April 29, 2004, from http://www.goalline.org/Goal%20Line/NatAtRisk.html#anchor807826

Porter, G., Epp, L., & Bryant, S. (2000). Collaboration among school mental health professionals: A necessity, not a luxury. *Professional School Counseling, 3,* 315–322.

Ripley, V., Erford, B. T., Dahir, C., & Eschback, L. (2003). Planning and implementing a 21st-century comprehensive developmental counseling program. In B. T. Erford (Ed.), *Transforming the school counseling profession* (pp. 63–120). Upper Saddle River, NJ: Pearson Education.

Rye, D. R., & Sparks, R. (1999). *Strengthening K-12 school counseling programs: A support system approach* (2nd ed.). Philadelphia, PA: Accelerated Development.

SCANS (2000). *Scans 2000: The workforce skills Web site*. Retrieved June 18, 2002, from http://www.scans.jhu.edu?NS/HTML/About Com.htm

Schmidt, J. J., & Ciechalski, J. C. (2001). School counseling standards: A summary and comparison with other student services' standards. *Professional School Counseling, 4,* 328–333.

Schwallie-Giddis, P., ter Maat., M., & Pak, M. (2003). Initiating leadership by introducing and implementing the ASCA National Model. *Professional School Counselor, 6,* 170–173.

Synatschk, K. O. (2002). Ensuring professionally relevant supervision and professional development: A district-level experience. In N. C. Gysbers & P. Henderson (Eds.), *Implementing comprehensive school guidance programs: Critical leadership issues and successful responses* (pp. 199–210). Greensboro, NC: ERIC.

Todd, R. J. (1999). Transformational leadership and transformational learning: Information literacy and the World Wide Web. *NASSP Bulletin, 83,* 4–12.

VanZandt, Z., & Hayslip, J. (2001). *Developing your school counseling program: A handbook for systemic planning.* Belmont, CA: Wadsworth/Thomson Learning.

6

The Professional School Counselor and Accountability

Mr. Karcher had been a vocational agriculture teacher in a small, rural high school for 18 years. Although he enjoyed teaching, he wanted to work with students in a different role. He decided to go back to graduate school to get a credential as a school counselor.

After completing his coursework, he was approached by the superintendent of a rural school district who asked him if he was interested in working as an elementary school counselor. At a meeting, Mr. Karcher learned that this was a new position approved by the school board and he would be instrumental in developing the first elementary school counseling program. At first he turned the offer down, but after he thought about it, he decided that this would be an excellent opportunity to work with younger children.

From the beginning, Mr. Karcher's worst fears were realized. He was not going to be placed at the one elementary school as he was told initially; he would be responsible for two elementary schools as well as the middle school—a population of well over 800 students. In addition, because he did not have a job description he found himself taking on such activities as bus duty, cafeteria duty, and substitute teaching.

At the end of the year he left the position discouraged and unconvinced that school counselors could actually perform the duties for which they had been trained. How can capable, energetic school counselors such as Mr. Karcher communicate his role and convince stakeholders that his training and skills can make a difference in the lives of others? The answer is related to the ability of school counselors to conduct research and evaluation (Whiston, 1996) and to communicate how their activities make a difference in the lives of youth.

In this age of school reform, the need for accountability is evident. The beneficial results of programming and counselor performance in leading school counseling programs are necessary to facilitate performance, remedy incompetence, and document student growth. Credentials alone do not prove competence (Loesch, 2000). Moreover, not being able to prove program effectiveness borders on unethical conduct (Gladding, 2000).

As early as the 1970s, educators were reminded to be accountable for the services they provided. However, school counselors did not spend much effort in collecting accountability information because many felt inadequately trained in program evaluation and efforts were too time-consuming and/or unnecessary (Fairchild & Zins, 1986). In the early 1990s, the cry for accountability was the cornerstone of educational reform, and society demanded that educational programs produce acceptable results. Those individuals and programs deemed as being fringe and ineffective were often eliminated when finances were low, and school counselors and school counseling programs were often among those that were eliminated (Gibson & Mitchell, 1999). Therefore, a need existed to justify and defend school counseling as beneficial and cost-effective (Gillies, 1993; Whiston, 2003). School boards require research and data to provide a defensible rationale for how school counseling programs benefit students.

Mediocre services may result when evaluation does not occur, and the opportunity to establish higher standards is lost. Unfortunately, school counselors have not consistently conducted research, and many have even questioned its usefulness. Counselors cite numerous reasons for their reluctance to engage in program evaluation:

1. Counselors report that they do not have the skills necessary to conduct research (Gladding, 2000) due to the erroneous belief that evaluation requires complex skills based on advanced statistical procedures. Much of this belief is credited to a heightened attention on research designs learned in graduate training that are problematical in a school counseling setting (Myrick, 1990). However many results can be obtained through uncomplicated data-gathering instruments in which sophisticated mathematical formulas are unnecessary (Allen, 2002; Frith & Clark, 1982; Gibson & Mitchell, 1999).
2. Many school counselors share the belief that other activities are more important. These professionals are not aware that school counselors are susceptible to external authorities such as school board members who have limited knowledge of the school counselor's tasks. Unless counselors engage in research to evaluate program effectiveness and measures of student competency, counselors will continue to perform duties that are outside of their training and skills (Whiston, 1996).
3. Some counselors state that evaluative studies will focus on their shortcomings or that a positive evaluation may lead to the assignment of additional activities outside of their training and education (Myrick, 1990).
4. Practitioners report that they do not feel research methodologies belong in the school system due to the faculty belief that children are not good sources of evaluative data or that soliciting information from parents is not worth the time

(Frith & Clark, 1982). However, students as the primary consumers of the counseling program are prime candidates for providing feedback. Furthermore, parents have a unique perspective that can be valuable to the assessment of the counselor program. When the opinions of parents who are often critics of the program are considered, these opponents may become the greatest counselor allies.

5. Counselors report a lack of time (Lee & Workman, 1992). Although the initial planning, designing, and implementation of an evaluative questionnaire do take time, once they are designed they can be used from year to year with revisions made as needed (Frith & Clark, 1982). In initially designing the evaluative instrument, it is helpful to administer it to a pilot group of individuals for their feedback for the purpose of making revisions.
6. Counselors report a lack of administrative support as a barrier to their efforts to engage in evaluative studies (Fairchild & Zins, 1986) not only because of the expense but also because of a misconception regarding counseling practices. Administrators keep an eye on budgetary issues and are concerned about the potential expense of evaluative studies, yet many evaluations can be conducted with minimal expense. This is particularly true if monies are solicited through grant writing. If administrators are kept informed about the value of the process and are provided with feedback from the evaluation, most will support evaluative procedures (Frith & Clark, 1982).

REASONS ACCOUNTABILITY HELPS SCHOOL COUNSELORS

Although counselors express their lack of enthusiasm in engaging in research, this process will provide proof that counseling programs do enhance the educational growth of K-12 students. According to Baker (2000), accountability may promote skills, improve program effectiveness, and provide positive feedback for performance. In addition, evaluations can validate or reject current practices, provide new insights, and identify individuals who are responsible for providing services (Gibson & Mitchell, 1999).

For too many years, studies were not available on the effectiveness of school counselors and their programs—a void that supported the belief that school counselors were helpful, fringe professionals, but expendable. Recent research reveals that the strategies implemented by the professional school counselors positively impact students (Whiston & Sexton, 1998, as cited in Whiston, 2003).

Because school counselors use a wide variety of strategies, it is important to know which services are most effective. For instance, one question often asked is, Is group work better than individual assistance, particularly when school personnel need to compete for the student's time? Based on several studies, group intervention with younger students reveals positive results (Whiston, 2003). Another group counseling intervention aimed at recognizing healthy relationships with at-risk, adolescent females revealed moderate to strong progress in attitude and relationship changes with others (Zinck & Littrell, 2000).

The trend today is to provide an integrated school counseling program that reflects the philosophy and mission of the school. In a study by Lapan, Gysbers, and Sun (as cited in Whiston, 2003), students who participated in a comprehensive, developmental school counseling program earned higher grades, reported greater preparation for future plans, and believed that their school had a more positive climate in comparison to peers who did not participate in a fully implemented counseling program.

Although it is clear that accountability is more important than ever in these times of diminishing monetary and personnel resources, there are some barriers in performing research in the schools. For one, some administrators are hesitant to approve of research projects in schools with youth due to the concern of litigious consequences. For example, students are minors who are unable to participate in studies without parental consent. Obtaining parental consent may be difficult due to perceived personal issues that may be revealed (Whiston, 1996). For example, at one point I was conducting research to determine whether or not the self-concept of children from different home structures (e.g., divorced parental homes, paternal-custodial homes, maternal-custodial homes, or intact families) was influenced by their family structure. Several parents refused to give consent for their children to participate in the study because of their belief that this information could be used to harm the family.

TYPES OF EVALUATION

Evaluation includes data about program and personnel leading the program. Through increased involvement with accountability studies, it is hoped that counselors will have a greater appreciation for its benefits. If counselors are not included in the evaluative procedures, then others will determine which methods are to be used even though these methods may not be best suited to the counseling process (Fairchild & Zins, 1986).

Formative and *summative evaluation* are two essential types of feedback that are performed for continuous program and personnel improvement. Since these assessment methodologies depend upon one another for providing vital information, neither one can be overlooked.

Formative evaluation includes utilizing data to determine the effects of services or programming during implementation. Data are used to alter, substitute, or eliminate ineffective strategies. Because it is an ongoing process, formative assessment guides summative assessment. For instance, an elementary counselor may ask students to evaluate their perceptions of a study skills group midway through the process to determine whether or not changes need to be made before the program terminates. *Summative evaluation* occurs at the conclusion of a program to determine the final effects of the counselor efforts and/or program (Baker, 2000; Gibson & Mitchell, 1999).

Using summative data, the counselor advisory committee can analyze available data to determine whether or not a counseling program is meeting its identified goals. It is possible that evaluations of the program and counselors are positive and that the activities need to continue, or it may be that programs and activities need to be modified or eliminated. Neither formative nor summative evaluation can be overlooked as each is interrelated to the other, and each provides valuable information for program effectiveness and personnel competence.

Action-based research is often used as an effective problem-solving method for gathering data (Gibson & Mitchell, 1999; Whiston, 1996) surrounding program results. This research method concentrates on a systematic application of the scientific method for solving problems (Allen, 2002; Gillies, 1993; Mills, 2000, as cited in Zinck & Littrell, 2000), service improvement, professional development, and survival of the counseling profession. Action-based research provides the foundation for solid program planning and decision making (Frith & Clark, 1982). The significant data obtained are vital sources of information for interested constituents. Examples of strategies that can be used for program assessment and school counselor performance are discussed subsequently.

EVALUATION OF PROGRAM EFFECTIVENESS

Although program planning, implementation, and evaluation are discussed in a previous chapter, this section more specifically focuses on the evaluation of a comprehensive, developmental school counselor program. As previously discussed, an understanding of target group demographics and characteristics and a needs assessment assist in identifying goals, competencies, and strategies for reaching the specified goals (Gibson & Mitchell, 1999; Schmidt, 1993). A program cannot be developed all at once, but a selection of priority needs is determined for long- and short-term planning. Evaluative strategies during and after implementation create an opportunity for careful program design.

Counselors complain about the lack of relevant measures that can be used in their work setting and have relied extensively on published standardized tests and inventories. Although these instruments provide valuable information, they are often cost prohibitive and time ineffective (Myrick, 1990). Since valid data are "determined not only by the research design itself but also by the nature of the measuring instrument" (Myrick, 1990, p. 22), counselors feel that self-designed tests may not provide legitimate results. At the same time, counselors need to obtain data upon which decisions are made. Such information has been obtained through comparative studies, follow-up studies of graduates, surveys, case studies, behavioral observations, retroactive measures, and student portfolios. Some knowledge of question construction is necessary so that the item intent is clear, scoring is easy, and the information is usable (Baker, 2000). Through these methods policy makers can receive evidence that assists in making decisions influencing counseling programming (Baker, 2000; Gillies, 1993).

TYPES OF PROGRAM EVALUATIONS

Comparative Studies

One method of obtaining data is through the use of comparisons that include pre-post assessments, experimental designs, and single-subject methodologies (Myrick, 1990).

Pre-Post Assessments Counselors may ask students to complete a pretest prior to participating in a program and a post-test upon completion of the program. The test results are compared to determine intervention effectiveness and subsequent student growth. For example, a pre/post test design was developed to study the acceptance of disabled students by their nondisabled peers following participation in a social skills program (Ciechalski & Schmidt, 1995). Fourth graders were randomly assigned to social studies classes. Students in the experimental group received training in social skills integrated into the regular social studies class, while the students in the control group received only instruction in the social studies curriculum. Both groups completed pre- and post-tests, which showed that the use of social skills training positively influenced the social interactions between the students with disabilities and their nondisabled peers. Studies such as this contribute an answer to the question, How do school counseling programs influence youth?

Experimental Action Research This research methodology compares equal groups of students. One group of students who have participated in a specific intervention (experimental group) are compared with a group of individuals who did not participate in the intervention (control group). In one study of middle-school students from an Appalachia community, three groups were compared to determine differences in interventions. Students referred by their teachers for tutoring were assigned to a group that received tutorial services only, to a group with tutorial services and counseling, or to a control group of students who did not wish to receive any type of tutoring. All groups of students were given the Coopersmith Self-Esteem Inventory to measure self-esteem, and classroom behavior was measured using the Behavior Rating Checklist (BRC). In addition, the grade-point average (GPA) of each student was determined as an additional pre-post test measure. Following the intervention, data revealed that the students receiving tutorial instruction and counseling improved significantly in self-esteem and classroom behavior in comparison with the other groups. On the measurement of academic achievement, the counseling/tutoring group had the highest GPA, while the GPA for the control group dropped from the pre-assessment to the post-assessment (Edmondson & White, 1998).

Single-Subject Methodologies Counselors are sometimes reluctant to assess individual counseling interventions due to the belief that one participant does not support good research design. A single-subject study by Yarbrough and Thompson (2002) was conducted to assess reality therapy and solution-focused behavior counseling with two elementary-aged children who exhibited behavior problems. One child received reality therapy, and the other received solution-focused brief therapy. Each child met with the same counselor once a week for a period of 5 weeks. Each child's behavior improved following the counseling sessions.

Graduate Follow-Up Studies

Graduates are able to provide extensive information, yet this is an area in which information is scarce. Counselors and members of the advisory committee have difficulty knowing how to conduct this type of study, where to obtain the financial resources, who should be responsible for the dissemination and collection of the study, and how the results will be used. One follow-up study of the 2000–2001 graduates conducted by the Anchorage School District (Graduate Follow-Up Survey, 2002) provides questions that may be considered in conducting a follow-up survey. A few of the questions follow:

1. How do you rate the overall academic program you received in Anchorage?
2. How do you rate the teachers who were teaching in your Anchorage high school?
3. How do you rate the counseling you received at your Anchorage high school?
4. Please rate the following aspects of the school program on a 5-point good-bad scale (subject areas listed).
5. Did you take classes in the career technology area?
6. Which classes in career technology were most useful to you?
7. Check the three of the following classes that were most important to you, the three least important, any area in which you would have liked to have more classes available, and any area in which tutoring would have been helpful to you (classes listed).

Surveys

Rating scales and questionnaires are used to obtain information from stakeholders. In a study by Fairchild and Zins (1986), among the counselors who did engage in accountability studies, student responses accounted for the largest group from whom information was gathered. Teachers were the second, followed by administrators and parents, and only a few counselors requested feedback from ancillary staff members. Open-ended questions allow respondents to provide personal opinions and generate intriguing information, but these surveys are difficult to score due to the wide range of answers. Some examples of *open-ended questions* follow:

1. One of the most important duties of a school counselor is . . .
2. One skill students should have upon graduating from high school is . . .
3. One of the biggest concerns adolescents face is . . .

Closed questions are easy to score and statistical data can be generated but may not reveal the wide range of responses as obtained through open-ended questionnaires. Some examples of *closed questions* follow:

1. Do you feel that students have too much free time? ___ yes ___ no
2. Do most students have difficulty with time management? ___ yes ___ no
3. Do students need to develop more social skills? ___ yes ___ no

Selected-response questionnaires provide a combination of statistical data and a wider variety of responses. Some examples of selected-response questions follow:

1. One of the greatest concerns adolescents face is
   a. peer relations
   b. stress
   c. family problems
   d. depression
   e. other
2. Teachers are most stressed by
   a. grade performance
   b. inattentive students
   c. time demands
   d. too many regulations
   e. other

Case Studies

School counselor practitioners also collect accountability data through case studies (Fairchild & Zins, 1986). In one case, counselors from a tri-county area in the Midwest each chose a student in their building who was identified as having AD HD. The counselors provided individual counseling and intervention for the identified student for a 9-week period and shared counseling results with each other. These interventions were published in a practitioner's handbook for counselors to consult whenever more information was necessary.

Behavioral Observations

School counselors are in an ideal position to observe student behavior in and out of the classroom. A baseline tracking system in which identified behaviors are noted and then compared following a particular intervention provides useful information for strategy assessment.

Portfolios

Portfolios showcase students' accomplishments to evaluate growth for college admission or future employers. The Kentucky Education Reform Act requires portfolios for certain grade levels in English/language arts and mathematics (Eastern High School Digital Portfolio, n.d.). The required contents of Grade 12 Portfolios follow:

English/Language Arts

1. Table of contents
2. A personal narrative
3. A short story, poem, or play
4. Three pieces of writing with designated criteria
5. Letter to the reviewer by the student that describes the portfolio's author and self-reflection

Mathematics

1. Table of contents
2. Entries that show an in-depth understanding of entries provided by various sources

Retrospective Assessment

A retrospective research method attempts to recreate the past events of an individual through the recollection of memories or events. The counselor constructs assessment items with a scale that is used as the response key. The student reads each item and is instructed to think back to a time prior to the intervention, (e.g., guidance lesson, assertiveness training, conflict mediation) indicate what his or her response would have been at that time, and to place an "X" somewhere along the scale. Then, the respondent is asked to think about the item as he or she perceives it at the present time. An "O" is placed on the scale to indicate the current perception. If there is a positive change in perception, then the counselor indicates this change with a "+" symbol next to the item. If the perception suggests a negative trend then the counselor places a "–" symbol next to the item. Case history procedures are frequently criticized because of their lack of reliability, but useful information may still be obtained. The numbers can be compared for accountability and evaluation of the strategy. An example of such an instrument designed for a student who was seeing a school counselor for stress relief is found in Box 6.1.

COUNSELOR PERFORMANCE EVALUATION

Closely related to program evaluation is an assessment of the counselors who lead the program. As previously discussed, counselors have not historically taken responsibility for documenting how their time is spent, leaving the job description and counselor activities up to the administrators to decide. The result is a

BOX 6.1 Example of a Retrospective Assessment for Stress Relief

Directions to student
Think back to how you were feeling when you first started counseling for stress. For each of the feelings found on the first chart, put an "X" next to the number that best indicates how you believe you would have rated yourself at the start of the counseling sessions for each of the following emotions. When you are finished look over the list in the second chart and place an "O" next to how you feel about each of the items at the present time.

Start of Counseling Session

	1	2	3	4	5
Angry			X		
Worried				X	
Frustrated			X		
Anxious				X	
Tense					X

End of Counseling Session

	1	2	3	4	5	Trend
Angry		O				+
Worried		O				+
Frustrated			O			No change
Anxious					O	–
Tense		O				+

Response Key: 1 = I rarely have this feeling 5 = I almost always have this feeling

battleground as administrators assign and assess duties based on personal experiences and knowledge about the counselor's training and role. Too often, administrators tie counselor performance to student growth, an unreasonable practice due to the numerous variables influencing the process. As the counselor actively communicates the value of a developmental school counseling program and the role he or she plays in this program, criteria that is collaboratively determined help decrease the number of noncounseling activities performed by counselors and allow the counselor to perform duties for which he or she has been trained. Too often, counselors feel vulnerable when they are involved with self-evaluative methods, but counselors who become involved in the process report more advantages than risks (Fairchild & Zins, 1986).

The establishment of a written job description provides school counselors with an opportunity to work proactively and to perform duties consistent with training (Baker, 2000). Knowledge of expectations, who will conduct the assessment, where and when it will take place, and the time frame for communicating results (Bleur, 2000) provides descriptive information that alleviates the "guesswork" surrounding the school counselor's role. Too often counselors are evaluated according to standards established for classroom teachers, an approach that is illogical for the school counselor who performs duties and tasks different from these professionals (Schmidt, 1993). An assessment instrument based on the counselor's job description and guided by the program development reflects the quality of the school counselor's performance. School counselor practitioners in the Western United States reported a performance evaluation based on a form designed for the teachers that included items such as the following:

1. The teacher has a neat, inviting classroom.
2. The teacher grades fairly.

3. The teacher is consistent in discipline procedures.
4. The teacher turns in grades on time.

These items had little relevance to the duties performed by the school counselors. They approached the president of the Teacher's Educational Association, the bargaining unit to which most counselors belong, about this problem, and they were told that the teacher evaluation form was a contract issue that could not be substituted. Furthermore, they were told that they were "minority members" of the association and the organization represented the "majority." This event and response highlighted their need to more vocally advocate and communicate for the integral role school counselors play in enhancing the growth of school-aged youth. An example of an assessment form based on the school counselor's job description is found in Table 6.1.

Supervisors, peers, students, self-assessments, the results of program outcome, or a combination form a more accurate picture of professional competencies, strengths, and weaknesses. Also, a decision as to whether the results will be used for promotion, pay increases, feedback, or for administrative decision making should be clear in advance.

Both objective and subjective measures are common in the assessment process. Objective assessments have an advantage of being structured, subject to psychometric properties, and more efficient (Loesch, 2000). These instruments can be a simple, straightforward, 1-page checklist in which each item measures a specific task; an instrument of several pages in which each task is broken down into component parts; or a Likert scale representing an identified behavior with clearly defined descriptors (Bleur, 2000). Subjective evaluations may include the use of rating forms and, in some cases, supervisors' judgments of actual counseling activities. However, these evaluative forms are not particularly effective indicators of performance, nor do they produce consistent results. Too often judgments are cluttered by personal perceptions with a reluctance of colleagues to provide any negative feedback (Loesch).

As the nature of education evolves, so do the assessment techniques that assist and complement each other in evaluating the professional school counselor. Other types of assessments include self, peer, student, enumerative data, and portfolios.

Self-Assessments

Self-improvement enhances services, promotes growth, and motivates counselors to pursue meaningful activities. When counselors are encouraged to establish professional goals at the beginning of each academic year with the understanding that they will be evaluated at the end of the year, the opportunity is provided for self-assessment. Moreover, these data hold the professional personally accountable for performance since personal motives are known better than those of anyone else. Unfortunately, these self-assessments are only useful to the counselor him or herself and do not have broad value. Furthermore, they are often not authorized by the administration as a valid performance indicator in comparison to those assessment instruments approved by the school board (Henderson & Gysbers, 1998).

Table 6.1 School Counselor Assessment Based on a Job Description

(Based on Job Description Identified by a Needs Assessment)

Delivery Services

Guidance Curriculum Structured Groups/Classroom Presentations	**Activities Identified**	Date	Satisfactory	Insufficient	In Progress	**Comments**
Planned and conducted financial aid night	• Scheduled date • Advertised event • Contact presenters					
Parent orientation	• Scheduled date • Notified parents • Contact speakers					
Conflict-mediation class lesson	• Schedule visit • Present lesson • Evaluate lesson					
Individual Planning Advisement Assessment Placement Follow-Up	**Activities Identified**					
Meet with each student	• Each student sets personal goals for year					
Interpret test results	• Discuss SAT results with each student					
Schedule classes	• Discuss career plans and assist in class registration based on career goals					
Graduate follow-up	• Conduct and communicate annual 5-year graduate survey					
Responsive Services Individual Counseling Small Group Counseling Consultation Referral	**Activities Identified**					
Provide individual counseling	• Meet with students for personal concerns					
Conduct groups	• Administer needs assessment to determine necessary groups • Facilitate group					
Meet with teachers	• Identify number of conferences with teachers					
Make referrals	• Identify number of referrals when appropriate					

Continued

Table 6.1 Continued

Guidance Curriculum Management Consultation Community Outreach Public Relations	**Activities Identified**	**Date**	**Satisfactory**	**Insufficient**	**In Progress**	**Comments**
Arrange department calendar	• Schedule yearly counseling activities					
Meet with administrator	• Monthly meeting with principal to discuss program concerns					
Community outreach	• Contact community agencies regarding school counseling program					
Public relations	• Design and distribute monthly newsletter					
Foundation Component	**Activities Identified**					
Philosophy and mission	• Review philosophy and mission					
National Standards	• Align competencies with SAT/ACT					
Management	**Activities Identified**					
Use of data	• Analyze evidence of competency					
Student monitoring	• Evaluate interventions					
Calendar	• Develop calendar of pertinent dates and distribute					
Accountability	**Activities Identified**					
Results report	• Report to school board members • Monthly report to building principal					
Performance evaluation	• Determine annual goals and assess • Meet with building principal for evaluation					
Program audit evaluation	• Analyze competency results					
Advisory council	• Meet with advisory board					

Peer Assessments

The best providers of peer assessment are those with expertise in the counseling field such as local counselor educators, counseling consultants, or program leaders. These identified evaluators assist counselors in enhancing their skills, facilitate program improvement, conceptualize cases (Henderson & Gysbers, 1998), and provide broader information support.

Student Assessments

Since counseling is a process, it is often difficult to recognize immediate results. However, several simple scales may be used to gauge progress immediately following a single counseling session and after a designated period of time following termination. Furthermore, scaling techniques that provide students with a visual depiction of their daily progress assist with goal attainment (see, for example, the thermometer in Figure 6.1) and are a gauge for counselors to assess their progress in working with these individuals.

An additional student assessment is illustrated in Box 6.2, and these accumulated data provide supporting evidence that the counselor is accountable to the students and school.

Other constituents are influential in assessment of counselor performance. Evaluative measures such as the one shown in Box 6.3 for parental feedback are encouraged.

Enumerative Data

Counselors use enumerative data to show how their time is spent. For example, counselors may tally their activities to determine the number of times a particular activity was performed (e.g. number of students seen for individual counseling, number of parents contacted regarding student concerns, number of consultations with educators, etc.) (Baker, 2000). In a study by Fairchild and Zins, (1986) of the counselors surveyed who engaged in collecting accountability information, enumerative data was the most commonly used due to the ease of data collection. See Table 6.2 as an example of how counselors document time spent.

Another essential source of enumerative data collection is conducting a time analysis to determine the amount of time devoted to a particular activity (Fairchild & Zims, 1986). As counseling programs are transformed to a comprehensive model, information on time spent based on data from the previous year can be gathered from calendars, lesson plan books, and notes, etc. (Hughes & James, 2001). These weekly reports can be transformed into monthly and then a yearly report (Hughes & James, 2001). The quantitative information obtained empowers the counselor for monitoring personal growth (McAuliffe & Erikson, 2000). An example of how time is monitored is shown in Table 6.3.

Circle the way you feel.

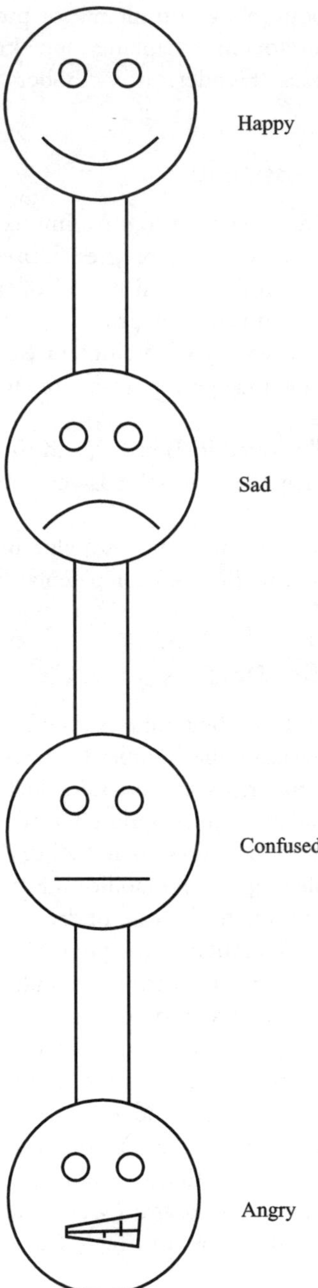

FIGURE 6.1 Client Assessment

BOX 6.2 Student Assessment

Directions

On a scale of 1 to 5, circle the number that best shows how you felt when you first saw your counselor. 1 = Bad 5 = Good

1 2 3 4 5

Now, circle how you felt when you left your counselor

1 2 3 4 5

BOX 6.3 Parent Evaluation

Directions

Your assistance is needed so that the school counseling department can provide the best services to you. Please respond to the following questions.

1. What services has the school counselor provided to you? (check all that apply)

   _____ consultation _____ referral

   _____ test interpretation _____ advice with concerns

   _____ information requested _____ other (please be specific)

2. How have you been informed of the school counselor duties?

   _____ individual contact _____ child

   _____ newsletter _____ teacher or other school person

   _____ another parent _____ other (please be specific)

3. What is one service provided by the school counselor that you found most helpful to you or your child?

   _____ information on parenting _____ consultation

   _____ group counseling _____ referral to another professional

   _____ classroom guidance _____ other (please be specific)

4. What comments, suggestions, or questions do you have regarding the counseling program?______________________________

   ____

Portfolio

The portfolio is another measure of effectiveness (Rhyne-Winkler & Wooten, 1996). A portfolio provides an individual with the opportunity to compile samples of achievements, personal growth experiences, philosophy, areas of interest, and self-reflection statements (Baker, 2000). Portfolio materials have the advantage of (a) documenting growth, (b) evaluating effectiveness of work, (c) reflecting on

Table 6.2 Analysis of Activities

Directions: Place a mark each time you perform an activity below.

Date ___________

Delivery System	**Tally**	**Total**
Guidance curriculum		
Individual planning		
Responsive services		
System Support services		
Foundation Component		
Philosophy & mission & beliefs		
Identified competencies		
Management		
Advisory Council		
Use of data		
Action Plans		
Calendar		
Accountability		
Results report		
Program evaluation		
Performance & evaluation		
Professional development		
Noncounseling Activities		
Administration		
Clerical		
Scheduling		

Comments:

____

____

____

____

Table 6.3 Analysis of Time

Directions: Place a mark each time you perform an activity below.

Date __________

	Delivery Services	**Foundation Components**	**Management**	**Accountability**	**Indirect Services**
Date	*Guidance Curriculum (GC) *Ind. Planning (IP) *Responsive Services (RS) *Support Services (SS)	*Philosophy & Mission (PM) *Competencies (C)	*Use of Data (D) *Student Monitoring (SM)	*Results Report (RR) *Performance and Evaluation (PE) *Professional Development (PD) *Program Audit (PA) *Advisory Board (AB)	*Clerical (C) *Scheduling (S) *Administration (A)
7:30–8:00					
8:00–8:30					
8:30–9:00					
9:00–9:30					
9:30–10:00					
10:00–10:30					
10:30–11:00					
11:00–11:30					
11:30–12:00					
12:00–12:30					
12:30–1:00					
1:00–1:30					
1:30–2:00					
2:00–2:30					
2:30–3:00					
3:00–3:30					
3:30–4:00					
4:00–4:30					
Total					

personal experiences, and (d) remediating problems. The following items may be considered for inclusion in a portfolio:

1. Transcripts and degrees
2. Certificates of attendance at workshops and conferences
3. Licenses and/or credentials
4. Letters of recommendation and commendation
5. Formal and informal assessments (based on results of guidance units or counseling strategies)
6. Professional disclosure statement (including areas of specialty)
7. Professional association memberships
8. Program development
9. Personal goals and checklist of accomplishments
10. Past job experiences
11. Miscellaneous (notes, thanks, cards)

The portfolio can take many forms such as placing materials in a notebook with dividers, a box, or an expandable folder, or it can even be digitized. This assessment tool is regularly updated to make certain that the information remains accurate and current (Steigerwald, 1997).

A combination of strategies is the best type of evaluation. Each district must determine the most time-effective assessment methods that will yield the best reflection of program and personnel effectiveness. Counselors have utilized numerous strategies that best answer the questions, Why are students different as a result of participating in a school counseling program? and What do school counselors do? In a study by Fairchild and Zins (1986), counselors used data to reveal the wide range of services provided, to enhance professional growth, and to monitor program delivery.

STRATEGIES FOR SHARING ACCOUNTABILITY INFORMATION

Sharing research results is a welcome opportunity for school counselors to influence public relations. The use of a chart that visually depicts time spent on activities can capture the attention of decision makers (Hughes & James, 2001) and form a foundation for public relations. *Public relations,* a fundamental element in counseling programs, includes ongoing activities that contribute to a mutual understanding among individuals and institutions (*The Public Relations Professional,* n.d.).

There are numerous strategies for communicating positive program results (Holcomb & Niffenegger, 1992). For instance, advisory committees can provide support and feedback for the counseling program. Administrators and school board members should be provided with a written report on weekly and/or monthly activities, then summarized in an annual report. Speaking to parent groups and teacher in-service meetings regarding the duties of the counselor is another method counselors can use to advocate for their profession (Schmidt, 1993). Additional considerations include: leaflets outlining the program and services, advertisements in local newspapers and radio, inviting the media to school programs sponsored by the counseling program, discussions on local talk shows, an informational parenting Web site, videotapes, or sponsoring a homework hotline (Holcomb & Niffenegger). Additional public relations ideas are included in Box 6.4.

With monetary concerns that often limit research efforts, funds and support are needed so that program continuity is not jeopardized. Counselors may strongly consider grant writing as a tool for program support to assist in meeting the needs of the students. The grant generates program visibility and public relations and promotes student advocacy.

BASICS OF GRANT WRITING

Money for grants comes from the government and public agencies such as foundations, corporations, and private philanthropy and are distributed in the form of gifts, grants, contracts, or cooperative research and development agreements. The necessary criteria for grant information are stated in a request for proposal (RFP) form, which generally includes the following information: (a) summary or abstract, (b) introduction, (c) problem statement or needs assessment, (d) program objectives, (e) methods, (f) evaluation, and (g) budget.

Summary or Abstract

The abstract is a concise, 1-page summary of the proposal that provides readers with a general idea of the grant proposal. Generally, the grant proposal will specify the length of this section.

Introduction

This part of the grant proposal includes background information such as the demographics of the school and community, qualifications of the individuals responsible for the project, and anecdotal data from reports. Research related to the proposal can convince grant readers that the grant writer is aware of current trends and developments in the field.

Problem Statement

The problem statement highlights the reason that this project needs to be undertaken at this time with an identified population. Too often, grant proposals are written based on emotional and political reasons rather than rational, factual, logical terms. Therefore, the grant should include convincing arguments as to the need for the proposal, and documentation should be included (particularly local statistics) to provide compelling evidence for the program. In addition, specifying the number of individuals who will be impacted by the grant will also assist in a persuasive case for the need for the grant.

BOX 6.4 Ninety-One Public Relations Ideas

1. Design a pamphlet that provides information on the role of the school counselor.
2. Work with teachers in designing and implementing a K-12 comprehensive school counseling program.
3. Give information to stakeholders about student achievement of all types.
4. Publish a monthly counseling newsletter.
5. Participate in radio and television programs to talk about your program.
6. Accept invitations to discuss your program, or invite yourself to local community groups.
7. Participate in in-service meetings.
8. Give immediate feedback to all coworkers, but make certain colleagues are aware of confidentiality issues.
9. Conduct in-service programs for faculty and staff on current topics such as suicide, self-mutilation, gang identification, and so on.
10. Turn in a monthly summary to your building principal.
11. Present accountability data to school board at least twice per year.
12. Encourage principals to observe classroom guidance lessons in action.
13. Identify and evaluate yearly goals.
14. Provide teachers with encouragement and positive feedback.
15. Seek exhibit space for a counseling program presentation at a shopping mall or store window. Inform the general public about services offered. Have students help with the exhibit.
16. Assist in designing a counselor evaluation form based on job description for administrator use.
17. Prepare a coloring book designed by students to explain guidance services to children and their parents.
18. Present a "career of the week." Briefly describe a career every Monday over the PA system.
19. Take your administrator to lunch.
20. Meet with new teachers to discuss the process of referring students.
21. Invite new teachers and staff members to the counseling facility to show them the materials and offices.
22. Send a guidance/counseling report card to parents to show student progress in meeting counseling objectives.
23. Share career bulletins and booklets with teachers to assist in relating careers to subject areas.
24. Place an informational insert on the counseling program in report cards (e.g., tips on time management).
25. Participate in the coordination of a career day for all students to shadow or observe community workers on the job. (School personnel usually arrange this type of program only for students in the upper percentile of their class.)
26. Develop a "logo" for your program. (A contest can be arranged for students.)
27. Keep a file of graduates and conduct a follow-up study.
28. Seek the assistance of senior citizens.
29. Develop a Web site for your program including a listing of courses and credits.
30. Subscribe to the local newspaper and acquaint yourself with the editors to cover special events or to publish counseling program information.
31. Attend school board meetings.
32. Accompany students when receiving scholarships or other awards.
33. Survey teachers, parents, and students to gain information on program effectiveness.
34. Publish accountability results.
35. Develop a video presentation about the school counseling program and make the video available to local realtors, interested parents, community agencies, and so on.
36. Public school materials to present to realtors to distribute to interested home buyers.
37. Display posters about the counseling services in laundry mats, grocery stores, and so on.
38. Speak to administrator groups.
39. Speak to or write letters to church groups about the counseling services.
40. Send get-well cards to students.
41. Order book covers, pens, and so on which "advertise" counselor services.
42. Arrange publicity for teachers who integrate counseling objectives in the classroom.
43. Urge administrators to permit counselors to attend professional meetings.

BOX 6.4 Continued

44. Send birthday cards to students.
45. Send thank-you notes to teachers who have been helpful.
46. Send a personal note to parents notifying them of the positive things their child has accomplished.
47. Publish a list of college representatives who are visiting the school and invite parents to attend.
48. Inservice staff (secretaries, bus drivers, cafeteria workers) on counseling services and things they can do to assist students.
49. Prioritize agenda items. Don't keep students waiting.
50. Keep appointments.
51. E-mail important information to students and/or parents.
52. Prepare a "senior fact sheet" with dates, events, important to seniors.
53. Schedule a summer time visit with new students.
54. Take pictures of new students and post in counselor offices with information about each new student.
55. Arrange and conduct sessions based on parent needs.
56. Assist in designing and revising a crisis management plan, and review plan with faculty and staff at least once a year.
57. Conduct group counseling sessions based on student needs.
58. Provide music in the office to provide a relaxed atmosphere.
59. Provide students with paper to write a thank-you note to a teacher, custodian, principal, or some other adult who has helped them.
60. Print and distribute business cards with your e-mail address.
61. Design special stationery with the counselor logo.
62. Design a "coupon book" to be exchanged for counselor services.
63. Participate in a computerized "Dear Counselor" program.
64. Visit each club and extracurricular activity to meet students.
65. Meet with each student at the beginning of the year to set personal goals.
66. Eat lunch with students.
67. Be available to students and teachers in the hallway during class change time.
68. Provide substitute teachers with information on counseling services and referral procedures.
69. Post a professional disclosure statement in office.
70. Cut out news articles featuring students and post in counseling offices.
71. Send students congratulatory letters on outstanding accomplishments.
72. Conduct a career and college day.
73. Provide convenient evening hours for family consultation.
74. Give faculty information on counseling services.
75. Form an advisory committee.
76. Teach counseling skills to teachers.
77. Organize a guidance breakfast for faculty and staff during National School Counseling Week.
78. Talk to school superintendent at least twice a year about the counseling program.
79. Keep informed on all school events.
80. Be active in community activities.
81. Join professional organizations.
82. Conduct research on counseling effectiveness.
83. Write grants for counseling materials.
84. Design bumper stickers advertising school counseling programs.
85. Personally know your juvenile judge and officers, understanding their program, and provide information about the counseling program.
86. Bring resource individuals into the school.
87. Visit teachers on a regular basis.
88. Publicize agencies and experts in the community for referral purposes.
89. Set aside one evening a month for parents to come to the school to discuss concerns.
90. Set up a counseling display table at the annual school open house.
91. Develop a Web site.

Program Objectives

Program objectives, often called *specific aims, goals,* or *purposes* are measurable and attainable. Therefore, action-oriented verbs such as *demonstrate, test,* or *develop* are advisable. The objectives need to be succinct, not ambiguous, and stated in a manner that determines the outcome, rather than as a description of the activity. Since the objectives are the basis for determining the methodology of the program, they are carefully formulated.

Methodology

The methodology includes the strategies by which the objectives are to be accomplished for grant readers to have a clear picture of *what* is to occur, to *whom, when* the project steps will take place, *where* they will occur, and *how* they will be implemented. This section is articulated clearly and logically, addresses staffing needs, and is written in a practical manner. This section is usually the most carefully read section of the whole proposal. Since the grant proposal is only one out of many that will be received and reviewed, it is helpful to write it in an interesting fashion so that it will be remembered by the grant reviewers. The use of professional jargon often confuses readers, particularly if these individuals are not familiar with the terminology of a certain profession.

Evaluation

Both formative and summative evaluative strategies are to be addressed including who will evaluate, how the project will be assessed, and the strategies for collecting the assessment data. A sound evaluation design will determine the extent to which the program will be effective in achieving its objectives. The following questions are to be considered in designing the evaluation: (a) Did the program accomplish its objectives? (b) Will the program operate as it was designed? and (c) What variables need to be considered in monitoring the program structure?

Budget

The budget is an operational statement of the project in monetary terms. Therefore, the program should not be designed to fit a budget, but, rather, the budget should be designed to fit the program. Since the budget mirrors the identified objectives, it requires attention to detail so that is reasonable, justifiable, and error free. Key elements of a program budget include: (a) a detailed salary rate structure for personnel, (b) identified fringe benefits for each category, (c) travel details such as purpose and description of trips, (d) an explanation of unusual requests and a justification for equipment items identified by model numbers.

Reasons as to why grant proposals are rejected include the following:

1. Failure to follow application instructions (even an overlooked signature may cause the application to be rejected)

2. The failure to respond to specific requests such as information about staffing, organizational qualifications, scheduling, technical issues, or any other form of information
3. Use of "flowery" terms and phrases to convey information that states claims rather than facts
4. Excessive use of citations and references to "prove" the importance of the project, possibly leading to a proposal that is viewed as unoriginal and left over from previous proposals
5. Lack of an effective evaluation scheme, or offering a weak procedure

Grants are promising methods by which school counselors can provide additional services and materials for their constituents and are an excellent resource for promoting the school counselor program.

SUMMARY

The benefits of research strategies for accountability are significant. Research and practice complement each other as both contribute to the professional growth of the professional. When the results of counselor interventions and program outcomes are not documented and communicated, school counseling programs will continue to be endangered. Historically, school counselors have been remiss in providing data to show program effectiveness, which has led to misconceptions of the counselor's role and a misunderstanding of the counselor's contribution to student academic achievement. Counselors need to take a more active role in program effectiveness and in defining tasks and methods for evaluating performance of these activities.

Information gathering alone is not enough. Counselors must educate their constituents about the importance of accountability information since proving effectiveness is more necessary than ever in this time of diminishing resources. In addition, public relations strategies including grant writing are included in this chapter for the purpose of communicating the role of the school counselor to the various program constituents.

REFERENCES

Allen, J. M. (2002). *Action-oriented research: Promoting school counselor advocacy and accountability*. Ann Arbor, MI: Eric Digests. (ERIC Document Reproduction Service No. ED347477)

Baker, S. (2000). *School counseling for the twenty-first century* (3rd ed.). Upper Saddle River, NJ: Merrill Prentice-Hall.

Bleur, J. (2000). *Assessing school counselor performance. In brief: An information digest from ERIC/CAPS*. Ann Arbor, MI: ERIC/CAPS Clearinghouse on Counseling and Personnel Services. (ERIC/CAPS ED260365)

Ciechalski, J. C., & Schmidt, M. W. (1995). The effects of social skills training on students with exceptionalities. *Elementary School Guidance & Counseling, 29,* 217–222.

Eastern High School Digital Portfolio. (n.d.). Retrieved September 24, 2003, from http://www.essentialschools.org/pub/ces_docs/resources/dp/eastern.html

Edmundson, J. H., & White, J. (1998). A tutorial and counseling program: Helping students at risk of dropping out of school. *Professional School Counseling Journal, 1,* 43–47.

Fairchild, T. N., & Zins, J. E. (1986). Accountability practices of school counselors: A national survey. *Journal of Counseling and Development, 65,* 196–199.

Frith, G. H., & Clark, R. (1982). Evaluating elementary counseling programs: 10 common myths of practitioners. *Elementary School Guidance & Counseling,* 17, 49–51.

Gibson, R. I., & Mitchell, M. H. (1999). *Introduction to counseling and guidance* (5th ed.). Upper Saddle River, NJ: Merrill Prentice-Hall.

Gillies, R. M. (1993). Action research for school counselors. *The School Counselor, 41,* 69–72.

Gladding, S. T. (2000). *Counseling: A comprehensive profession (94th ed.).* Upper Saddle River, NJ: Merrill Prentice Hall.

Graduate Follow-Up Study (2002). Retrieved Sept. 24, 2003 from http://www.asdk12.org/depts/assess_eval/gradsurvey/AppendixBIV.asp

Henderson, P., & Gysbers, N. C. (1998). *Leading and managing your school guidance program staff.* Alexandria, VA: American Counseling Association.

Holcomb, T. F., & Niffenegger, P. B. (1992). Elementary school counselors: A plan for marketing their services under the new education reform. *Elementary School Guidance & Counseling, 27,* 56–63.

Hughes, D. K., & James, S. H. (2001). Using accountability data to protect a school counseling program: One counselor's experience. *Professional School Counseling, 4,* 306–309.

Lee, C. C., & Workman, D. J. (1992). School counselors and research: Current status and future direction. *The School Counselor, 40,* 15–19.

Loesch, L. C. (2000). *Assessing counselor performance. Highlights: An ERIC/CAPS Digest.* Ann Arbor, MI: Clearinghouse on counseling and personnel services (ERIC/CAPS Digest No. ED304635).

McAuliffe, G., & Erikson, K. (2000). *Preparing counselors and therapists: Creating constructivist and developmental programs.* Virginia Beach: Donning Company.

Myrick, R. D. (1990). Retrospective measurement: An accountability tool. *Elementary School Guidance & Counseling,* 25, 21–29.

Rhyne-Winkler, M. C., & Wooten, H. R. (1996). The school counselor portfolio: Professional development and accountability. *The School Counselor, 44,* 146–150.

Schmidt, J. J. (1993). *Counseling in schools: Essential services and comprehensive programs.* Boston, MA: Allyn and Bacon.

Steigerwald, F. (1997). Portfolio development: Documenting the adventure. *Counseling Today.* Alexandria, VA: American Counseling Association.

The public relations professional. (n.d.). Retrieved July 26, 2003, from http://www.prsa.org

Whiston S. C. (1996). Accountability through action research: Research methods for practitioners. *Journal of Counseling & Development, 74,* 616–623.

Whiston, S. C. (2003). Outcome research on school counseling services. In B. T. Erford (Ed.), *Transforming the school counseling profession* (pp. 435–448). Upper Saddle River, NJ: Merrill Prentice-Hall.

Yarborough, J. L., & Thompson, C. L. (2002). Using single-participant research to assess counseling approaches on children's off-task behavior. *Professional School Counseling, 5,* 308–314.

Zinck, K., & Littrell, J. M. (2000). Action research shows group counseling effective with at-risk adolescent girls. *Professional School Counseling, 4,* 50–59.

7

The Professional School Counselor's Role in Career Development

JUDITH A. SOMMERS, PH.D.
Retired High School Counselor/Adjunct Professor, Heidelberg College

Nearly a century of social change has brought about an increased interest in career development. Career education is no longer just for seniors in high school to decide if they are going to college or not. As our society makes its transition into the 21st century and computer technology is becoming more widespread, the professional school counselor's role becomes very important in career development for students of all ages across all cultures.

HISTORY OF CAREER DEVELOPMENT

The Industrial Revolution provided the catalyst for the need for vocational guidance since the revolution brought about many changes in the manufacturing industry, thus creating the need for new jobs. The roots for career education were developed in 1908 when Frank Parsons, considered to be the father of vocational guidance, provided the basis for the trait/factor theory in his book *Choosing a Vocation* (1909). The *trait/factor theory* states that occupational choice is based upon matching personal traits such as aptitudes, abilities, and interests to job characteristics such as skills and attitudes needed, opportunities available, and educational requirements. According to Parsons' theory, the greater the match between personal traits and job factors the greater the probability that satisfaction will result.

The first vocational education act passed by Congress was the Smith-Hughes Act of 1917 (Pub. L. 64-347) that established vocational education and separated Agriculture, Homemaking and Trade, and Industrial Education from other vocational programs, as well as academic curriculum areas. This act led to the development of separate teacher training programs and organizations for both teachers and students. Before a state could receive federal funding under the Smith-Hughes Act, the state had to establish a state board for vocational education.

The Depression Era shifted the emphasis from occupational information to personal traits since the Depression produced a need to help dislocated workers to retrain and find new jobs. During the 1920s and 1930s the concern was with finding occupations for White males. In the 1940s women took over many jobs formerly held by males who were fighting in World War II. This presented a whole new picture of the workforce, while creating many new social dilemmas such as child care issues and maternity and paternity leaves.

The 1950s brought another era of concern to the United States after Russia launched *Sputnik I* into space. It became obvious to governmental officials that the United States was lagging behind in education, particularly in mathematics and science. The National Defense Education Act of 1958 (NDEA) created incentives for students to attend college with low interest rates, and students who went into the teaching profession had reduced loan payments back to the government. It was during this time period that many more school systems were hiring guidance counselors to help high-school students with vocational planning.

The civil rights and women's movements during the 1960s and 1970s emphasized the need for minority groups to be given equal consideration for available jobs. In 1990 the Americans with Disabilities Act (Pub. L. 101-336) was passed. This act gave civil rights protection to individuals with disabilities similar to those provided to individuals on the basis of race, color, sex, national origin, age, and religion. This act guaranteed equal opportunity for individuals with disabilities.

During the 1980s and 1990s many legislative changes impacted career education as it is known today. In 1990, during President George W. Bush's administration and as part of his America 2000 Goals for Education platform, the secretary of labor, Elizabeth Dole, formed a commission to look at the readiness of youth to assume roles in the workplace. This commission was called the Secretary's Commission on Achieving Necessary Skills (SCANS). In 1991 the SCANS report described a generation of undereducated students who had received little or no career guidance and who lacked the skills necessary to enter an increasingly competitive workplace. Because of this inadequate preparation, youth that were transitioning from school to work faced struggles in the labor market, unemployment, and jobs that lacked opportunity for advancement.

In response to the SCANS report and as part of a comprehensive educational reform, the School-to-Work Opportunities Act of 1994 (Pub. L. 103-239) was passed in order to prepare students for jobs in high skill and high-wage careers and to expose students to a broad array of career opportunities. This act signaled the beginning of a new role for counselors in assisting students with the transition from school into the workplace. The federal funding for School-to-Work programs was phased out in October 2001 due to federal budget cuts.

The Carl Perkins Vocational-Technical Education Amendment of 1998 (Pub. L. 105-332) was a legislative initiative designed to provide funding and programming ideas, as well as assessments of current career education programs such as tech prep that is described later in the chapter. Congress also passed the Workforce Investment Act (WIA) of 1998 (Pub. L. 105-220). This law reformed federal employment, adult education, and vocational rehabilitation programs to create a "one-stop" system of workforce investment and educational activities for adults and youth.

CAREER DEFINITIONS

Part of the problem in defining career development is that, although there is some overlap, there are two distinct philosophies. One is the workforce development and jobs search philosophy that is reinforced by computer technology and labor market information. This philosophy speaks to the economic and placement functions of preparing people to work toward keeping the nation's competitive edge in the global marketplace. The second philosophy focuses upon career and human development, emphasizing growth and development of the whole person for work and other life roles across the life span. Both philosophies are needed, but the former economic philosophy receives more emphasis (Hiebert & Bezanson, 2000).

The following definitions take on the essence of the second philosophy, using a human growth and development approach. *Career* (http://www.careernet.state.md.us) can be defined as the totality of work and life roles that an individual takes on in life through which the individual expresses him or herself. *Jobs* (http://www.careernet.state.md.us) are paid positions within a work environment that are similar in nature, whereas *occupations* are groups of similar jobs within a work environment that connote the kinds of work a person is pursuing. Occupations are definable and exist independently from the person.

Another significant term is *career development*. It has been defined as the interaction of psychological, sociological, economic, physical, and chance factors that shape the sequence of jobs, occupations, or careers that a person may engage in throughout a lifetime (Zunker, 1997). It is expressed through the job, occupations, leisure activities, and the avocations that we choose. It is how we experience ourselves in all of our roles. It is part of human development. According to Donald Super (1957b), it is lifelong and continuous. An *avocation* can be defined as a hobby or a pastime (*Encarta World English Dictionary,* 2003). It is a chosen activity, not necessarily pursued for money, that gives a person satisfaction and fulfillment.

Career counseling is a one-on-one process that focuses on what a person can do, what the person likes to do, and what the person is willing to do. Career counseling (Krumboltz, 1996, p. 61) "facilitates the learning of skills, interests, beliefs, values, work habits, and personal qualities that enable each client to create a satisfying life within a constantly changing work environment."

Sam makes an appointment to see his counselor. He is a senior in high school and knows that he needs to make a decision about his future career. Many of his friends have already applied to college, but Sam doesn't feel that he has the "grades" to go to a 4-year college. In a counseling session the professional school counselor reviews some earlier interest and abilities assessments that Sam had taken. The counselor discusses with Sam some of the activities and school subjects that Sam enjoys and has some skills in. They also discuss career options and how to make career decisions. In a follow-up session Sam decides that he is good working with people, enjoys science, and has always received good grades in that subject. The counselor suggests that Sam might want to explore the possibility of attending a nearby community college and getting an associate's degree in one of several medical programs available. The counselor schedules a visit to the community college for Sam. On a third visit Sam excitedly tells the counselor about the college visit and his decision to major in the registered nursing program.

CAREER THEORIES

Frank Parsons (1909) developed the trait/factor theory that is still being utilized today in many counseling arenas. The trait/factor theory, introduced earlier, states that a wise occupational choice consists of matching personal traits to job characteristics. According to Parsons, there are three factors that influence a vocation: (a) an understanding of self, including aptitudes, abilities, interests, ambitions, resources, and limitations; (b) knowledge of requirements and conditions for success, advantages and disadvantages, compensation, and opportunities and prospects in different lines of work; and (c) true reasoning about the relationships between a person's traits and job factors. The greater the match between personal characteristics and job requirements, the greater the probability that satisfaction will result.

The trait/factor theory was very prominent through the 1950s when other career theories began to be developed, but the trait/factor influence is still apparent today. The federal government, through the U.S. Department of Labor, Bureau of Statistics, developed the *Occupational Outlook Handbook (OOH)* (rev. 2000) and the *Dictionary of Occupational Titles (DOT)* (rev. 1991), which has now been replaced by the *Occupational Information Network (O*Net)* (2001). The U.S. Department of Defense developed the *Alpha and Beta Test,* later called the *Armed Services Vocational Aptitude Battery (ASVAB)* (rev. 1993) that utilized the trait/factor theory in both its design and interpretation. This test, originally designed during World War I to determine who could be enlisted in the armed services, is still being widely utilized throughout the country today. It is being used not only for enlistment purposes but also as a tool to help high-school students match information they learn about themselves with career possibilities.

More recent theories not only look at interests and abilities but also take into account family background, personality traits, developmental stages, values, sociological conditions, and decision-making skills. Although there are many new career theories being introduced, this chapter only discusses the career theorists that are most applicable for school counselors.

One such theorist, Anne Roe (1956), began her research during the 1950s. Her career development theory consisted of two major premises: (a) Her theory was based upon Maslow's hierarchy of needs; that is, needs at the lower end of the hierarchy need to be met in order to move up the hierarchy. (b) Occupational choice is the result of personality, which is the result of early parent-child relationships. Roe concluded that some personality differences evolve from child-rearing practices such as over-protecting, rejecting, democratic and that these differences are related to the kinds of interactions that such people ultimately establish with other people. A career genogram is a student-oriented activity described in the following exercise.

Exercise

This is an individual activity that is designed to involve the students in their family heritage as it relates to career development. Students will make their own genograms and then be able to discuss career values exhibited in their family's work history. Other life roles may also be exhibited and discussed. One limitation of this activity might occur if the student comes from a single-parent home.

Materials and Preparation

Students will need newsprint, rulers, and magic markers. Students will be asked to get family career history in advance of the actual project/discussion.

Activity

1. Students will be asked to get information about the careers that members of their family have been involved in, getting as much information as possible about parents, grandparents, aunts and uncles, and great grandparents.
2. A week later students will be asked to construct a genogram of their family, using the career information that they obtained, with the materials supplied.
3. Students will then be asked to complete a worksheet.
4. Once the students have completed their family genogram and the worksheet, they will be asked to explain some information about their family's career history.

Discussion

1. Can the students make any conclusions about their family's work history?
2. Can the students identify any stereotypes or other self-imposed limitations that may have occurred?
3. Are there cultural issues that arise out of the family's career background?
4. Are the students aware of how the family's career history impacted upon their own career development?
5. Are there specific work values that seem to have been passed down from other family members?

6. Can the students make conclusions about the implications of their family's career history as it relates to current and future career and life-planning roles?
7. Are the students able to ascertain family perceptions of role relationships, leisure, work, and other life roles?

The Genogram Worksheet

Please answer the following questions as completely as possible. You may do this on your own paper if you are writing your answers on the computer.

1. What did your parents model?
2. What did your grandparents model?
3. Were people happy in their roles?
4. What job values have been passed on?
5. List the relatives that you like most and then list a work value that person has (had).
6. List the relatives that you liked least and then list a work value that person has (had).
7. Are your work values similar/dissimilar to the liked/unliked relatives?
8. What stereotypes about careers and yourself have been transmitted to you from your relatives?

Roe developed a classification system for occupations that consisted of eight categories of occupations with six levels based upon the degree of responsibility, skills, and abilities. This became known as her *8 × 6 matrix.* Roe's contributions to career counseling are her classification system and the attention to early childhood experiences influencing career development. The *Career Aptitude Placement Survey (CAPS),* the *Career Occupational Preference Survey (COPS),* and the *Career Orientation Placement and Evaluation Survey (COPES)* (EdITS, 1996) are assessments that have been designed utilizing Roe's matrix.

Another important career theorist is John Holland (1985). Holland made the assumption that the individual is the product of heredity and environment. Holland decided that there were six kinds of occupational environments and six matching personal orientations. These six types include realistic (R), investigative (I), artistic (A), social (S), enterprising (E), or conventional (C). There are four assumptions that underlie Holland's theory: (a) In our culture most people can be categorized as R, I, A, S, E, or C. (b) There are six kinds of environments: R, I, A, S, E, or C. (c) People search for environments that will let them exercise their skills and abilities, express their attitudes and values, and take on agreeable problems and roles. (d) People's behaviors are determined by an interaction between their personality and the characteristics of their environment. Holland's hexagon model (Figure 7.1 in the following exercise) provides a visual presentation of the interrelationship of personality styles and occupational environment correlation. An activity that correlates with Holland's six personality types is called "The Party." This activity, described in the following exercise, can be done with middle-school and high-school students and readily illustrates the correlation between personality and career.

Exercise

This game is designed to match your interests and skills with several skills. This game will also help you to begin thinking about how your personality will help you to fit in with certain careers.

Imagine that you are attending a party. When you walk into the room, you notice that people with similar interests are all gathered in different corners of the room, as described in Figure 7.1.

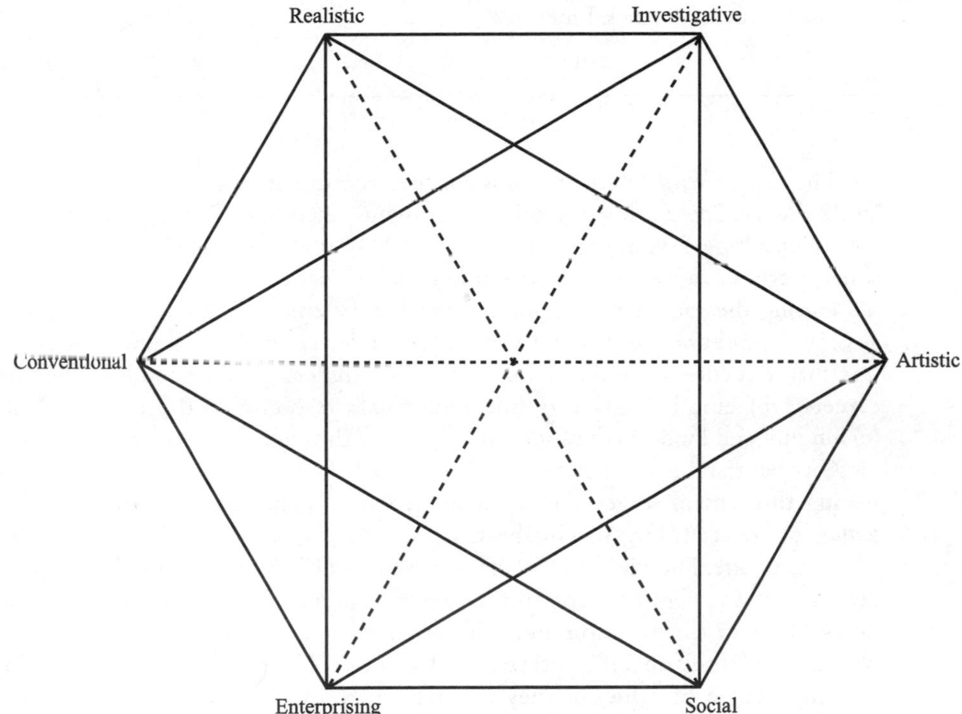

FIGURE 7.1 Holland's Model of Relationships Among Personality Types and Work Environments

1. In which corner of the room are the people you most enjoy being with for the longest period of time? Write the letter for that group on the line here: ______
2. After 15 minutes everyone in that corner leaves to attend another party. Of the groups remaining, which one would you most likely go to? Write the letter here: ______

3. After 15 minutes this group also leaves, except for you. Which group would you now choose to go to of all the groups remaining? Write the letter here: ______

4. In this last step, underline the skills that are described in the three groups that you said you liked best.

   Note. This RIASEC model of occupations is the copyrighted work of John Holland (1985) and his publisher, Psychological Assessment Resources, Inc. The hexagon shape is reproduced by special permission of the publisher, Psychological Assessment Resources, Inc., 16204 North Florida Avenue, Lutz, FL 33549, from *Making Vocational Choices,* 3rd edition, Copyright 1973, 1985, 1992, 1997 by Psychological Assessment Resources, Inc. All rights reserved. *The Party* is adapted from the World Wide Web: http://www.career.missouri.edu/ Once this page is found place the pointer on "Career Interests Game" under "Quick Links."

The *Self-Directed Search* (1994) is a career assessment that is a product of Holland's theory. There are many other assessments, such as the *Strong Interest Inventory* (Consulting Psychologists Press, Inc., 1994), that also use Holland's six personality types as a basis for determining which career choices are preferred.

During the early 1950s another career theory emerged. Eli Ginzberg and his associates Ginsburg, Axelrad, and Herma (1951) determined that there are four factors that influence vocational choice: (a) values (differing values result in differing careers), (b) emotional factors (the individual's response to the environment), (c) amount and kind of education, and (d) reality through environmental pressures.

Ginzberg and his associates (1951) pictured the vocational choice process as having three main stages: fantasy stage, tentative stage, and realistic stage. The *fantasy stage,* according to Ginzberg, occurs during the ages of birth to about 11 years of age. The child can make unrealistic choices and usually has no concept about the requirements for a specific career. During the *tentative stage* (ages 11 to 17), maturation and self-awareness occur. In this stage the person begins to identify specific interests and abilities. The person begins to realize the importance of values as they affect choices. In the final *realistic stage* (ages 17 through adulthood), choices are made and steps are taken to carry out these choices. Compromises become prevalent.

In 1984 this theory underwent several modifications. Since all three of his colleagues had died, Eli Ginzberg (1984) is given sole credit for this theory, which indicates that values orientation plays a major role in the career search. The implication of this theory is that, when a professional school counselor works with a student, that individual's values need to be explored as part of the career decision-making process. An example of Ginzberg's *career values theory* is illustrated in the activity "The Survivor," described in the following exercise.

Exercise

The Survivor is a group activity to make students more aware of their values and to allow students to share their values with others. It takes approximately 30 minutes to complete this activity.

Materials and Preparation

Students need to design a job description for one or more careers.

Activity

1. All participants are asked to stand.
2. Explain that they will be hearing a description of a job that is being offered to them. Begin reading through the job description one point at a time.
3. Students are to remain standing until they decide that they no longer want the job.
4. Students that remain standing through the entire job description are asked what they think the job is. The students who are seated are also asked why they decided to sit down.
5. Students are then told what the job is (the example is a *blackjack dealer in a Las Vegas casino*).

Discussion

1. What thought process did the students go through to make their decisions?
2. On what value did you decide to sit down?
3. How did the students feel about being given limited information with no alternatives?
4. When the students decided to sit down, how did they feel?
5. How did the students feel who chose to remain standing throughout when they found out what the career was?
6. Why are values important in the career decision-making process?

Sample Job Description

1. You will make an annual salary of $40,000+ per year.
2. You will work in plush, beautiful surroundings.
3. You will live in a warm, dry climate.
4. The job involves working with people.
5. You will have a boss.
6. You will work 6-hour shifts, 6 days a week.
7. Your work hours will be from 8 P.M. until 2 A.M.
8. You will hear many complaints.
9. Your work will involve standing most of the time.
10. Some people will think your job is immoral.

Note: Adapted from the University of Louisville Faculty Guide for Gen 101, 1996–97.

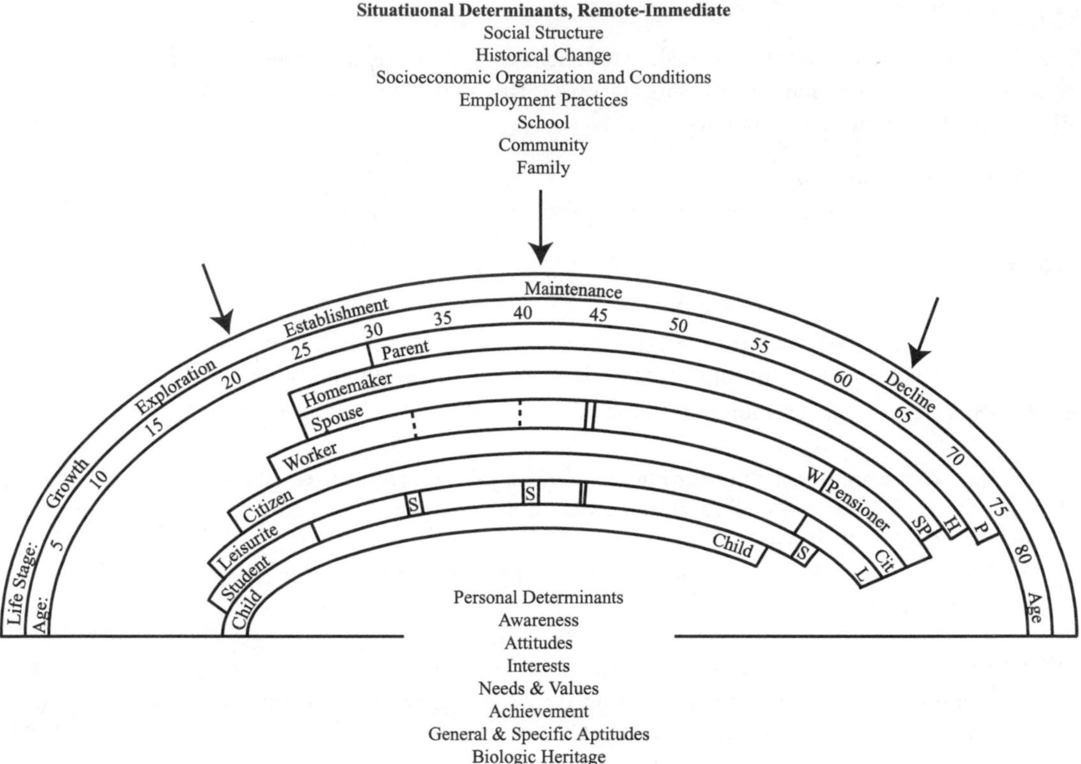

FIGURE 7.2 The Life-Career Rainbow: Nine Life Roles in Schematic Life Space

From Super, Donald E. "A Life-Span, Life-Space Approach to Career Development," Journal of Vocational Behavior 16 (1980): 282–298. Reprinted with permission.

Donald Super (1957a) was another career theorist who discussed development stages. His theory for vocational development focused on four elements: (a) People go through life stages. (b) Vocational tasks must be mastered. (c) The fundamental aspect of vocational choice is self-concept, and self-concept is translated into a vocational choice. (d) Career patterns such as occupational level attained, psychological and physiological attributes, and environmental conditions determine sequences and duration of jobs. According to Super, the five developmental stages in a life span are known as *maxi-cycles.* These stages include growth, exploration, establishment, maintenance, and disengagement. There are also *mini-cycles* within each of these stages. Super indicated that career selection is not a stable choice but is a result of cumulative past decisions. His model was called the "rainbow model" and is shown in Figure 7.2. Super developed the *Adult Career Concerns Inventory* (1988) to assist with career counseling for adults.

John Krumboltz (1979) developed the social learning approach to career development as a protest to trait/factor thinking. According to Krumboltz, the trait/factor theory totally disregarded feelings, attitudes, and values. Career counseling, in order to be effective, must be separated from the trait/factor theory. Krumboltz developed four propositions: (a) The more reinforcement received, the more likely it is that a person will go into a specific occupation. (b) Role models influence choices. (c) A valuable person points out the advantages to a specific career. (d) An individual will be successful in an occupation if that person is exposed to positive words and phrases associated with a specific career. Krumboltz developed three laws of learning to support his theory: (a) Instrumental—there are rewards and punishments. (b) Associative—people learn by association. (c) Vicarious learning—career choice is influenced by several factors that are different for all individuals. Krumboltz theorized that career beliefs appear independent of personality factors, and so he developed the *Career Beliefs Inventory* (1997) to address these concerns. Krumboltz's inventory contains statements like "I am content to maintain my present skill level" and "When I have a career problem I like to take action to solve it." The assessment examines the person's beliefs about him or herself and the world of work. The following activity assists students in addressing faulty beliefs.

Exercise

In the activity known as Faulty Beliefs, the discussion leader provides the following examples and asks the class to discuss these scenarios. The purpose of this activity is to help students understand that faulty beliefs often stand in the way of appropriate career decision making.

1. Drawing faulty generalizations: "I am the only one who doesn't understand this Math problem."
2. Making self-comparisons with a single standard: "I'm not as good as Michael Jordan."
3. Exaggerating the emotional impact of an outcome: "I'd just die if I didn't get an A."
4. Drawing false causal relationships: "The only way to get ahead is to be at the right place at the right time."
5. Being ignorant of relevant facts: "All high-school teachers make a ton of money."
6. Giving undue weight to low-probability events: "I won't go to college because I may not be able to get a job when I graduate."

As we move into the 21st century, new career theories have emerged. The *social cognitive career theory (SCCT)* (Brown & Lent, 1996; Lent, Brown, & Hackett, 1996) builds upon earlier assumptions that cognitive factors are very important to career development and career decision making. This theory is closely linked to Krumboltz's (1979) social learning theory. One approach used by Brown and Lent (1996) to facilitate interest exploration is the use of a card sort, as explained in the following exercise.

Exercise

A student is given a deck of cards that have one occupation listed on each card. The student sorts the cards into stacks that include headings from careers most likely to be chosen to careers least likely to be chosen. Once all of the cards are sorted, students then go back through the cards of those careers most likely to be chosen, identifying those careers that they might select if they had the appropriate skills (self-efficacy beliefs) and those careers they might choose if the careers offered them things they might value (outcome expectations). The careers remaining would then be examined further.

Another new theory is the *cognitive information processing (CIP)* approach (Peterson, Sampson, Reardon, & Lenz, 1996), which emphasizes the relationships among self-efficacy beliefs, outcome experiences, goals, and interests. According to Peterson and colleagues (p. 436), students must ask themselves two questions: "What am I thinking and feeling about my career choice at this moment?" and "What do I hope to attain as a result of career counseling?" Once a student recognizes that a career problem exists, he or she can work toward the resolution of the problem, possibly through more self-assessment, the use of additional resources, or acquiring more information.

A third new theory, that of Hansen (1997), is called the *integrative life-planning model (ILP)*. This model is similar to Super's life-space theory but takes a more holistic approach, drawing upon psychology, sociology, economics, multiculturalism, and constructivism. The ILP model seems most useful for teaching an approach to life planning that emphasizes connectedness and wholeness. It is one of the few models to include spirituality as part of the career development process, as well as the impact of career choice on others and on the environment.

These emerging career theories fill many gaps in previous career development theories. While more extensive research needs to be conducted by the more modern theorists, it is certainly hoped that the newest career development theories will more clearly define career development as it relates to all of our populations. These new career theories will also be invaluable to professional school counselors as they work with school-age youth in today's world.

CAREER ASSESSMENTS

Many of the career theorists developed assessments that were outgrowths of their specific career theories. The Career Occupational Preference System (EdITS, 1996), which includes the *Career Occupational Preference Survey (COPS),* an interest survey; the *Career Aptitude Placement Survey (CAPS),* an aptitude assessment; and the *Career Orientation and Placement Evaluation Survey (COPES),* a work values survey, was designed under the influence of Anne Roe's 8 × 6 matrix.

Michael is a junior in high school who makes an appointment with the counselor to discuss his future. Michael is very unsure about what to do after he graduates from high school. After some discussion the counselor suggests that Michael take some assessments to see where his interests, values, and aptitudes lie. The counselor administers the COPS System to Michael that consists of an interest, a values, and an abilities assessment. Once the assessments are completed, the counselor meets again with Michael to discuss the results of each of these individual assessments and look at the collective picture. The results indicate that Michael is very interested in science and technology, that he did very well in the related aptitudes, and that he has values appropriate to a career in the Science Professional field. The counselor then suggests that Michael should look further at some of the careers suggested in the COPS System. A discussion specifically about Michael's work values might also ensue. During another meeting with Michael the counselor might suggest that Michael could interview people in science-related careers to see if any of these careers seem interesting to him. Michael could also shadow some science professionals to see what they actually do in their positions. In another session the counselor might assist Michael with finding Web sites that could provide him with beneficial information. If Michael's interest in the science field continues, he would then probably need to be directed to colleges that offer science majors in the areas he is most interested in. In a follow-up session the counselor could also meet with Michael and his parents to answer any questions that they might also have.

Another career theorist, John Holland, developed the *Self-Directed Search* (1994), which is widely used today. The *Strong Interest Inventory* (Consulting Psychologists Press, 1994), the *Campbell Interest and Skills Inventory* (Campbell, 1996), and the interpretative guide of the *Armed Services Vocational Aptitude Battery* (U.S. Department of Defense, 1993) also use Holland's model of six personality types when assessing the individual's career interests. The *Harrington O'Shea Career Decision-Making System* (Harrington & O'Shea, rev. 2000) is another interest assessment that is appropriate for high-school-age students. Other interest assessments for elementary and middle-school-age children include *E-WOW* (*Explore the world of work,* 1991), *Job-O* (Cutler, Ferry, Kauk, & Robinett, 1994) and *The Career Game* (2000).

In addition to interest and personality assessments, there are many abilities tests that can be useful to students to determine their specific abilities as they relate to career decision making. Some examples of ability assessments include the *Armed Services Vocational Aptitude Battery* (U.S. Department of Defense, 1993), the *General Aptitude Test Battery* (U.S. Department of Labor, 1979) and the *Differential Aptitude Test* (Bennett, Seashore, & Wesman, 1982).

There are also many personality assessments available to assist in counseling an individual about career possibilities. Some of these include the *Myers-Briggs Type Indicator* (Myers & Myers, 1993), the *Kiersey Temperament Sorter II* (Kiersey, 1998), and the *Personal Style Inventory* (Taggart & Taggart-Hausladen, 1993). The National Career Development Association (Kapes & Whitfield, 2002) publishes a guide that provides comprehensive reviews of over 50 of the leading instruments and 250 annotations of additional instruments. Obviously, there are many assessments available, including such activities as "card sorts" that prove invaluable in counseling individuals. Many of these inventories are listed in the reference section of this book.

TECHNOLOGY

The onset of computer technology has brought about many computer software packages that contain a wealth of career information. Counselors, as well as their students and the general public, can access career information, take interest inventories, determine what careers best fit their individual needs, look at educational institutions that offer training for a variety of career requirements, list financial aid resources, and even learn to write a resume and have a job interview. Many of these software programs now provide a crosswalk between career information and educational institutions where an individual can go from the career segment to an educational institution's Web site and apply to that institution online.

There are several computer software systems that currently are being used in school systems throughout the country. A summary of some of these comprehensive programs is described in the following paragraphs. Further information about these computer software packages can be found in the reference section of the student workbook.

Discover (ACT, 1998) is a comprehensive career and educational computer and software package that is published by the American College Testing program. This system includes information about careers, career inventories, self, and major training institutions. This computerized system also assists the individual in planning for a career, making transitions, and finding occupations that match the individual's unique characteristics.

The *Guidance Information System (GIS)* (2002) includes information on over 1,450 occupations; more than 3,400 two- and four-year colleges, as well as other training institutions; 650 national financial aid resources; and 200 military occupations. This system can also be used to match a person's personal aptitudes and interests with job characteristics.

The *Career Information System (CIS)* (2003) begins with a survey of the individual's aptitudes, interests, and specific career preferences such as desired salary. Based upon the individual's responses, a list of occupations is formulated that can be further explored. Additional units of this software package include ways to prepare for an occupation, publications to provide further research, and listings of postsecondary programs and colleges.

The *System of Interactive Guidance and Information (SIGI Plus)* (Educational Testing Service, 1994) is based upon the idea that an individual needs to know his or her values in order to make effective career decisions. *SIGI Plus* consists of nine sections including an introduction, self-assessment, occupational search, career information, skill rating, preparing, coping, decision-making strategies, and next steps.

The *Education and Career Opportunities System (ECOS)*(Princeton Review Publishing, 2002) is another example of a career software program. This program, however, has its own Web site with access by students and parents alike. In addition to components useful to the students, this site also contains information that is intended to support the school counselor's career development efforts.

Occupational information is becoming increasingly available on the Internet, or the World Wide Web (www), the most popular branch of the Internet. Most career sites on the Internet are concerned with job postings, resumes, and individual company research. However, many online sites are providing excellent occupational information such as the *Occupational Outlook Handbook,* now published online by the U.S. Department of Labor (2000). The *Occupational Information Network (O*Net)* (2001) is also a valuable database for counselors to use with students.

Other Web sites provide information about national programs such as "Job Shadow Day." Additional Web sites offer interest inventories that can be taken online. Some of these interest inventories require a fee to take them. Individual states also provide occupational information as well as job postings that might be available within that state.

Isabella, a high-school junior, presents herself to the counselor seeking information about career possibilities. The counselor shows Isabella how to use a computer software program that is available at their school. This program assists students with occupation sorts as well as provides additional career information when the student inputs certain interest assessment results. In addition, the school counselor explains to Isabella that their school will be involved in a career shadow day in February that matches the National Groundhog Shadow Day. He suggests that Isabella sign up for this shadowing opportunity. The counselor further suggests that Isabella involve her parents in the computer technology as they are interested in her future as well. A follow-up session is scheduled to discuss Isabella's career choices after she has used the computer software program.

Another use of technology is the *interactive video distance learning (IVDL)* that allows individuals to be in separate locations and still listen to, speak to, and see the people in the other location. In terms of career education this new technology can be used for videoconferencing, career information with speakers across the country sharing their specific areas of expertise, as well as job interviews, and even college-level career classes.

MODEL SCHOOL-BASED CAREER EDUCATION PROGRAM

Career development needs to be an ongoing integral part of the entire K–12 school curriculum. According to the American School Counselor Association's (ASCA) National Standards for School Counseling Programs (1998, p. 11), "the standards for career development guide the school counseling program to implement strategies and activities to support and enable the student to develop a positive attitude toward work and to develop the necessary skills to make a successful transition from school to the world of work, and from job to job across the life span." The three career standards developed by the ASCA National Standards include: Standard A. Students will acquire the skills to investigate the world of work in relation to knowledge of self and to make informed career decisions; Standard B. Students will employ strategies to achieve future career success and satisfaction; Standard C. Students will understand the relationship between personal qualities, education and training, and the world of work.

The National Occupational Information Coordinating Committee (NOICC) (1992), although no longer operational, has identified areas of career development by career stage and grade level. A model career education program that could be used within any school setting might include the following goals, objectives, and strategies.

Grades K–5 Career Motivation and Awareness

Career motivation develops pride in accomplishments, varied interests, awareness of the dignity of work, sense of self-worth, and a positive attitude toward task completion. In order to accomplish this goal, students need to

1. Become aware of and develop positive attitudes about themselves and their relationships with others.
2. Appreciate all levels and types of work in our society.
3. Develop awareness that work is a way of life and a necessary element in the free-enterprise system.
4. Foster appropriate work habits and attitudes.
5. Develop necessary decision-making skills.

Strategies and activities that could be implemented include the following:

- Safe and structured school environment
- Strong family, community, and school partnerships
- Field trips that relate to careers
- Community speakers
- Entrepreneurial activities within the school setting
- Curriculum integration using every subject area to foster careers
- Looking at the student's own interests, skills, and talents through grade-appropriate career inventories
- Community volunteer service
- Job shadowing with parents or others
- Use of parents within the classroom
- Fostering health, fitness, teamwork, and cooperation
- Participating in such programs as Kids and the Power of Work (KAPOW)
- Looking at nontraditional careers and equity

Grades 6–8 Career Orientation and Exploration

The goal of career orientation and exploration is to emphasize the wide range of occupations available, various worker characteristics, the relevancy of school subjects to the occupational area, and self-evaluation. The objectives for this goal include the following:

1. Students will understand their importance as individuals in our technological society and be motivated to participate as productive members of society.
2. Students will evaluate their interests, aptitudes, and abilities.
3. Students will understand the relationship between formal education and occupational requirements.
4. Students will become aware of the scope and nature of the world of work.

Strategies and activities in order to accomplish these objectives might include the following:

- Career exploration through job shadowing, short internships, targeted field trips, career research, career interviews, and entrepreneurial projects
- Career portfolios
- Individual assessments and personal investigations
- Curriculum integration utilizing every subject area emphasizing work concepts and career awareness
- Individual counseling
- Use of parents within the classroom
- Community volunteer service
- Group dynamics, team building, and leadership skills
- Adaptive learning and instruction strategies to accommodate individual needs and learning styles
- Instruction in problem-solving, decision-making, goal-setting, and communication skills
- Planning a tentative sequence of courses for grades 9–12 consistent with career interests and aptitudes

Grades 9–12 Career Planning and Preparation

The goal for high-school students in the planning and preparation stage is to have actual work experiences, value and interest clarification with a heavy emphasis on decision making, and preparation for immediate employment or postsecondary education. Students at this level will

1. Develop appropriate career attitudes and employability skills.
2. Make appropriate selections of courses of study based upon their career interests and aptitudes.

3. Explore a variety of occupational options.
4. Participate in planned activities for continued career exploration and career decision making.
5. Understand the value of preparing up-to-date and accurate information for the transition from high school to postsecondary education, other training, or employment.

Strategies and activities that can be used to accomplish these objectives might include

- Internships
- Mentoring
- Apprenticeships
- Work experience
- Vocational programs
- Tech prep programs
- Community volunteer service
- Goal setting, long-term planning seminars
- Career portfolio
- Job getting, keeping, and coping skills
- Problem solving and real-world-based activities
- Use of technology
- Curriculum integration
- Assessments and inventories
- Use of parents and community members
- Establishing advisor/mentor opportunities for students
- Access to comprehensive information about labor markets and workplace trends

One of the suggested program strategies for high-school students is "tech prep," which is a federally initiated program (School-to-Work Opportunities Act of 1994) intended to expand students' academic and occupational skills. This program tends to target the "neglected majority" but does include all students by creating a learning environment that is more student-centered, participatory, and contextual through an enhanced curriculum as well as applied teaching methodologies. The intent of this program is to integrate academic and occupational curricula while expanding career awareness and providing career-planning activities. Tech prep programs also provide opportunities to blend classroom and worksite learning, as well as advanced standing opportunities into community college programs.

Another program that connects school to work is *High Schools That Work (HSTW),* developed by the Southern Regional Education Board (SREB) in 1987. HSTW is based upon the belief that most students can learn complex academic and technical concepts if schools create an environment that encourages students to make the effort to succeed. The SREB's studies indicate that when high-school students are challenged and motivated and understand how their school subjects relate to careers, 90% or more can complete a rigorous program of academic and technical study without increasing the school dropout rate.

The HSTW program has two major goals: to increase mathematics, science, communication, problem-solving and technical achievement, and the application of learning for career-bound students to the national average of all students; and to blend the essential content of traditional college preparatory studies—mathematics, science, language arts, and social studies—with quality vocational and technical studies by creating conditions that support school leaders, teachers, and counselors in carrying out the key practices. There are 10 key practices that are being utilized to accomplish these goals:

1. Setting higher expectations and getting career-bound students to meet them
2. Increasing access to challenging vocational and technical studies with a major emphasis on using high-level mathematics, science, language arts, and problem-solving skills in the context of modern workplace practices
3. Increasing access to academic studies that teach the essential concepts from the college preparatory curriculum through functional and applied strategies, enabling students to see the relationship between school and work
4. Having students complete a challenging course of study with an upgraded academic core and a major
5. Providing students with access to a structured system of work-based and high-status school-based learning collaboratively planned by educators, employers, and workers
6. Having an organizational structure and schedule enabling academic and vocational teachers to have the time to plan and provide integrated instruction aimed at reaching high-status academic and technical content
7. Having each student actively engaged in the learning process.
8. Involving each student and his or her parents in career guidance and individualized advising aimed at ensuring the completion of an accelerated program of study
9. Providing a structured system of extra help to enable career-bound students to successfully complete an accelerated program of study that includes high-level academic content and a major
10. Using student assessments and program evaluation data to continuously improve curriculum, instruction, school climate, organization, and management to advance student learning.

MULTICULTURAL ISSUES

There are several reasons why a multicultural perspective of career development is essential:

1. Current models of career counseling do not take into account the impact of social and economic barriers. Economic hardships, racial discrimination, and culturally related career behaviors are not commonly addressed in career theories. Such barriers, however, have severely affected both the actual and perceived career choices of "people of color" (Brown, Brooks, & Associates, 1990).

2. Existing career theories are actually limited in their basic philosophical principles, as these relate to culturally different groups. Most theories of career development are based upon a Eurocentric culture that may well be very different from the perspectives of those from non-Eurocentric cultures of the world. For example, in some cultures such as African American, Asian, and Hispanic, the family is as important or even more important in deciding whether to enter a specific occupation than is the desire and experience of the jobseeker (Leong & Leung, 1994).
3. Many career assessment instruments that have been commonly used in career counseling were both developed and normed for the white majority population. Such norming may well make these instruments inapplicable to representatives of diverse cultures.

Mei Ling is an academically gifted eighth grader who is Chinese American. She comes to the school counselor to discuss the classes that she will register for her ninth grade. She is very concerned that her parents will not allow her to enroll in the advanced science and math courses available to ninth graders in this school system. She indicates that in the Chinese culture parents select the career field for their children, and they may not even want her to go to college at all. Mei Ling fears that her parents will not permit her to eventually pursue a degree in engineering. The counselor first suggests that they take a look at Mei Ling's skills and interests, using some of the career assessments that are available. Then the counselor suggests that Mei Ling and she should meet with Mei Ling's parents in order to provide them with this same information. If the parents still do not feel that Mei Ling should enroll in the advanced classes, the counselor might then discuss possible compromises as well as some alternate careers that might meet with her parents' approval as well as Mei Ling's. The counselor does need to be aware that in the Chinese culture the parents oftentimes make the decision as to what career path their child will follow.

School counselors are the most likely school-based personnel to deal effectively with increasing the career options for people of color and other ethnic backgrounds, for disabled persons, and for women. If, as the research suggests, one of the major concerns for career development for culturally diverse people is limited career aspirations, the professional school counselor can certainly have an impact. The traditional three Cs of school counseling—that of counselor, coordinator, and consultant—become crucial tools for changing the career options for people who are not members of the dominant culture:

1. *Counselor* for both individuals and groups to aid the student in working through the process of education and making the transition to work
2. *Coordinator* of programs to create effective links between "minority" students and the world of work
3. *Consultant* with teachers, administrators, parents, and students to create the best opportunities for students to access information they most need to develop appropriate career skills

SUMMARY

In order for our future career holders to lead happy and productive lives, school counselors at all grade levels need to recognize that our youth need career guidance, including establishing a work ethic by being on time for school, turning in homework assignments, and having good attendance. Our students need to be given the opportunity to take a variety of assessments at several age levels in order to have the "best fit" for their future career choices. Since research indicates that people now change careers at least five times during their lifetime, it is essential that school counselors recognize this fact and prepare our youth for making appropriate career decisions by providing them with a wide variety of career information.

REFERENCES

ACT (1998). *Discover* (computer software). Iowa City, IA: Author.

American School Counselor Association. (1998). *Vision into action: Implementing the National Standards for school counseling programs*. Alexandria, VA: American School Counselor Association.

Americans with Disabilities Act of 1990, Pub. L. No. 101-336.

Bennett, G. K., Seashore, H. G., & Wesman, A. G. (1982). *Administrator's handbook for Differential Aptitude Test, forms V and W*. San Antonio, TX: The Psychological Corporation, Harcourt Brace Jovanovich.

Brown, D., Brooks, L., & Associates. (1990). *Career choice and development* (2nd ed.). San Francisco, CA: Jossey-Bass.

Brown, S. D., & Lent, R. W. (1996). A social cognitive framework for career choice counseling. *Career Development Quarterly, 44,* 211–223.

Campbell, D. (1996). *Campbell Interest and Skills Inventory*. Minneapolis, MN:Pearson Assessments.

The Career Game. (2000). New Hope, PA: Rick Trow Productions.

Career Information System (CIS). (2003). University of Oregon, OR: into CAREERS.

Career planning concepts and definitions. (2001). Retrieved on September 9, 2003, from Maryland's Career Net on the World Wide Web: http://www.careernet.state.md.us

Carl Perkins Vocational-Technical Education Amendment of 1998, Pub. L. No. 105-332.

Consulting Psychologists Press, Inc. (1994). *Strong interest survey*. Palo Alto, CA: Author.

Cutler, A., Ferry, F., Kauk, R., & Robinett, R. (1994). *Job-O*. Auburn, CA: CFKR Career Materials.

Educational and Industrial Testing Service. (1996). *COPS system*. San Diego, CA: EdITS.

Educational Testing Service. (1994). *SIGI Plus*. Princeton, NJ: Author.

Encarta World English Dictionary. (2003). Microsoft Corporation, Bloomsbury Publishing Plc.

Explore the world of work (E-Wow). (1991). Auburn, CA: CFKR Career Materials.

Ginzberg, E. (1984). Career Development. In D. Brown & L. Brooks (Eds.), *Career choice and development* (pp. 169–191). San Francisco: Jossey-Bass.

Ginzberg, E., Ginsburg, S. W., Axelrad, S., & Herma, J. L. (1951). *Occupational choice: An approach to general theory*. New York: Columbia University Press.

Guidance Information System (GIS). (2002). El Cajon, CA: Grossmont College.

Hansen, I. S. (1997) *Integrative life planning: Critical tasks for career development and changing life patterns*. San Francisco: Jossey-Bass.

Harrington, T., & O'Shea, A. (2000). *Harrington O'Shea Career Decision-Making System*. Circle Pines, MN: American Guidance Service.

Hiebert, B., & Bezanson, L. (Eds.). (2000). *Making waves: Career development and public policy*. Ottawa, ON: Canadian Career Development Foundation.

Holland, J. L. (1985). *Making vocational choices: A theory of vocational personalities and work environments* (2nd ed.). Englewood Cliffs, NJ: Prentice-Hall.

Holland, J. L. (1994). *Self-directed search*. Odessa FL: Psychological Assessment Resources.

Kapes, J. T., & Whitfield, E. S., (Eds.). (2002). *A counselor's guide to career assessment instruments*, 4th ed. Tulsa, OK: National Career Development Association.

Kiersey, D. (1998). *Kiersey temperament sorter II*. Del Mar, CA: Prometheus Nemesis Book Company.

Krumboltz, J. D. (1979). A social learning theory of career decision making. In A. M. Mitchell, G. B. Jones, & J. D. Krumboltz (Eds.), *Social learning and career decision making* (pp. 19–49). Cranston, RI: Carroll Press.

Krumboltz, J. D. (1996). A learning theory of counseling. In M. L. Savickas & W. B. Walsh (Eds.), *Handbook for career counseling theory and practice* (pp. 55–80). Palo Alto, CA: Davies-Black.

Krumboltz, J. D. (1997). *Career beliefs inventory*. Palo Alto, CA: Consulting Psychologists Press, Inc.

Lent, R. W., Brown, S. D., & Hackett, G. (1996). Career development from a social cognitive perspective. In D. Brown, L. Brooks (Eds.), *Career choice and development* (3rd ed.) (pp. 373–416) San Francisco, CA: Jossey-Bass.

Leong, F. T. L., & Leung, S. A. (1994). Career assessments with Asian Americans. *Journal of Career Assessment, 2*, 240–257.

Mitchell, J. M., Jones, G. B., & Krumboltz, J. D. (1979). *Social learning and career decision making*. Cranston, RI: Carroll Press.

Myers, I. B., & Myers, K. D. (1993). *Report form for the Myers-Briggs type indicator*. Palo Alto, CA: Consulting Psychologists Press.

National Child Labor Committee. (1991). *Kids and the power of work (KAPOW)*. New York: Author.

National Occupational Information Coordinating Committee. (1992). *National career development guidelines: Local handbook for high schools*. Washington, DC: Author.

Parsons, F. (1909). *Choosing a vocation*. New York: Agatha Press.

Peterson, G. W., Sampson, J. P., Reardon, R. C., & Lenz, J. G. (1996). A cognitive information processing approach. In D. Brown, L. Brooks, & Assoc. (Eds.), *Career choice and development* (3rd ed., pp. 423–476). San Francisco, CA: Jossey-Bass.

Princeton Review Publishing. (2002). *Education and Career Opportunities System* (computer software). Princeton, NJ: Author.

Roe, A. (1959). *The psychology of occupations.* New York: Wiley.

School-to-Work Opportunities Act of 1994, Pub. L. No. 103-239.

Secretary's Commission on Achieving Necessary Skills. (1991, June). U.S. Department of Labor. *What work requires of schools: A SCANS report for America 2000.* Washington, DC: U.S. Government Printing Office.

Smith-Hughes Act of 1917, Pub. L. No. 64-347.

Southern Regional Education Board. (1987). *High schools that work.* Atlanta, GA: Author.

Super, D. E. (1957a). *The psychology of careers.* New York: Harper & Row.

Super, D. E. (1957b). Vocational adjustment: Implementing a self-concept. *Occupations, 30,* 88–92.

Super, D. E. (1988). *Adult Career Concerns Inventory.* Palo Alto, CA. Consulting Psychological Press.

Super, D. E. (1990). A life-span, life-space approach to career development. In D. Brown & L. Brooks (Eds.), *Career choice and development* (2nd ed., pp. 197–261). San Francisco: Jossey-Bass.

Taggart, W., & Taggart-Hausladen, B. (1993). *Personal Style Inventory.* Odessa, FL: Psychological Assessment Resources, Inc.

U.S. Department of Defense. (1993). *Armed Services Vocational Aptitude Battery.* Washington, DC: U.S. Government Printing Office.

U.S. Department of Labor. (1979). *General Aptitude Test Battery.* Washington, DC: U.S. Government Printing Office.

U.S. Department of Labor. (1991). *Dictionary of occupational titles* (4th ed. revised). Washington, DC: U.S. Government Printing Office.

U.S. Department of Labor. (2000). *Occupational outlook handbook.* Washington, DC: U.S. Government Printing Office.

U.S. Department of Labor. (2001). *Occupational information network (O*Net).* Available from http://www.doleta.gov/program/onet

www://online.onetcenter.org

Workforce Investment Act of 1998, Pub. L. No. 105-220

Zunker, V. G. (1997). *Career counseling: Applied concepts of life planning.* Pacific Grove, CA: Brooks/Cole.

PART III

Knowledge and Skill Requirements for School Counselors

SECTION I: PROGRAM DEVELOPMENT, IMPLEMENTATION, AND EVALUATION

In this age of testing to document achievement, school counselors are significant professionals with knowledge of tests and assessment procedures. This information assists in providing essential information to students, teachers, and families. Furthermore, as technology becomes a part of our daily lives, the Internet has also influenced the profession of school counseling. Effective school counselors have the skills to effectively utilize the Internet to benefit the many stakeholders with whom they work.

The chapters in this section include: The Professional School Counselor's Role in Testing and Assessment and The Internet's Influence on the School Counseling Profession.

SECTION II: COUNSELING AND GUIDANCE

As our society witnesses increased levels of violence, schools are not immune from acts of aggression. School counselors teach preventive and intervention strategies to reduce the risk of violent behaviors, and are among the first to respond and to assist students in crisis. Furthermore, students benefit when school counselors collaborate with families to teach parents and/or guardians new ways of responding when children and adolescents have difficulties. In addition to creating partnerships to influence student growth, school counselors use a variety of creative, developmentally appropriate approaches to assist youth through individual and group counseling interventions.

The chapters in this section include: Crisis Counseling and Critical Incident Management, The School Counselor and Family Partnership, Planning and Implementing Group Work in the Schools, and Expressive Arts in Counseling Children and Adolescents.

8

The Professional School Counselor's Role in Testing and Assessment

Mrs. Lisa Brown is a school counselor in an urban, midwestern senior high school. She loves working with the students and was devastated when a state law was passed requiring all students to pass a competency exam before graduating from high school. She was even more frustrated when she was told that she would be the testing coordinator for the district, a task she did not want since it would take her away from the time she would be able to spend with students. School counselors are often designated as the test coordinators in schools because of their knowledge of tests and measurements. Mrs. Brown tearfully explained how much she disliked this task when administering the competency exam to a senior who had difficulty taking tests. This football linebacker received passing grades in all of his classes and met all of his graduation requirements, but he just was not able to pass this exam despite numerous attempts in the past. Lisa recalled an upsetting situation in which the senior was visibly shaking and sobbing while attempting to pass this exam because he knew that his future depended upon this last-time effort.

What is the school counselor's role in testing and assessment, and how can this professional work with teachers and students to assist in the assessment process?

Key pieces of legislation brought about a resurgence of tests for school accountability. The Goals 2000: Educate America Act (Pub. L. 103-227), signed into law on March 31, 1994, required higher student achievement and established a framework to measure student progress. The No Child Left Behind (NCLB) Act of 2001, signed into law January 8, 2002, mandated states to develop assessment standards based on the goal that all children will be proficient in math and reading by the year 2014 (Education Trust, n.d.; Legislative Handbook, n.d.).

Testing and assessment are significant aspects of the professional school counselor's role at all grade levels (Neukrug, 1999; Whiston, 2000). In fact, with the exception of the school psychologist, who is often assigned to many school buildings in the district, school counselors are often the only individuals in the school with a background in testing; in many cases administrators and teachers may have never even taken a testing course (Neukrug).

The terms *testing, assessment, evaluation,* and *appraisal* create confusion. *Assessment* is a broad term that describes a method by which information is gathered to identify people, programs, or objects and often includes the use of tests (Anastasi, 1992; Hood & Johnson, 1997; Whiston, 2000). The term *evaluation* refers to the process in which various measurements are compared (Vacc & Loesch, 1994). *Appraisal* is a term synonymous with evaluation (Vacc & Loesch). A *test* is a task people are asked to perform to their greatest ability (Hood & Johnson) to measure a sample of behavior (Anastasi & Urbina, 1997). For the purposes of this chapter, the terms *testing, assessment, evaluation,* and *appraisal* are used interchangeably.

The Association for Assessment in Counseling (AAC), a division of the American Counseling Association, provides test-related information such as the effective use of tests, ethical use of instruments, and test qualities. Originally named the Association for Measurement and Evaluation in Guidance, the AAC publishes the journal *Measurement and Evaluation in Counseling and Development* (Gladding, 2000). Organizations such as AAC are helpful resources for school counselors because tests in schools today are more popular than ever and school counselors are asked to coordinate, administer, and interpret test results with greater frequency (Schmidt, 1993).

WHY USE TESTS?

Although a test score is simply a reflection of performance at a given moment in time, tests are valuable in that the information received may not be provided using any other type of assessment (Gladding, 2000). Yet, caution is urged in using a single test score for making decisions that influence individuals (Anastasi, 1992).

The American School Counselor Association (ASCA) position statement on testing "recognizes the use of standardized testing as one in a range of measures used to assess student performance and learning" (ASCA, 2002) and opposes the use of a "high-stakes" test, or a single measure in educational decision making that influences students. Multiple assessment results assist in goal setting, placement, diagnosis, and program evaluation.

Goal Setting

Many students have never received any instruction on goal setting and have no idea how to begin this procedure (House, Martin, & Ward, 2002). Professional school counselors assist students in determining goals for problem solving, facilitating personal growth, and identifying areas of improvement. Using the results of multiple measures may assist in identifying goals.

Placement

Educators continually debate the merits of *homogeneous* grouping (placing students in groups with similar characteristics) versus *heterogeneous* grouping (categorizing students with dissimilar characteristics). Students' achievement or aptitude test results are often used for group assignments that label students. Unfortunately, some students are rarely reevaluated, leaving little opportunity for reassignment (Baker, 2000). Although gender, ethnicity, language, and culture are often factors that interfere with the test results, these characteristics are not always considered in making placement decisions, and unsound placements may result.

Diagnosis/Diagnostic and Statistical Manual of Mental Disorders

Diagnosis is one essential element of the decision-making process that determines thoughts, feelings, and behaviors that may negatively hinder growth. Counselors recognize that many assessments, "such as intelligence tests, personality assessments, substance abuse assessments, eating disorder inventories, and depression assessments . . . are useful to the counseling profession" (Giordano, Schwiebert, & Brotherton, 1997, p. 203). Although school counselors successfully use diagnostic instruments, there is a need for additional training to be competently trained in administering and interpreting many specialized instruments (Giordano et al.).

In 1840 only one disorder, "idiocy/insanity," was known; and in the 1880 census data, seven recognized forms of mental illness were identified. In 1952, the American Psychiatric Association (APA) published the first edition of the *Diagnostic and Statistical Manual: Mental Disorders (DSM)* for clinical use. The *DSM-II* was published shortly afterward, followed by the *DSM-III* in 1980 (Sterba & Dowd, 1998). The *DSM-III-R,* which contained revisions of the previous publications, was released in 1987; and the *DSM-IV* was published in 1994 (House, 2002) with new data regarding mental illnesses. The newest revision is the *DSM-IV-TR*. The *DSM* codes are in agreement with the *International Classification of Diseases, Ninth Edition, Clinical Modification (ICD-9-CM),* used throughout the world to aid in making congruent medical diagnoses.

The main purpose of the *DSM* is to assist as a guide for mental health professionals as they diagnose individuals, to facilitate communication between other professionals, and to document individual planning (House, 2002). Through a greater understanding of the criteria that compose a diagnosis, school counselors can more effectively communicate with other mental health professionals and work in a partnership for the benefit of youth.

The *DSM-IV-TR* contains a multiaxial assessment system that includes the following:

Axis I	Clinical Disorders and Other Conditions
Axis II	Personality Disorders and Mental Retardation
Axis III	General Medical Conditions
Axis IV	Psychosocial and Environmental Problems
Axis V	Global Assessment of Functioning

Axis I is classified as "Clinical Disorders" or "Other Conditions That May Be a Focus of Clinical Attention." Most Axis I disorders are generally assumed to be the problem that brought the client to the mental health professional (House, 2002; Sterba & Dowd, 1998).

Axis II is classified as Personality Disorders and Mental Retardation. The information on these first two axes provides the mental health diagnosis, with the remaining three axes used to provide information for a better understanding of the individual.

Axis III describes general medical conditions and current physical conditions that may provide a better understanding of the individual's mental disorder. For instance, an individual may have high blood pressure, which in turn may contribute to mental health conditions. These disorders are often difficulties that emerge in early childhood and adversely influence many areas of an individual's life (House, 2002).

Axis IV provides for psychosocial and environmental problems that may be occurring at the time of diagnosis such as the death of a family member, moving to a new state, divorce, or the birth of a new family member.

Finally, Axis V provides a professional judgment of the individual's overall level of functioning on a scale known as the Global Assessment of Functioning (GAF) scale. The mental health professional can take into account a wide spectrum of issues influencing an individual's life using this scale.

A mental disorder is associated with a group of related characteristics. These include a *sign* (a measurable characteristic about the person such as an increased heart rate) or a *symptom* (a subjective report from the individual being diagnosed). A sign and symptom together form a *syndrome,* which is thought of as the defining characteristics of a mental disorder (House, 2002). The *DSM-IV-TR* is organized by groups of signs and symptoms that are generally associated with specific diseases.

Diagnosing children and adolescent is difficult for several reasons. For one, children are generally referred by adults and rarely seek counseling on their own. In addition, what children most worry about it not necessarily what these referring adults are most concerned about. Moreover, youth seem to be more influenced by circumstances beyond their control than adults.

Program Evaluation

Counselors are accountable for the quality of their services and face increasing demands to show effectiveness. School counseling programs prove results through collecting, analyzing, and communicating data upon which program decisions are based (Steenbarger & Smith, 1996).

Although tests are valuable tools and provide useful information, counselors must also consider some of the limitations in selecting, administering, and interpreting appraisal instruments. These limitations include practicality, cultural bias, and counselor misuse.

Practicality With budgetary concerns, school districts need to be frugal in their choice of testing instruments. Although a test may provide good results, the cost of the instrument, the administration time, the length of the test, and interpretation could make a difference in selecting one test over another. For instance, for many years school counselors administered the *General Aptitude Test Battery (GATB)* to help students with career decisions. The performance portion of the test, in which only 10 students can be tested at one time, assesses such skills as finger and manual dexterity and eye-hand coordination, skills useful in many occupations. In addition, the paper-and-pencil part of the test measures mathematics, verbal, and spatial aptitude. This battery, although useful in providing a wide variety of career options, was time-ineffective, required costly equipment, and consumed a large portion of the school counselor's time that may have been more beneficially used in performing other career aptitude assessment activities.

Cultural Bias Testing is a dehumanizing experience for many. Minority students may spend years in ineffective or inappropriate programs as a result of inaccurate test scores, or due to the results of a single test score. Since test bias is nearly impossible to eliminate, multiple data provide a more complete picture for decision making regarding students (Gladding, 2000; Guindon, 2003).

Counselor Misuse Unless knowledgeable counselors are trained to interpret test results, the scores are of little value (Gladding, 2000). Shertzer and Stone (1980, as cited in Gladding, 2000) contend that without consideration of other sources of information, it is possible that the counselor could be influenced by a student's test score and make uninformed, inappropriate decisions. In addition, without an explanation of test limitations, the student may believe that the test results are a true reflection of his or her ability without examining other sources of information.

TYPES OF TESTS

Student assessments may be classified into two distinct categories—*standardized* or *nonstandardized*. Standardized tests must meet uniform procedures of design, administration, scoring, and interpretation (Anastasi & Urbina, 1997; Whiston, 2000). Nonstandardized tests are usually more flexible and often provide greater insight into an individual's personality, behavior, and cognition—not always available from the standardized assessments (Drum, 1992). As stated by Goldman (1992), "I . . believe there is a whole world of assessment methods other than standardized tests and . . . many of them have more to offer in the work of counselors." Too often, these instruments are criticized due to the lack of empirical data surrounding the test attributes (Gladding, 2000).

Many of the standardized instruments do not always answer the questions asked by parents, teachers, and counselors. For this reason, school counselors need to be aware of assessments that are better suited to the student's learning style, cultural background, and emotional and cognitive maturity (Vernon, 1993). Various types of inventories used by school counselors for gaining additional information about students are discussed in the following sections.

Intelligence Tests

Intelligence is defined differently by numerous individuals (Anastasi, 1982, as cited in Gladding, 2000). Two widely respected, individually administered intelligence tests are the *Stanford-Binet Intelligence Scale,* 4th ed., published by Riverside Publishing Company, and the *Bender-Gestalt,* also published by Riverside (Anastasi & Urbina, 1997; Whiston, 2000).

Although the words *intelligence* and *aptitude* are used interchangeably, they are not the same. Intelligence measures one specific type of aptitude, commonly known as scholastic aptitude, but other types of aptitudes exist.

Aptitude Tests

An *aptitude* is a capability for a particular task or type of skill that predicts future performance or learning ability (Whiston, 2000). Aptitude tests, sometimes known as ability tests, measure a single skill such as spatial ability or eye/hand coordination. Multiaptitude batteries consisting of several aptitude subscales (Guindon, 2003) are also given. The *Differential Aptitude Test,* one example of an ability test published by the Psychological Corporation, measures eight aptitudes for vocational guidance (Whiston, 2000). Traditionally, aptitude and achievement tests have been treated differently; however, distinct differences between these tests cannot be rigidly applied (Anastasi & Urbina, 1997). Test items may appear identical, but the major differences are test purpose and how the results will be used.

Achievement Tests

An achievement test measures an individual's knowledge of a subject or task (Aiken, 1997, as cited in Gladding, 2000) and provides students with information on their performance compared with a group of similar individuals. Achievement tests are among the best appraisal instruments for obtaining individual performance scores and aggregate school achievement scores (Guindon, 2003). The *Iowa Tests of Basic Skills,* an achievement test published by Riverside, is a battery of tests designed to assess student progress in basic skills (Domino, 2000).

Interest Tests

An interest inventory is a test or checklist that assesses a person's preference for activities and topics and is one of the most commonly used interventions in career counseling (Savickas, 1998, as cited in Gladding, 2000). Counselors report frequent use of *The Career Occupational Preference Survey (COPS)* (Giordano et al., 1997) and the *Strong-Campbell Interest Inventory,* available through the Consulting Psychologists Press.

Career Inventories

Middle-school and high-school counselors use career inventories for career exploration and decision making (Giordano et al., 1997; Guindon, 2003). A common career instrument used in the middle and high school is the *Self-Directed Search (SDS)* developed by John Holland (Hood & Johnson, 1997). This instrument is often used in conjunction with computer career-based systems such as the *DISCOVER* program developed by the American College Testing Program, or *SIGI-Plus* available through the Educational Testing Services (Whiston, 2000).

Personality Assessments

Personality inventories measure personal characteristics, emotional and social traits, behaviors, attitudes, emotions, and opinions (Anastasi & Urbina, 1997). These assessments are either structured or unstructured (Hood & Johnson, 1997). Although the many-sided nature of personality makes assessment difficult, there are many structured instruments including self-report inventories that are easily administered and interpreted. For example, the *Myers-Briggs Type Indicator* published by Consulting Psychologists Press is an example of a personality test based on Jungian theory that is easy to interpret and understand (Domino, 2000; Whiston, 2000).

Unstructured assessments such as projective tests including the *Rorschach,* the *Thematic Apperception Test (TAT),* and the *House-Tree-Person (H-T-P) Test* (Gladding, 2000) are not generally used by professional school counselors (Guindon, 2003) due to the intense in-depth training that is necessary for administration and interpretation. These projective assessments require complex scoring procedures and are more difficult for the client to falsify, but they are informative in that personality aspects may be revealed that are not apparent in other types of personality tests. A referral to a professional trained in this type of assessment may be in the best interest of the student being assessed; or the school counselor may wish to receive specialized training in administering and interpreting these assessments due to the valuable information obtained.

Diagnostic Assessments

Many counselors, including noted counselors such as Dr. Carl Rogers, do not consider diagnostic skills to be congruent with an effective counseling relationship. However, Dr. Rogers did acknowledge that if the student wishes to take a test, or the institution requires the test, diagnostic tests are acceptable for the enhancement of decision making (Bozarth, 1992).

Many inventories are available that can be used without specialized training. School counselors find these instruments useful in assessing student mental and emotional health. For instance, because suicide risk, substance abuse, and eating disorders are common concerns among youth, assessment instruments assist counselors in finding the best ways to intervene. The *Beck Hopelessness Scale* measures the presence and intensity of depression (Domino, 2000), and the *Suicide Ideation Questionnaire* is an instrument that provides information about suicidal behaviors (Whiston, 2000). The *Adolescent Substance Abuse Subtle Screening Inventory (SASSI-2),* available through Psychological Assessment Resources, identifies the probability of substance use disorder (Whiston, 2000). The *Eating Disorder Inventory-2* by Western Psychological Services is designed for male and female adolescents and is easily administered in about 20 minutes (Domino).

In addition, measures of self-concept and self-esteem can be indicators of emotional well-being. The *Tennessee Self-Concept Scale,* published by Western Psychological Services, written at a sixth-grade reading level, assesses self-image (Domino, 2000). The *Piers-Harris Self-Concept Scale* is an inventory in which the child responds to questions that best represent him or herself; the inventory helps identify aspects of self most troublesome to the individual being tested (Domino).

Interviews

Interviews are a powerful information-gathering technique. *Unstructured interviews* are more individualized and can be a useful "rapport builder" with resistant students (Clark, 1995); but because of the random selection of asking questions, valuable information could be overlooked (Vacc & Juhnke, 1997). An interview composed of incomplete sentences is one type of unstructured format:

I like . . .

Sometimes I feel . . .

My friends are . . .

My family is . . .

One thing I would most like to accomplish is . . .

School is . . .

Another unstructured interview format is to have students identify adjectives or phrases that they feel best describe them, such as in the following exercise.

Exercise

Circle the words or phrases that best describe you.

Happy	Sad	Disappointed	Likes to be alone	Neat
Neat	Lonely	Studies hard	Excited	Follower
Friendly	Smart	Pays attention	Generous	Poor student

Athletic	Frustrated	Irritable	Stupid	Bored easily
Leader	Shy	Silly	Likes to play	Irritable
Popular	Angry	Serious	Sloppy	Organized

Structured interviews tend to be more thorough in that information is obtained in a designated order, which prevents the omission of certain questions. An example of a structured interview form is provided in Box 8.1.

Performance Assessments

Performance or work samples are assessments of learning that involve observation and professional evaluations about the student's performance without the use of a pencil-and-paper test (Whiston, 2000). The counselor evaluates a student's skill such as presenting an oral report, performing in a career interview, or demonstrating conflict-mediation skills. Or, a counselor may ask a younger individual to perform a behavior such as clapping, standing on one foot, or drawing a picture to evaluate performance with a comparable group.

Since a performance evaluation is more difficult than evaluating a paper-and-pencil test, a rating form designed in advance, based on skills that can be directly observed, with procedures that have been field tested (Whiston, 2000), provides a consistent format. Counselors can assist teachers with performance test construction and scoring so that evaluation is not a haphazard exercise but, rather, one in which predetermined criteria are known in advance (Popham, 1995). For instance, if a test taker is requested to classify shapes in a designated period of time, the rating scale may include items such as attention to task, number of corrections, and comments made by the test taker during the process.

Portfolios

A portfolio is another alternate assessment that is more individualized and provides a more accurate picture of the individual. The purpose is to make the educational process as meaningful and authentic as possible (Anastasi & Urbina, 1997). Although many disagree as to the definition of a portfolio, there is agreement that this type of assessment is a purposeful, cumulative compilation of student work that shows growth, accomplishments, and acquired knowledge. A portfolio generally contains predetermined items such as transcripts, written scholarly reports, personal/career goals, test results, and letters of recommendation.

Observations

Student appraisal does not necessarily need to be based on an assessment instrument. The counselor is in an ideal position to observe the student's behavior and verbal style, note inconsistencies between the two, and monitor patterns. Teachers or coaches are valuable individuals who constantly observe students and are able to provide additional information. The observation form in Box 8.2 can be adapted to reflect the purposes of an activity.

BOX 8.1 Structured Interview Form

Identification

Name____________________ Age __________ Grade ________

Address ________________ Phone Number ____________________ (home) ____________________ (office)

Father or Guardian ________________ Occupation ________________

Mother or Guardian ________________ Occupation ________________

Person to Contact in Emergency ________________ Number ________________

Family Member ____________ Relationship _____ Age _____

Family Member ____________ Relationship _____ Age _____

Family Member ____________ Relationship _____ Age _____

Family Member ____________ Relationship _____ Age _____

Family Member ____________ Relationship _____ Age _____

Others Living With Family ____

A. FAMILY STRUCTURE

________ Divorced _______ Married

________ Separated _______ Other ____________________________________

(Description of Family)

B. HEALTH

1. Height ______ 2. Weight _______

3. Serious Illnesses ____

____

Number of Days Absent From School __________________ Days Tardy __________

Medications ____

Sleep Patterns ___________________________________ Eating Habits __________________________________

Physical Appearance ____

C. ACADEMICS

1. Grades in Classes English _____ Science _____ Mathematics _____

P.E. _____ Social Studies _____

2. Subjects Liked the Most____

____

3. Subjects Liked Least ____

____

4. Favorite Teacher ____

BOX 8.1 Continued

D. RELATIONSHIPS

Best Friends ______________________ Relationship ______________________

______________________ ______________________

______________________ ______________________

E. ACTIVITIES

Favorite Activities ____

____

Clubs or Extracurricular Activities ____

____

F. PRESENTING CONCERN

Academic ____

Career ____

Personal/Social ____

G. GOALS

Goals That You Would Like to Have Happen This Year

Academic

Career

Personal/Social

BOX 8.2 Observation Form

NAME ________________________________ DATE OF BIRTH ______________________

DATE OF OBSERVATION ____

PRESENTING CONCERN ____

BACKGROUND HISTORY

BEHAVIORAL OBSERVATIONS

Relationship with Examiner

Verbalizations

Motor Skills

AFFECTIVE OBSERVATIONS

Emotions Observed

Affect Matches Behavior/Thinking

Relationship with Others

COGNITIVE OBSERVATIONS

Appropriate Problem-Solving Skills for Age

Displays Critical-Thinking Skills

Problem-Solving Strategies Used

PATTERNS OBSERVED

Organization

Creativity

Developmental Appropriateness

Themes

Personality Characteristics

Other Observations

RECOMMENDATIONS

Note. Source unknown.

Another observational technique that combines many of the preceding assessment techniques is mask making. Students can be asked to create an image of their face using plaster of Paris. (See Figure 8.1 for instructions.) When the medium is dry the students can create an image of (a) how they see themselves, (b) how they wish to be seen, or (c) how they would like to be seen at a designated time in the future. (The photo in Figure 8.2 is of a completed mask.) This activity can lead to self-understanding, can provide information to the counselor, and can serve as a rapport-building strategy.

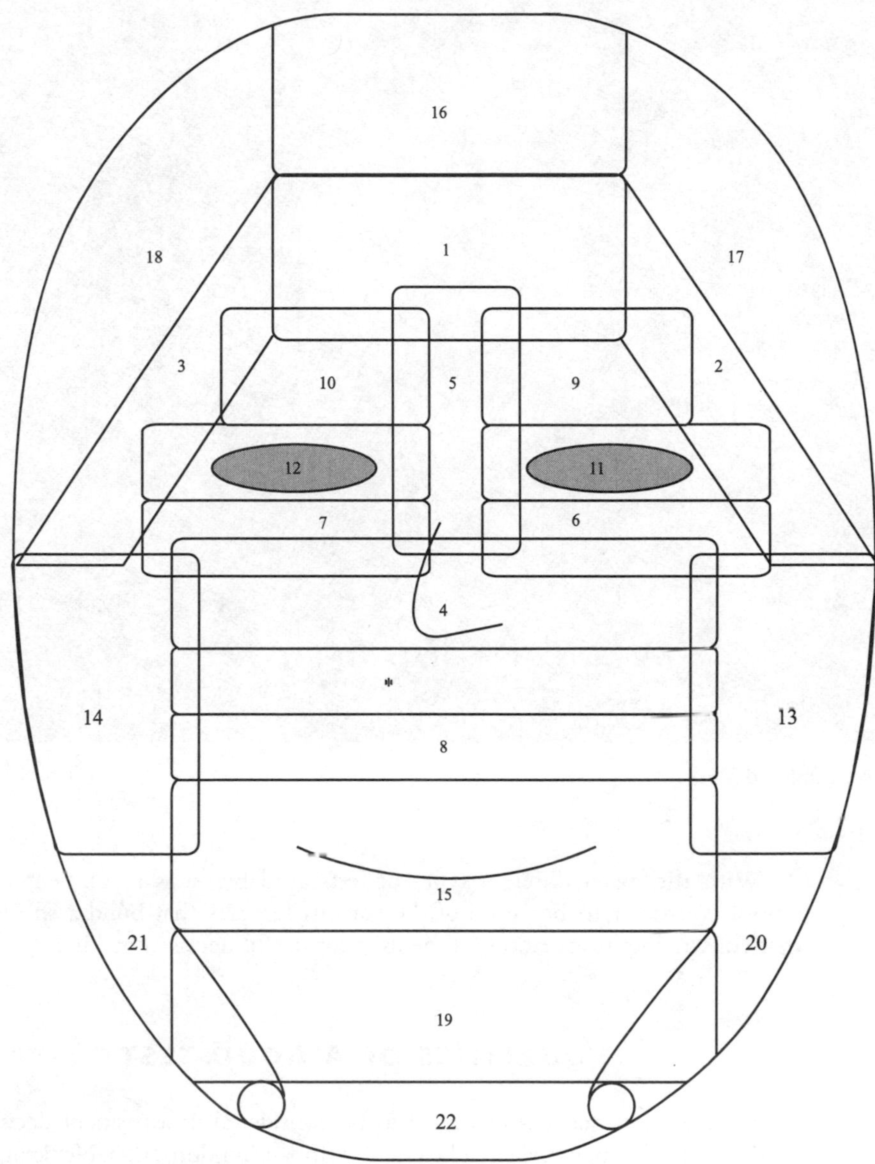

FIGURE 8.1 Constructing a Mask
Directions:
Vaseline entire face
Cover eyes with gauze before covering with strips of plaster of Paris
22 to 24 strips of plaster of Paris, approximately 1½″ wide
Cover the nose of the mask with strip of plaster of Paris after the mask is removed from the face.

FIGURE 8.2 A Completed Mask

With the many different types of tests available, it is incumbent upon the school counselor to be aware of the various features that build a strong test so that convincing information can be used for useful decision making.

QUALITIES OF A GOOD TEST

Some of the test qualities that need to be considered in assessment decisions are: validity, reliability, practicality, and cultural factors (Guindon, 2003; Neukrug, 1999).

- *Validity.* Validity determines whether or not a test measures what it is supposed to measure. It is often considered the most important test quality (Gladding, 2000; Hood & Johnson, 1997).

- *Reliability.* Reliability is a measure of the degree to which a test produces consistent test scores. Although reliability is related to validity, a test score may be reliable but may not necessarily be valid (Gladding, 2000; Hood & Johnson, 1997).

• *Practicality.* Practicality refers to the ease of test orientation, administration, and interpretation. A test may provide useful results; but if it is too expensive, lengthy, and difficult to administer, it may not be the best choice. A budget and calendar developed in advance with testing dates built into the regular school calendar of events help assist with testing decisions and provide money for consistency of test purchasing and replacement of items (Guindon, 2003).

• *Cross-Cultural Fairness of Tests.* Tests should consistently measure what they are intended to measure for all groups of people. The *Code of Fair Testing Practices in Education* was established to safeguard test takers from unfair testing practices (American Psychological Association, 1988), including instrumentation that discriminates among groups of individuals. Attempts have been made to develop culture-fair tests that eliminate or reduce cultural language and content for justifiable score interpretation (Hood & Johnson, 1997).

With all the elements of a good test to consider and the rapid rate in which tests are being published, it is essential that the school counselor stay knowledgeable about available tests, new instruments developed for testing needs, and revisions of existing tests.

WHERE TO FIND TESTS

The Buros Institute was established by Oscar Krisen Buros with the mission of communicating the significance and limitations of available tests. The publication of the *Mental Measurements Yearbook (MMY)* in 1938 was initiated to inform test users of testing qualities and good test practices. In 1961 *Tests in Print (TIP)* emerged as a cumulative index to the information within the *MMY* (Guindon, 2003; Plake, Conoley, Kramer, & Murphy, 1992). Tests may also be located through publisher resource catalogs, journals in the field, and the Internet.

With the advent of computer usage and tests available online, counselors have the opportunity to administer and interpret online tests; but there are also disadvantages to using this tool. Computers allow the test taker to receive instant results, yet the tests that appear on the computer have not necessarily been examined as thoroughly as other tests in regard to test qualities, leading to questionable results. Although computerized testing is convenient, test interpretation by the school counselor is essential so that norms, basic test statistics, and test qualities can be explained to the test taker (Neukrug, 1999). Too often, counselors have relied on untrained clerical staff to distribute and interpret results to students and parents because of time demands, yet this practice creates ethical and legal concerns. Moreover, counselors are to be aware of the security of test results so that scores are not accessible to other individuals (Guindon, 2003). This concern pertains to scores printed and distributed to students, as well as to scores stored on the computer.

One high-school counselor served over 750 students in grades 9–12. She was obviously overworked and felt that she was not able to make a difference in the lives of students because of her overwhelming schedule. In order to accomplish her many tasks, she made an error in judgment when she decided to leave the American College Test (ACT) results in a box outside of her office so that students would be able to individually and conveniently pick up their scores. She realized her mistake when students complained that their peers were broadcasting each others' composite scores throughout the classrooms.

School counselors obviously have a huge responsibility in regard to knowledge of testing and skills, orientation, administration, and interpretation to provide students with the best possible testing situation.

APPRAISAL SKILLS OF THE COUNSELOR

Counselors report being uncomfortable with testing instruments due to limited training (Giordano et al., 1997) in administering or interpreting tests (Tinsley & Bradley, 1986, as cited in Guindon, 2003). For these reasons and others, the process of testing can be mechanical and frustrating, leading to a psychological distance between the counselor and student. Counselors can make the testing process more comfortable through

1. Understanding norming, administration, reliability and validity, scoring results, and test strengths and weaknesses (Gladding, 2000)
2. Establishing rapport
3. Interpreting scores through graphs or charts that are more easily understood
4. Using multiple measures to provide a more complete picture of the individual

In addition, using a five-step model developed by Miller (1998, as cited in Guindon, 2003) with the acronym SCORE can assist the counselor in interpreting test results:

Strategize ways to reach an identified goal.

Connect test scores with other types of data.

Open-ended questions are helpful in determining what the test results mean to the student.

Review how the test scores are presented (percentile ranks) and to whom the student is being compared.

Emotions that were apparent on the day of the test that could interfere with test results should be identified by the test taker.

MANAGEMENT AND ADMINISTRATION OF THE SCHOOL TESTING PROGRAM

The professional school counselor is often given the task of managing the school or district testing program, which includes securing the tests in a safe place, making a testing schedule, training test administrators, assuring proper test procedures, and providing information to teachers on how to interpret the test results (Keys & Green, 2001, as cited in Guindon, 2003).

One concern debated by psychometricians is whether or not the test taker should be involved in the test selection and, if so, the amount of involvement that is necessary, particularly when minor students are involved. Test results are more likely to be accepted if the test taker is allowed to be involved in selecting the test, an opportunity that may lead to other decision-making opportunities (Goldman, 1971, as cited in Gladding, 2000).

The administration of tests, particularly standardized tests, requires specific test conditions such as the type of room to be used for optimal performance, number of individuals to be tested at one time, specific timing for test sections, explicit procedures for individuals who finish prior to the allotted time, and guidelines for a student who needs to leave the testing situation early.

In many cases, when tests are administered the regular school schedule is disrupted and rooms designated for testing need to be assigned in advance. A schedule needs to be available well in advance to allow teachers to make arrangements for their students. Parents should be notified if the regular bus schedule or the school-day schedule is altered, and students need to be oriented to the test purposes and how the results will be used. Counselors have a responsibility to inform students and others that test performance is affected when the test taker

1. Responds to questions in a manner thought to be acceptable to the test administrator rather than providing an accurate reflection of what he or she believes to be the true answers
2. Experiences factors such as fatigue, illness, noise in the room, or uncomfortable temperatures
3. Is aware of how the test will be scored (For instance, there is no penalty for incorrect answers in the ACT, but students are penalized for incorrect responses in the SAT.)

Professional school counselors have reported the usefulness of the counselor advisory committee in assisting in test selection and establishing the calendar. Some school districts have even sought assistance in test administration and interpretation by the members of this committee who are appropriately trained. This committee is valuable in designing a policy for registering concerns or complaints surrounding the test (American Psychological Association, 1998); and, since these members serve a dual function of assisting with public relations, other functions may include

- Informing students and their parents and/or guardians with the rights of test takers such as opportunities to obtain copies of the test and answers, and investigating possibilities to retake tests, rescore tests, or to have scores declared invalid
- Educating concerned individuals regarding special tests and accommodations for students with handicapping conditions
- Communicating how long scores will be kept on file and who will have access to these scores
- Informing the public about "high-stakes" testing

MORE ABOUT HIGH-STAKES TESTING

With the passage of the No Child Left Behind Act, many individuals are questioning the increased use of testing, particularly the high-stakes tests that determine promotion and high-school graduation. Well-informed advisory committee members can serve as the voice of the school in educating the public about the issues surrounding these tests. Competency tests tied to graduation were developed with the good intentions of challenging students and improving the schools in the United States, but these well-meaning purposes also bring about consequences that are becoming evident as more states are adopting these exams as a graduation requirement (*Dangerous Consequences,* n.d.; *National Testing,* n.d.):

1. Students with high test anxiety do not always perform in a way that best reflects ability. The greatest, negative impact of these tests will be with students with learning disabilities, those whose first language is not English, students of color, and low SES students. These individuals tend to fail these tests more regularly (Heubert, 2000).
2. The examinations do not improve educational standards since objective test questions such as multiple-choice questions do not measure high-level learning, and the curriculum is narrowed or "watered-down" in those subjects not measured on the examination such as life skills or vocational programs.
3. A higher dropout rate is associated with high-stakes testing since retained students may lose interest in learning and suffer from a damaged sense of self due to the belief that meeting graduation standards is futile.

ADDITIONAL STRATEGIES FOR INTEGRATING COUNSELING TECHNIQUES INTO THE ACADEMIC MISSION

Counselor support of the school educational goals and student achievement is essential, particularly as the nation is consumed with tests as a foundation for success. The school counselor's role is one that assists students to develop the attitudes, values, knowledge, and skills that contribute to effective learning (Rowell &

Hong, 2002). Counselors can utilize numerous interventions to realize this goal including test anxiety reduction, cognitive therapy, visualization, and test preparation classes.

Test Anxiety Reduction

With the apprehension that often accompanies tests, students often experience *test anxiety,* which is considered a barrier to academic success (Cheek, Bradley, Reynolds, & Coy, 2002). Test anxiety has been considered an "invisible disability" in that academic success may be jeopardized (Hill & Wigfield, 1981, as cited in Cheek, et al.). The need for school counselors to implement test anxiety reduction strategies increases as the demand for tests escalates. Relaxation paired with art, music, and imagery has been shown to be effective in reducing apprehension. In a study by Cheek and colleagues, students experiencing test anxiety were taught relaxation exercises using the strategy "stop, drop, and roll." Stop: put down pencils and concentrate on something else when experiencing test anxiety; drop: put head forward so that the chin is tucked into the neck; and roll: roll head around while taking deep breaths.

Cognitive Therapy

Rational-emotive therapy techniques are used effectively in identifying and changing irrational beliefs. In an intervention by Hobson (1996), students were taught to identify debilitating thoughts that negatively influenced performance; these thoughts were written on blue paper representing raindrops. Students were then asked to draw an umbrella (to represent a preventive strategy) with rational thoughts to counteract the negative thoughts. Students were taught to rehearse the rational, positive thoughts whenever they caught themselves thinking irrationally. Or, an alternative technique is to have students draw darts representing irrational thoughts and a shield to represent the preventive thoughts. This activity is illustrated in Figure 8.3.

Visualization

Mental imagery also helps students gain a better understanding of themselves while exploring new behaviors. Students are taught to visualize a time in which they were completely relaxed and to use their senses to picture this relaxing scene. Students are taught to verbalize what they hear, see, smell, taste, and touch. Deep, relaxing breaths and visualization are taught to counteract the tension and stress experienced due to the test. Box 8.3 is a script that can be used for the counselor and student to practice together.

Test Preparation Groups

Test preparation workshops have emerged throughout the nation not only for improving performance on tests but also for teaching strategies that can help reduce the anxiety that accompanies tests. In a study by Wiggins (1992), students participated in a 6-hour Saturday program that was based on Donner's 1981

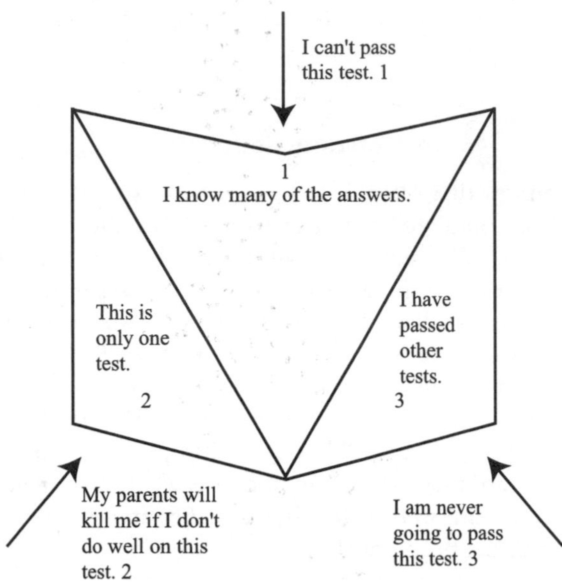

FIGURE 8.3 Cognitive Therapy Strategy for Reducing Test Anxiety

BOX 8.3 Visualization

Close your eyes

Take a deep breath and imagine the following scene.

You are floating on a cloud. (Imagine this picture while taking a few deep breaths.)

You feel warm, comfortable, and relaxed (Take a few deep breaths).

The softness of the cloud is silky and relaxing, and you feel good all over. (Take a few deep breaths).

You are relaxed and happy. What do you see? What do you hear? What do you touch?

Pay attention to these senses while you take in deep, relaxing breaths of air.

From now on, whenever you feel tension, take deep breaths and think of yourself floating on a cloud until you feel that the tension is gone.

book, *How to Beat the SAT.* This program instructed participants to apply game strategies while taking the SAT. Data revealed participants' scores increased as a result of this workshop. Furthermore, students were able to transfer and apply test-taking strategies to other test-taking situations. Counselors may develop similar programs for students who desire to learn these strategies.

SUMMARY

School counselors are key players in the school testing and assessment process, a role that has significantly increased in this age of accountability and documentation. Tests are valuable sources of information about students, and multiple measures provide an even better picture of the student than does the result of one single test score. "High-stakes" tests, developed to improve student achievement, are not fulfilling the intended purpose and, in some cases, are responsible for student dissatisfaction and ultimately dropping out of school.

Various types of tests can be utilized with students including both standardized and nonstandardized assessments. School counselors need to be aware of their scope of training and the requirements for test administration and interpretation.

School counselors are to be aware of the qualities that comprise an effective test, where to locate tests, and the elements of school testing management and administration. Educating and utilizing the skills of the advisory committee members can assist in test selection, help with administration, and serve as a channel from which regulations and laws surrounding testing standards can be communicated. Furthermore, counselors can help fulfill the academic mission by developing strategies for reducing test anxiety and enhancing test performance.

REFERENCES

Anastasi, A. (1992). What counselors should know about the use and interpretation of psychological tests. *Journal of Counseling & Development, 70,* 610–615.

Anastasi, A., & Urbina, S. (1997). *Psychological testing.* Upper Saddle River, NJ: Prentice-Hall.

Arter, J. A., Spandel, V., & Culham, R. (1995). *Portfolios for assessment and instruction.* Office of Educational Research and Improvement. (ERIC Document Reproduction Service No. ED388890)

American Psychological Association. (1988). *Code of fair testing practices in education.* Joint Committee on Testing Practices. Washington, DC: Author.

American School Counselor Association. (2002). *Position statement: High-stakes testing.* Alexandria, VA: Author.

Baker, S. B. (2000). *School counseling for the 21st century* (3rd ed.). Upper Saddle River, NJ: Prentice-Hall.

Bozarth, J. D. (1992). Person-centered assessment. *Journal of Counseling and Development, 69,* 458–465.

Cheek, J. R., Bradley, L. J., Reynolds, J., & Coy, D. (2002). An intervention for helping elementary students reduce test anxiety. *Professional School Counseling Journal, 6,* 162–164.

Clark, A. J. (1995). Projective techniques in the counseling process. *Journal of Counseling & Development, 73,* 311–316.

Dangerous consequences. (n.d.). Retrieved August 21, 2003, from http://www.fairtest.org

Domino, G. L. (2000). *Psychological testing: An introduction.* Upper Saddle River, NJ: Prentice-Hall.

Drum, D. J. (1992). A review of Leo Goldman's article "Qualitative assessment: An approach for counselors." *Journal of Counseling and Development, 70,* 622–623.

Education Trust. (n.d.) 1725 K Street, NW, Suite 200, Washington, DC 10006. Author.

Giordano, F. G., Schwiebert, V. L., & Brotherton, W. D. (1997). School counselors' perceptions of the usefulness of standardized tests, frequency of their use, and assessment training needs. *The School Counselor, 44,* 198–205.

Gladding, S. T. (2000). *Counseling: A comprehensive profession* (4th ed.). Upper Saddle River, NJ: Merrill.

Goldman, L. (1992). Qualitative assessment: An approach for counselors. *Journal of Counseling & Development, 70,* 616–619.

Guindon, M. H. (2003). Assessment. In B. T. Erford, (Ed.), *Transforming the school counseling profession* (pp. 331–356). Upper Saddle River, NJ: Merrill Prentice-Hall.

Heubert, J. P. (2000, September/October). *High-stakes testing. Opportunities and risks for students of color, English-language learners, and students with disabilities*. Retrieved August 21, 2003, from National Center on Accessing the General Curriculum Web site: *http://www.cast.org/ncac/*

Hobson, S. M. (1996). Test anxiety: Rain or shine. *Elementary School Guidance and Counseling, 30,* 316–318.

Hood, A. B., & Johnson, R. W. (1997). *Assessment in counseling. A guide to the use of psychological assessment procedures* (2nd ed.). Alexandria, VA: American Counseling Association.

House, A. E. (2002). DSM-IV *diagnosis in the schools*. New York: The Guilford Press.

House, R., Martin, P. J., & Ward, C. C. (2002). *Changing school counselor preparation: A critical need*. (Report No. CG031701). Washington, DC: Department of Education. (ERIC Document Reproduction Service No. ED464281)

Legislative handbook: Quick facts. Retrieved August 22, 2003, from http://www.nsta.org/ncibquick.html

National testing: Measuring learning does not improve learning. (n.d.). Retrieved August 21, 2003, from http://www.fairtest.org

Neukrug, E. (1999). *The world of the counselor: An introduction to the counseling profession*. Pacific Grove, CA: Brooks/Cole.

Plake, B. S., Conoley, J. C., Kramer, J. J., & Murphy, L. U. (1992). The Buros Institute of Mental Measurements: Commitment to the tradition of excellence. *Journal of Counseling and Development, 69,* 449–455.

Popham, W. J. (1995). *New assessment methods for school counselors*. (Report No. NC 27412-5001). Greensboro, NC: Clearinghouse on Counseling and Student Services. (ERIC Document Reproduction Service No. ED388888)

Rowell, L., & Hong, E. (2002). The role of school counselors in homework intervention. *The Professional School Counseling Journal, 5,* 285–291.

Schmidt, J. J. (1993). *Counseling in schools: Essential services and comprehensive programs*. Needham Heights, MA: Allyn & Bacon.

Steenbarger, B. N., & Smith, H. B. (1996). Assessing the quality of counseling services: Developing accountable helping systems. *Journal of Counseling and Development, 75,* 145–150.

Sterba, M., & Dowd, T. (1998). *Treating youth with* DSM-IV *disorders: The role of social skill instruction*. Boys Town, NE: Boys Town Press.

Vacc, N. A., & Juhnke, G. A. (1997). The use of structured clinical interviews for assessment in counseling. *Journal of Counseling & Development, 75,* 470–480.

Vacc, N. A., & Loesch, L. C. (1994). *A professional orientation to counseling* (2nd ed.). Levittown, PA: Accelerated Development.

Vernon, A. (1993). *Developmental assessment and intervention with children and adolescents*. Alexandria, VA: American Counseling Association.

Whiston, S. C. (2000). *Principles and applications of assessment in counseling*. Belmont, CA: Wadsworth/Thomson Learning.

Wiggins, J. D. (1992). Beating the SAT: Playing the game. *The School Counselor, 39,* 300–303.

9

The Internet's Influence on the School Counseling Profession

DR. CAROLE S. ROBINSON

School counselors are more often than not the only school professionals who have completed formal training in both mental health and education. School counseling responsibilities encompass conceptualizing and putting a comprehensive school counseling program into operation (Bowers & Hatch, 2002). Keeping the interdependence between computer technology and school counseling in mind, establishing an accomplished student counseling service relies on counselors establishing instructional, informational, and ethical toolsets to best meet demands for quality support of "academic, career, and personal/social" domains (Bowers & Hatch, p. 12). Technology assists school counselors in implementing these three domains.

This chapter primarily focuses on information literacy. In a nutshell, *information literacy* is the efficient use of the Internet and its resources. Now the confusing part comes in. Information technology skills are altogether different from information literacy. *Information technology skills* provide individuals with the knowledge "to use computers, software applications, databases, and other technologies to achieve a wide variety of academic, work-related, and personal goals" (*Information literacy competency standards for higher education,* 2002). These technology skills are the workhorse of information literacy, as well as of a school counseling service.

School counseling graduates are expected to be able to use technology to search information, that is, information literacy. Information literacy relies on information technology skills; however, the information literacy skill set is distinctly different from computer hardware and software application knowledge.

Competence requires an extensive proficiency to "recognize when information is needed and have the ability to locate, evaluate, and use effectively the needed information . . . an intellectual framework for understanding, finding, evaluating, and using information" (*Information literacy competency standards for higher education,* 2002). One could oversimplify the two definitions by relating to informational literacy as the *brain* and informational technology as the *brawn*.

COMPUTERS AND COUNSELING: A HISTORY

Counseling, programmers, and computers appear to be a strange mix. Nevertheless, their relationships go back half a century. The product of collaborations is electronic communication and a seemingly endless informational resource—the Internet—for school counselors, parents, guardians, and students.

In the 1950s the leading behaviorist psychologist, B. F. Skinner, at Harvard developed precedent setting experimental dialogue between computer and user. Skinner's Teaching Machines Project explored student learning with the help of a computer. A special typewriter transmitted teaching instructions from a huge International Business Machines (IBM) computer to a mathematics student. The student "user" was able to type answers to the math problems and relay the answers to the computer for checking. Corrections were returned to the student with minimal delay. Computer-to-user communication was limited to a fixed, question-and-answer-type linear sequence (*The hypertext history of instructional design* (n.d.)).

Massachusetts Institute of Technology (MIT) programmers in the late 1960s created the ELIZA (named after George Bernard Shaw's fictitious cockney flower seller Eliza Doolittle) program to emulate reflective comments of a Rogerian person-centered therapist and a client (user). Basically, ELIZA responded to the user by recognizing key words submitted in typed text, then analyzing the statement and producing a typed, preprogrammed response. Continuous dialogue between user and computer resembled a nondirective counseling session (Weizenbaum, n.d.). ELIZA's limitations in terms of interpreting natural language with cumbersome computer programming language became clear rather quickly. Technology replacing counselors was not yet considered a viable service.

During the same time frame that (MIT) was working with ELIZA, the leadership in the U.S. Department of Defense was formulating the Advanced Research Project Agency (ARPA) (*Life on the Internet timeline,* 2000). ARPA began envisioning the creation of a computer network system to serve as a vehicle to encourage U.S. researchers in think tanks like RAND and major universities like Stanford to share the massive room-sized super computers. This network-sharing (host-to-host) communicating with independent equipment was named ARPANET—the precursor to today's Internet. In conjunction with ARPANET, other similar projects were also making progress. For the sake of simplicity, *host* will be a synonym for *computer* in the next few paragraphs (Gray, 1996b).

Throughout the 1970s AT&T installed cross-country ARPANET links between computers used by think tanks and universities. Government agencies joined into the network (Zakon, 2003). Before too long, visionaries created an e-mail (electronic mail) program to send and manage messages across a network of computers. In the next 10 years, ARPANET included 213 hosts and was growing at the rate of one new host added every 20 days (*Basic concepts of distributed database systems* (n.d)).

At the 1972 International Conference on Computer Communication (ICCC), the first computer-to-computer chat between linked computers (one at Stanford University in California and the other at BBN Technologies in Cambridge, Massachusetts) simulated an online psychotherapy session. Stanford's computer psychotic "PARRY" discussed its problems with the BBN's "Doctor" computer (Zakon, 2003). ICCC's "PARRY" and the BBN's "Doctor" demonstration introduced the potential of the Internet and set the stage for today's expanding online facilitated services in counseling communication.

With the Internet as we now know it on the horizon, practical computer size and language evolved into the personal computers (PCs) recognizable by today's standards. Computer-building hobby kits of the 1970s led the way until IBM introduced the first commercially manufactured PC in 1981. IBM's computer (microcomputer) was small, programmable, reasonably inexpensive, and simple enough for the general public to operate. Throughout the 1980s, PCs became more readily available to the public at large. Original research-oriented Internet scientific presence decreased as the number of public users increased exponentially, seeking online access to everything from communication to information.

Cornell University had the insight in the mid-1980s to put the Internet to work for its students. Speaking to the demands for accessibility to health information, Cornell's Jerry Feist, former director of the Cornell Counseling Center, and Steve Worona of University Computer Services, designed *Dear Uncle Ezra,* the world's first organized student-oriented online counseling service in continuous service since its inception in 1986 (*History of Dear Uncle Ezra,* 2003). This service remains a confidential query-based resource; computers communicate questions and return responses, as well as archiving all information in a database for searchable future reference. *Dear Uncle Ezra* is a classic example of e-mail-based individual Internet counseling involving "asynchronous distance interaction between counselor and client using what is read via text to communicate" (*The practice of Internet counseling,* 2001). In other words, communication between counselor and client is conducted *not* in real time. E-mail is the primary communication tool. The following exercise provides a firsthand look at *Dear Uncle Ezra.*

Exercise

Explore Cornell's *Dear Uncle Ezra* Web site (http://ezra.cornell.edu), including the links Ask Uncle Ezra, Latest Questions, and Question Archive. Then investigate Dr. John Grohol's *Psychcentral* (http://www.psychcentral.com) and Dr. Ivan Goldberg's *Depression Central* http://www.psycom.net/depression.central.html#contents).

Write a couple of paragraphs that compare and contrast the informational content found on each Web site. Describe similarities or qualities that resemble each other. Describe dissimilarities or differences.

As the ability to create and link computer networks increased from over 100,000 hosts to 1.3 million in 1991 (Gray, 1996a), ARPANET disbanded and the World Wide Web, as we know it, was born (*History and development of the Internet a timeline: The 1980s,* 2002). The 1990s ushered in extraordinary Internet growth and significant transformation of online counseling "technology was truly recognized as a force impacting both the education and practice of counselors" (LaTurno-Hines, 2002, May).

Psychiatrist and clinical psychopharmacologist Ivan Goldberg, M.D., created an online presence in 1993 called *Dr. Ivan's Depression Central. Depression Central* was designed as an educational Web-based kiosk providing educational information on depressive disorders and their treatment to generate "self-help skills of those with depressive disorders, to increase the clinical skills of professionals, and to reduce stigma and discrimination against those with depressive disorders . . ." (Goldberg, 2002). Dr. Ivan Goldberg was clear when putting his information online that the Web site functioned as a support tool and not as an alternative to professional care. For over a decade, the quality of information provided by *Depression Central* has been held in high regard as a significant educational resource pertaining to mood disorders.

The 1990s became the decade of public and media focus on the Information Super Highway and, in turn, advanced Internet use for online counseling. Many therapists independently pioneered new forms of technology-assisted counseling employing the computer as a communication medium between themselves and clients. Each therapist contributed to the development of online services. Their services contributed to today's school counseling services involving "asynchronous and synchronous distance interaction among counselors and students using e-mail, chat, and videoconferencing features of the Internet to communicate" (*The practice of Internet counseling,* 2001).

John Grohol, a young psychology student long fascinated by computers and online communication, soon realized that the Internet was a viable psychology and mental health public venue. In 1992 he created *Psychcentral.com,* today's oldest psychology and mental health directory on the Internet, indexing mental health and support newsgroups and free weekly mental health advice in a public online chat room. *Psychcentral* may be viewed at

http://www.psychcentral.com

Eventually trained and educated as a clinical psychologist, Dr. John Grohol, Psy.D. is considered to be a groundbreaker in technology-assisted distance counseling and is given credit for coining the term *e-therapy*—a term universally used to "describe using an Internet-mediated technology to foster a helping relationship online" (Grohol, 2003a).

Computer technology, the Internet, and the phenomenon of online counseling continue to directly have an effect on the school counseling field. Traditional meanings of ethics are continually being redefined and are challenging counselors to investigate the essence of their professional beliefs. Information technology and information literacy skills are more important than ever for present and future school counselors. The Internet demands stakeholders to evaluate new approaches toward conducting counseling programs.

TOOLS NECESSARY TO MIGRATE TOWARD TECHNOLOGY-ASSISTED COUNSELING

Basic technology literacy is subject to as many interpretations as there are accrediting and professional organizations overseeing technology-assisted counseling. A comparison of leading organizations' current technology standards guidelines highlights two areas of competencies—information technology skills and information literacy.

Information Technology Skills

Information technology skills are essential to attain information literacy. Keep in mind that information technology skills encompass the "use computers, software applications, databases, and other technologies to achieve a wide variety of academic, work related, and personal goals" (*Information literacy competency standards for higher education,* 2002). A basic information technology skills model does exist. The model is the result of a "national consensus" outlining technology competencies based on teacher education preparation programs (*NETS PT3 project overview,* 2002). From the original 17-point *General Preparation Performance Profile for Technology-Literate Teachers,* a majority of preparation steps can readily serve as a competency checklist for the school counselor community (*Profiles for technology-literate teachers,* 2002). Box 9.1 defines basic information technology literacy skills.

Information Literacy Competency Standards

In the current information age facilitated through computers, an extraordinary amount of questionable information exists in our evolving global society linked together through the Internet. Information is everywhere creating information overload. Individuals, especially counselors, must be empowered to effectively select, search, and evaluate those abundant sources. Information literacy helps separate the quality informational treasure from the massive collection of cyber trash harbored on the Internet.

BOX 9.1 General Preparation Performance Profile for Technology-Literate Teachers

- Demonstrate a sound understanding of the nature and operation of technology systems.
- Demonstrate proficiency in the use of common input and output devices; solve routine hardware and software problems; and make informed choices about technology systems, resources, and services.
- Use technology tools and information resources to increase productivity, promote creativity, and facilitate academic learning.
- Use content-specific tools (e.g., software, simulation, environmental robes, graphing calculators, exploratory environments, Web tools) to support learning and research.
- Use technology tools to process data and report results.
- Use technology tools and resources for managing and communicating information (e.g., finances, schedules, addresses, purchases, correspondence).
- Use a variety of media and formats, including telecommunications, to collaborate, publish, and interact with peers, experts, and other audiences.

Note. From *Profiles for technology-literate teachers,* (2002). Retrieved March 12, 2003, from http://cnets.iste.org/teachers/t_profile-gen.html

The Association of College and Research Libraries (ACRL) is actively soliciting support and dissemination of the *Information Literacy Competency Standards for Higher Education* for learning information management skills in K–16 and in professional preparation programs (see Box 9.2). These ALA driven standards address Information Literacy competencies including ethical issues required by counseling organizations including the Association for Counselor Education and Supervision (ACES), the Council for Accreditation of Counseling and Related Educational Programs (CACREP), and the American School Counselor Association (ASCA). (See discussions and tables later in this chapter.)

Information Literacy: Internet Search Strategies

Internet search skills are essential to school counselors. ACES technical competencies and CACREP standards for counselor education students (discussed in more detail later in the chapter) prioritize the ability for counselors to use the Internet to locate electronic resources for career, training, financial assistance, and personal guidance. However, the most prominent frustration about accessing specific online information is compounded by unproductive searches and time-eating misdirection. The second point found in the information literacy competencies "access the needed information effectively and efficiently"—entails effective Internet search strategies. Productive searching guidelines are available on authoritative Web sites.

Many excellent online informational sources are available only mouse clicks away. A variety of superior Web sites supply sound approaches to finding the exact information in a timely manner. Each one has a unique approach to guiding and informing.

BOX 9.2 Association of College and Research Libraries Information Literacy Competency Standards for Higher Education

An information-literate individual is able to

- Determine the extent of information needed
- Access the needed information effectively and efficiently
- Evaluate information and its sources critically
- Incorporate selected information into one's knowledge base
- Use information effectively to accomplish a specific purpose
- Understand the economic, legal, and social issues surrounding the use of information, and access and use information ethically and legally

Note. From *Association of College and Research Libraries Information Literacy Competency Standards for Higher Education.* (2000). Retrieved March 9, 2003, from the ACRL Web site.

- *Search Engine Showdown: Learning About Searching* is a private Web site created and maintained by a Montana State University reference librarian/associate professor (Notess, 2003). The Web site may be viewed at

  http://www.notess.com/search/strat

- San Diego State University's *Four NETS for Better Searching* (2003) is informative, entertaining, multilingual, and appropriate for all ages of cyber searchers. The Web site may be viewed at

  http://webquest.sdsu.edu/searching/fournets.htm

- The Rice University Fondren Library *Internet Search Strategies* (2001) is another excellent resource for fine-tuning your search skills. The Web site may be viewed at

  http://www.rice.edu/fondren/etext/howto/search.html

Information Literacy: Web Site Evaluation Procedures

Once searching the Internet becomes productive, evaluating the information can be daunting. Anyone exploring any given subject on the Internet soon realizes the overwhelming amount of information available on any given search. Understanding logical procedures for discerning high-quality Web sites from the inferior ones requires assessment. Table 9.1 shows six steps necessary in determining a valid Website resource. Whether a school counselor is searching for professional development information or helping a student choose a college, Internet resource reliability and credibility are necessary for providing students, parents, and guardians quality, timely information.

The Quick List is another valuable Internet search tool. After evaluating each Web site, positive results can be documented using a simple table. Instructions for creating such a table are given in the following exercise. Table 9.2 documents Web sites that are useful to a counseling program.

Table 9.1 Six-Step Web-Site Evaluation Criteria

Who	• is the author?
	• sponsors the page?
What	• is the purpose of the Web site?
	• credentials and/or qualifications are listed for the author(s) and/or publisher?
	• institution (if any) publishes this Web site?
When	• was the Web site produced?
	• was the Web site last updated?
Where	• can you contact the author and/or publisher?
	• does the URL domain direct you? (For example: Is it .gov, .edu, .net, .com?)
Why	• was this Web site produced and for whom?
How	• accurate and/or objective is the information?
	• precise is spelling and grammar?
	• current is the information?
	• well is the Web site content presented?
	• up-to-date are the hyperlinks?
	• correct are the citations enabling content verification?
	• easy is it to differentiate advertising from informational content?
	• properly can information be viewed without limitations of fees, browser technology, and/or software requirements?

Table 9.2 Professional Counseling Resources Quick List Example

Professional Organizations/ Resources	**Description**	**Internet Address**
National Association for College Admission Counseling (NACAD)	Dedicated to serving students for postsecondary education choice	http://www.nacac.com
Career/Vocational Sites	**Description**	**Internet Address**
Office of Vocational and Adult Education (OVAE)	Career and technical education information	http://www.ed.gov/about/offices/list/ovae/pi/cte/index.html
Disabilities/Disorders	**Description**	**Internet Address**
Learning Disabilities (LD) Online	Information supporting educational competence of LD children	http://www.ldonline.org/index.html

Exercise

1. Create a table in a Word document with three columns.
2. Categorize the subject of your search on the list.

3. Evaluate each Web site using the Six-Step Web-Site Evaluation Criteria from Table 9.1 prior to adding the Web site to the list.
4. Copy and paste the name of the Web site in the first column.
5. Add a brief description of the Web-site content in the second column.
6. Copy and paste the Internet address in the third column.

Write a short paper justifying your outstanding Web site choices. Present evidence to support how each high-quality Web site met the Six-Step Web Site Evaluation Criteria where other Web sites failed.

SCHOOL COUNSELOR PROFESSIONAL ORGANIZATIONS AND THE INTERNET

After reviewing the abridged history of computers and the interesting relationship to counseling at the beginning of this chapter, one can appreciate how constantly emerging technology advancements combined with the evolution of and exponential growth rate of the Internet have impacted counseling in general and school counseling specifically. Communication and counseling are mutually dependent—joined at the hip, so to speak. As communication evolves digitally, growing demands for reliable counseling resources and information have become an important component of the counseling process.

Establishing instructional, informational, and ethical competencies regarding the Internet have been subject to debate and discussion for many years within governing organizations, including the Association for Counselor Education and Supervision (ACES); the Council for Accreditation of Counseling and Related Educational Programs (CACREP); the American School Counselor Association (ASCA); the American Counseling Association (ACA); and the National Board for Certified Counselors (NBCC). Understanding the competencies and standards established by these governing organizations is an important part of becoming an informed professional school counselor.

The Association for Counselor Education and Supervision

The Association for Counselor Education and Supervision (ACES), one of the gatekeepers of counselor education standards, diligently puts forth great efforts to improve counselor education, credentialing, and supervision. By 1999, the organization members published a 12-point list of guidelines addressing the technology standards counselor educators should integrate into their curriculum. Integrating

Table 9.3 ACES Competencies Category Overview

Categories	ACES Technology Interest Network
Information Technology Skills	Be able to • Use productivity software to develop Web pages, group presentations, letters, and reports. • Use such audiovisual equipment as video recorders, audio recorders, projection equipment, videoconferencing equipment, and playback units. • Use computerized statistical packages. • Use computerized testing, diagnostic, and career decision-making programs with clients. • Use e-mail. • Subscribe, participate in, and sign off counseling-related listservs. • Access and use counseling-related CD-ROM databases.
Information Literacy	Be able to • Help clients search for various types of counseling-related information via the Internet, including information about careers, employment opportunities, educational and training opportunities, financial assistance/scholarships, treatment procedures, and social and personal information. • Use the Internet for finding and using continuing education opportunities in counseling. • Evaluate the quality of Internet information.
Legal/Ethics: Technology-Assisted Counseling	Be knowledgeable about the • Legal and ethical codes that relate to counseling services via the Internet. • Strengths and weaknesses of counseling services provided via the Internet.

Note. From *Technical competencies for counselor education students: Recommended guidelines for program development.* (1999). Retrieved February 24, 2003, from http://www.acesonline.net/competencies.htm

standards into the curriculum ensures that educational programs will bring counseling students up to technological par prior to graduation. The 12 *Technical Competencies for Counselor Education Students: Recommended Guidelines for Program Development* (1999) consist of information technology skills (sometimes referred to as computer literacy), information literacy, and e-therapy ethics. A complete list of all 12 competencies is provided in Table 9.3 and may be reviewed at the following Web site:

http://www.acesonline.net/competencies.htm

Seven of the 12 ACES competencies focus on information technology literacy. In a similar vein, three of the ACES competencies speak to information literacy. Aware of trends, the ACES clearly addresses counselor educators with educating students about making informed decisions about the strengths and weaknesses of Internet-provided counseling services including professional legal and ethical guidelines. The following exercise will help to familiarize you with the information literacy competencies.

Exercise

Review the Information Literacy requirements listed in Table 9.3: ACES Competencies Category Overview.

Examine your ability to meet each of the Information Literacy competencies at this moment in your school counseling program.

Write a few brief paragraphs identifying your Information Literacy strengths and weakness in meeting each listed competency. Indicate the degree to which you meet each competency and write a proposal of how to improve your competence by the last semester of your school counseling program.

The Council for Accreditation of Counseling and Related Educational Programs

The American Counseling Association (ACA) organized the Council for Accreditation of Counseling and Related Educational Programs (CACREP) in 1981 (*About CACREP,* 2002). It is an accreditation organization independent of the ACA. Organizational responsibilities include reviewing and evaluating counselor education program alignment with national standards outlined in the *CACREP 2001 Standards.* These standards "ensure that students develop a professional counselor identity and also master the knowledge and skills to practice effectively" (*Council for Accreditation of Counseling and Related Educational Programs: The 2001 Standards,* 2001).

Counselor technological competence and ethical standards set by the other professional organizations are highlighted throughout this chapter. However, CACREP-endorsed information technology skill sets are generalized and not as specific as the ACES. Endorsed examples can be viewed in Table 9.4 under Section II Program Objectives and Curriculum. Legal and ethical issues surrounding technology-assisted counseling are not directly addressed. Section III Clinical Instruction (not shown) also speaks to technology requirement and is worth online investigation.

The National Certified School Counselor (NCSC) certification/licensure is a product of the shared governance of three national associations: the ACA, the ASCA, and the NBCC. One of the first steps on the road to a successful career in school counseling is becoming familiar with ethical, information literacy, and information technology standards set by these three organizational bodies. Standards were designed to ensure the appropriate knowledge base concerning the use of technology in counseling settings.

The American School Counselor Association

The American School Counselor Association (ASCA), comprised of graduate school counselor educators, credentialed school counselors, and school counselor supervisors, published a second revision of the *ASCA Ethical Standards for School Counselors* in 1998 (Table 9.5). It may be viewed online at

http://www.schoolcounselor.org/content.cfm?L1=1&L2=15

Table 9.4 Council for Accreditation of Counseling and Related Educational Programs 2001 Standards

Categories	Section II Program Objectives and Curriculum
	Professional Identity
Information Technology Skills	• Technological competence and computer literacy
Legal/Ethics	• Ethical standards of ACA and related entities, and applications of ethical and legal considerations in professional counseling
	Career Development
Information Literacy	• Career, avocational, educational, occupational and labor market information resources, visual and print media, computer-based career information systems, and other electronic career information systems • Technology-based career development applications and strategies, including computer-assisted career guidance and information systems and appropriate World Wide Web sites
	Helping Relationships
Information Literacy	• Integration of technological strategies and applications within counseling and consultation processes
	Research and Program Evaluation
Information Technology Skills	• Use of technology and statistical methods in conducting research and program evaluation, assuming basic computer literacy

Note. Council for Accreditation of Counseling and Related Educational Programs: The 2001 Standards. (2001). Retrieved January 6, 2003, from http://www.counseling.org/cacrep/2001standards700.htm

Table 9.5 American School Counselor Association Ethical Standards for School Counselors

Categories	Ethical Standards for School Counselors (1998)
Information Technology Skills	A.10. Computer Technology • Computer applications are appropriate for the individual needs of the counselee.
Americans with Disabilities Act	• The counselee understands how to use the application. • Members of underrepresented groups are assured equal access to computer technologies and are assured the absence of discriminatory information and values in computer applications.
Legal/Ethics: Technology Assisted Counseling	A.10. Follow the NBCC *Standards for Web Counseling.*

Note. From *Ethics.* (2002). Retrieved December 12, 2002, from the ASCA Web site.

Table 9.6 National Model for School Counseling Programs

Categories	Preconditions
Information Technology Skills	• School counselors use technology daily in their work, including the Internet*, word processing, student database systems and presentation software. • School counselors use data regarding their school population to work with the principal, teachers and the advisory council in making recommendations to improve academic achievement. • School counselors receive yearly training in all areas of technology advancement and updates. • School counselors use technology in the planning, implementation and evaluation of the school counseling program. • School counselors use technology as a tool to gather**, analyze and present data to drive systematic change.
Information Literacy	• School counselors use technology to help students perform career and advanced educational searches and create online portfolios.

**including the Internet* refers to information literacy.

***gathering data* refers to information literacy.

Note. From Bowers, J., & Hatch, P. (2002). *ASCA* National Model for School Counseling Programs (p. 64). Retrieved September 15, 2003, from the North Carolina School Counselor Association Web site.

Computer technology "promotes the benefits of appropriate computer applications and clarifies the limitations of computer technology" (*Ethics,* 2002). Technology literacy is addressed as the responsibility of the school counselor to educate/train clients (counselees) on technology applications used in counseling sessions as well as monitor equal access to computer technologies and applications. Counselors must also have the ability to evaluate computer application appropriateness in relationship to individual client needs. The ASCA refers school counselors to the National Board for Certified Counselors (NBCC) *Standards for Web Counseling* when integrating Internet-facilitated, technology-assisted distance counseling into their counseling procedures.

The *National Model for School Counseling Programs* draft published by the ASCA in 2002 recognizes counselor information technology and informational literacy skills within the preconditions necessary to effectively implement and support feasible school counseling programs. Table 9.6 breaks down the technology-related preconditions. Observe the reiteration of Internet search skills in the areas of student career and educational search and counselor data collection. Providing the most up-to-date and reliable information to students, parents, and the school stakeholders helps fulfill the ultimate goal of a school counseling program—supporting the school's academic mission.

Table 9.7 American Counseling Association Ethical Standards for Internet Online Counseling

Categories	Ethical Standards for Internet Online Counseling (1999)
Information Technology Skills	A.12 a.; 12 c. Computer technology
	A.12 b. Explain the limitations of computer technology.
Legal/Ethics: Technology-Assisted Counseling	Adherence to: Appropriateness of online counseling; Counseling plans; Continuing coverage; Boundaries of competence especially determining minor or incompetent clients

Note. From *Confidentiality.* (2003). Retrieved February 22, 2003, from the ACA Web site.

The National Board for Certified Counselors and the American Counseling Association

Even though the National Board for Certified Counselors (NBCC) and the American Counseling Association (ACA) standards largely speak to counselors in a private practice setting, these organizations set standards that serve as touchstones for school counseling guidelines. Awareness of organizational interconnectivity is important to a productive counseling career.

The NBCC is a credentialing body establishing, monitoring, and promoting national counselor certification. More than 30,000 certified counselors have met NBCC "predetermined standards in their training, experience, and performance on the National Counselor Examination (NCE) for Licensure and Certification." The NBCC published *Standards for the Ethical Practice of Internet Counseling* in 2001. Not only is this document a definitive resource for definitions, the 14 standards speak to Web-based counseling subtleties and nuances (*The practice of Internet counseling,* 2001).

The ACA, with over 50,000 members, is a professional and educational organization representing counselors. In efforts to advance the profession and enhance client service, members also work on public policy and legislation. Instrumental in establishing professional and ethical counseling standards, the "association has made considerable strides in accreditation, licensure, and national certification" (*Confidentiality,* 2003). Educational programs and organizational publications are representative of the services used for promoting the development of practicing counselors. The 1999 ACA *Ethical Standards for Internet Online Counseling* publication (see Table 9.7) establishes guidelines "for the use of electronic communications over the Internet to provide online counseling services" *(Confidentiality).*

EQUAL ACCESS ISSUES

The NBCC details the area of equal access: "Within the limits of readily available technology, Internet counselors have an obligation to make their Web site a barrier-free environment to clients with disabilities" (*The practice of Internet counseling,* 2001). Equal access is not only an *ethical* issue; counseling Web sites have a *legal* obligation to be compliant with Section 508 of the Disabilities Act and *The World Wide Web Consortium's (W3C) Web Content Accessibility Guidelines (WCAG).* The WCAG help the disabled find information on the Internet more quickly. Compliance requires Web-site content (electronic and information technology) to be accessible to people with disabilities no matter what devices they may choose to use to access information (*508 Law,* 1998). Information concerning Section 508 compliance measures is readily available both online and through software purchase.

Counseling Web Sites and Section 508 Compliance

Placing scholarship/financial aid college information, transcript request forms, career information, online counseling communications, and a myriad of other counseling specific content on the school Web site requires careful planning. Counselors must thoughtfully consider accessibility barriers and strategically design the site to be Section 508 compliant. *User Agent Accessibility Guidelines 1.0* (2002) is a great reference for determing Web-site functionality and interoperability. The guidelines and may be viewed at

http://www.w3.org/TR/2002/REC-UAAG10-20021217

This document may be a bit daunting to novices who "just want to put up a Web site" for parents, guardians, and students. However, equity and access issues are a counseling program priority. The World Wide Web Consortium (WC3), created in 1994 at the Massachusetts Institute of Technology, is dedicated to many facets of universal Web access including language barriers, societal issues, and technical requirements. Organizational goals not only include addressing equal Web access tools but also encompass "differences in culture, . . . education, ability, [and] material resources . . ." (*About the World Wide Web Consortium,* 2003). Members are global. The WC3 comprehensive Web site may be viewed at

http://www.w3.org/Consortium/#mission

Bobby is a free online service provided by Watchfire, a "for-profit" software and management company. Bobby may be viewed at

http://bobby.watchfire.com/bobby/html/en/index.jsp

The service was created to encourage the design of equal access Web sites. It provides Web developers with a central Web site where they may test Web pages for accessibility compliance prior to placing content online. Bobby analysis highlights critical Web design problems and possible ways to repair barriers. The following exercise can be used to learn more about the Bobby Web site.

Exercise

Locate the Bobby Web site (http://bobby.watchfire.com/bobby/html/en/index.jsp) and copy a counseling organizational Web-site address into the URL box. Run a Bobby test using both *Web Content Accessibility Guidelines 1.0* and then *U.S. Section 508 Guidelines.*

Americans with Disabilities Act (ADA) compliant software options for monitoring Section 508 and WCAG compliance are on the market. Two of the most used software are InFocus (*InFocus,* 2003) and AccVerify (HiSoftware, 2003). These products scrutinize Web sites and applications with a complete accessibility standards checklist. Individual Web pages are automatically checked for any accessibility violations and errors. Specific steps necessary for violation and error remediation are also reported to achieve compliance.

INTERNET ACCESS TO VIABLE SOFTWARE FOR COUNSELING PROGRAMS

Technology is becoming an increasingly efficient way to support school counseling programs in the area of accountability. According to the ASCA National Model (Comprehensive Developmental Guidance Model), programs are data-driven and responsible for accurate reporting of student outcomes (Bowers & Hatch, 2002). Operating a school counseling program depends on action plans, time use audits, and master calendars. Collected data are important for examining student achievement and achievement variances between students, as well as for planning, monitoring, evaluating, and modifying interventions. Electronic databases are rapidly replacing pencil-and-paper records and calendars. The spreadsheet/database programs such as *Microsoft® Excel, Microsoft Access,* and *Filemaker Pro,* usually found in basic computer software package bundles, are simple, inexpensive tools for maintaining documentation of the number of students seen for counseling, official presentations, group work, and so on.

Technology in the form of e-mail (Internet communication) and informational Web sites can become important to individual client communication and enhance communication between school and home—supporting dialogue between students, parents, and yourself. Internet communication might be a viable alternative to face-to-face individual conferences difficult to schedule within a typical school year. Always remember that you have an ethical obligation to address equal access issues when using electronic communication in any form, including Web-site postings. Supplemental online counseling materials including school district calendars and forms, career search information, career/vocational planning, and referral/information Web-site links serve to broaden interactions and influence parental involvement along with student motivation and self-reliance. The following are examples of district school counseling Web-site content based on the ASCA National Model. These sites include materials helpful in realizing and authoring your own counseling program Web site.

- *Tucson Unified School District School Counseling Program:*

  http://instech.tusd.k12.az.us/counsel/counselor/handbook.htm

- *Moreno Valley School District School Counseling Program:*

  http://www.mvusd.k12.ca.us/Departments/Educational/Student_Services/Program_Information/program_information.html

Unless your school district provides an exceptionally well equipped technology-based counseling office, software-specific tools (i.e., data collection, documentation, scheduling, client communication, and Web-site authoring software) are made available for downloading onto your computer at little or no cost to you. Literally hundreds of these download access sites may be found by strategically searching the Internet for freeware, shareware, and public domain software.

Before you search for or download software, it is important to understand the difference between freeware, shareware, and public domain software. The Ohio State University Office of Information Technology provides straightforward definitions of the terms:

> *Freeware:* Copyrighted software available for downloading without charge; unlimited personal usage is permitted, but you cannot do anything else without express permission of the author. Contrast to
>
> *Shareware:* Copyrighted software that requires you to register and pay a small fee to the author if you decide to continue using a program you download (Ohio State University Office of Information Technology, 2003a).
>
> *Public domain software:* Any noncopyrighted program; this software is free and can be used without restriction; often confused with *freeware* (free software that is copyrighted by the author) (Ohio State University Office of Information Technology, 2003b).

The University of California at Los Angeles School of Engineering and Applied Science maintains an archived database of searchable public domain software at

http://aixpdslib.seas.ucla.edu/index.html

Many shareware/freeware searchable sites require a membership fee to proceed toward downloading the chosen software. So consider this capitalistic tactic in your Internet search. An example of a nonmembership Web site is ZDNET at

http://downloads-zdnet.com.com

ZDNET provides perspective and resources PC and Macintosh reviewed, rated, and categorized software. Numerous freeware, shareware, and public domain software sites are available to you by honing your Internet researching skills. Review "Information Literacy: Internet Search Strategies" in this chapter before going into cyberspace.

Once you locate downloadable software, the next step is evaluating the product. The Northwest Regional Educational Technology Consortium's (NWREL) Web site at

http://www.netc.org/software

provides information about software selection and evaluation criteria. *Seven Steps to Responsible Software Selection* is located at

http://www.netc.org/software/eric_software.html

Clearinghouse Web links are also provided for reviewing software products. Happy searching! The following exercise will help you get started.

Exercise

Use your Internet research skills and find examples of freeware, shareware, and public domain software you can use to improve your school counseling program. Begin by searching for a calendar for scheduling appointments. Use the *Seven Steps to Responsible Software Selection* Web site to explain the reasons you chose each software package to download: http://www.netc.org/software/eric_software.html

If you have problems with productive Internet searching, locate the *Four NETS for Better Searching* Web site:

http://webquest.sdsu.edu/searching/fournets.htm

Read and work through the Net 1–Net 4 practice involving an Internet search on a topic: Start Narrow, Find Exact Phrases, Trim Back the URL, and Look for Similar Pages.

SUMMARY

Societal and technological influences are creating a rapidly expanding demand for technology-assisted counseling practice. The Internet offers an exciting format for delivering and receiving services and the potential to assist more students and their families—especially those who are time- and place-bound due to a variety of circumstances. It is important to remember that this digital format is still in its formative years. Many questions concerning migrating traditional services to technology-assisted counseling are yet to be considered, let alone answered. Professional organizations are conscientiously constructing guidelines and instructional/informational/ethical competencies providing quality Web-based counseling services and best practices for educating students.

Your overall responsibility as a school counselor is protecting the privacy of client data and communication. Be sure you are informed of legal and ethical guidelines when using e-mail, Web-site postings, or computer-based data collection. Review Box 9.2, Table 9.3, Table 9.4, Table 9.5, and Table 9.7 in this chapter. These resources provide a summary of legal and ethical points regarding technology use in school counseling programs. For more detailed information, use the Association of College and Research Libraries (ACRL), the Association for Counselor Education and Supervision (ACES), the Council for Accreditation of Counseling and Related Educational Programs (CACREP), the American School Counselor Association (ASCA), and the American Counseling Association (ACA) Web-site addresses (URLs) provided in this text.

If you venture into supplementing your future school counseling program with online resources, guidance, and communication, the journey will be more informed.

REFERENCES

About CACREP. (2002). Retrieved January 6, 2003, from http://www.counseling.org/cacrep/aboutCACREP.htm

About the World Wide Web Consortium. (2003). Retrieved March 3, 2003, from the World Wide Web Consortium Web site: http://www.w3.org/Consortium/#mission

Association of College and Research Libraries Information Literacy Competency Standards for Higher Education. (2000). Retrieved March 9, 2003 from the Association of College and Research Libraries Web site: http://www.ala.org/ala/acrl/acrlstandards/informationliteracycompetency.htm#ildef

Basic concepts of distributed database systems. (n.d.) Retrieved May 17, 2004 from http://www.deakin.edu.au/~scc762/s762s1.pdf

Bowers, J., & Hatch, P. (2002). *ASCA National Model for School Counseling Programs*. Retrieved September 15, 2003, from North Carolina School Counselor Association Web site: http://www.nccounseling.org/NCSCA/modeltext.pdf

Confidentiality. (2003). Retrieved February 22, 2003, from the American Counseling Association Web site: http://www.counseling.org/site/PageServer?pagename=resources_internet

Council for Accreditation of Counseling and Related Educational Programs: The 2001 Standards. (2001). Retrieved January 6, 2003, from http://www.counseling.org/cacrep/2001standards700.htm

Ethics. (2002). Retrieved December 12, 2002, from the American School Counselor Association Web site: http://www.schoolcounselor.org/content.cfm?L1=1&L2=15

Ethics. (2003). Retrieved February 22, 2003, from the American Psychological Association Online Web site: http://www.apa.org/ethics/stmnt01.html

Four NETS for Better Searching. (2003). Retrieved September 21, 2003, from San Diego State University Web site: http://webquest.sdsu.edu/searching/fournets.htm

Goldberg, I. (2002). *Mission statement*. Retrieved November 24, 2002, from Dr. Ivan's *Depression Central* Web site: http://www.psycom.net/depression.central.mission.html

Gray, M. (1996a). *Internet growth: Raw data.* Retrieved December 20, 2002, from the Massachusetts Institute of Technology Web site: http://www.mit.edu/people/mkgray/net/terminology.html

Gray, M. (1996b). *Web sites, hostnames and IP addresses, oh my.* Retrieved May 12, 2004, from the Massachusetts Institute of Technology Web site: http://www.mit.edu/people/mkgray/net/internet-growth-summary.html

Grohol, J. (2003a). *eTherapy essays.* Retrieved January 5, 2003, from Dr. John Grohol's *Psych Central* Web site: http://psychcentral.com/best/s

Grohol, J. (2003b). *Dr. John Grohol's Psych Central.* Retrieved January 5, 2003, from Dr. John Grohol's *Psych Central* Web site: http://psychcentral.com

HiSoftware. (2003). *HiSoftware and Microsoft present.* Retrieved January 5, 2003, from http://www.hisoftware.com/msacc

History and development of the Internet: A timeline: the 1980s. (2002). Retrieved November 24, 2002, from San Antonio Public Library: Government Documents Web site: http://www.sat.lib.tx.us/Displays/it80.htm

History of Dear Uncle Ezra. (2003). Retrieved September 21, 2003, from Cornell University, *Ask Uncle Ezra* Web site: http://ezra.cornell.edu/history.php

InFocus. (2003). Retrieved February 25, 2003, from SSB Technologies Web site: http://www.ssbtechnologies.com/products/InFocus.php

Information literacy competency standards for higher education. (2002). Retrieved November 28, 2002, from the American Library Association, Association of College and Research Libraries Web site: http://www.ala.org/acrl/ilintro.html#iltech

Internet search strategy. (2001). Retrieved November 30, 2002, from Rice University Fondren Library Web site: http://www.rice.edu/fondren/etext/howto/search.html

LaTurno-Hines, P. (2002, May). Student technology competencies for school counseling programs. *Journal of Technology in Counseling.* Available: http://jtc.colstate.edu/vol2_2/hines/hines.htm

Moreno Valley School District School Counseling Program. (2003). Retrieved December 30, 2003, from the Moreno Valley School District School Web site: http://www.mvusd.k12.ca.us/Departments/Educational/Student_Services/Program_Information/program_information.html

NETS PT3 project overview. (2002). Retrieved March 12, 2003, from http://cnets.iste.org/teachers/t_overview.html

Northwest Educational Technology Consortium. (2003). Retrieved December 30, 2003, from the NETC Web site: http://www.netc.org/software

Notess, G. (2003). *Learning about searching.* Retrieved January 5, 2003, from Search Engine Showdown Web site: http://www.notess.com/search/strat

Ohio State University Office of Information Technology. (2003a). Retrieved December 29, 2003, from the Ohio State University Web site: http://www.oit.ohio-state.edu/glossary/gloss2.html#f

Ohio State University Office of Information Technology. (2003b). Retrieved December 29, 2003, from the Ohio State University Web site: http://www.oit.ohio-state.edu/glossary/gloss2.html#p

Presidential Committee on Information Literacy. Final Report. (1989). Chicago: American Library Association. Retrieved March 11, 2003, from the American Library Association Web site: http://www.ala.org/acrl/nili/ilit1st.html

Profiles for technology-literate teachers. (2002). Retrieved March 12, 2003, from http://cnets.iste.org/teachers/t_profile-gen.html

Rabasca, L. (2000). Self-help sites: A blessing or a bane? *Monitor on Psychology, 31* (4). Retrieved December 5, 2002, from http://www.apa.org/monitor/apr00/selfhelp.html

Seven steps to responsible software selection. (2003). Retrieved December 30, 2003, from the NETC Web site: http://www.netc.org/software/eric_software.html

Technical competencies for counselor education students: Recommended guidelines for program development. (1999). Retrieved February 24, 2003, from http://www.acesonline.net/competencies.htm

Telehealth and the Internet. (2002). Retrieved November 28, 2002, from the U.S. Department of Health and Human Services, Office for the Advancement of Healthnet Web site: http://telehealth.hrsa.gov/pubs/inter.htm

The ASCA National Model: A framework for school counseling programs. (2002). Retrieved September 24, 2003, from the American School Counselor Association Web site: http://www.schoolcounselor.org/library/ExecSumm.pdf

The hypertext history of instructional design (n.d.) Retrieved May 12, 2004 from the University of Houston College of Education Web site: http://www.coe.uh.edu/courses/coin6373/idhistory/ibm.html

The practice of Internet counseling. (2001). Retrieved February 14, 2003, from the National Board for Certified Counselors Web site: http://www.nbcc.org/ethics/webethics.htm

Tucson Unified School District School Counseling Program. (2003). Retrieved December 29, 2003, from the Tucson Unified School District Web site: http://instech.tusd.k12.az.us/counsel/counselor/handbook.htm

University of California at Los Angeles School of Engineering and Applied Science. (2003). Retrieved December 30, 2003, from the UCLA Web site: http://aixpdslib.seas.ucla.edu/index.html

User Agent Accessibility Guidelines 1.0. (2002). Retrieved September 30, 2003, from the World Wide Web Consortium Web site: http://www.w3.org/TR/2002/REC-UAAG10-20021217

Weizenbaum, J. (n.d.). *ELIZA—A computer program for the study of natural language communication between man and machine.* Retrieved December 20, 2002, from the New York University Web site: http://i5.nyu.edu/~mm64/x52.9265/january1966.html

Welcome to the Bobby online services. (2003). Retrieved January 24, 2003, from Bobby Web site: http://bobby.watchfire.com/bobby/html/en/index.jsp

W3C: World Wide Web Consortium. (2003). Retrieved February 24, 2003, from http://www.w3.org

Zakon, R. (2003). *Hobbes' Internet timeline v6.0.* Retrieved January 2, 2003, from http://www.zakon.org/robert/Internet/timeline

ZDNET. (2003). Retrieved December 30, 2003, from ZDNET Web site: http://downloads-zdnet.com.com

508 Law. (1998). Retrieved February 14, 2003, from Section 508 Web site: http://www.section508.gov/index.cfm?FuseAction=Content&ID=3

10

Crisis Counseling and Critical Incident Management

As a new counselor in a rural high school located in the Midwest, several female students approached me because of their concern about their friend, "Susan," who was talking about suicide. They were particularly concerned because she had made an attempt the previous year. I was not sure how to handle this since my counselor education program did not really cover the topic of suicide and self-destructive behaviors; nor did I really know the students of this school or even Susan. I at least had the foresight to call Susan into my office and ask her if she was thinking of harming herself. Susan angrily denied having ever engaged in these thoughts and angrily left my office. Several minutes later Susan reappeared and stated furiously, "If this is what you think I am going to do, then I will." With these words she quickly pulled a knife out of her purse and slit her wrists in front of me.

After this incident I realized my lack of education regarding destructive behaviors and decided at that point that I had a responsibility to learn more about students in crisis and my role as a school counselor.

The frequency with which conflicts occur in our community and schools affirm the increasing incidents of violence by school-aged youth. More than ever before, schools have a responsibility to respond to these events.

When a person is faced with a problem that he or she cannot resolve, a crisis results (Aguilera, 1990; James & Gilliland, 2001; Kanel, 1999). Crises are a normal part of life experienced by everyone. As depicted by the Chinese *konjii,* a crisis represents both danger and opportunity (Caplan, 1964, as cited in Kanel). The symbol represents danger in that the situation may be so overwhelming that pathological behavior such as homicide and suicide may result, but it may also be an opportunity for learning new skills and coping strategies (James & Gilliland).

Crises are classified as developmental, situational, existential, or environmental. *Developmental* crises are naturally occurring events in human development that produce anxiety. Erik Erikson defined developmental crises as a gradual maturation process in which individuals confront a crisis that must be mastered. When the strategies are successful, the individual is stronger, healthier, and better equipped to handle future difficulties (Santrock, 1996). If a task within a life stage is not accomplished, the individual remains stuck and developmental growth is hindered (Kanel, 1999). Transitional events within the developmental stages are normal, expected events that can create stress even though these events may be positively regarded. Examples include: pregnancy, introduction of a new family member, death of a family member, graduation, or marriage.

Situational crises are events that are unpredictable, unexpected, and beyond an individual's control. Examples include: crime, rape, accidents, or school/community disasters (Kanel, 1999). An *existential* crisis includes conflicts that accompany issues of purpose and/or responsibility. Leaving home, going to college, or being a teen parent are examples of opportunities in which one may reflect on life's meaning. An *environmental* crisis includes a natural disaster such as hurricanes, floods, earthquakes, blizzards, or forest fires.

Incidents of violence and conflicts are becoming increasingly evident in our society's secondary, middle, and elementary schools (D'Andrea & Daniels, 1996). Counselors are increasingly relied on to provide assistance in prevention and intervention to combat the aggressive responses and subsequent trauma experienced by school-aged youth. This chapter covers a model for counselors to use in crisis intervention; children's reactions to trauma; programs for at-risk youth; and, finally, a critical incident management model for schools to adapt.

MODEL OF CRISIS INTERVENTION

A crisis is time limited and usually lasts anywhere from 4 to 6 weeks (Kanel, 1999) to 6 to 8 weeks (James & Gilliland, 2001). Because of the acute characteristics evident when one is in a crisis situation, immediate assistance is needed. Resolution may be hastened when youth share their distress as explicitly as possible and to the best of their ability. In many cases, the child is experiencing so much chaos that his or her normal routine, relationships, and behaviors are disrupted

(Johnson, 1989). An assessment is crucial to determine the extent to which the child's life has been impacted.

Assessment

Assessment is an action-oriented, time-limited approach in which the school counselor determines the crisis severity. A child who is experiencing a traumatic reaction will show extremes of behavior by either underresponding or overresponding cognitively, affectively, behaviorally, and physiologically (Johnson, 1989).

The ABC model (James & Gilliland, 2001; Kanel, 1999) is a useful strategy for the counselor to assess the student's *a*ffective, *b*ehavioral, and *c*ognitive state.

- *Affect.* Anxiety, anger, or depression is commonly expressed when an individual is in crisis (Crow, 1977, as cited in James & Gilliland, 2001). The counselor is to determine whether or not the displayed affect is disproportionate to the situation and/or if the emotional state is further exacerbated by other individuals or events. For example, think of a time when you or someone else you know well was in a crisis situation. What were some of the features that made this situation unique from other events in your life cognitively, affectively, and behaviorally?
- *Behavior.* Behaviorally, an individual in crisis is more or less stuck in a static behavioral pattern and rendered immobile. Providing structure is an opportunity to actively do something (e.g., take a walk, call mom, etc.).
- *Cognition.* Cognitively, the crisis is perceived as a catastrophic threat or loss, producing irrational thinking that narrows the individual's ability to clearly define the problem and to generate solutions. The better the problem is defined, the more rapidly the student can be assisted. One difficulty for school counselors is that youth are not always able to communicate their discomfort clearly and often communicate their distress through physical symptoms such as complaints of a headache or stomachache. The school nurse is a key person with whom the counselor may consult to receive important information regarding the student's health.

The counselor assesses the student's *balancing factors,* or the variables that serve as protective buffers. These balancing factors include the perception of the event, the support system, and existing coping skills. These factors protect the individual from additional stress, assist in growth through a new understanding of the event, and result in more productive coping strategies to promote resiliency (Aguilera, 1998).

Perception of the Event

The significance of an event is different for every student. Some students will perceive an event realistically and engage in appropriate resolution strategies, and others will pretend that the event was insignificant or even deny its reality. How realistically the individual views the event aids the counselor in reframing the significance to the individual (Kanel, 1999). Some questions for the counselor to ask include: "What meaning does this event have for you?" or, "What are some of the thoughts you have been having since the event?" One essential question is, "What happened that made you come in to see me today?" Since the crisis usually occurs 10 to 14 days before the student actively seeks assistance (Aguilera, 1998), the counselor needs to know the triggering event that served as the catalyst for the student to seek assistance at that particular time (Aguilera; Kanel).

Kellie came to see her counselor because she learned that her parents were getting a separation and, ultimately, a divorce. Although Kellie knew that their marriage was not the best, she really hoped that her parents could work things out. Kellie spoke to the counselor about her fears and the difficulties she was having sleeping, eating, and concentrating on her school work. Together, they worked out some strategies that Kellie felt she could try, and Kellie left the office feeling a little better. However, 1 week later, Kellie burst into the counselor's office in tears, out of breath, and having difficulty talking. After a few minutes of uncontrollable sobbing, she was able to tell her counselor that she was upset that her parents were breaking up the family.

Since they had previously discussed the situation, the confused counselor asked, "What happened that you came in to see me right now?" This question brought a bewildered look to Kellie's face as she replied, "I thought you wanted me to tell you when I was upset!" The counselor replied, "Yes, and we've talked about this situation before, and I'm wondering what happened that made you come to see me right now. What has just happened that is different?"

Kellie immediately explained that she had walked to school that morning and when she had stopped in a local bakery for a bagel, she had seen her father and another woman in deep, intimate conversation. It was this scene that finally brought about the reality of her parents' divorce.

Support System

People in crisis need support from others, and in most cases the family is the primary source of support for children. However, if the family is in a state of turmoil, this system is often ineffective (Johnson, 1989). When confronted with a difficult situation, children have confused feelings, memories, and troublesome reactions but often feel isolated because adults rarely talk to children when they are caught up in their own reactions (Johnson). People rarely think in terms of "whom could I contact if . . ." situations, particularly in the event that a major support person is absent or not able to be contacted. When thinking and affect are impaired, identifying significant alternative people to replace the people who were previously available is difficult.

One activity that may assist students identify support systems before a crisis erupts is described in the following exercise.

Exercise

- Ask the student to draw a circle on a piece of paper representing him or herself and to write his or her name in the circle. The student usually asks questions such as "Where should I put the circle?" or "How big should it be?" The counselor should simply respond that it can be placed wherever he or she chooses and the size is whatever he or she wants it to be.

- After the student has drawn the circle, the counselor instructs the student to draw circles representing anyone who comes to mind, to place the name of the individual in each circle, and to continue drawing circles representing people who come to mind until finished.
- The counselor then discusses the location of the selected individuals, whether there is significance to the size and location of the identified individuals, and any people who may be missing from the illustration.
- Following this discussion, the student is asked to think of the people in the illustration with whom he or she has a strong, positive relationship and to draw a solid line from that individual's circle to the student's circle. The student is next asked to think of people with whom he or she has a relationship that is sometimes good but at times tension appears. A dotted line is to be drawn from the identified individual's circle to the student's circle to represent a tenuous relationship. Finally, for the individuals in which the relationship is characterized by opposition and turmoil, a jagged line is drawn.
- Last, the identified persons with whom a solid, strong relationship exists are to be listed along with their contact phone numbers. The student is instructed to place this list in a safe place that can be easily accessed if there is an emergency. The counselor may want to follow up with the student after several months to review this list for changes. Figure 10.1 depicts this process.

Another method to identify a support system is to present a problem situation, ask what a person would need in that situation, and ask who or what would be able to meet those needs (Johnson, 1989). The following situations can be adapted to help students prepare for a difficult situation:

- Suppose a fire broke out in your house. Who would be helpful to you?
- Your best friend just told you that she is thinking of killing herself because life just isn't worth living anymore. Whom would you contact?
- You have just witnessed a car accident in which several people you know have been severely injured and they have been rushed by ambulance to the hospital. Whom could you call to help in this situation?

Coping Ability

Throughout life, people use many strategies to reduce anxiety. Coping skills influence the way that a person deals with a stressful event (McWhirter, McWhirter, McWhirter, & McWhirter 1998). Many individuals have positive ways of dealing with stress such as talking with a friend or going for a long walk, and they call upon these strategies whenever they experience distress. However, other children and adolescents cope poorly with crisis and use behaviors such as acting out, withdrawal, or aggression (Aguilera, 1998). The counselor's role is to

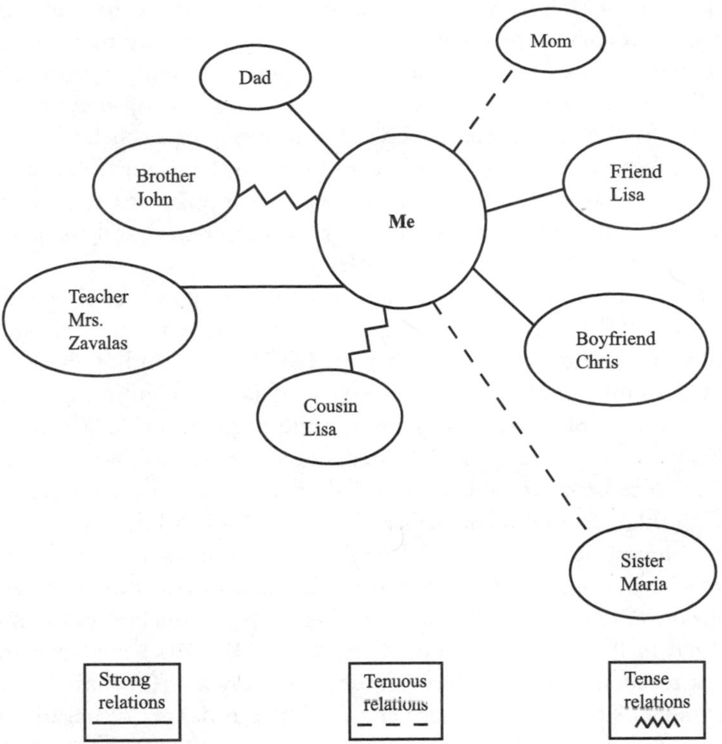

FIGURE 10.1 Who is my support system?

assess the student's strengths and coping abilities (James & Gilliland, 2001) and/or teach successful, positive coping skills to replace unhelpful strategies.

To determine coping strategies that have been valuable, the counselor may ask the student, "What has helped you in past situations when you were feeling stressed?" If the student is unable to think of any helpful coping techniques, the counselor can go one step further and ask, "If you were to give advice to someone who was upset, what would you tell him or her to do?" (James & Gilliland, 2001).

REACTIONS TO TRAUMA

Because children express anxiety differently than do adults, it is difficult to recognize children who are traumatized. Children in crisis sometimes have difficulty setting priorities, acting effectively, and distinguishing between trivial and important information. Furthermore, they may appear confused or overly calm in making sense of the event.

Children under the age of 12 have not yet mastered time orientation. Therefore, sequences of events may be distorted as they struggle to understand incoming sensory information (Johnson, 1989). Symptoms in response to the event are sometimes immediately observable; and, in other cases, reactions to crisis may persist for hours or days after the event or even appear suddenly at some point in the future. These latter responses are known as *delayed stress responses* or *post traumatic stress disorder* (PTSD) (Johnson). The situation may be even further exacerbated as the child reflects upon his or her reactions to the event (Johnson). Identifying youth who have witnessed traumatic events is a huge first step in assisting these individuals since they are not only at risk for physical and mental illness but also may be at risk for perpetuating violence.

Rod Paige, Secretary of Education, stated that the issue of school violence has gone "beyond metal detectors" and emphasized the need to identify and assist school-aged youth at risk for violent behavior (CNN, 2001). Although early identification is desirable, counselors run the risk of falsely identifying aggressive youth. The "accuracy of the school shooter profile is questionable" (Reddy et al., 2001, p. 162, as cited in Daniels, 2002). Media descriptions of lower-class, minority youth as the predators of violence lead authorities to target the wrong population. In reality, the youth who have killed—such as Mitchell Johnson and Andrew Golden from Jonesboro, Arkansas, and Kip Kinkel from Springfield, Oregon—were White youth from middle socioeconomic families and not members of a minority group (Breland, 2000). However, there are personality and contextual factors that aid in the identification of at-risk youth. Box 10.1 contains a sample checklist that teachers and counselors can use to identify at-risk youth.

Past or present situations that place an individual in danger of negative future events are *risk factors* (McWhirter et al., 1998) for destructive future growth and development. Despite deleterious situational, developmental, familial, or personal crises, many individuals grow up to be healthy, productive citizens, which is known as *resiliency.*

Mental health professionals are curious about the variables that promote resiliency. It is of great interest to note how differently children grow and succeed when raised in the same chaotic, dysfunctional family. Some of these individuals grow into productive, responsible citizens while other siblings may grow into unlawful members of society.

Matt and Mark were the two oldest brothers in a family of three boys who all lived with their father. Their parents were divorced, and the brothers rarely had any contact with their mother who lived in a different state. Mark told his school counselor that he hated his father and often wished he were dead. Mark further expressed his unhappiness and pain when he revealed that there were several times he thought about taking a gun from his father's gun rack, coming to school, and shooting anyone that got in his way. Mark continued telling his counselor that following this plan he would go home, shoot his father, and then kill himself to end it all. The counselor contacted the appropriate authorities: but, despite the efforts to help Mark, he eventually dropped out of school. Throughout the years Mark had many arrests and is well known by the community social services and police.

Mark's brother, however, turned out quite differently. Matt graduated from high school, majored in business in college, and now has an MBA degree. Matt is also well known in the community but in a far different way than Mark. Matt is a prominent businessman and is a productive, contributing member to society.

BOX 10.1 Age-Appropriate Reactions of Children in Crisis

Childhood (Ages 5–11)

- Sadness & crying
- Difficulty concentrating
- Fearful
- Enuresis
- Confusion
- Physical complaints
- Regression
- Aggressive behaviors
- Withdrawal
- Attention-seeking
- Irritability
- Difficulty sleeping
- Anxiety
- Eating difficulties

Early Adolescence (Ages 11–14)

- Sleeping problems
- Withdrawal
- Eating difficulties
- Loss of interest in activities
- Disinterest in the future
- Rebelliousness
- Anxiety
- School problems
- Fearful
- Physical complaints
- Depression
- Attention difficulties

Adolescence (Ages 14–18)

- Intrusive memories
- Anxiety and guilt
- Eating difficulties
- Aggressive behaviors
- Substance abuse
- Depression
- Difficulty concentrating
- Decrease in energy level
- Numbing
- Difficulty sleeping
- Apathy
- Peer problems
- Withdrawal

Note. From Lerner, M. D., Volpe, J. S., & Lindell, B. (2003). *A practical guide for crisis response in our schools* (5th ed.). Commack, NY: A Publication of the American Academy of Experts in Traumatic Stress. Reprinted with permission.

FACTORS CREATING AGGRESSION IN AT-RISK YOUTH

Counselors have often discussed the variables that lead one individual to an industrious, satisfying life and another individual to a troubled, unproductive life. Some characteristics of youth at risk for violent behavior include attachment difficulties, family violence, media depictions, lower socioeconomic status, peer group influence, personality characteristics, lack of empathy, academic performance, self-esteem issues, and poor interpersonal communication skills. Youth who display some of these characteristics, particularly at a young age, may be identified and taught skills to promote resiliency.

Attachment

Attachment is the "propensity of human beings to make strong affectional bonds with others" (Bowlby, 1977, p. 201, as cited in Sandhu, Underwood, & Sandhu, 2000). The early experiences infants have with their parents or guardians become the foundation for relationships that may be formed with others in the future (Sandhu et al.). Therefore, relationship difficulties later in life could be linked with insecure attachment earlier in life (Santrock, 1996).

One successful strategy for working with individuals with attachment disorder is to direct the child to carry a picture of his or her prominent caregiver when they are separated during the day. This picture serves as a concrete reminder that the child and caregiver will be reunited. This reminder may be kept in the child's locker, cubbyhole, or other personal storage area to be viewed whenever the child feels vulnerable and lonely.

Family Violence

The family can either buffer or reinforce aggressive tendencies (McWhirter et al., 1998). Family violence appears to be one of the most underreported crimes in the United States, and boys who witness this violence have a greater tendency for becoming abusers themselves (Kratcoski, 1984, as cited in Ibrahim & Tran, 2000). Violence is also associated with low parental investment. Stepchildren are more likely to be abused than children raised in homes with two biological parents (Troost & Filsinger, 1992, as cited in Wyatt, 2000).

Media

Research is mixed on the effects of violent programming and aggressive behavior. In a study by the Gallup Organization, 6 in 10 adolescents reported that "gangsta rap" encouraged violence (The Federal Trade Commission and the Surgeon General, as cited in Gay, Lesbian and Straight Education Network, 2001). Studies like this conclude an association between violent programming and aggressive behaviors. Other researchers report no direct correlation between media portrayals of violence and aggressive behavior. Lower intelligence and noncensorship of programming by parents (Ibrahim & Tran, 2000) are identified as the intervening factors linked with violent tendencies, rather than the actual exposure.

Ethnic Minority Families

Ethnic minorities are disproportionately represented in the lower income brackets, and young female-headed households with children are especially vulnerable to poverty. Although there is not a direct association between socioeconomic status and delinquency, ethnicity, neighborhood, parents' educational levels, and income do have an effect on anti-social behaviors (Tolan & Guerra, 1994, as cited in McWhirter et al., 1998). Furthermore, parent irritability, negative disposition, and depression due to financial concerns may negatively impact the development of children.

Peer Group Influence

A sense of belonging is an important step in development, and positive peer influence is considered as a significant factor in decreasing violence (Leffert et al., 1998, as cited in Bauer, 2000). Since peers are the foundation for the formation of attitudes, beliefs, and behaviors, delinquent peers reinforce aggressive behaviors (Beauvais, 1996; McWhirter et al., 1998). Youth who do not feel part of sanctioned school activities feel alienation and anger toward school, personnel, and peers (Baker, 1998, as cited in Ibrahim & Tran, 2000) and tend to associate with other peers who feel on the "outside of the mainstream." Gangs emerge as youth seek belonging, acceptance, and approval.

Personality Characteristics

Resilient children have certain personality characteristics such as a well-developed sense of humor, an ability to delay gratification, and empathy for others (James & Gilliland, 2001). Violent youth often suffer from episodes of sadness to severe depression, sometimes leading to suicide. Counselors may determine depression by inquiring about long- and short-term goals, since individuals suffering from depression have few goals for the future.

Lack of Empathy

Empathic individuals more easily understand others' perspectives and are more tolerant of others. Violent youth tend to display anger to perceived hostile incidents without regard to other motivating factors (Sandhu, Underwood, & Sandhu, 2000). In recent school killings, the killers planned the event methodically with no compassion or caring built in to the implementation (Leffert, 1998, as cited in Bauer, 2000). This lack of emotional identification is also associated with insensitivity and cruelty to animals and others.

Academics

Research is mixed on the cognitive abilities of aggressive youth. Some researchers reveal a correlation between aggressive behaviors and poor academic performance (McWhirter et al., 1998). Others state that the plans executed by violent children require average to above average intelligence (Sandhu et al., 2000). These same researchers explain that, for the most part, these students are academic underachievers and experience academic problems not because of their intelligence but, rather, due to a lack of motivation and nonparticipation in school activities (Good & Brophy, 1995, as cited in Sandhu et al.).

Self-Esteem

There is disagreement as to the relationship between aggressiveness and self-concept. Self-esteem is defined as the value one places on his or her concept of self (Santrock, 1996). Some researchers (McWhirter et al., 1998) point out that low self-esteem is a determinant of at-risk behavior. Children who have had few successes in life may engage in antisocial behavior to increase self-esteem. On the other hand, when others back down, retreat, or cater to demands, the immediate reinforcement of these acts enhances the aggressor's sense of self (James & Gilliland, 2001)

Communication with Others

Interpersonal skills are related to adjustment in later life. Good social functioning in childhood and adolescence has been related to academic success and adequate interpersonal adjustment; at-risk children have distorted perceptions of situations and lack skills to make satisfying social relationships (James & Gilliland, 2001). School counselors are in an ideal position to identify these youth, to implement strategies to prevent future negative behaviors, and to intervene when deleterious behaviors and attitudes are evident.

Counselors report that suicide is one of the school counselor's greatest fears and is an experience that is never forgotten (Austin, 2003). Youth suicide is ranked as the third leading cause of death, ranking below accidents and homicides. The student workbook that supplements this chapter contains information concerning the issues most commonly confronting children and adolescents in our society. However, because of the high numbers of youth with suicidal ideation and completion, more detailed information on factors associated with suicide and assessment follows.

SUICIDE AND YOUTH

Because suicide within the adolescent population is ranked as a leading cause of death in our society today, counselors have the responsibility to be familiar with the factors associated with youth suicide and to assess suicidal risk factors.

Factors Associated with Adolescent Suicide

- *Parenting and family issues.* Family discord caused by parental separation, divorce, caretaker changes, or abuse contributes to suicidal behaviors. Each of these factors is associated with poor communication (Aguilera, 1998).
- *Problem-solving skills.* Suicidal youth experience a greater number of stressful events compared with their nonsuicidal classmates, which impairs cognition and reduces the ability to make decisions (Brown, Overholser, Spirito, & Fritz, 1991).
- *Hopelessness.* Hopeless, one component of depression, is associated with suicidal ideation. Hopelessness is often a better indicator of suicidal intent because of the difficulty in diagnosing depression (Cole, Protinsky, & Cross, 1992). A counselor may be able to determine hopelessness by asking the student about long- and short-term goals. An absence of goals, along with other warning signs, could be an indication of suicidal ideation.
- *Running away.* In a study by Wagner, Cole, and Schwartzman (1995), suicide attempters were more likely to have run away from home than their nonsuicidal peers. This trend is higher among middle-school students than among high-school students.

- *Stressors.* Suicidal youth display behaviors that may be detected as early as age 5 (Reinherz, Giaconia, Silverman, & Friedman, 1995). These individuals have had numerous, negative life events that overburden the ability of adolescents to cope. Some of the stressors associated with suicidal youth include: family turmoil, concerns with sexual identity, lack of supportive adults, sexual abuse, physical violence, children with disabilities, gifted students, pregnancy, and abortion (Henry, Stephenson, Hanson, & Hargett, 1993).
- *Identity issues.* Gender identity issues are associated with suicide attempts. It is difficult enough establishing a sense of self, but for youth who are gay or lesbian, identity is even more difficult. Negative attitudes, poor self-esteem, verbal and physical abuse from family members, and substance abuse are all associated factors contributing to suicidal ideation among youth who are gay or lesbian (McFarland, 1998).
- *Cognitive development.* Individuals with learning disorders often have poor problem-solving skills, and when faced with problematic situations these individuals have even more difficulty solving difficult dilemmas (Wagner et al., 1995).
- *Loss.* A significant loss is associated with adolescent suicide ideation and attempts. These losses may include a divorce or death, an accident, the loss of a scholarship, or the failure of not making a team (McWhirter et al., 1998).

Assessment of Suicidal Ideation

It is not unusual for the adolescent to be reluctant to disclose suicidal intentions due to its taboo nature. A counselor who directly asks the student if he or she is thinking of harming him or herself brings about a sense of relief and permission to discuss this topic. Checklists available to assist counselors determine suicidal risk are often unreliable because of the faulty results that are obtained in the form of a false positive or false negative. Directly asking a student if he or she is thinking of "harming self" provides a much more reliable assessment (McWhirter et al., 1998). The acronym STRESS serves as a concrete tool to assist in the assessment.

- **S***pecifics of the plan.* The more specific the plan, the higher the suicidal risk. An adolescent with unclear plans and few details as to how the suicide will be carried out is at a lower risk than an individual who has clear, detailed plans for how, when, and where it will occur.
- **T***iming of the last attempt.* One of the greatest predictors of suicidal ideation is a previous attempt. The more recent the last attempt, the greater the danger for future attempts. Ambivalence is commonly expressed by suicidal youth in that they do not want to live but they do not want to die either. In addition, behavioral and verbal warning signs often precede attempts. However, as the student appears to be improving, the next 90 days are crucial because ambivalence may be replaced with a decision to kill oneself (Kanel, 1999).

- **R***escue available.* When an individual describes a previous attempt, the school counselor is to consider whether the student allowed time in the attempt for someone to stop the attempt and rescue the student from further harm.
- **E***xternal locus of control.* Suicidal youth perceive life events as outside of their control, with little power to change situations. Feelings of helplessness often accompany loss. Taking one's life may be the only situation the adolescent feels he or she can control.
- **S***kill deficits.* Poor social skills, insufficient problem-solving strategies, and poor communication skills are linked to suicidal behaviors (McBride & Siegel, 1997). Prevention strategies taught in elementary school assist youth in learning appropriate skills to apply for productive problem solving.
- **S***upport system.* The availability of positive, supportive individuals in the lives of adolescents is associated with a lower risk of suicidal behaviors. It could be that the school counselor is the only positive, supportive individual in a student' s life (Aguilera, 1998).

PREVENTION AND INTERVENTION

Numerous programs have been developed to reduce aggressive behaviors that can be viewed as both prevention and intervention (Larson, 1994). For example, a counselor may provide an intervention for an angry youth that later becomes a preventive strategy in future events. A preventive measure may be viewed as an intervention if a violent incident is avoided because of the training and skills that were presented and acquired. Goldstein and Glick (1987) have categorized the various primary prevention strategies into a comprehensive program that includes social/cognitive training, anger management, moral reasoning, or what is more commonly referred to as empathy building, and relaxation.

Social/Cognitive Training

Understanding the influence of children's cognitive processing and its role in aggressive behavior assists the school counselor in providing appropriate programming (Buckley, 2000). The focus of these programs is on developing social competence and facilitative coping for all children, not just those at risk. These programs commonly include problem solving, identification of feelings, stress management, assertiveness training, and conflict mediation and have been successful when incorporated into the K-12 curriculum (Durlack, 1995, as cited in McWhirter et al., 1998).

- *Problem solving.* At-risk youth usually have a rigid thinking style that prevents generating alternative solutions (McWhirter et al., 1998). When children have gained experience in decision making, they are in a better position to handle the stressors. A sense of control and personal responsibility is the outcome when children are given the opportunity to make choices.

BOX 10.2 Fish for Feelings

The counselor cuts fish from construction paper and writes an emotion on each of these paper fish. A magnet is attached to the back side of the paper fish so that the magnet is on one side and the printed emotion on the other. A child is given a fishing pole with a magnet at the end of it as a "hook." The fishing pole magnet will "catch" a fish. The child is to read the emotion printed on the underside of the fish and tell of a time he or she experienced that particular feeling.

- *Identification of feelings.* At-risk children tend to ignore feelings because recognizing and acknowledging these emotions cause pain and turmoil. Being immune to affect not only assists an individual in producing acts of violence and hostility but also allows a better opportunity to commit these behaviors. A person cannot engage in criminal activity if he or she has feelings and is able to empathize. One activity a counselor can use to facilitate feeling identification is the "Fish for Feelings" activity (Box 10.2).
- *Stress management.* Children often feel that no one else feels the stress that they are experiencing. People differ in their reaction and vulnerability to stress as well as their accompanying reactions. Some symptoms may never disappear, or periods of time may go by and then symptoms reappear (Johnson, 1989). Teaching relaxation skills helps youth to manage stress.

The deep-breathing exercises used by athletes before an important play (Goldstein & Glick, 1987) are easily adaptable strategies for reducing excessive anxiety in children and adolescents. The following procedure can be taught and practiced:

> Slowly inhale while counting to 10, hold your breath for the count of 3, and then exhale to the count of 10. Repeat the sequence.

Another relaxation technique is illustrated in Box 10.3.

• *Assertiveness skills. Assertion* is the ability to express oneself but at the same time to respect the rights of others (Feindler, 1995). Alberti (1986) designed a four-step model to assist individuals identify and rehearse assertiveness skills:

Step 1. "*When* . . ." (The speaker describes the other individual's behavior.)

Step 2. "*The effects are* . . ." (The speaker describes how the other's actions influenced him or her.)

Step 3. "*I feel* . . ." (The speaker reports his or her feelings.)

Step 4. "*I would like* . . ." (The speaker specifies what he or she would like to see occur.)

These four steps are illustrated in the following hypothetical scenario: Your friend is always asking for your homework to copy.

Step 1. "*When* you ask me for my homework to copy . . ."

Step 2. "I am afraid *the teacher will lower my grade* . . ."

BOX 10.3 Relaxation Through Imagery

Age: 6 to adult

Materials: Pen and paper, tape recorder, and tape

Directions

Ask the child to think of a time that he or she was happy and relaxed. Have the child explain the scene in as much detail as possible and pay attention to all of the senses. As the child describes his or her "happy" place, write the story. Prompt the student with questions such as, "What did you see?" "Who was with you?" "What did you hear?" "What did you do?" "What did you feel?" "Did you smell anything?" "Do you remember tasting anything?"

After the story is written, read it to the child and make any revisions. Before the script is ready to record, teach and practice relaxation and deep breathing exercises. Record the script and direct the child to listen to the tape whenever he or she feels stressed.

The following is a script that was written from a scene visualized by an eighth-grade student.

> Imagine that you are going to the beach. Take a deep breath and let it out slowly. You are walking onto the sand and enjoy feeling the warm sand crunch between your toes. As you are stretching out your toes and digging your feet into the soft sand, you take a long look at the beautiful, blue water stretched out before you. (Pause.) You are listening to the sounds of the beach; sea gulls are loudly calling to each other, the water is lapping gently up on the shore, and your friends are calling out to you. (Pause.) You are happy and content, and you have a smile on your face as you run to the water's edge to join your friends. A game of catch has begun, and everyone is laughing and having fun.
>
> You momentarily join them and laughingly splash your friend and dive into the water. You feel the gentle, warm breeze against your face and you decide to lie down on the towel that is spread out on the sand. You hear the waves somersault on the beach and you feel rested, relaxed, almost as if you are floating in space. It is beautiful and you are happy and content. (Pause.) What else do you hear? What else do you see? Relax for a minute and just pay attention to what is around you that makes you feel relaxed and at peace. (Pause.) When you are ready to leave the beach, stretch your arms over your head and take a few deep breaths.

Step 3: "I *feel* used and frustrated when you copy my homework . . ."

Step 4: "and I *would like* you to do your own work so I don't have to worry about getting in trouble."

Assertion, aggression, and unassertive behaviors are often difficult to distinguish from one another. Research has shown the value of practicing assertive responses and related social skills while recognizing how this response is different from aggressiveness and nonassertiveness (Takaka-Matsumi, 1995). Providing students with different scenarios, allowing them to practice assertive responses in the counseling setting, and assigning these skills outside the counselor's office reinforce these skills.

• *Conflict mediation.* Conflict management programs in which peers influence, mediate, and resolve conflicts among classmates assist school-aged youth in resolving troublesome behaviors (Buckley, 2000; Short & Talley, 1997). Conflict mediation teaches students cooperation, communication, negotiation, compromise, and acceptable resolutions to a problem situation (Levy, 1989). There are many suc-

FIGURE 10.2 A Commitment to Peace

Reprinted with permission.

cessful models designed to resolve school-based conflict. One successful resolution model designed by Schrumpt, Crawford, and Udadel (1991) outlines six phases:

1. *Opening the session,* in which introductions are made, ground rules are stated by the mediator, and the disputants agree to abide by the outlined rules
2. *Gathering information,* which includes providing each disputant uninterrupted time to tell his or her side of the story
3. *Finding commonalities,* which serves as the basis for an agreement
4. *Creating options,* which allows each disputant to identify how the problem should be resolved
5. *Evaluating and choosing a solution* from the list generated in Step 4
6. *Writing an agreement* and providing a copy to each disputant and the mediator.

School personnel reveal that students in conflict resolution programs demonstrate greater understanding and ability to model problem solving after participation in such a program (Johnson & Johnson, 1995).

Acceptable methods of assisting others and preventing violence are demonstrated through student commitment to nonviolence. In one such method students are asked to trace their hands, decorate this outline, autograph it, and show their commitment to a "safe" environment by writing the words,. "These hands are for helping not hurting." These pictures are displayed throughout the building or classroom (Figure 10.2).

Anger Management

Anger and aggression are frequent in the workplace, home, and school. Most people report being mildly to moderately angry anywhere from several times a day to several times per week (Anastasi, Cohan, & Spatz, 1984, as cited in Kassinove & Sukhodolsky, 1995). In fact, anger is reported as being the most universal emotion among humans (Izard, 1977, as cited in DiGuiseppe, 1995). Strong, negative feelings often disrupt behavior, physiological responses, and cognition.

Children who display temper tantrums have a set of personal beliefs and thoughts that create a tendency to misinterpret all social interactions as hostile intentions, which in turn leads to retaliation (Feindler, 1995; Kassinove & Sudhodolsky, 1995). These individuals often feel that anger is justified, have no knowledge of alternative emotions other than anger, and believe that anger is an acceptable response (DiGuiseppe, 1995). In addition, angry people have an external orientation to the source of anger and believe, "I would be fine if he (she) didn't make me mad." This view makes it difficult for individuals to accept personal responsibility for their actions and/or reactions (DiGuiseppe). Furthermore, it is the rare student who seeks assistance for his or her anger. Instead, students generally seek out the counselor not because they want to change their behavior but, rather, to change the behavior of others who make them angry; or they are forced to seek treatment by authority figures (DiGuiseppe) without an investment in changing.

When an individual is angry, thoughts, feelings, and physical responses occur that cause changes in the endocrine, cardiovascular, and skeletal muscular physiological systems (Feindler, 1990, as cited in Feindler, 1995). These changes increase heart rate, breathing, muscle tension, and skin temperature. These responses are responsible for emotional blockage associated with neurotransmitters (Zajonc, 1985, as cited in Kassinove & Sukhodolsky, 1995) and erroneous affect labeling. Since youth are inclined to label any situation that creates physiological arousal as hostility as opposed to other emotions such as sadness, fear, guilt, or tension (Kassinove & Sukhodolsky), anger-reduction techniques focus on reframing social information processing situations. The following exercise may be used to help students assess and process responses to anger. Students can be presented with a situation that may produce anger, discuss typical responses, and then discuss alternative prosocial behaviors.

Exercise

Situation 1

You have been anticipating prom for a long time. Your dress is beautiful, you bought new shoes, and you have a hair appointment with the best stylist in town. You feel so lucky that the "best looking, most popular guy" in school has asked you to be his date. The phone rings and it is your prom date telling you that he is really sorry but he won't be able to take you to the dance that weekend. He gives no additional explanation and says, "Maybe I'll see you around." What would you do? How do you feel? What are you thinking? What are your physiological reactions?

Feelings	Physical Response
_____Feel relieved	_____Rapid heart rate
_____Feel hurt	_____Tense up
_____Feel happy	_____Feel hot
_____Feel mad	_____Start to cry
_____Other	_____Tired
Behavior	**Thinking**
_____Yell and scream	_____Think you deserve it
_____Run away	_____Think he is getting to you
_____Start hitting things	_____Think you hate him
_____Talk it over	_____Think there is a good reason
_____Immobile	_____Think about getting even

Situation 2

You are excited about a summer job that became available, a position you had been hoping would open up. You tell your best friend about the job, and that friend applies and is hired for the job you wanted. What would you do? How do you feel? What are you thinking? What are your physiological responses?

Feelings	Physical Response
_____Feel relieved	_____Rapid heart rate
_____Feel hurt	_____Tense up
_____Feel happy	_____Feel hot
_____Feel mad	_____Start to cry
_____Other	_____Tired
Behavior	**Thinking**
_____Yell and scream	_____Think you deserve it
_____Run away	_____Think he is getting to you
_____Start hitting things	_____Think you hate him
_____Talk it over	_____Think there is a good reason
_____Immobile	_____Think about getting even

Counselors may also choose to incorporate feeling "as if" exercises for students to practice alternative ways of behaving. For instance, actors and actresses trained in the Stanislavsky Method are asked to think and behave "as if" they are angry, sad, happy, and so on. Counselors can adapt this strategy in their work with youth. If making an angry expression prompts one to feel angry, then counselors can work with students in acting the exact opposite way by smiling and acting happy as substitutions for more appropriate ways of behaving (Kassinove & Sukhodolsky, 1995).

Cognitive restructuring techniques in which one's irrational, negative beliefs are restructured are effective with children and adolescents (McWhirter et al., 1998). The following exercise can be used with children and adolescents. Youth are instructed to write down their irrational thoughts and to think about changing these unconstructive thoughts into positive thoughts.

Exercise

Harmful Thoughts of Student ⟶	**Positive Thoughts**
This is going to be awful.	I can handle it.
He is trying to make me look bad.	No one can make me look bad.
I am such an idiot and I never get things right.	I got an A in math class.
____________________	____________________
____________________	____________________
____________________	____________________

Recognizing and changing harmful thoughts into constructive thoughts assist students to think about a new way of behaving and feeling.

Finally, self-monitoring techniques allow for a continuous recording of anger triggers accompanying cognitive, affective, behavioral, and physiological responses. One such monitoring method is an "anger log" that provides a rich source of data as the basis for counseling sessions. Box 10.4, Anger Log, can be adapted for use with students.

Empathy Building

Empathic, perspective-taking situations in which there are no clear-cut answers invite students to gain insight, develop personal problem-solving skills, advance reasoning skills, and understand another's perspective (Buckley, 2000; Goldstein & Glick, 1987). The following open-ended dilemmas are examples that may be used in a discussion for feeling identification associated with empathy building.

BOX 10.4 Anger Log (Copy as Needed)

Anger Log

When did it happen?
_____ Morning
_____ Afternoon
_____ Evening

Where did it happen?
_____ Classroom
_____ Hallway
_____ Cafeteria
_____ Home
_____ Restroom
_____ On the job
_____ With a friend
_____ After-school activity

What happened?
_____ Someone took something of mine.
_____ Somebody told me to do something.
_____ Someone was being mean.
_____ I did something to someone.
_____ Other

Who else was involved?
_____ Another student
_____ Teacher
_____ Parent
_____ Another adult
_____ Brother
_____ Sister
_____ Other

How did you react?
_____ Clenched fists
_____ Increased heart rate
_____ Sweaty palms
_____ Shaky legs
_____ Rapid breathing
_____ Change of voice
_____ Other

What did you think?
_____ Someone is making me mad.
_____ Someone thinks I'm stupid.
_____ Someone is hurting my feelings.
_____ Other

How did you do?
_____ I didn't control my anger.
_____ I need improvement.
_____ I did a good job.

Anger Log

When did it happen?
_____ Morning
_____ Afternoon
_____ Evening

Where did it happen?
_____ Classroom
_____ Hallway
_____ Cafeteria
_____ Home
_____ Restroom
_____ On the job
_____ With a friend
_____ After-school activity

What happened?
_____ Someone took something of mine.
_____ Somebody told me to do something.
_____ Someone was being mean.
_____ I did something to someone.
_____ Other

Who else was involved?
_____ Another student
_____ Teacher
_____ Parent
_____ Another adult
_____ Brother
_____ Sister
_____ Other

How did you react?
_____ Clenched fists
_____ Increased heart rate
_____ Sweaty palms
_____ Shaky legs
_____ Rapid breathing
_____ Change of voice
_____ Other

What did you think?
_____ Someone is making me mad.
_____ Someone thinks I'm stupid.
_____ Someone is hurting my feelings.
_____ Other

How did you do?
_____ I didn't control my anger.
_____ I need improvement.
_____ I did a good job.

Theresa knows that her best friend, Maria, has been shoplifting from several stores in the local mall. Theresa knows that Maria has already been caught once, warned, and told that if she is caught again that she will spend some time in the juvenile detention center. On one shopping spree Maria takes an expensive watch and places it inside Theresa's purse when Theresa is not looking. When they walk out of the store, the alarm sounds and they are apprehended by store security. When security checks their purchases Maria has receipts for everything, but they find the stolen watch in Theresa's purse. If Theresa confesses that Maria placed the watch in her purse, she knows that her best friend will go to the detention center. However, if she confesses that she lifted the item, she will just have a record and be placed on probation but her friend will be able to go home.

What should Theresa do? Why?

What if Maria were not her best friend? Should this make a difference?

Should a friend take the punishment for a friend? Why or why not?

What should Maria do?

How do you think Theresa feels?

How do you think Maria feels?

Zeke and Amanda had been dating for several months and were spending Saturday evening at Amanda's house watching videos. Suddenly, two local gang members broke into the house and held the couple at knife point. One of the gang members took a switch blade and cut a small line across the young man's neck drawing a ribbon of blood. The gang members said that they would let him go if he would leave the girl to them.

What should Zeke do?

What do you think Zeke is feeling?

What should Amanda do?

What is Amanda feeling?

If Zeke and Amanda weren't in a serious relationship, should it make a difference in his decision?

Relaxation

Relaxation reduces stress and anxiety by decreasing muscle tension. Children can take responsibility for recognizing and managing tension as a self-management tool whenever they experience physiological signs of stress. For example, exercises such as the following are easily taught to children so that they are rehearsed in other settings.

Exercise

Imagine you are squeezing a tennis ball in your hand. Squeeze as hard as you can, harder, now even harder. Now, pretend that you drop the ball. Notice how different your hands feel. Now, pretend you are picking up the ball again. Squeeze even harder. Hold it for just 5 seconds, and count "one, two, three, four, five." Now drop the ball, and again notice the difference.

In Conclusion

Prevention and intervention are only a few considerations to help prevent violence from entering the schools. Intervention and prevention programs that aim at social-cognitive, anger management techniques, and empathy building have produced positive results (Shure & Spivack, 1988, as cited in McWhirter et al., 1998) when incorporated in a developmental, comprehensive school counseling curriculum.

SCHOOL-BASED CRITICAL INCIDENT MANAGEMENT PROGRAMS

Since no school is immune from a critical incident entering the lives of school-aged youth, preparation is essential for alleviating the negative consequences when they do occur. Charles Andrew Williams, charged with the deadly shooting at Santana High School located near San Diego, had reportedly told others about his plans for violence. Not one person took him seriously (CNN, 2001). Since violence is not always an impulsive action but, rather, the result of careful planning, violent acts can be prevented (Daniels, 2002) and the school can be prepared when disaster strikes.

Crimes and violence occur in schools or on school grounds (Jenkins, 1997, as cited in Sandhu et al., 2000). Crisis plans designed, implemented, and rehearsed in the same manner as tornado or fire drills can mitigate the negative psychological effects that too often disrupt students' growth (Nims, 2000). Although many states have legislated school districts to have a crisis plan in place, many have given only cursory attention to the directive by highlighting rudimentary procedures in a manual that is placed on a shelf to be forgotten until a crisis occurs. Some school districts argue that having a plan in place promotes the idea that a crisis is imminent and needlessly frightens children; others state that it is a community security concern rather than an educational issue; and still others reveal that they do not have the resources or the time to delve into a critical incident plan (Nims). An effective crisis intervention plan includes the following components: training and planning, responding, debriefing and defusing, and evaluating.

Training and Planning for a Crisis

A school crisis response needs a board-approved delivery system that includes written policies of what to do when a crisis occurs, physical resources to carry out the policy, and trained personnel to implement the plan. Initially, a needs assessment will determine what the school faculty/staff and community members need in the way of training. A clear plan for dealing with potentially violent behavior is established so that personnel are confident as to what is going to happen, when procedures take place, who is responsible for parts of the plan, and how evaluative strategies will occur. When a crisis is of such magnitude that local staff are overwhelmed or devastated because of personal involvement, a planned program should include external support prior to the occurrence of a crisis (James & Gilliland, 2001).

Links between school crisis intervention teams and the community are not always well established, but these connections will increase the chances of successful referral and normalization following a traumatic event. Therefore, the response planning committee should be composed of two teams (Guthrie, 1992). One team is communitywide representing a cross section of social services and government institutions. The second is a school response team representing a cross section of personnel within the school such as teachers, administrators, school counselors, custodians, secretaries, and bus drivers. Careful consideration should be given to team composition, people, and roles, including a duplication of roles, because if the media liaison is a principal who is being held hostage, someone else needs to be familiar with that role. Part of the design is to include individuals who are recognized with an appropriate level of training to prevent unknown volunteers whose training level is uncertain from arriving at the school unannounced.

The crisis intervention coordinator is often the school counselor who has a clear understanding of the objectives and methods of the crisis intervention plan and is able to deal with a variety of crises that range from individual suicides to natural and human disasters. Other crisis team roles include a media liaison, a community/medical liaison, and a parent liaison.

Media Liaison Media cannot be excluded from the crisis planning. One designated role is to keep relationships with the media positive and to determine what and how information is to be shared. The worst possible scenario is to allow a randomly selected individual to talk with the media because false information may be provided. Oftentimes, reporters wish to talk with students. Instead of allowing reporters to interview the first student out of the building, a student (usually a student leader) should be chosen ahead of time and parent/guardian permission obtained to speak with the media in the event a critical incident occurs. If the student is unable to answer some of the questions, the designated media liaison can be available to assist with the interview. Furthermore, it is helpful to obtain the fax numbers of the media since phone lines may be disrupted and/or cell phones may not receive a clear transmission. An additional task for the media monitor is to oversee national and local news to determine areas of misinformation, concern, and community reactions.

Community/Medical Liaison Links with local emergency, fire, medical, and mental health systems are essential for the plan to succeed. This community/medical liaison is to have advance knowledge of the building to interpret the plans to emergency personnel called to the scene.

Parent Liaison Parents need to be kept provided with information, support, facts of the incident, information as to the signs children exhibit when undergoing stress, how to communicate with their children and adolescents, and referral resources if their child needs additional assistance. Moreover, translators to assist parents who do not speak English as a first language are helpful resources.

Physical Requirements A great deal of rescheduling and shuffling of rooms and assignments will be necessary, and alternate buildings such as churches may need to be used if hazardous conditions exist within the school building. Additional phone lines, supplies, and furniture are considerations. Furthermore, message boards are needed, and food and drink should be provided or arrangements made for delivery on site. Box 10.5 has sample guidelines that school personnel may choose to adapt.

Frequent in-service sessions that are updated on a regular basis are necessary for the plan to succeed. Immediacy of response is built into the plan for a greater chance of a favorable outcome. For instance, if a situation occurs on a Friday night, waiting until Monday morning to respond is too much of a time delay. Responsive services are most effective when they are provided at the time and place of the crisis, when they are flexible, and when they are ready and where they are needed. This could include morning, evening, or weekends. Personnel services provided at a school familiar to students and parents are more likely to be utilized than those provided at an unfamiliar agency.

Responding

When news of a crisis that involves students outside of the school such as a suicide, accident, or murder, the principal or a designated person gathers the information and verifies the facts with the police. A calling tree established in advance notifies faculty and staff as soon as possible; a crisis response team meeting is held to determine the impact of the crisis on the school; and a meeting of faculty and staff is arranged.

At the faculty and staff meeting, information will be shared with the school personnel, questions answered, and a list of characteristics associated with stress distributed for identifying students displaying these signs and symptoms (Guthrie, 1992). Teachers are requested to allow classroom time for open dialogue and expressions of grief. Crisis team members will be assigned rooms, a debriefing room available for the crisis workers, and a "drop-in" room designated for students who need additional assistance. One crisis plan goal is to return the school to a state of normalcy as quickly as possible, and one way of facilitating this objective is to have school counselors in their own offices so that students know where to find them. Furthermore, a common student reaction is to leave school and go home immediately upon hearing of a tragic incident. This request will only permit students to go home to an empty house without a support system and should be discouraged even if parental permission is granted.

BOX 10.5 Guidelines for Crisis Intervention Team

Components of Plan

A. Training and planning

B. Responding

C. Debriefing and defusing

D. Evaluating

Training and Planning Sessions

Who should be a member of the school-based crisis team?

Name **Title** **Phone Number** **Assignment**

(Principal) ____________________

(Counselor) ____________________

(Teachers 3–5 who work well with students in crisis) ____________________

Who should be a member of the community-based crisis team?

Media Source **Contact Person** **Phone** **Fax**

Radio/TV/Newspaper ____________________

Ambulance ____________________

Police ____________________

Mental Health Professionals ____________________

Others ____________________

What should be the tasks of the crisis team members?

- Designate person to gather personal effects of deceased. ____________________
- Designate person to contact family. ____________________
- Designate person to communicate with media (usually central office person).____________________
- Designate person to communicate with other schools that have relatives, close friends, or teammates of the deceased. ____________________
- Determine central location and supervisor of the "Drop-in Room." (Location) ____________________ (Supervisor) ____________________
- Determine who will keep list of area experts. ____________________
- Determine person to keep calendar of events.____________________
- Determine person to monitor chart lines. ____________________
- Determine media monitor. ____________________
- Determine who can cover classrooms in an emergency. ____________________
- Determine individuals for debriefing.____________________

BOX 10.5 Continued

- Identify one person from crisis team to brief secretaries as to what should be said to family/friends calling for information.____________________
- Identify one person from the crisis team to be responsible for writing and distributing a newsletter to be sent home to parents. ____________________

Responding

How will the faculty and staff be informed of the incident?

Verify information.

One person from the crisis team will verify information.

Designated person ____________________

Notify superintendent (phone). ____________________

Notify faculty and auxiliary staff.

Designated person ____________________

Faculty and staff should be informed of

- Nature of crisis
- Time and place of meeting

How will the students be informed of the incident?

- Determine the wording of the announcement to be made to students and staff. "We are sad to learn that _________ of _____ grade, died _________ , due to _________. If you need more information about the funeral, ask your teacher, or your parents may call the school."
- Determine how concerned individuals can refer high-risk students for counseling.

What should be communicated with the school, community, and parents?

Communicating with Faculty and Staff

If the crisis occurs during school, crisis team members may make rounds with information. (Special color-coded paper for written information is suggested.)

If the crisis occurs at the end of the day, call meeting as soon as possible. The following information should be included:

- Update on facts.
- Review possible reactions of students.
- Review how to respond to students.
- Review signs of students at risk.
- Inform faculty and staff of grieving/counseling rooms available for students and how to transport students to this area.
- Inform faculty and staff of grieving rooms for themselves.

continued

BOX 10.5 Guidelines for Crisis Intervention Team *(continued)*

- Discuss the written statement to be read to their students.
- Inform faculty and staff that an information sheet will be distributed to parents.

Communicating with Parents

The following information may be included in the newsletter to parents:

- Facts of the event
- Procedure for allowing students to leave school
- Time of funeral and procedure for students attendance
- Ways to help their child to cope with the crisis situation
- List of available support groups in the area
- Time and place of parents' meeting (if scheduled)

Debriefing and Defusing

Debriefing and defusing designed to assist people in returning to normalcy.

Who will debrief faculty and staff?

- Identify individuals who will present the defusing meeting. ____________________
- Determine how the meetings will be organized. ____________________
- Identify a room for the meetings to be held. ____________________

Evaluation

How often should a crisis plan be evaluated?

The crisis plan should be reviewed following the tragedy. Feedback from both the community and school are important.

The crisis plan should be reviewed at least once a year with the faculty and staff.

At the end of the day, a *triage* is conducted to determine which individuals are most directly affected by the crisis and which are only indirectly affected. It is not to be assumed that just relatives, survivors, witnesses to the event, and close friends are those who will need immediate help; individuals just hearing about the event may be rendered immobile (James & Gilliland, 2001). School counselors are particularly vulnerable as they listen to the pain of others, often without the luxury of having someone available to care for their needs. School personnel who have a close relationship with any of the identified students can be requested to make a contact to determine individual needs.

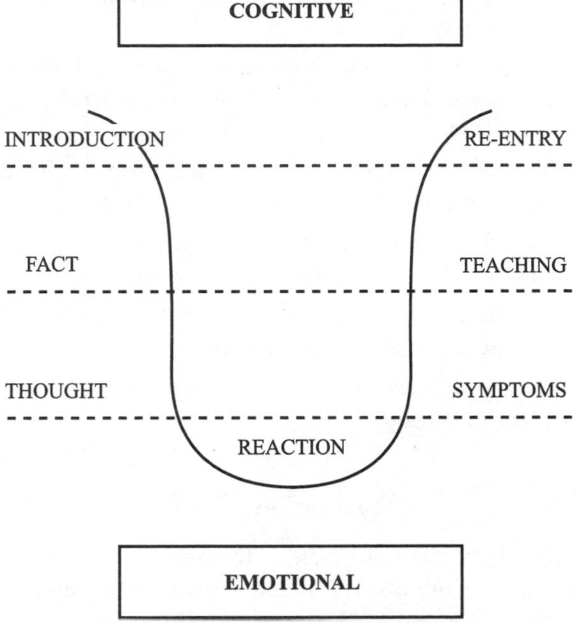

FIGURE 10.3 A critical incident stress defusing and debriefing model (CISD)

Note. From Mitchell, J. T., & Everly, G. S. (2003). *Critical Incident Stress Management (CISM): Basic group crisis, intervention* (3rd ed). Ellicott City, MD: International Critical Incident Stress Foundation. Reprinted with permission.

Debriefing and Defusing

Critical incident stress debriefing and the shortened version, defusing, are used to buffer the psychological effects of the trauma for the individuals involved in the devastating event (Mitchell & Everly, 1998). Defusing, a three-stage process implemented immediately following the crisis, is shorter in length (1 hour) and more flexible. The purpose of defusing is to eliminate or to strengthen a formal debriefing. The process includes seven stages that fluctuate from a cognitive phase to an emotional process and then back to a cognitive orientation (Mitchell & Everly). The debriefing occurs within 72 hours of the event and takes approximately 2 to 3 hours to implement. The stages of this model, which is illustrated in Figure 10.3, include the introduction, fact, thought, reaction, symptoms, teaching, and re-entry phases (Mitchell & Everly).

Stage 1: Introduction. The leader is to explain the process, inform the participants of confidentiality, and ask for questions.

Stage 2: Fact. In a methodical "go around," each participant is to introduce him or herself, state what role they had in the incident, and state the facts of the incident from his or her view.

Stage 3: Thought. Once again the leader systematically asks each member about his or her thoughts about the incident or what first occurred to him or her when the event occurred.

Stage 4: Reaction. The leader asks members to reveal the worst part of the experience and what continues to be most difficult for them.

Stage 5: Symptom. Participants share the affective, cognitive, behavioral, or physiological symptoms they are experiencing as a result of the incident.

Stage 6: Teaching. This phase provides the opportunity for members to share the strategies used to cope successfully with the stress.

Stage 7: Re-Entry. Participants may bring up new material, issues, or questions that may occur prior to leaving.

Evaluation

At some point in the future the crisis team is to meet to evaluate and revise the effectiveness of the plan. A "fish bowl" technique may be implemented in which two concentric circles are arranged. The community team members sit in the center circle and discuss the plan success and areas of improvement while the school team members, who are seated on the outside circle, listen and take notes. After a period of time the team members switch places, and the school team members discuss their concerns while the community team members listen and take notes. Plans are revised accordingly and reviewed several times throughout the school year.

SUMMARY

This chapter summarizes characteristics of individuals who may be expressing distress, strategies for assisting these individuals, and a crisis management plan schools may adapt for their own situation. A school crisis in any school district, building, or classroom is inevitable. We can no longer "wait and see" if a crisis will occur; schools are to be ready for any eventuality. Because it is sometimes difficult to identify students who may display violent behaviors, school counselors are pivotal individuals who assist in the identification of at-risk individuals and provide prevention and intervention so that all students can be equipped to handle crises when they occur.

REFERENCES

Aguilera, D. C. (1990). *Crisis intervention: Theory and methodology* (7th ed.). St. Louis, MO: Mosby.

Aguilera, D. C. (1998). *Crisis intervention: Theory and methodology* (8th ed.). St. Louis, MO: Mosby.

Alberti, R. E. (Speaker). (1986). *Making yourself heard: A guide to assertive relationships* (Cassette Recording No. 29532). New York: BMA Audio Cassette.

Austin, S. (2003). Multiple lessons from multiple suicides. *ASCA School Counselor, 41,* 22–27.

Bauer, A. L. (2000). Violence prevention: A systematic approach. In D. S. Sandhu & C. B. Aspy (Eds.), *Violence in American schools: A practical guide for counselors* (pp. 139–152). Alexandria, VA: American Counseling Association.

Beauvais, F. (1996). Trends in drug use among American Indian students and dropouts, 1975–1994. *American Journal of Public Health, 86,* 1594–1598.

Breland, A. M. (2000). The "true" perpetrators of violence. The effects of the media on public perceptions of youthful violent offenders. In D. S. Sandu & C. B. Aspy (Eds.), *Violence in American schools: A practical guide for counselors* (pp. 109–120). Alexandria, VA: American Counseling Association.

Brown, L. K., Overholser, J., Spirito, A., & Fritz, G. K. (1991). The correlates of planning in adolescent suicide attempts. *Journal of the American Academy of Child and Adolescent Psychiatry, 30,* 95–99.

Buckley, M. A. (2000). Cognitive-developmental considerations in violence prevention and intervention. *Professional School Counseling, 4,* 60–70.

CNN. (2001, March 8). *An epidemic of violence.* Retrieved April 6, 2001, from http://www.cnn.com/2001/us/03/08/alarming.incidents/index.html

Cole, D. E., Protinsky, H. O., & Cross, L. H. (1992). An empirical investigation of adolescent suicidal ideation. *Adolescence, 27,* 813–818.

D'Andrea, M., & Daniels, J. (1996). Promoting peace in our schools: Developmental, preventive, and multicultural considerations. *The School Counselor, 44,* 55–63.

Daniels, J. A. (2002). Assessing threats of school violence: Implications for counselors. *Journal of Counseling and Development, 80,* 215–218.

DiGuiseppe, R. (1995). Anger disorders: Basic science and practice issues. In H. Kassinove (Ed.), *Anger disorders: Definition, diagnosis, and treatment* (pp. 1–26). Philadelphia, PA: Taylor & Francis.

Feindler, E. L. (1995). Ideal treatment package for children and adolescents with anger disorders. In H. Kassinove (Ed.), *Anger disorders: Definition, diagnosis, and treatment* (pp. 173–195). Philadelphia, PA: Taylor & Francis.

Gay, Lesbian, and Straight Education Network. (2001). *Do words hurt? A guide for discussing Eminem and the Grammys with students.* New York: Author.

Goldstein, A. P., & Glick, B. (1987). *Aggression replacement training.* Champaign, IL: Research Press.

Guthrie, S. (1992). Crisis intervention teaming: A participant's perspective. *The School Counselor, 40,* 73–76.

Henry, C. S., Stephenson, A. L., Hanson, M. F., & Hargett, W. (1993). Adolescent suicide and families: An ecological approach. *Adolesence, 28,* 291–308.

Ibrahim, F. A., & Tran, P. (2000). School violence: An ecological, social, and cultural perspective. In Sandhu & Aspy (Eds.), *Violence in American schools: A practical guide for counselors* (pp. 167–183). Alexandria, VA: American Counseling Association.

James, R. K., & Gilliland, B. E. (2001). *Crisis intervention strategies* (4th ed.). Belmont, CA: Wadsworth/Thomson Learning.

Johnson, D. W., & Johnson, R. T. (1995). *Teaching students to be peacemakers* (3rd ed.). Edina, MN: Interactive Book.

Johnson, K. (1989). *Trauma in the lives of children.* Alameda, CA: Hunter House.

Kanel, K. (1999). *A guide to crisis intervention.* Pacific Grove, CA: Brooks/Cole.

Kassinove, H., & Sukhodolsky, D. G. (1995). Anger disorders: Basic science and practice issues. In H. Kassinove (Ed.), *Anger disorders: Definition, diagnosis, and treatment* (pp. 1–26). Philadelphia, PA: Taylor & Francis.

Larson, J. (1994). Violence prevention in the schools: A review of selected programs and procedures. *School Psychology Review, 23* (2), 151–164.

Levy, J. (1989). Conflict resolution in elementary and secondary education. *Mediation Quarterly, 7,* 73–87.

McBride, H. E. A., & Siegel, L. C. (1997). Learning disabilities and adolescent suicide. *Journal of Learning Disabilities, 30,* 652–659.

McFarland, W. P. (1998). Gay, lesbian, and bisexual student suicide. *Professional School Counseling, 1,* 26–29.

McWhirter, J. J., McWhirter, B. T., McWhirter, A. M., & McWhirter, E. H. (1998). *At-risk youth: A comprehensive response.* Pacific Grove, CA: Brooks/Cole.

Mitchell, J. T., & Everly, G. S. (1998). *Critical stress management: The basic course workbook* (2nd ed.). Ellicott City, MD: International Critical Incident Stress Foundation, Inc.

Nims, D. R. (2000). Violence in our schools: A national crisis. In D. S. Sandhu & C. B Aspy (Eds.), *Violence in American schools: A practical guide for counselors* (pp. 3–20). Alexandria, VA: American Counseling Association.

Reinherz, H. Z., Giaconia, R. H., Silverman, A. B., & Friedman, A. (1995). Early psychosocial risks for adolescent suicidal ideation and attempts. *Journal of the Academy of Child and Adolescent Psychiatry, 34,* 599–611.

Sandhu, D. S., Underwood, J. R., & Sandhu, V. S. (2000). Psychocultural profiles of violent students: Prevention and intervention strategies. In D. S. Sandhu & C. B. Aspy (Eds.), *Violence in American schools: A practical guide for counselors* (pp. 21–41). Alexandria, VA: American Counseling Association.

Santrock, J. W. (1996). *Adolescence.* Dubuque, IA: Brown & Benchmark.

Schrumpt, F., Crawford, D., & Udadel, H. C. (1991). *Peer mediation: Conflict resolution in schools.* Champaign, IL: Research Press.

Short, R. J., & Talley, R. C. (1997). Rethinking psychology and the schools: Implications of recent national policy. *American Psychologist, 52,* 234–240.

Takaka-Matsumi, J. (1995). Cross-cultural perspectives on anger. In H. Kassinove (Ed.), *Anger disorders: Definition, diagnosis, and treatment* (pp. 81–108). Philadelphia, PA: Taylor & Francis.

Wagner, B. M., Cole R. E., & Schwartzman, P. (1995). Psychosocial correlates of suicide attempts among junior and senior high school youth. *Suicide and Life Threatening Behavior, 25,* 358–372.

Wyatt, V. H. (2000). A social ecology approach to violence in American schools. In D. S. Sandhu & C. B. Aspy (Eds.), *Violence in American schools: A practical guide for counselors* (pp. 43–64). Alexandria, VA: American Counseling Association.

11

The School Counselor and Family Partnership

As a school counselor, I realized how much of my time was consumed with parents wishing to talk with me about the difficulties they were experiencing with their son or daughter. At the same time, more students were talking with me about their home lives that could only be characterized as chaotic and tumultuous. When more of my time was being spent calling parents in the evening, I recognized that if my day hours were extended into the evening hours, I would be able to meet face to face with more parents.

When I spoke with my building principal about the feasibility of rearranging my daytime hours for evening hours 2 days a week, the principal was reluctant since this was an unusual request that did not fit into the regular school schedule. It did not occur to me until later that perhaps the results of my request would have been different if I had taken the time to provide data about successful family programs implemented in schools.

It has long been acknowledged that a strong relationship between parents and/or guardians and the school assists in student success. Research has repeatedly pointed out that family dynamics are significant factors in the academic and personal growth of children and adolescents. In fact, most data reveal that the family influences school achievement more than school variables (Hinkle & Wells, 1995). School counselors are key individuals to work with families, appreciate the effectiveness of counseling interventions with families, and promote family involvement in schools.

Because the families of today are as diverse as is our society, and the structures far removed from the traditional two-parent family, this group of individuals is difficult to define (Hall, 2003). The school and the family are two distinct but interconnected systems, each with the responsibility of educating and socializing youth (Edwards & Foster, 1995). Students will benefit when these two institutions collaborate.

School counselors have traditionally worked from an individual counseling approach that required large amounts of time and little discernible improvement (Hinkle, 1993). Because change is uncomfortable, family members persist in behaviors that are familiar, constant, and predictable, even if these behaviors are a problem. In the 1980s and 1990s, *systems* or *interactional theory* began to attract the interest of professionals as a way of working with school-aged youth (Sexton, 1994). The systems approach to working with children emphasizes that when a child's problems persist despite interventions, the problems are related to family interactions and counselors can intervene before additional problems occur (Hinkle). Ineffective counseling strategies are apparent when a school counselor assists a child without consideration of the family influence on the problem behaviors and (Davis, 2001; Kraus, 1998); and, likewise, students not coping within the school find it difficult to manage within their family system (Aliotti, 1992, as cited in Hinkle & Wells, 1995; Lewis, 1996). When a child's problems continue and specific school-related causes have been eliminated, it is wise to include the family and school in a partnership (Hinkle). When school counselors pay insufficient attention to the influence of families on academic and/or behavioral problems, there is the risk of implementing inappropriate or even counterproductive interventions.

It is not my intention to propose that school counselors work with families therapeutically. School counselors do not typically provide family counseling because generally they have not received the necessary training for in-depth family counseling. Nevertheless, by keeping a systems approach in mind when working with a child, the school counselor initiates problem solving and change within the family. If administrators and school board members believe that family counseling provided by school counselors is an essential component to fulfill school goals, scheduling, training, time, political support, and money are considerations in meeting this need.

FORMING A PARTNERSHIP

School counselors do not have the luxury of extended time to work with families. Therefore, brief interventions are recommended. The interventions can be used in a parent-counselor conference or in limited individual counseling meetings. Golden (1998) suggests that families may be more receptive to meeting with the school counselor if the contacts are referred to as a *consultation,* with the understanding there will be no more than five *conferences* (not *sessions* due to the connotation associated with counseling and therapy). If the problem is more extensive and pathological, then an alternative option such as an outside referral is needed. If a referral is made, the school counselor may show support by attending the first session with the family (Hinkle, 1993). As in all counseling approaches, culture needs to be respected and honored, particularly when a strong focus is placed on the hierarchical structure and roles of extended family members within the Asian, African, and Hispanic American cultures (Davis, 2001).

Before working with families, self-reflection about one's own personal beliefs, values, and behaviors provides insight about family influences on your personal life. The following self-reflection exercise is designed to provide an opportunity to think about your family of origin and the influence of this system on your life.

Exercise

1. Take a moment to reflect on a time in your life in your family of origin that you wish to explore.
2. Once you have identified this period of time, try to recall each of the following:
   a. Who was living in the household at the time? Ages?
   b. What kinds of family interactions were common?
   c. How close or distant were parents and siblings?
   d. Was there conflict between any family members?
3. Write each person's name and an adjective that describes that person. Be sure to include yourself.
4. Reflect on the rules and boundaries in the household.
5. How is your family life now different or similar to this period of time you are recalling?

After reflecting on your family of origin, think in terms of the traits exhibited in your family. A list of common characteristics found in healthy families is found in the following chart. Check the traits that were evident in your family of origin and in your family today.

Traits of Healthy Families			
Sense of fun together		Willingness to work through conflicts productively	
Encourages and supports one another		Cooperative relationship	
Respectful attitude		Expresses anger appropriately	
Talks about feelings		Willingness to negotiate and compromise	
Equality among males and females		Celebration of positive events	
Freedom to make mistakes		Honesty among members	
Respectful of privacy behavior		Known consequences for inappropriate	

Note. Adapted with permission from Hinkle, J. S., & Wells, M. E. (1995). *Family Counseling in the Schools.* Greensboro, NC: ERIC/CASS.

THE PROCESS

Counselors and teachers have come to appreciate the enormous influence of the family on the student's behavior. Parents and/or guardians are not always aware of their enormous impact on their child's educational accomplishments. When the goals of the educational institution and the family are similar, the child will benefit. When the goals are incompatible, the child may face social, emotional, and educational difficulties (Widerman & Widerman, 1995). Parent/guardian resistance is a predictable natural emotional reaction to the helping process due to: (a) negative experiences they may have had with the school (Campbell, 1993), (b) defensiveness in that parents/guardians feel they are to blame when their child is in trouble, (c) only being summoned to the school when their child is in trouble, (d) negative past experiences as a student, or (e) the work schedules of the parents/guardians (Evans & Hines, 1997). Resistance may be lessened when parents are contacted for positive events or behaviors (Edwards & Foster, 1995). Initiation of the process, assessment, interventions, and termination guide the parent/guardian partnership.

Initiation of the Process

A phone call initiated either by the counselor or parent/guardian is generally the first contact between the two institutions (Haley, 1987, as cited in Widerman & Widerman, 1995). From the moment this contact occurs, change is already happening. The counselor will begin to formulate a hypothesis as to what the problem is, who is involved, and what information is available through the school records, teachers, coaches, and so on. The family members are already making decisions about the problem and what they will or will not reveal. It is not unusual for parents/guardians to arrive at the school without an appointment, making advanced planning impossible. But, valuable information is still obtained through observation of the parents'/guardians' interactions, attitudes, and behaviors (Widerman & Widerman). Negative attitudes that the parents/guardians and school have of each other may obstruct the counseling session; or, based on past negative school experiences, caregivers may enter the school with hostile attitudes. Altering these long-standing beliefs is a challenge for the school counselor. Listening, validating experiences, and allowing time for parents/guardians to vent their frustrations help create a caring partnership (Davis, 2001). In addition, the counselor's acknowledgment that the parents/guardians are the experts of their child (Aponte, 1976, as cited in Edwards & Foster, 1995) and a valuable resource may ease the tension and enhance the relationship. The informational sheet in Box 11.1 assists in documentation and tracking family interventions and progress.

Assessment

A main task of the school counselor is to observe and assess the ability of the family to change, recognize how family members define the problem, and identify family strengths. The acronym TRACE assists with the assessment (Golden, 1998):

BOX 11.1 Tracking Family Interventions and Progress

Contact Information Sheet

Date ______________________

Student's name ______________________________________ Age __________

Grade ______________________ Homeroom teacher ______________________

Name of contact person ______________________________________

Phone number ______________________________________

Reason for contact _______________ Teacher _______________ Child _______________ Principal _______________ Coach _______________ Family member_______________ Other

Lives with: Biological parents __________ Guardians __________ Parent/Step-parent __________

Other __________

Marital status of caregiver ____________________

Family structure (check members who are in the home)

____ Biological father (name)______________________________ Age __________

____ Step-father (name) ______________________________ Age __________

____ Biological mother (name) ______________________________ Age __________

____ Step-mother (name) ______________________________ Age __________

_____ Guardian (name) ______________________________ Age __________

Relationship to child ______________________________________

____ Other adult (name) ______________________________ Age __________

Relationship to child ______________________________ Age __________

______ Grandfather ______________________________ Age __________

______ Grandmother ______________________________ Age __________

______ Brother ______________________________ Age __________

______________________________ Age __________

_______ Sister ______________________________ Age __________

______________________________ Age __________

_______ Others in home ______________________________ Age __________

______________________________ Age __________

_______ Siblings not in home ______________________________ Age __________

______________________________ Age __________

_______ Others in home ______________________________ Age __________

_______ Others not in home ______________________________ Age __________

Notes: ____

____

____

Note: Source unknown.

Team: Are the caregivers and counselor able to work together as a team in which goals and strategies are mutually agreed upon? Are the caregivers motivated to follow through on suggestions and strategies?

Resources: Is the family able to take care of the needs of their child? Do parents/guardians have adequate, effective coping skills with a capacity to make changes?

Authority: Do parents/guardians have adequate parenting skills so that they have control of their children? Are rules understood with consequences for breaking these rules?

Communication: Can all family members communicate and express concerns in a healthy manner? Are members' views respected?

Extent of problem: When did the problem begin? Has it been an issue for awhile, or is the problem a reflection of a transitional phase? How has it affected each family member?

The school counselor's main task is to support educational concerns and academic progress. Therefore, these issues are to be addressed first, followed by other issues impacting the child's educational performance. At times, a school-related problem is resolved when all individuals recognize a problem exists and all individuals are motivated to resolve the issue. Finding a common goal is assisted by asking each family member the following questions:

1. Would you like to tell me why you are here today?
2. What do you see as the difficulty?
3. When did the problem begin?
4. How did the problem start?
5. How have you been affected by the problem?
6. How have you dealt with the problem?
7. What has worked effectively?
8. Who do you think talks the most in the family?
9. Who do you think talks the least?
10. Do you find it easy to talk about your feelings in the family?
11. What do you do together as a family?
12. When was the last time the family spent time together?

During the meetings the counselor provides interventions to assist in problem solving, and between conferences homework assignments are suggested for the family to try. A creative approach designed by Downing (1983) provides caregivers with a homework intervention for gathering information and observing their child's positive behaviors rather than focusing on negative responses (see Table 11.1).

Table 11.1 Parent Observation Form

Behavior I Like	My Response to This Behavior	Behavior That Is Acceptable	My Response to This Behavior	Behavior That Needs to Change	My Response to This Behavior	Behavior That Is Unacceptable	My Response to This Behavior

Interventions

School counselors have successfully used the following interventions with families.

- *Reframing.* Parents or guardians often come to counseling because of their negative view of their child's behavior. For example, a caregiver's presenting concern may be, "My child is lazy" or "My child is disrespectful." Productive change is difficult with these negative perceptions. These harsh labels can be reframed by the counselor to (a) avoid pathological connotations, (b) normalize the characteristic, (c) allow people to see the situation from a different paradigm, (d) look at the behavior as having a positive purpose (Hinkle & Wells, 1995), or (e) work toward cooperative means (Carns & Carns, 1997). Change is possible when a positive connotation is assigned to a negative label (Andolfi, 1979). For example, parents/guardians who state that their child is "withdrawn" might look at the problem differently if this label were reframed to "likes to be by him or herself." Or, a child who is labeled as "impulsive" may be perceived differently if relabeled as "acting before thinking of consequences." The following exercise provides an example of reframing.

Exercise

The following labels are commonly used to describe the behavior of youth. Look at these labels and reframe the term with a more positive, acceptable term.

Delinquent	Depressed	Hyperactive	Defensive	Anxious
Loner	Rebellious	Apathetic	Resistant	Angry
Shy	Unfriendly	Complainer	Worrier	Unconfident

- *Enactment.* Enactment is the process by which the counselor teaches new communication patterns. The counselor may direct the family to interact with each other differently, direct the parent/guardian to converse with the child in another way, or ask a child to sit apart from his or her overinvolved parent/guardian (Kemenoff, Jachimczyk, & Fussner, 1999).
- *Sculpting.* Family sculpting is a creative, active, nonverbal technique in which each family member provides a representation of his or her perception of the family relationships, interactions, and position within the family system (Andolfi, 1979). This technique is most successful when all members of the family are present and each family member is physically placed in a position according to the perceptions of the "sculptor." A school counselor can adapt this technique by providing miniature figurines that represent family members. The child is asked to choose a figurine that represents a family member and to physically place each of the figures according to his or her view of the family dynamics. For example, the sculptor who feels isolated

Family Sculpting Using Figurines

from the family may place the figurine representing him or herself facing away from the family. A brother who is viewed as the "ideal" son may be placed next to the parents/guardian, and a younger sibling who has formed an alliance with the "ideal" child may be placed next to him. Participants communicate their thoughts and feelings regarding the placement of each family member after finishing the sculpture. Finally, the counselor can ask the child or parent/guardian to position the family members as they would like each family member to look at some point in the future (Andolfi).

- *Acting and Reflecting "As If."* Adlerian psychology uses the technique of acting "as if," a technique in which the student is asked to begin acting as if he or she is the ideal person he or she would like to be (Watts, 2003). The following exercises provide adaptations of this technique.

Exercise

The school counselor asks the child and parent/guardian to think about the ideal family and how each family member would be interacting (Watts, 2003). The counselor asks the following questions to aid the process:

1. If you were acting like the ideal family member, what would you be doing differently? How would the other family members interact?

2. If I were to see you 6 months from now, how would you be acting differently?
3. What would be some of the signs that the family is acting in the way you would like them to be behaving?

The parents/guardian and child can select one or two behaviors to practice during the week.

Exercise

1. Choose an aspect of your life that you would like to improve. It could be work, family, friends, or so on.
2. Think of an ideal person in this aspect of your life.
3. Visualize what this person would be doing, saying, thinking, and so on.
4. Role-play this ideal individual for a brief period.
5. What was this experience like for you?

Termination

When the conferences have ended, it is critical for the counselor to assess the progress the family members have made. If a homework assignment or suggestion was not followed or did not achieve the desired results, it is important to discuss the reasons it was unsuccessful. Telephone calls, e-mails, letters, and periodic follow-up meetings are all methods to stay connected after the family conferences have ended (Bilynsky & Vernaglia, 1999).

CONSIDERATIONS FOR A SUCCESSFUL PARTNERSHIP

There are many compelling reasons for assisting children and adolescents using interactional approaches. At the same time, there are many reasons for the reluctance of practitioners to work with families in the school: (a) educators are often viewed as public servants, and parents/guardians sometimes have difficulty accepting the guidance and directives of a counselor in the school (Whitaker & Bumberry, 1988, as cited in Cerio, 1997); (b) the extended family system can sabotage counseling by persisting in the view that the problem belongs to the child rather than to the family; (c) many school counselors do not feel comfortable with a systems approach and have not had appropriate training (Cerio; Hinkle & Wells, 1995); and (d) administrators and policy makers may believe that the school counselors need to be in attendance during regular school hours (Carlson & Sincavagae, 1987, as cited in Hinkle & Wells). For this approach to be successful, a belief in its effectiveness is necessary for sufficient support in terms of money, time, scheduling, and accommodations.

The school counselor is a key individual to initiate, promote, and deliver family/parenting education (ASCA, 2003). The role the school counselor plays in fulfilling this position varies according to the needs, resources, and political climate of the educational community. Counselors have designed and implemented successful psychoeducational programs and collaborative interventions for parents and guardians within schools across the nation.

PSYCHOEDUCATIONAL INTERVENTIONS

Psychoeducational strategies can be adapted to any family in any setting. Educational training can be delivered to families—individually or in groups—and covers a wide variety of topics such as parenting, changing family structures, developmental issues of children, or concerns of children and adolescents in divorced-parent homes. Families with younger children may require more of a "hands-on" training, while families with older children may prefer a more instructional, interpersonal method. Psychoeducational interventions are time-limited with goals and objectives identified ahead of time and evaluated for effectiveness.

With all the many tasks counselors perform, why would counselors agree to take on additional duties? Not only are counselors natural helpers, but counselor-led programs can supplement already existing curricula to prove program effectiveness. Moreover, counselors have an ethical obligation to work with students and their families (Benshoff & Alexander, 1993) and counselors can design and implement these programs by recruiting interested parents.

Parenting Education

In one North Texas School District, an educational program was implemented to determine whether parents are able to assist counselors in leading psychoeducational groups for other parents in the community (Kottman & Wilborn, 1992). Sixteen parents were trained to serve as leaders of parenting groups for parents of elementary-aged students. Intensive 2-hour, 6-week training sessions were conducted that covered Adlerian parenting strategies, basic counseling skills, and group dynamics. Instructional activities included role play, listening activities, demonstration and modeling, and discussion from the selected text. Following the training, the parents were partnered and placed in eight elementary schools to train other parents. The results revealed that the parents who participated had significantly different attitudes toward their children; and because parents were effective leaders, counselors were available to perform other duties.

Sexuality Education

Research reports that both students and parents/guardians want the primary caregiver to be the primary source of sex education (Sanders & Mullis, 1988, as cited in Benshoff & Alexander, 1993). Yet, caregivers are either unwilling or unable to provide this information to their children. A program entitled Family Communication Project (FCP) was designed with elementary and middle-school counselors serving as project trainers to help interested parents and children improve communication about sexuality. Results showed increases in participants' knowledge and ability to communicate about sexual issues (Benshoff & Alexander).

Filial Education

Filial education is another psychoeducational strategy that teaches communication skills and improves parent/guardian and child relationships. Filial education is used to teach parents how to read the child's language through play (Thompson, Rudolph, & Henderson, 2004). Filial education is designed to

1. Reduce children's problem behaviors by teaching parents/guardians how children communicate through their play
2. Assist parents to learn and apply new ways of communicating (Skills surrounding limit setting, active listening, building self-esteem, and reflection of feelings are all interpersonal skills used by counselors and applicable to good parenting.)
3. Improve the parent-child relationship (Thompson et al.), particularly when the child is encouraged to express him or herself freely and the parents are taught new ways of responding,

In one school the counselor taught skills in groups of six to eight parents of children under the age of 10. The parents/guardians learned how to connect to their child through verbalizations and to acknowledge the child's thoughts, feelings, and desires (Stollack, 1982). Following the training, play sessions were conducted in the home, and follow-up educational sessions provided an opportunity for the parents to discuss their experiences and to receive feedback from the counselor. Child and caregiver interactions changed as a result of the consistency in playtime and time spent between the parent/guardian and child (Stollack).

Career and Academic Development

School counselors are in the unique position to assist parents and children in career and academic concerns. Students' academic and career goals and the caregiver/child relationship may be enhanced when the families are provided assistance in decision making that is respectful of the family culture and values (Hall, 2003). In some instances, a student's career choice is one that disrupts family beliefs. School counselors provide academic and career counseling to students that maximizes the student's potential without creating more tension or stress in the home.

COLLABORATIVE PARTNERSHIPS

Comprehensive services that commonly combine health care, day-care programs, tutoring, and parent education and provide opportunities for parents and children are becoming more common in today's schools (Porter, Epp, & Bryant, 2000). In fact, some studies predict that family centers will be housed in schools of the future (Cetron, as cited in Peeks, 1993). Too often social services, medical professionals, and other helpers provide help to families with little coordination and much duplication of services (Downing, Pierce, & Woodruff, 1993). Collaborative teaming addresses learning barriers and educational needs of parents, strengthens ties between the school and community, and contributes to the growth of youth (Taylor & Adelman, 2000). School counselors are ideal leaders to coordinate these interconnections with other helping professionals and programs in a school-based setting (Keys, 2000).

As agents of school reform, school counselors can smooth the delivery of services by communicating with school administrators and teachers and closely supervising and coordinating the services of the team professionals (Bemak, 2000) without program redundancy.

SUMMARY

Traditionally, school counselors have worked with students from an individual counseling approach. Rarely is the school counselor able to intervene successfully in the lives of students without consideration of the systems that influence the student's life. Systems theory began to attract the attention of counselors as a viable method of working with youth and their families. Counselors in the school, although not typically trained in a systems approach to assisting others, have more success in problem solving and change when a partnership is formed between the counselor and the child's family with consideration of systems theory concepts.

Although counselors do not have the time to work with families extensively, limited consultations using basic systems concepts have been successful in school settings. In forming a partnership the counselor is to acknowledge that resistance may be common among parents and/or guardians. With basic attending and listening skills and by acknowledging the position of the parents/guardians, a workable, respectful alliance is possible and cooperation is created.

School counselors are first and foremost responsible for the academic growth of their students. Therefore, academic issues are to be discussed first, and other issues can be addressed later. Family interactions, beliefs, and behaviors provide an opportunity for assessment and formulating strategies for intervention. Reframing, enactment, sculpting, and acting "as if" are just a few of the interventions counselors can implement to bring about change. Psychoeducational programs including parenting, sexuality education, career development, and filial education are a few of the many programs counselors have implemented to connect the relationships between the family and the school. Furthermore, collaborative strategies with the school counselor as the coordinator of these programs are projected to be a common venture for schools of the future. Counselors are key individuals to provide education, collaboration, and consultation to assist parents; and when parents connect with the school, measurable gains in student growth are realized.

REFERENCES

Andolfi, M. (1979). *Family therapy: An interactional approach.* New York: Plenum Press.

ASCA. (2003). *Family Education Position Statement.* Alexandria, VA: Author.

Bemak, F. (2000). Transforming the role of the counselor to provide leadership in educational reform through collaboration. *Professional School Counseling, 3,* 323–331.

Benshoff, J. M., & Alexander, S. J. (1993). The family communication project: Fostering parent-child communication about sexuality. *Elementary School Guidance and Counseling, 27,* 288–300.

Bilynsky, N. S., & Vernaglia, E. R. (1999). Identifying and working with dysfunctional families. *Professional School Counseling, 2,* 305–313.

Campbell, C. (1993). Strategies for reducing parent resistance to consultation in the schools. *Elementary School Guidance and Counseling, 28,* 83–91.

Carns, A. W., & Carns, M. R. (1997). A systems approach to school counseling. *The School Counselor, 44,* 218–223.

Cashwell, C. S., & Vacc, N. A. (1996). Family functioning and risk behaviors: Influences on adolescent delinquency. *The School Counselor, 44,* 105–114.

Cerio, J. (1997). School phobia: A family systems approach. *Elementary School Guidance and Counseling, 31,* 180–191.

Davis, K. M. (2001). Structural-strategic family counseling: A case study in elementary school counseling. *Professional School Counseling, 4,* 180–185.

Downing, J. (1983). A positive way to help families. *Elementary School Guidance & Counseling, 17,* 208–213.

Downing, J., Pierce, K. A., & Woodruff, D. (1993). A community network for helping families. *The School Counselor, 41,* 102–108.

Edwards, D. L., & Foster, M. A. (1995). Uniting the family and school systems: A process of empowering the school counselor. *The School Counselor, 42,* 277–282.

Evans, J. E., & Hines, P. L. (1997). Lunch with school counselors: Reaching parents through their workplace. *Professional School Counseling, 1,* 45–47.

Golden, L. B. (1998). *Case studies in child and adolescent counseling* (2nd ed.). Upper Saddle River, NJ: Merrill.

Hall, A. S. (2003). Expanding academic and career self-efficacy: A family systems framework. *Journal of Counseling and Development, 81,* 33–39.

Hinkle, J. S. (1993). Revolutions in counseling and education: A systems perspective in the schools. *Elementary School Guidance and Counseling, 27,* 252–257.

Hinkle, J. S., & Wells, M. E. (1995). *Family counseling in the schools.* Greensboro, NC: ERIC/CASS.

Kemenoff, Jachimczyk, & Fussner, (1999). Structural family therapy. In D. M. Lawson & F. F. Prevatt (Eds.), *Casebook in family therapy.* Pacific Grove, CA: Brooks/Cole.

Keys, S. G. (2000). Living the collaborative role: Voices from the field. *Professional School Counseling, 3,* 332–338.

Kottman, T., & Wilborn, B. L. (1992). Parents helping parents: Multiplying the counselor's effectiveness. *The School Counselor, 40,* 10–14.

Kraus, I. (1998). A fresh look at school counseling: A family systems approach. *Professional School Counseling, 4,* 12–17.

Lewis, W. (1996). A proposal for initiating family counseling interventions by school counselors. *The School Counselor, 44,* 93–99.

Peeks, B. (1993). Revolutions in counseling and education: A systems perspective in the schools. *Elementary School Guidance and Counseling, 27,* 245–251.

Porter, G., Epp, L., & Bryant, S. (2000). Collaboration among mental health professionals: A necessity not a luxury. *Professional School Counselor, 3,* 315–322.

Sexton, T. L. (1994). Systemic thinking in a linear world: Issues in the application of interactional counseling. *Journal of Counseling and Development, 72,* 249–259.

Stollack, G. E. (1982). Elaborations and extensions of filial therapy. In E. T. Nickerson & K. B. O'Laughlin (Eds.), *Helping through action: Action-oriented therapies* (pp. 237–242). Amherst, MA: Human Resource Development Press.

Taylor, L., & Adelman, H. S. (2000). Connecting schools, families, and communities. *Professional School Counseling, 3,* 298–307.

Thompson, C. L., Rudolph, L. B., & Henderson, D. (2004). *Counseling children.* Belmont, CA: Brooks/Cole.

Watts, R. E. (2003). Reflecting "as if": An integrative process in couples counseling. *The Family Journal, 11,* 73–75.

Widerman, J. L., & Widerman, E. (1995). Family systems-oriented school counseling. *The School Counselor, 43,* 66–73.

12

Planning and Implementing Group Work in the Schools

Tabitha Devlin is a school counselor at a junior high school. Mrs. Devlin is aware of groups in schools that were formed to increase group members' self-esteem and were associated with increased student members' academic performance. She was hoping that the group she would form would have similar results. After she identified eight students who were interested in being part of the group, she made a schedule, received parental permission, designed activities, and was ready to begin. From the beginning, the students were motivated and excited about participating in the group, but gradually their attendance slacked off. When Tabitha spoke with them about their nonattendance, the students replied that their teachers refused to release them from class to attend the group. Tabitha spoke to the teachers, who responded, "We can't allow the students to miss class because they would miss out on important information that would hurt their performance on state standardized tests."

Mrs. Devlin was frustrated and disheartened because she knew how this type of group could benefit youth, but she was unable to convince the teachers that this type of group would also help students perform better in class.

How can school counselors convince others of the advantage of groups and how this method assists in student growth? How can school counselors work around the issues that most concern teachers?

Although most counselor education programs require a separate course on group work, this chapter provides vital information for school counselors to consider when using groups in the educational setting. In addition, this chapter includes helpful strategies for counselors to convince their various constituents as to how teachers, as well as the students, will benefit from group work in a school setting, and procedures for sharing students' time with teachers.

WHAT IS A GROUP?

A *group* is a collection of two or more individuals who meet face-to-face, with mutual awareness that each is a group member participating to achieve consensual group goals (Johnson & Johnson, 1994, as cited in Gladding, 1999) and personal goals.

Group work first emerged following World War II when there was a shortage of trained therapists and increasing numbers of returning veterans who needed assistance (Capuzzi & Gross, 1998; Posthuma, 2002). New counseling methods were needed to close this gap in services and needs. Dr. Carl Rogers and his colleagues were asked to create a brief intensive course to teach counselors strategies to connect with larger numbers of veterans than could be reached through individual counseling. Interestingly, at this time many had a suspicious view of group work since it was believed to be a form of brainwashing and thought control inspired by Communist dogma (Rogers, 1970). However, by the 1950s, group work was viewed more favorably (Posthuma). Teachers had the responsibility of conducting group work during homeroom, commonly referred to as the "guidance hour," with themes that centered on personal and vocational concerns. In time, group counseling replaced group guidance as an approach for improving attitudes and behavior in the educational setting (Gladding, 1999).

Groups continued to proliferate in the 1960s and 1970s and became more popular and accepted as a way of working with individuals (Terres & Larrabee, 1985). As stated by Rogers (1970) ". . . [A group], in my judgment, is the most rapidly spreading social invention of the century, and probably the most potent— an invention that goes by many names." Interestingly, despite the advantages of groups, this methodology still remains controversial even into the 21st century.

PURPOSES OF GROUPS

A lack of formal research on the positive aspects of groups, poorly trained leaders, and the emergence of questionable groups with controversial goals and purposes led to inaccurate beliefs about group work with school-aged youth. It cannot be assumed that all groups are good for all children, nor is it the treatment of choice for all students (Terres & Larrabee, 1985). Yet, groups can provide several benefits:

1. Groups are more time-effective than individual counseling since they reach a greater number of students (Gladding, 1999; Posthuma, 2002). Peers are influential in the lives of their peers in that they share common problems and often serve as excellent providers of feedback and support that may not be available in individual counseling (Trotzer, 1989).
2. Students sometimes find it easier to share feelings, concerns, attitudes, and beliefs with peers than with a counselor in an individual session. Each group member can observe the problems, coping skills, and attitudes of others and use this information as a gauge for comparing self with others.

3. Since the group is a reflection of the attitudes, values, and behaviors of society, members feel a sense of belonging. In a supportive environment, new behaviors may be attempted and transferred to the outside world with the encouragement and confirmation of the group members.
4. Children and adolescents gain new information when personal sharing is understood and feedback is provided by more than one person. The group member may choose to ignore or deny feedback given by one individual, but information consistently given by several members tends to be taken more seriously.

The main purpose of counseling, whether individual or group, is to bring about change through personal awareness. Through active participation, members acquire new attitudes, values, skills, and behaviors as they interact with others. Despite positive characteristics and satisfying outcomes, counselors have been hesitant to use this method of reaching youth (Schnedeker, 1991) in part due to the

- confusion as to the various types of groups,
- lack of support for group work by administrators, and
- attitudes toward the dubious groups birthed in the 1960s with questionable practices and leadership.

Yet, group work is endorsed and encouraged by the ASCA. As stated in the *American School Counselor Association Position on Group Counseling* (2002), "Every school district and every institution of higher learning should include and support the group counseling concept as an integral part of a comprehensive developmental guidance and counseling program."

TYPES OF GROUPS

The various types of groups are categorized as task, guidance/psychoeducational, counseling, or psychotherapy groups. All but psychotherapy groups are utilized effectively in K–12 schools.

Task/Work Groups

Task or work groups are also referred to as task forces, committees, or planning groups. Regardless of the title, task/work groups include normally functioning individuals who work together on a common issue. These groups do not focus on changing individuals but, rather, focus on interacting collaboratively to discuss and resolve a concern. Task/work groups work best with less than 12 people (Gladding, 1999).

Example of a task/work group Task/work group was formed in a suburban middle school in upstate New York with the purpose of obtaining student perceptions of the school climate. Students were administered the *Survey of School Climates Questionnaire,* reactions were assessed, and strategies were developed for improving the school environment (Goldberg & Chandler, 1992). Other examples of task groups implemented in schools include groups formed for the development of a new student orientation, for tutoring, or for planning a career day.

Guidance/Psychoeducational Groups

Guidance or psychoeducational groups were originally developed for educational settings with the purpose of presenting information to group members. Group members, in turn, could apply this knowledge to developmental and/or situational issues that would be faced in the future (Gladding, 1999).

The size of these groups varies across settings from a self-contained classroom to a large lecture hall, but a range of from 20 to 40 individuals is common. Discussion and skill practice are most valuable in small groups of 10 adolescent or adult members, with fewer numbers for groups of children. These groups are most helpful when there is a regular meeting time such as once a week. Common themes in school psychoeducational/guidance groups involve teaching coping skills and supplying information that facilitates an understanding of self and others, such as dealing with an interpersonal crisis, or transitional issues such as leaving for college, moving away from parents, or preparing for the work world.

Example of a Guidance Group A group guidance model was conducted with underachieving, low self-esteem, junior-high-school students. Twelve lessons were developed and delivered in English class by two counselors who met with the students twice a week. Lessons included such topics as the development of organizational skills, study skills, evaluating academic performance, peer pressure as related to social and academic problems, and future concerns. Students who wished to continue instruction with the counselors were given the option to participate in an additional counseling group outside of the class (Schnedeker, 1991) to further enhance self-esteem and academics.

Example of a Psychoeducational Group An alcohol and drug prevention psychoeducational training program called Project BASIC Training was developed for school mental health workers. These individuals were provided with information on the identification, prevention, and intervention of students involved with alcohol and drugs. This 8-hour training session consisted of experiential learning, role playing, supervision, homework assignments, and sensitivity training for assisting Mexican American students. The evaluation of this psychoeducational group revealed greater knowledge of methodology and improvement in participants' clinical skills (Mason, 1996).

Another psychoeducational group was used to help fifth-grade students prepare for the transition to middle school. The counselors capitalized on peer influences to provide information and to practice skill building for a smoother move into a new school with different rules, procedures, faculty, and expectations (Akos & Martin, 2003).

BOX 12.1 Request for Classroom Guidance or Small Group Counseling (Circle One)

Teacher ______________________________ Grade ____________________ Room ______________

Topic requested ____

Best class period ____

Best date/day of week ____

Names of students for small group counseling ____

Counseling Groups

Counseling groups are preventive, growth enhancing, and remedial in nature. Group counseling participants are generally experiencing problems that are interfering in same aspect of their lives. Since counseling groups are formed around a specific issue rather than a general concern, group members usually share similarities. A counseling group for children from homes in which there has been a parental divorce can assist students in coping with such topics as myths surrounding divorce, common feelings youth experience when parents divorce, games parents play, assertiveness skills, and communication skills. Other common topics are developmental or situational issues such as adjustment to school, eating disorders, or relationship issues (Gladding, 1999).

Example of a Counseling Group A counseling group was formed at an elementary school with the purpose of promoting peer relationships. Participants were a diverse group of children, from members displaying deficiencies in social skills to students who were skilled in interpersonal relations, and role models. The group met for 8 weeks for a half hour each week and covered the specific skills of inviting, sharing and cooperating, participating, conversing, giving information, asking questions, smiling, complimenting, and joining—skills deemed important to satisfying peer relationships. An evaluation following the group revealed improved peer relationships (Mehaffey & Sandberg, 1992).

Psychotherapy Groups

Psychotherapy groups are normally found in a mental health facility with the goal of remediating psychological problems or reconstructing major personality characteristics (Capuzzi & Gross, 1998; Trotzer, 1989). The duration of the group is measured in months or years, and the group is led by a mental health expert who has training in assisting people with severe emotional problems. School counselors do not normally have the training or the time to lead these groups in the schools.

Teachers and students are great sources of information for topics to be addressed in group work. Box 12.1 contains a request that a counselor can use to gather information on the type of group to conduct.

GROUP STAGES AND CHARACTERISTICS

Regardless of the type of group implemented in the school, it is important to note that the members' maturity and verbal ability may facilitate or debilitate the group process (Vernon, 1999). Since groups do not always progress in a consistent linear fashion, it is common to shift from earlier to later stages and sometimes back again. Within each stage, individual members may also be at different stages due to differences in trust, acceptance, and responsibility. Open groups are particularly susceptible to rapid recyling due to the fluctuating membership (Trotzer, 1989). The various group stages include: pregroup, initial, transition, working, and termination.

Pregroup Stage

Group membership is often considered as the most vital element influencing group success (Bergin, 1999). Some individuals may respond better to group work than others. For example, some individuals may be so disruptive that the entire group process is jeopardized. Therefore, even though the counselor may believe that he or she knows students well because of previous contacts (Terres & Larrabee, 1985), it is important for the counselor to have an individual pregroup meeting with each prospective member. This session is to determine the individual's motivation to set individual goals and to assist in helping other members reach their goals (Vernon, 1999). This is also the ideal opportunity to discuss the purposes of the group; group logistics such as meeting time, place, and group schedule; and group expectations such as attendance and confidentiality. Also, during this interview the prospective member will be asked to establish a personal goal that he or she would like to accomplish as a group participant. Putting the personal goal in writing often leads to a greater commitment to achieve the goal (Corey, 2000).

Confusion often exists among school counselors as to whether or not parent or guardian permission needs to be obtained for a child or adolescent to participate in group work. According to the ASCA position statement, "providing written information about the school counseling program is essential to legal functioning of the professional school counselor. A full understanding of the relationship and process tends to increase the sense of trust between the counselor, student, and parents. School counselors obtain parental permission for service according to local law or policy" (ASCA, 1999). School counselors should provide parents with written information regarding their services and an explanation of limits to confidentiality. In fact, holding an orientation session for parents supplements the written information and provides an opportunity to discuss the benefits of group work (Vernon, 1999). Or, attending a PTA meeting and discussing group work may also generate interest, support, and enthusiasm for this strategy for working with students. An example of an informed consent form is shown in Box 12.2.

BOX 12.2 Informed Consent for Group Participation

Dear Parent or Guardian,

Being an adolescent today is difficult. In order to help our teens learn better ways of dealing with life's difficulties, I am running a group on social skills for any student who is interested in participating. We will be covering topics such as assertiveness, coping with anger, relaxation, communication skills, refusal skills, and self-esteem issues.

What is the group like? The beginning sessions will be spent getting to know each of the group members. As trust between members develops, common problems and reasons for joining the group will be discussed. All the information that is discussed in the group will remain confidential except in the circumstances that a group member reveals that he or she is going to harm him or herself or another person. Each participant will identify one personal goal he or she would like to achieve as a result of being in the group.

How often will the group meet? The group will meet for 9-weeks on a rotating schedule during the length of the grading term. The meetings will be one time a week for 50 minutes at a different time and day each week so that students will not be missing the same class each week.

Who is the group? There will be approximately 8 to 10 students with similar interests and a counselor who will serve as the leader.

Who will lead the group? I have had training in group processes through my graduate work at Harvey University and I will be leading the group.

What are some group topics that have been covered in the past?

Getting along with family

How to study smarter

How to cope with problems

How to choose a career

Friends and relationship

How to express feelings appropriately

Dealing with parents' divorce

If you need additional information regarding this group, please contact me at ______________. Please sign below giving permission for your child to participate in the group.

______________________________ ____________________

(Parent/guardian signature) (Date)

______________________________ ____________________

(Student's signature) (Date)

Orientation/Initial Stage

Ambiguity, anxiety, suspicion, resistance, discomfort, and other emotional reactions characterize the orientation/initial stage (Gladding, 1999; Trotzer, 1989). As in any new situation, commonly asked questions are: "Will people like me?" "Can I fit in with the others?" "Am I going to sound stupid?" "What can I say in the group?" and "Can I really trust others with personal problems?" (Terres & Larrabee, 1985). A variety of behaviors may be seen in response to these concerns. For example, some members may form an alliance with others to feel safe, others may talk too much about inconsequential people and things, and still others may be passive and withdrawn.

Rules, group goals, and confidentiality are discussed to assist members in feeling comfortable and trusting. To establish common ground, icebreakers are used. As members move to deeper levels of interaction, comfort is developed and group cohesiveness allows members to work on personal goals that were set during the pregroup phase (Trotzer, 1989).

The following exercises can be used as icebreakers but may need to be modified to fit the needs or age of the participants.

Exercise

Title:	Pieces of Information
Objective:	To learn something about members in the group
Ages:	7 to adult
Materials:	A roll of toilet paper

Directions

The instructor will instruct each member of the group to tear off as many sheets from the roll of toilet paper as he or she desires. The roll is passed to every group member until all the members have had the opportunity to tear off the tissue sheets. The instructor then tells the members that for every sheet of paper they have torn off they will have to tell one thing about themselves. For example, if a person tore off five sheets of toilet paper, then that person will have to disclose five things about him or herself.

Evaluation

Class participants will share one thing they learned about each group member.

Exercise

Title:	If I Could Be . . .
Objective:	To provide the opportunity for each member to think about who he or she is
Ages:	7 to adult
Materials:	Instruction sheet for leader

Directions

The leader will go around the group and ask each group member to complete the following sentence.

If I could be an animal, I'd be a(n) . . .	because. . . .
If I could be a boat, I'd be a(n) . . .	because. . . .
If I could be any flower, I'd be a(n) . . .	because. . . .
If I could be a color, I'd be . . .	because. . . .
If I could be any person in the world, I'd be . . .	because. . . .
If I could be a country, I'd be . . .	because. . . .
If I could be a street, I'd be . . .	because. . . .
If I could be a car, I'd be a(n) . . .	because. . . .
If I could be an actor/actress, I'd be . . .	because. . . .
If I could be a movie, I'd be . . .	because. . . .

Evaluation

Each person will state one thing he or she learned about him/herself.

Exercise

Title:	A Haiku About Me
Objective:	To learn about group members
Age:	9 to adult
Materials:	Paper and pencil for each member

Directions

A haiku is a Japanese form of poetry divided into three lines. The first and third lines contain five syllables, and the second line contains seven syllables. Using this format, each member is asked to create a haiku that will introduce him or her to the group.

Example

I like to make friends.

Sharing with others is great.

I want to know you.

Evaluation

Each person will go around the group and tell other members what he or she learned.

Movement to the next stage may be either a smooth or bumpy path. Much of the movement depends on how the goals of the previous stage were completed.

Dissatisfaction or Transition Stage

Frustration, conflict, lack of unity, and "testing out" behaviors are commonly seen during this phase because members are not sure of each other, nor are they completely at ease with the leader (Vernon, 1999). Much of the conflict has to do with the discrepancy between what the member wants to have happen and what is actually happening. Members bring to the group preconceived notions as to what the group process is all about based on past experiences with group work, things their peers have told them about groups, and/or portrayals of group work in the media.

Sometimes the leader will step back and allow the group to assume responsibility for the group process, but when this happens members may feel lost, uncertain as to their role, and disappointed that the group is not proceeding as hoped. Questions commonly asked are, "Who is going to direct us?" "What are we supposed to do?" and "What is the purpose of this group?" During this phase members tend to become argumentative, anxious, ambivalent toward the leader, and negative toward the other members. Children express their opposition to leadership through such behaviors as fighting, making noises, moving chairs, and showing disinterest (McClure, Miller, & Russo, 1992). With the group members expressing dissatisfaction, it is not unusual for the counselor to completely discontinue the group altogether. Yet, this situation is often more readily accepted if the leader remembers that dissatisfaction is part of the process and that conflict can actually facilitate group closeness at times. For example, in a 1985 study by Maynard, social conflict among first-grade group members actually assisted in building group cohesion (McClure, Miller, & Russo).

What can the counselor do to alleviate the stress and tension? The leader can remind group members of the group goals and ask each member to reexamine personal goals that he or she has identified. Sometimes participants feel as if they are the only people feeling a certain way. The leader may normalize feelings by discussing the various stages of the group and the common behaviors found in each stage to better understand typical feelings. Additionally, leader modeling of behaviors and responses may also teach group participants acceptable conduct. For instance, members may be taught to change questions into statements that elicit more information about personal perceptions, observations, or feelings. For instance, instead of asking, "Do you like music?" the question can be restated as, "Tell me about the type of music you like."

Since group members are learning to express themselves, the leader can help members distinguish the difference between "I should . . ." statements and "I choose to . . ." statements for the purpose of showing that change is within each member's control.

Another technique for dealing with conflict during this stage includes planning activities that take advantage of group members' energy through physical movement such as stretching, dancing, role-play, or drama. In addition, cooperative problem-solving activities such as deciding on a group name or choosing group rules are also useful in discharging energy (McClure et al., 1992). The leader may consider the following exercise to promote cooperation during this phase.

Exercise

Title:	A Creation of Us
Objective:	To create collaboration and cooperation
Age:	7 to adult
Materials:	Music, recorder, paper, and crayons

Directions

Give a piece of drawing paper to each group member. Each member is asked to turn the paper over and write his or her name on the back. Then ask the members to turn the paper to the front side; and, as music is playing, ask the members to draw whatever they wish. When the music stops they are to pass the drawing to the person on the right. The music is turned back on, and the members begin drawing on the picture in front of them. When the music is stopped, the drawings are again passed to the person on the right until all group members have their original work.

Evaluation

Each member is to share what it felt like to have his or her picture shared with other group members.

Working or Production Stage

The working or production stage is reached when the group goal is addressed and participants help each other reach their personal goals. During this stage, trust is elevated and members feel comfortable self-disclosing and providing feedback to other members. An opportunity exists for the exploration of interpersonal conflicts. Members feel free expressing themselves without seeking permission from the leader; a side benefit is that they are taking responsibility for their own behaviors.

At this stage, the members are now working together with the purpose of accomplishing personal goals and achieving the group task (Corey & Corey, 2002; Trotzer, 1989). Since members are willing to share, confront, encourage, and support new behaviors, practicing these new behaviors outside of the group is encouraged. The following exercise can be implemented in this stage.

Exercise

Title: New Beginnings
Objective: To practice new behaviors outside of the group
Age: 10 to adult
Materials: Cardboard, brads

Directions

A large, sturdy, cardboard wheel can be constructed with eight identified behaviors to practice outside of the group. A sturdy, cardboard arrow is attached to the wheel with a brad to allow for members to spin the wheel. When a member spins the wheel and the arrow lands on a behavior, the member must perform that behavior at least once outside of the group.

Evaluation

Each group member will describe the experience to other group members.

Termination Stage

The termination stage assists members to evaluate their personal progress and choose strategies for continuing their growth outside of the group (Vernon, 1999). Termination is believed to be as important as the initial group stage (Corey & Corey, 2002). Typically, counselors view termination as something that occurs during the final few sessions and pay little attention to the conclusion of each session. It is helpful for the leader to announce that the group is ending approximately 5 to 10 minutes prior to the end of every session; the conclusion may be conducted in numerous ways:

1. The leader summarizes highlights of the group session and personal perceptions of the group members.
2. Each member highlights personal goals and efforts to achieve these goals, what transpired in the group, or personal important insights that occurred within the session.
3. A group discussion of the significance of the group is held as each member comments on the highlights of the session or the group experience.
4. Individuals in dyads share their experiences and reactions to the group session(s).
5. Members take a few minutes to write personal reactions and efforts in achieving goals in their journals. In addition, the leader may wish to provide members with written personal reactions.
6. Incomplete sentences are presented for members to complete. For example:

   One thing I did today to help me reach my goal was. . . .

   One of the highlights of the group was. . . .

   One thing that could have been improved in today's session was. . . .

During termination, members review their personal goals and evaluate whether or not they have been achieved. The counselor encourages members to decide how they want to continue their new behaviors outside of the group. Group members commonly express feelings of loss or sadness since group relationships as a whole are ending. Comments are made such as, "I don't know what I am going to do without the group," "I feel as if you are one of my best friends," or "I hope I can find friends like you outside of the group." Some members, especially those who feel close to the leader, may feel a sense of abandonment (Posthuma, 2002). Usually two to four sessions are focused on termination issues in closed groups (Corey & Corey, 2002).

To help with feelings about termination, the leader may provide an opportunity for students to role-play the newly acquired behaviors with member feedback in anticipation of future events outside of the group (Corey & Corey, 2002; Jacobs, Masson, & Harvill, 2002). An exercise follows that can be utilized during this stage.

Exercise

Title:	A Picture of Me 10 Years in the Future
Objective:	To identify goals and strategies for reaching these goals
Age:	12 to adult
Materials:	Pencil or pen and paper

Directions

The leader is to discuss how goals help us guide our lives. Provide each member with a piece of paper and pencil or pen, and ask them to draw a picture of something they would like to see themselves doing 10 years in the future in the personal, career, family, or academic area. After the picture is complete, ask the members to list activities they need to do to reach this goal.

Evaluation

Each member will discuss his or her goal for the future.

Post-Group Stage

The post-group stage is one that is often overlooked by group leaders but provides a rich opportunity to analyze long-term behavior change and to evaluate the reasons learned behaviors were not continued. Evaluating individual and group experiences is best accomplished after members have had the opportunity to practice their newly acquired behaviors outside of the group. Scheduling a follow-up session is helpful for members to practice newly learned skills; but it should not be too far in the future, or members will not be able to receive member feedback on new behaviors. Gladding (1999) recommends a follow-up session approximately 3 months after the termination of the group. However, in the school setting, the age of the group members, the school calendar, and scheduling considerations will influence the post-group date. When group members are aware that they will be asked to report on progress in the future, they are more likely to take responsibility for continuing with their commitments (Corey, 2000).

An evaluation of the group at termination and again during the post-group session helps to determine whether or not the group experience fulfilled its purpose. If a pretest was administered at the orientation stage to determine attitudes, beliefs, values, and personal concerns, this is an ideal time to administer a similar post-test to assess personal change.

Some group leaders believe another one-on-one, individual follow-up session between the counselor and each group member provides even more feedback. This session can be formal, with structured questions, or informal, with a discussion of how the group helped the group members. The additional benefits of this session are to provide each member with the opportunity to share additional information not disclosed in the group, to show leader concern for each member after the group has ended, and to reveal any additional personal insights of the group experience (Corey, 2000; Corey & Corey, 2002).

TYPES OF EVALUATION

The use of the same instrument for pre- and post-testing provides useful evaluative information, as do teacher baseline scales and scales following the intervention for comparative purposes. Sociometric measures, self-reports, or observation of students in the classroom or playground can also assess group effectiveness (Mehaffey & Sandberg, 1992). Typical evaluative measures are shown in Box 12.3 through Box 12.7.

BOX 12.3 Likert Scales

Some evaluations include questions regarding the facilities and leadership.

Directions
Use the following scale to rate each of the items in the questions that follow the scale:

1 = poor 2 = average 3 = good

1. How did you feel about the group leadership? ______
2. Rate how well the group accomplished its purpose. ______
3. Rate how you feel about the group room accommodations. ______
4. How well do you feel you accomplished your personal goal? ______
5. How well do you feel you can continue fulfilling your goal? ______

BOX 12.4 Open-Ended Questions

Directions
Complete the following sentences.

1. One of the best things about the group was. . . .
2. One of my greatest successes in group was. . . .
3. One thing I wish I had done differently in group was. . . .
4. If I were to be a member of this group again, one thing I would do differently would be. . . .
5. One thing I learned about myself is. . . .

FORMING A GROUP

A critical concern for group success depends on the ability of the school counselor to convince teachers and administrators how groups can support their academic goals and objectives. School counselors work with an impossibly large caseload of students, and group work has the potential to be the future of counseling. Groups are often more powerful and time-effective than individual counseling and can reach more students (Kottler, 2000). This prospect is promising for school counselors, but advocating for group work is difficult since teachers are often reluctant to excuse students from classroom instruction due to the strict curricular standards that must be mastered and competency exams that must be passed. Scheduling, time constraints due to class period length, and selecting appropriate group members are all concerns school counselors encounter when planning for group work (LaFountain, Garner, & Eliason, 1996).

BOX 12.5 Scaling Questionnaire

A scaling questionnaire can be used as a quantitative source of information.

Directions
Circle the number that best describes your feelings.

1. On a scale of 1 to 10 with 1 being the lowest score and 10 being the highest score, circle the number that indicates your feelings about your group experience.

   1 2 3 4 5 6 7 8 9 10

2. Circle the number that indicates how confident you feel about continuing your goal without the group support.

   1 2 3 4 5 6 7 8 9 10

3. Circle the number that indicates how you were feeling about yourself before the group experience.

   1 2 3 4 5 6 7 8 9 10

4. Circle the number that indicates how you are feeling about yourself as a result of the group experience.

   1 2 3 4 5 6 7 8 9 10

BOX 12.6 Pre- or Post-Test

This is an example of how a pre- or post-test may be used to evaluate the effectiveness of a study skills group.

Directions
Put an X in the box that best describes how you feel about your ability in each of the following areas.

		Always	Usually	Sometimes	Never
1.	I am seated and ready to listen when it is time to begin.	1	2	3	4
2.	I am in class regularly.	1	2	3	4
3.	I spend enough time preparing for class assignments/tests.	1	2	3	4
4.	I finish all my assignments.	1	2	3	4
5.	I do my homework.	1	2	3	4
6.	I pay attention in class.	1	2	3	4
7.	I come to class prepared with pencil, textbook, and paper.	1	2	3	4
8.	I listen to and follow directions.	1	2	3	4
9.	I make up my work when I am absent from class.	1	2	3	4
10.	I complete my work on time.	1	2	3	4
11.	My work is organized in my notebook.	1	2	3	4
12.	I have a place to write down my assignments.	1	2	3	4
13.	My classwork and homework are neat.	1	2	3	4
14.	I ask questions when I don't understand something.	1	2	3	4

BOX 12.7 Faces and Feelings

Faces and Feelings can be used for younger children to describe how the group influenced them.

Directions

Draw a face that best describes how you feel about being a new member of this group. (Select a face from those illustrated in the following pretest/post-test.)

Project Respect Pretest/Post-Test Ages 5–7

1. How happy are you with how you are doing with grades and behavior at school?

2. How much do you like yourself?

3. How important do you think you are to your family?

4. How much do you like the way you look?

5. How much do you think you are liked by other children?

6. How happy are you with the way that you behave and cooperate at home?

7. What is the one thing that you do the best?
8. What is one thing that you would like to improve on?

Not all students will react favorably to group counseling because of ethnic and cultural beliefs. For example, Asian American students may be reluctant to disclose personal information for fear of disrespecting the family. Likewise, a Hispanic male may be hesitant to release information that may reflect negatively on his family or masculinity (Baruth & Manning, 2003).

BOX 12.8 Group Survey

Dear ______________________________

Please circle the area you feel is of the greatest concern among students in our school.

Study skills	Drugs and alcohol	Other concerns
Interpersonal relationships	Self-esteem	
Anger management	Test-taking skills	
Tolerance	Anxiety	
Communication	Eating disorders	
Conflict and aggression	Loss and divorce	

Please place this survey in my mailbox. Thanks for your help.

Yours in education,

Mrs. Johnson, Counselor

NUTS AND BOLTS OF GROUP WORK IN SCHOOLS

To gain encouragement and support for group work, a proposal should be presented to faculty, staff, and administration with evidence as to group effectiveness. Other information that is appropriate to share includes group purpose, goals and objectives, and practical considerations.

What Is the Purpose of the Group?

The counselor's task is to enrich the educational mission of the school. Before teachers will be convinced of the group concept, they need to have an understanding of how a counselor-led group can strengthen academics as a whole and augment specific subject objectives. Therefore, a needs assessment to determine an area of focus is the first step in designing and planning a group. This assessment may be distributed to teachers, students, and parents for input. A sample survey that can be modified for specific audiences is shown in Box 12.8.

After the surveys have been tallied and the primary needs identified, the counselor should provide a clear rationale as to the reason this group is necessary. Too often groups are not even launched because they lack a convincing plan and supporting data (Jacobs et al., 2002). Statistics may be obtained from a number of sources: attendance records, discipline reports, counselor referrals, number of parent complaints, report cards, referrals, and so on. Once concrete data have been obtained, an investigation into similar groups that have been successfully conducted assists to

1. learn of possible strategies and activities that have been successful,
2. provide a foundation for group objectives and goals, and
3. reproduce evaluative techniques.

What Are the Group Goals and Objectives?

Without a specific purpose the group will probably break up (Corey & Corey, 2002; Jacobs et al., 2002). Goals and objectives are a reflection of specific group member needs as well as the type of group to be conducted. For instance, in an anger management group, one goal may be to have members identify the people, events, or situations that trigger anger. Objectives are to be measurable, attainable, performed in an identified time period, and evaluated at the group termination. If the group goal is not fully understood, members will lose interest and express this indifference through absenteeism, tardiness, or simply dropping out.

What Practical Considerations Need to Be Taken Into Account?

Meeting Room Think of a time you were in a room that just did not seem quite right for the purpose of the meeting. Was the room too large or too small? Did it influence your ability to express yourself? The meeting room can influence communication and participation and is a particularly vital consideration if members will be involved in activities requiring movement. The room should be easy to locate and accessible to all students; but, at the same time, too much noise created by the activities could disrupt academic classes in progress.

The physical appearance of the room may facilitate or detract from group progress. For instance, I was leading a group in a room that had windows that overlooked the student parking lot and had a door with a window. Students who were not members of the group would often pass by and curiously look in the door window to see what was going on in the room. This compromised confidentiality. At the same time, the parking lot windows were a distraction as group participants were often curious as to who was leaving and entering the parking lot.

Although windows may create distractions, they can also provide a feeling of openness. A windowless room may feel "closed in." Enough space should be considered to organize the group comfortably. Chairs may need to be maneuvered, which may be problematic in rooms in which the chairs are bolted to the floor. A room that is neither too big nor too small is ideal since a large room can detract from feelings of closeness and cohesion, and too small a room can cause members to feel confined. A group organized in one corner of a room with protection on two sides may provide a sense of security for hypervigilant students.

Overcrowded schools often have few available rooms, creating a need to share a room with a faculty member who is not scheduled to use the room at the time the group is meeting. This may create resentment if a faculty member is barred from the room while group is in session. If it is possible to designate a room as a group room, students will know where the group will be meeting on a consistent basis and territorial issues will not develop. A common meeting room is essential for elementary-aged students, in particular, due to their developmental issues.

Seating Arrangements Where people choose to sit is important, and the counselor should pay attention to the participants who consistently sit next to each other. "Best friends" or "enemies" can interfere with group cohesiveness (Bergin, 1999). Therefore, the counselor may consider mixing up the seating arrangement to create interaction with different students during each group meeting to foster the development of trust. Too informal an arrangement sometimes encourages a relaxed behavior that may disrupt the group process. Even providing snacks to the participants may be distracting because members may be more interested in the food available than the group purpose. The use of chairs with hard backs, seating on the floor, or providing "bean-bag" chairs may facilitate group cohesiveness.

Furthermore, sitting in a circle in which chairs are of an equal height encourages and facilitates communication especially without the barrier of a table. However, a table is necessary for task groups due to the working nature of the group.

Sound Confidentiality is a significant variable in making the group work successfully. Schools sometimes do not have walls that protect from noise; and, if members are uncertain how much can be heard outside of the room, sharing information may be avoided. Noise often makes it difficult for members to hear one another or may be distracting. A relatively inexpensive noise filter that masks room sounds is a good investment if there is any question of what can be heard outside of the room.

Duration and Frequency of Sessions The duration of any one session affects the degree to which members become familiar and trusting of one another, as well as their willingness to take risks. As the group comes to an end, it is common for group members who are enjoying a group to try to convince the counselor to extend the number of sessions. This request is particularly persuasive for school counselors, but it is to be avoided. Group members often postpone working on personal issues if the time period is extended; and if the group ending is continually postponed, students may delay working on their goals.

Groups in a school setting are usually dictated by the school calendar. A designated grading period (such as a 9-week grading quarter) and the length of a classroom session are often the gauge by which the sessions will be conducted. Although the classroom period is practical, it is not always the most ideal. Class periods tend to be 45 to 50 minutes in length, and members hardly have time to warm up and work on their goals before the time is up. Yet, time should not be a reason for eliminating group work because much progress can still be made in a short time frame. In some schools, longer sessions are arranged before or after school, or even on weekends, depending on the group purpose and member needs.

BOX 12.9 Classroom Pass/Reminder

Dear ______________________________ Date ______________

______________________________ is scheduled to meet with

______________________________ during your classroom period. Please excuse this student from your class. Any work missed will be completed prior to the next classroom meeting. If you feel that the student needs to remain in class at this time due to activities that cannot be made up, please let the counselor know for attendance purposes. Thank you for your assistance.

____

(Counselor's Name)

Scheduling Since teacher "buy in" to the group is essential for group success, teacher suggestions and feedback are vital. Teachers need to be aware of when the group will be meeting, how often, and the expectations for students. Distributing a list of student participants to the teachers may be perceived as problematic in that group members may feel that this procedure breaks confidentiality. Conversely, others feel that members are protected if the students are aware that their teachers are informed of group participation without revealing the personal nature and proceedings of the group.

The best time to schedule groups is during students' study hall or free time. However, this is not always possible. Teachers feel better about relinquishing a student if the counselor and student are willing to work with the teacher regarding tests that may be missed or assignments that may be late. Clear guidelines are to be established so that the student knows the consequences if work is late or missing. A rotating schedule so that a student will not continually miss the same class is recommended; but with younger students, a constant time and day is preferred for better management of their daily schedule. If the decision is made to provide teachers with the names of group participants, it is helpful to have the student remind the teacher of the class that will be missed prior to the group meeting. A sample classroom pass/reminder is shown in Box 12.9.

Group Composition Based on the purpose of the group, the counselor may have either a *homogeneous* group of students who share similarities or a *heterogeneous* group with a variety of differences to better reflect the outside world. As an example of a homogeneous group, children and adolescents who live in homes with alcoholic parents are more likely to relate to each other and share common concerns than is a student who lives in a home in which alcoholism is not present.

As an example of a heterogeneous group, suppose the school counselor wanted to begin an anger management group. A group of individuals all with anger problems may simply promote additional aggressive responses (Posthuma,

2002). Members who have been selected due to their appropriate manner of handling anger can teach acceptable behaviors to those who display inappropriate anger. Those members serving as role models can work on other personal goals within the group and possibly gain insight as to the reasons some individuals exhibit anger and aggression.

Size Researchers disagree on the number of members to include in a group (Postuma, 2002). Some researchers believe that a group of five to eight members is ideal, yet other groups have been successful with as many as 12 members (Jacobs et al., 2002). Since preschoolers and primary-school students feel natural in play and other activities that allow them to release their boundless energy, small groups of two to four members may be more appropriate (Bergin, 1999). Too large a group may make members feel uncomfortable sharing personal concerns and limit the amount of attention the leader can provide to each individual member. In contrast, a small group may create too much pressure for participation. When children reach elementary and middle-school age, they are better able to communicate; but because of the wide developmental differences, some participants may need additional training in social skills. Therefore, activities for participants to role-play and practice listening skills assist in learning these skills. Adolescents often respond more favorably to group work due to their need for peer acceptance, and group activities provide an environment for feedback and encouragement (Bergin). The group size is determined by the group purpose, age of members, and type of group.

Open Versus Closed Groups Members in an *open group* rotate in and out as the group progresses. Membership in a *closed group* is fixed, and members stay together from the beginning to the end. The type of group will dictate whether or not membership is fixed or flexible. For example, a study skills group in which the counselor instructs students on test taking, following directions, organizing homework, and so on may accommodate an open-group configuration since members may enter and leave based on their needs (Corey & Corey, 2002). The advantage to an open group of this type is that there is an increased opportunity for members to meet new members who can share new ways of studying. However, a closed group would be better suited to individuals working on personal issues such as improving self-esteem, since the introduction of new members at various points may cause the group to recycle to earlier phases without ever reaching the working stage.

Rules Greater trust and security are facilitated by the use of ground rules generated either by the counselor or by the group members at the initial meeting. The rules inform members of their rights, responsibilities within the group, the importance of confidentiality, and consequences if rules are broken. The rules are more meaningful when members place their signature to a written document specifying their agreement to the stated rules. Common rules used in groups are shown in Box 12.10.

BOX 12.10 Sample Group Rules

I agree to

1. Focus on accomplishing personal goals
2. Take turns talking
3. Not interrupt others
4. Not "put down" others
5. Feel free to pass
6. Attend group sessions and be on time

I understand that if I fail to follow the rules, I will be dismissed from the group.

Signature of Group Member ______________________________ Date __________

GROUPS AT VARIOUS AGE/GRADE LEVELS

Many different types of groups have been successfully developed in schools. Group counseling has been effective in working with at-risk students (Becky & Farren, 1997) and has been associated with academic achievement as well as improved interpersonal relationships (Schectman, 1993). The following section summarizes a few of the groups at each grade and age level.

Groups with Primary and Elementary Students

Fourth- and fifth-grade students from an urban public elementary school participated in a group designed to improve the self-concept of children of alcoholics. Students were randomly assigned to either the counseling intervention group or the control group. Control group members were not provided with any treatment but were given the opportunity to receive assistance following the group study. The Piers-Harris Self-Concept Scale was administered to both groups as a pre- and post-test to determine each participant's self-concept. Activities in the experimental (intervention) group included role playing, group discussion, relaxation training, guest speaker presentations, drawing, problem solving, and personal planning using a decision-making model. The study results showed an overall total improvement in self-concept and lower anxiety levels following the group intervention (Riddle, Bergin, & Douzenis, 1997).

In another study, coping strategies were taught to second-grade students. Forty-four second-grade students participated in a teacher-led intervention that focused on teaching relaxation skills and maintaining positive perspectives. Students participated in pre- and post-testing that involved measuring heart rate to determine relaxation, and an assessment of students' positive experiences. Students were given a logbook to record coping strategies, to identify highlights, and to verify heart rates. Four, 15- to 20-minute sessions for 9 consecutive weeks included relaxation activities and concepts about stress and stress control through audiotapes, games, and other activities. Post-test results were significant in that students were able to apply personal highlights and stress-relief skills even after the conclusion of the group (Gilbert & Orlick, 1996).

Groups with Middle-School-Age Students

Students in grades 6, 7, and 8 were referred for tutorial help. Students were placed in either a tutoring-only group or a tutoring-with-counseling group, and students who chose not to participate were placed in a control group in which tutoring was not provided. At the conclusion of the study, the researchers revealed that students who received tutoring combined with counseling scored significantly higher in gains in self-esteem, classroom behavior, and academic achievement (Edmondson & White, 1998).

Groups with Adolescents

Nine African American women in 11th and 12th grades formed a group to discuss feelings and experiences with racism, expectations, relationships, and future goals. The 12 weekly sessions that met for 45 minutes each week were led by two European American leaders. Topics ranged from influential women in the lives of the members to expectations of others, to events and people that made them angry, to relationship concerns, to future goals. The group evaluation indicated that the members found the group to be effective in all areas assessed (Muller, 2000).

SUMMARY

Although the use of groups in the schools is a relatively recent counseling method with positive results, it is still met with skepticism. Without a clear understanding of how groups can assist the academic community, groups may be viewed as acceptable but not necessary. Professional school counselors can assist more students through group intervention but need to be clear about group purposes, personal level of expertise, and group stages. Teachers and other stakeholders need to be convinced that group work will assist in their educational mission and is a viable method in which students' growth will be enhanced. An overview of groups and types of groups implemented in the school setting and activities that can be incorporated within the group phases are included in this chapter.

REFERENCES

Akos, P., & Martin, M. (2003). Transition groups for preparing students for middle school. *Journal for Specialists in Group Work, 28,* 139–154.

American School Counselor Association. (1999). *Professional school counselor and parent consent for services.* Alexandria, VA: Author.

American School Counselor Association. (2002). *Professional school counselor and group counseling.* Alexandria, VA: Author.

Baruth, G. L., & Manning, M. L. (2003). *Multicultural counseling and psychotherapy: A lifespan perspective* (3rd ed.). Upper Saddle River, NJ: Merrill Prentice-Hall.

Becky, D., & Farren, P. M. (1997). Teaching students how to understand and avoid abusive relationships. *The School Counselor, 44,* 303–307.

Bergin, J. J. (1999). Small-group counseling. In A. Vernon (Ed.), *Counseling children and adolescents* (2nd ed.). Denver: Love.

Cappetta, L. K. (1996). The effectiveness of small group counseling for children of divorce. *The School Counselor, 43,* 317–318.

Capuzzi, D., & Gross, D. R. (1998). *Introduction to groups* (2nd ed.). Denver: Love.

Corey, G. (2000). *Theory and practice of group counseling* (5th ed.). Belmont, CA: Wadsworth/Thomson Learning.

Corey, M. S., & Corey, G. (2002). *Groups: Process and practice* (6th ed.). Pacific Grove, CA: Brooks/Cole.

Edmondson, J. H., & White, J. (1998). A tutorial and counseling program. Helping students at risk of dropping out of school. *Professional School Counseling, 1,* 43–47.

Gilbert, J. N., & Orlick, T. (1996). Evaluation of a life skills program with grade two children. *Elementary School Guidance and Counseling, 31,* 139–151.

Gladding, S. T. (1999). *Group work: A counseling specialty* (3rd ed.). Upper Saddle River, NJ: Prentice-Hall.

Goldberg, A. D., & Chandler, T. J. (1992). Academics and athletics in the social world of junior high school students. *The School Counselor, 40,* 40–45.

Jacobs, E. E., Masson, R. L., & Harvill, R. L. (2002). *Group counseling: Strategies and skills.* Pacific Grove, CA: Brooks/Cole.

Kottler, J. A. (2000). *Nuts and bolts of helping.* Boston, MA: Allyn and Bacon.

LaFountain, R. M., Garner, N. E., & Eliason, T. E. (1996). Solution-focused counseling groups: A key for school counselors. *The School Counselor, 43,* 256–267.

Mason, M. J. (1996). Evaluation of an alcohol and other drug use prevention training program for school counselors in a predominantly Mexican American school district. *The School Counselor, 43,* 308–316.

McClure, B. A., Miller, G. A., & Russo, T. J. (1992). Conflict within a children's group: Suggestions for facilitating its expression and resolution stages. *The School Counselor, 39,* 268–272.

Mehaffey, J. I., & Sandberg, S. K. (1992). Conducting social skills training groups with elementary school children. *The School Counselor, 40,* 61–67.

Muller, L. E. (2000). A 12-session, European-American-led counseling group for African-American females. *Professional School Counseling, 3,* 264–269.

Posthuma, B. W. (2002). *Small groups in counseling and therapy: Process and leadership* (4th ed.). Boston: Allyn and Bacon.

Riddle, J., Bergin, J. J., & Douzenis, C. (1997). Effects of group counseling on the self-concept of children of alcoholics. *Elementary School Guidance and Counseling, 31,* 192–203.

Rogers, C. (1970). *Carl Rogers on encounter groups.* New York: Harper & Row.

Schectman, Z. (1993). School adjustment and small-group therapy: An Israeli study. *Journal of Counseling and Development, 72,* 77–81.

Schnedeker, J. A. (1991). Multistage group guidance and counseling for low-achieving students. *The School Counselor, 39,* 47–51.

Terres, C. K., & Larrabee, M. J. (1985). Ethical issues and groupwork with children. *Elementary School Guidance and Counseling, 19,* 190–197.

Trotzer, J. P. (1989). *The counselor and the group: Integrating theory, training and practice* (2nd ed.). Muncie, IN: Accelerated Development Inc.

Vernon, A. (1999). *Counseling children and adolescents* (2nd ed.). Denver: Love.

13

Expressive Arts in Counseling Children and Adolescents

The coursework was over, and now theory was ready to meet reality as Lynn came face to face with her first student in her practicum site. She tried to remember the various theories and specific techniques but was overcome with anxiety as she tried to reconcile her own feelings and concerns for the student sitting in front of her. Lynn was particularly anxious since many of the theories she learned seemed unsuited for younger or nonverbal students.

Most programs that offer credentials for school counselors offer a separate course in counseling theories with a comprehensive knowledge base. This chapter is not intended to substitute for this in-depth information. However, the purpose of this chapter is to provide school counselors with creative counseling strategies that are suited to the developmental level of school-aged children and adolescents since most counseling theories were developed for use with adults and relied primarily on "talk therapy." School counselors do not provide therapy, but they do provide counseling to students. When school counselors make the decision to implement creative counseling techniques, political ramifications are considerations. For instance, *counseling with toys* and *play counseling* are terms that are often preferred by school counselors in explaining their counseling program. These terms are also easily misinterpreted. Therefore, in-service sessions with program stakeholders are helpful for a clear understanding of how these approaches help children and adolescents. Furthermore, data that reveal the effectiveness of these strategies will help convince others that the child goes to the counselor not just to have a good time but to develop and grow through play.

COUNSELING STAGES

Regardless of the counseling theory or strategies counselors choose to use with youth, counseling goes through several stages that include: building a relationship, assessment, intervention, and termination. Assessment during the counseling sessions, and again at some point at termination, assists in determining goal identification and achievement.

Building a Relationship

Establishing rapport and trust, particularly with youth who have been referred by a teacher or parent, is essential during the initial sessions. Since students often express resistance or reluctance when requested to see a counselor, the counselor may explain that creative techniques such as art or play are useful in getting to know one another and are another way of communicating. When a counselor provides creative materials and strategies that are appropriate to the child and allows the child to freely choose the materials, trust may be more readily achieved (Rubin, 1988). Furthermore, consideration of the youth's developmental stage, culture, and the basis for the referral assist in building a relationship (Newsome & Gladding, 2003).

Taking the time to explain what counseling is all about, including the limits of confidentiality, relieves some of the anxiety children and adolescents bring to the counseling session. Simply making statements like, "We have some time to spend together and you can spend it however you wish. What you talk about is between us and stays between us, unless you tell me something that is harmful to you or to someone else. Then I will have to tell someone" (Muro & Kottman, 1995). Sometimes it is helpful to say, "Your mom wanted me to see you because she was concerned about your grades in school. Is her concern something you are worried about too?"

Assessment

Counselors who work in mental health clinics use an intake interview to obtain information about the individual seeking counseling. School counselors typically do not conduct a formal interview but do gather information in other ways. For instance, the school counselor has access to student records, teacher reports, parent concerns, and so on. Information may also be gathered in an informal session using the acronym HELPING. This informal assessment, designed by Keats, is based on Lazarus's multimodal model (Baker, 2000; Schmidt, 1999). The counselor assesses by answering the following questions:

H = Health concerns such as illnesses, hospitalizations, and physical complaints. Is the student missing school?

E = Emotions and feelings. Are emotions appropriately expressed?

L = Learning and school. Do grades match ability?

P = Personal relationships. Who are the significant people in the child's life?

I = Imagery and interests. How does the student see him or herself?

N = Need to know. How well does the student learn?

G = Guidance of acts and behaviors. How well does the student recognize the consequences of responses?

Intervention

A wide range of theoretical approaches for assisting students is available, with no one particular approach more effective than another. Multicultural issues, personality, and developmental level are all considerations in matching appropriate interventions to the needs of the student (Erk, 2004). These factors and the developmental level of the student create difficulty for school counselors in deciding whether to use a cognitive, affective, or behavioral intervention (Gladding, 1992). School counselors have reported that Adlerian counseling approaches, control therapy, cognitive-behavioral, solution-focused, and narrative approaches are most useful with school-aged youth (Schmidt, 1999). Creative techniques that guide the chosen theoretical model serve as the foundation of this chapter. Nevertheless, despite the counseling theory selected, *goal setting* is at the heart of the counseling process (Erk, 2004).

It is not unusual for students to talk with a counselor about several problems they are facing simultaneously. With the many events disrupting the student's life, it is often difficult to focus on the one problem creating the most concern. Counselors working with youth report that shifting the focus from the problem to future possibilities assists in goal identification. Types of questions include, "What would you like to see happen?" or "When is what you want to have happen occurring now in your life?" The use of the *miracle question,* borrowed from solution-focused counseling, assists in viewing life without the problem. For instance, the counselor can ask the student, "Suppose a miracle happened and your problem was solved. What would you be doing differently? Thinking? Feeling?"

Another adaptation of this technique is the use of the *magic wand* or *crystal ball* (DeShazer, 1985). "Suppose I were to wave a magic wand and all your problems were solved. What would you be doing differently?" Or, "Look into the crystal ball and tell me what life is like without the problem." Each of these questions helps to focus the student on what he or she has a desire to have happen.

Termination

Throughout the counseling process, assessment is continually occurring; and when interventions are not providing the desired results, the counselor makes changes. Termination occurs at the end of each counseling session and again when the sessions are over. At the end of each session, the last 5 minutes provide an opportunity for transition between the session and life outside the office door. The student and counselor may use this time to discuss the information that can be shared with parents or teachers. Honoring this request is important, particularly for students who are referred by teachers or parents (Hollis, 1998).

BOX 13.1 Three Affirmations and a Wish

Directions
The counselor writes a note to the student that lists three strengths or attributes the student possesses. Following these positive statements, the counselor concludes with a wish or a desire that he or she has for the student.

To Katie

I have enjoyed getting to know you better. During the time we have spent together I have noticed that

You have motivation to make changes.

You are able to take risks.

You are able to take responsibility for your actions.

My hope for you is that you continue to use the skills you have learned to meet your goal.

Sincerely,

Mrs. Yousaf

Counselors prepare students for termination by reinforcing the progress they have made, asking students to summarize what they have learned, and providing resources that may be useful in the future (Newsome & Gladding, 2003). One counselor found the strategy shown in Box 13.1 particularly affirming for students when terminating counseling.

Termination is often difficult, and the counselor can remind the student that just because the counseling sessions are over the relationship is not, and that the student is invited to return at any point. Sometimes dependency is an issue. The counselor will need to set guidelines if the student is making frequent visits to the counselor's office (Doyle, 1992). In a school setting students generally have a designated number of minutes to pass from each class. I learned a valuable lesson in boundary setting as a new school counselor when the students would unexpectedly "drop in" at my office after the tardy bell rang. It finally occurred to me that these students really did not want to see me; they simply wanted a pass to take to the teacher to excuse them from being tardy to class. Clear procedures for how and when students are able to contact the counselor assist in creating a partnership of trust and respect among personnel.

Determining counseling effectiveness during the sessions and again at termination can be obtained through checklists, self-reports, and scaling methods. At times, counselors find that a second, follow-up assessment at some point in the future is a valuable technique to determine how well the student has continued to apply the lessons learned from the counseling sessions. Constructive information is also received from follow-up letters to the student, reports from teachers, follow-up counseling sessions, or parent reports.

Creative counseling techniques provide an opportunity for school-aged youth to concretely explore who they are, recognize interpersonal relationships, and determine how they would like their lives to be different (Erford, 2003; Muro & Kottman, 1995). Moreover, counselors who use these strategies are able to recognize the student's patterns of behavior, relating, and solving problems. For example, through observation it becomes readily apparent whether or not the student can follow directions, how he or she responds to winning and losing, and how well he or she is able to cooperate (Nickerson, Maas, & O'Laughlin, 1982).

School counselors who wish to use different strategies with children do not normally have the training that is needed for "therapy" (Muro & Kottman, 1995). For example, the American Art Therapy Association (AATA) and the American Music Therapy Association (AMTA) have outlined training and supervision requirements for individuals who desire to be licensed to use these theoretical tools. School counselors do not use these tools for therapy. However, applying these strategies appropriate to their level of training assists in rapport building and learning. Some of the expressive arts in counseling include play, sand play, art, imagery, movement and dance, music, bibliocounseling (Webb, 1991), and games.

USING PLAY AS A COUNSELING INTERVENTION

Counseling through play is not a new approach to working with children. Erik Erikson viewed play as a means of achieving mastery over a difficult situation (Webb, 1991). In addition, Alfred Adler used play as an intervention with children (Wagner, 2003) and Dr. Carl Rogers believed in play as an expression of self within a safe environment (Gladding, 1992). In fact, interventions with children began with Sigmund Freud and little Hans, a boy who had developed a phobia of horses and other large animals. Interestingly, Freud did not have direct contact with little Hans but, instead, worked with this boy through consultation with Hans's father (Wagner).

Play assists in developing rapport and serves as a substitute for spoken language in that emotions, perceptions, and events in the lives of children can be expressed (Garbarino, Stott, & others, 1992) through nonverbal means. Just as adults talk about experiences over and over again to make sense of an upsetting issue, children repeatedly play out disturbing events. Play allows children to deal with a situation "as if" it were another person's feelings and thoughts and by pretending the situations were happening to someone else (Garbarino et al.). Since children are often confused about the differences between thoughts, feelings, and behaviors, play can assist the child in distancing him or herself from these negative thoughts and feelings.

The child's play in itself does not create change; the counselor interventions bring about growth. The counselor may choose a *nondirective role* in which the child sets up, directs, and enacts the situation (Webb, 1991) or a *directive style* that the counselor creates to focus the counseling session (Gil, 1994). One of the most frequent play technique mistakes counselors make is allowing the child to play arbitrarily over an extended period of time, ignoring the child's play, or providing distracting toys that do not promote growth (Gil). Although play techniques are most commonly used with children under the age of 12 who have difficulty expressing themselves, adolescents can also relate to play through such activities as games (Gladding, 1992). Video games, ball games, board games, and so on all provide natural outlets for older children.

The value of play was documented in a study by Johnson, McLeod, and Fall (1997). Nondirective play therapy was conducted in a school setting with children with special needs between the ages of 5 and 9. The participants met individually for six, 30-minute sessions in which they were able to choose the type of play in a nurturing environment. The resulting increase in coping skills transferred into other areas of their lives.

Toy Selection

Counselors do not need to have a fully furnished room for counseling using play strategies. Not all counselors have the luxury of a permanently assigned room for counseling, and many have to travel from room to room or from building to building. This arrangement necessitates a flexible means to transport toys, which some counselors handle by filling movable suitcases with a combination of toys that are readily available at all times.

A few well-chosen toys can accomplish the goals of counseling, particularly when the counselor predetermines the toys and situation in advance. A consistent arrangement of toys in the counseling room helps provide for a predictable atmosphere and makes cleanup easier. For counselors with a portable supply of counseling materials, arranging the toys in a consistent place each time a session occurs provides reliability and stability (Kottman, 1999).

Toys that represent family members and common household items allow a child to act out common household situations and to choose dolls or figures that represent various members of their family, classmates, or other significant people in their lives. A play telephone is a method of communicating in that a child can indirectly "talk to the counselor" in a nonthreatening manner.

Providing toys that are associated with violence is controversial. Some authors believe that providing toys that permit children to act out angry feelings in a safe environment assist children learn appropriate ways to express aggression (Muro & Kottman, 1995). Other individuals believe that exposure to aggressive toys such as toy knives and guns encourages hostility. Furthermore, many schools have a "zero tolerance" policy enforced, and policy makers may oppose objects representing aggression being present at any place in the school building. A discussion with the building administrators is necessary before introducing toys of this nature.

BOX 13.2 Observation Worksheet

Student's name ________ Date ________

Directions
Place a mark next to all that apply in the following chart.

Behavior	**Affect**	**Play**
Cooperative	Appropriate to play	Organized
Activity level	No affect	Developmentally appropriate
Impulsive	Inappropriate	Repeated themes
Resistant	Apathetic	Creative
Other	Other	Other

Sand Play

A different type of play is expression through sand in which no previous knowledge or skill on the part of the child is needed. Two waterproof trays, one filled with wet sand and the other with dry sand, that are approximately 20″ × 30″ × 4″ are provided. Both trays have a painted blue interior to represent water (Gladding, 1992) and are placed on a waist-high work surface for a comfortable work area. Other materials are often substituted for sand, such as cornmeal, beans, split peas, rice, popcorn, and aquarium gravel (Carmichael, 1994). Because of the consistency of these media, the school counselor may find it more convenient to store the sand in a plastic container with a lid.

Miniature objects including plants, minerals, buildings, vehicles, natural objects, animals, and people that represent all facets of life are provided. The student selects objects based on personal meaning and has the opportunity to direct the play, correct placements of objects, and observe his or her creation all at the same time.

The counselor is to make note of the child's affect and observe for an emerging theme after at least three or four constructions. The observation sheet shown in Box 13.2 may be adapted by the counselor using this technique.

ART TECHNIQUES IN COUNSELING

Art materials that encourage children to express themselves in a creative manner include such things as paint, crayons, markers, or colored pencils (see Table 13.1). Materials that can be manipulated and used in various ways include play dough, pipe cleaners, or clay. These materials can provide an outlet for youth to express their feelings, reveal personality, and use their imagination (Kottman, 1999). Some commonly used strategies include drawing, painting, sculpting, self-portraits, or family portrayals.

Table 13.1 Art Materials

Paint	**Clay**	**Printing**
Tempera	Ball clay	Silkscreen
Acrylic	Porcelain	Batik
Watercolor	Play dough	Potato
Food coloring	Bread dough	Sponge
Sculpture	**Handwork**	**Crafts**
Plaster	Knitting	Leather
Wax	Crochet	Popsicle sticks
Wood	Macrame	Models
Metal	Doll making	Beading
Wire	Needlepoint	Pipecleaners
Papers	**Utensils**	**Other materials**
Drawing	Crayon	Elmer's glue
Construction paper	Pencil	Rubber cement
Tissue	Ink pen	Sandbox
Foil	Pastels	Videotape
Cardboard	Brushes	Tape recorder
Newspaper	Sponge	Digital camera
Wax paper	Markers	CD player
Paper towels	Palette knife	Computer

Through art the student's talent, physical and mental developmental levels, personality, and relationship to others can be determined in a nonthreatening, nonjudgmental environment. Art strategies such as the Squiggle Technique (Winnicott, 1971, as cited in Webb, 1991), shown in Box 13.3, assist the child in uncovering buried feelings and thoughts while building rapport with the counselor.

Art techniques can also be used with adolescents as a creative outlet in a nonthreatening atmosphere without their feeling the pressure to express themselves through words (Kahn, 1999).

The Lifeline Exercise (Coleman, 1998), shown in Box 13.4, may help students explore their past, present, and future.

Children may be reluctant to share their concerns or worries for fear that it may create more turmoil for a significant person. The Worry Doll Exercise, shown in Box 13.5, is designed for children ages 5 to 10, to share their worries and to give themselves permission to talk about concerns (Korenblat-Hanin, 1998).

Students who have difficulties in their lives due to disruptive behaviors are often not aware of how their destructive behaviors and attitudes influence significant people in their lives. The art activity in Box 13.6 is designed for adolescents, with the purpose of building an awareness of how continuous inappropriate behaviors can create relationship problems.

BOX 13.3 The Squiggle Art Technique

Both the counselor and the student have a paper and pencil, and each person draws a squiggle on his or her own paper. Each person makes a picture out of the other individual's squiggle and tells a story about it. When the story is finished, the second person can ask questions about the story. In the following illustrations, a child drew a squiggle and the counselor added additional marks on the student's squiggle and told a story about a lonely bird. This story served as a metaphor about the importance of not going along with peer pressure. The story as told by the counselor follows the illustrations.

Child's squiggle

Counselor's addition to squiggle and story

Once upon a time there was a baby bird who felt different from all the other birds in his neighborhood. He tried to fit in by doing things the other birds wanted him to do, even though he knew it was wrong. He finally realized that when he acted like himself he was happier and he had more true friends that liked him for who he was.

A counselor using art in counseling with a student

BOX 13.4 The Lifeline Exercise

The student is asked to draw a horizontal line. The student is then asked to indicate his or her date of birth at one end of the line and, at the other end, to identify a year at least 5 years into the future.

1. The student is asked to recollect significant events in his or her life and to indicate these events at the appropriate place on the lifeline.
2. After the events are identified, the following coding system is used:
   O = Satisfying decision
   E = Emotionally significant event, positive or negative
   X = Poor decision
   / = A barrier that frustrated goal attainment
   ? = Future event
3. Following the lifeline completion the counselor discusses and clarifies the illustration with the student. Themes, events, and emotional experiences are discussed, in addition to possible consideration of future goals.

Birth	E	X	/	0	X	E	x	?	?
1988	1994	1996	1998	1999	2000	2002	2004	2007	2009

BOX 13.5 The Worry Doll Exercise

Materials: Popsicle sticks, yarn, colored markers

Directions
The counselor talks to the students about the importance of discussing concerns with others. The students are given art materials to make a worry doll out of the popsicle stick. The students are able to decorate their dolls however they wish and to name the doll. Students are instructed to take their doll home and to tell their worries to the doll before they go to sleep each night.

BOX 13.6 The Heart Activity

The student is given a piece of paper and is asked to draw a heart and to cut it out. The student is asked to section the heart in four either by drawing lines or folding the heart. Once this is completed, the student is asked to write the names of the four most important people in his or her life—one name for each section of the heart. Next, the student is to choose one of the people from the heart that they are most willing to sacrifice right now (indicating that this person has isolated him or herself from the student because of the student's inappropriate behavior). The student is to tear this person's name off of his or her heart and give it to the counselor. This process continues until all the people from the heart have been torn off. The following questions facilitate an understanding of how people's lives are affected:

1. What was it like for you to have to choose which person to give up?
2. What would your life be like without this special person?
3. What thoughts and/or feelings did you have as you had to face life without this person?

Imagery in Counseling

Imagery. Imagery is a method in which students are taught skills to assist in connecting with the senses of sight, hearing, touch, smell, and taste. Guided fantasy imagery was used to uncover work values and how these values support career decisions. In a study by Krumboltz, Blando, Kim, and Reikowski (1994), participants were asked to imagine themselves in the future workplace and to record how they envision their role in an ideal occupation for skill in career decision making.

Another imagery technique for students with academic difficulties is to request the student to visualize an "ideal student," and then to ask the student to describe what the ideal student is "doing," "saying," "hearing," etc. The student is then requested to practice these behaviors.

Or, if a student is having difficulty solving a personal problem or the counselor may ask, "What do you *imagine* you might tell a person who is having a similar problem to say?" "Do?" "Think?" The individual can be asked to apply these responses to resolve his / her issues.

Imagery is sometimes associated with misconceptions and unfair conclusions. Before using imagery with children in the school setting, it is important to check with state and local policies regarding the use of this technique (Bradley & Gould, 1999).

MOVEMENT AND DANCE IN COUNSELING

Emotion is expressed through movement. Dance and movement assist the student in identifying feelings, viewing personality, improving body image, and communicating with others (Warren, 1993). For instance, children can be asked to walk as if they were happy, sad, embarrassed, etc. to understand how body movements influence affect.

The movement activity shown in Box 13.7 may be used to build group cohesiveness.

BOX 13.7 Let's Get Moving

Directions
Group members either sit or stand in a circle. The group leader will start a movement (jumping, skipping, waving hands, etc.). All members are to repeat this movement until the leader calls "NEXT!" The student to the right of the leader then becomes the new leader until he or she calls the word "NEXT!" This new leader begins a different movement that is imitated by all the group members. The leadership is passed around the circle (Warren, 1993).

Evaluation
Members will discuss what it was like being the leader and the follower.

MUSIC AS AN EXPRESSIVE COUNSELING TECHNIQUE

Music as a method of helping others has been used throughout history. The Bible mentions that harp playing was used to lift King Saul's mood (Nickerson, 1982). In the 19th century music was used in mental hospitals, and today we find music in dentist's offices to alleviate anxiety, and in malls to induce shopping. Music is also used to help people become more self-aware, as a learning tool, and as a way of communicating (Gladding, 1992) Prior musical ability is not needed with this expressive counseling technique.

The counselor can use music in such activities as listening and learning, performing, or even composing (Gladding, 1992), and the counselor should determine whether or not music is an appropriate intervention based on the student's personality. A student may bring music that is meaningful to him or her to the counseling session. Together the counselor and student can listen to the music to build rapport, to discover personal meaning, or to discover personal values.

Lessons can be incorporated into music. For instance, there are songs that teach students about the different parts of the body, geography, and other concepts. A counselor can ask a student or a group of students to compose a song based on a particular theme such as making friends, or following rules, etc. Other students may simply wish to perform a favorite song or piece of music based on their particular talent.

Another counseling strategy using music entitled, *Musical Feelings,* assists children ages 5–12 to explore and express feelings (Korenblaat-Hanin, 1998). (See Box 13.8.)

BIBLIOCOUNSELING

Bibliocounseling is defined as a method to assist individuals with problem-solving skills, self-understanding, developmental growth, and attitude change (Borders & Paisley, 1992). As counselor programs shift to a developmental focus, counselors team with teachers and librarians to integrate biblio-techniques in the classroom. For example, in one study using bibliocounseling, fourth- and

BOX 13.8 Musical Feelings

Materials Needed
Musical instruments

Directions
1. Children are asked to select an instrument that reflects their feelings on a specific issue (divorce, school, friends, family, etc.).
2. Each group member is asked to play the instrument that best represents how he or she is feeling.
3. Group members will guess the feeling represented.
4. Each child discusses his or her musical composition and feelings.

Evaluation
Students will identify feelings.

fifth-grade students showed promising growth in motivation and personal growth after participation in a bibliocounseling-based classroom guidance curriculum (Borders & Paisley).

Other creative counseling approaches using bibliocounseling include finishing stories or poems, writing a story that takes place in the future, or drawing a personal emblem and writing a story about it. For example, a student may be asked to finish the following open-ended situation:

The Wandering Soldier

The war was over
Now what could the soldier do?
His experiences made him bolder,
He could now start his life anew.
Should he travel?
See his family?
Go back to school?
Visit his friends?

Finish the story of what you think the soldier should do.

GAMES

The use of games in counseling provides an opportunity to teach children and adolescents strategies for paying attention, keeping an interest in school work, learning and remembering, and studying (Moore & Serby, 1988). As the student is learning the rules of the game and developing strategies for winning, he or she learns that paying attention facilitates winning. Many word games such as *Boggle* helps word understanding and spelling, and students can increase math comprehension and apply classroom concepts through other games such as *Dominoes* or *Cribbage.* Furthermore, games such as *Memory* create participation and strategies for remembering items, and concentrating on the placement of game cards. These skills are readily transferred into strategies for studying.

Other games increase social, motor, directional, and visual skills. For instance, *Jenga* is a game in which the object is to remove blocks placed within a stack, and replaced on the top of the stack while preventing the stack from falling. Judgment and eye-hand coordination are developed while partners participate in a competitive, challenging game (Moore & Serby, 1988).

THE SCHOOL COUNSELOR'S OFFICE

In this age of accountability, counselors find themselves in competition with teachers for the student's time, with good reason. Teachers, responsible for student achievement of standards identified for each grade level, are reluctant to release students from class. When teachers are convinced that school counselors share their mission, and are partners in the educational process collaboration, sharing students, and cooperation are the end results. Only then will students be released from class.

Individual counseling and appropriate times for a student to meet with a counselor is a procedure to be determined collaboratively. Some teachers wish to know in advance when a child is missing their class. Other teachers will not release a student without written permission from the counselor, and still others will not release a student if an important test or assignment will be missed. Students also need to be aware of the rules of contacting a counselor, and the consequences for violating the guidelines.

For example, novice counselors complain that some students will come to their office to seek out counseling, only to find out later that the student missed a test or didn't have an assignment ready for a particular class. Other counselors state that students have taken advantage of the counselor by requesting a pass for class admission only to avoid being tardy to class.

Creative, expressive arts as strategies for counselors are effective with children and adolescents. The greater the counselor communicates his or her skills and educational training that serve as a basis for helping students, the greater the support for the counseling program. The following suggestions promote counseling success using creative arts in counseling in the schools.

The Counselor's Role in the Use of Creative Counseling Techniques

1. Inservice educators and parents about the purpose and goals of play, sand, and art in counseling so its therapeutic value and the relationship to developmental stages can be emphasized.
2. Provide an opportunity for educators and parents to experience the process of play, sand, art, or music.

3. If a permanent station is available, displaying art, sand, and play materials on open shelves that are securely attached to the wall will prevent children from knocking over the shelves. Traveling counselors using portable equipment should find a place to arrange the materials in an open, easily viewed location (Muro & Kottman, 1995). If possible, space and location are to be considered. A counseling room that is too small may limit movement in play, and a room that is too large may also distract from the session. Ideally, a counseling room that is separated from the academic classes is recommended since play, especially in groups, may generate noise that could disrupt the regular educational process.
4. Remind students that expressive art or play will not be evaluated, but is instead an opportunity to communicate in a creative fashion.
5. Counseling departments have limited funds that are usually designated for testing materials, supplies, and educational resources and generally exclude items for expressive arts. Funds for play items may not be allocated. Therefore, counselors who wish to use play in counseling may solicit funds from the PTO or other parent organizations, obtain toys second-hand through friends or neighbors, or attend garage sales to purchase items at a low cost.
6. The issue of ownership of the artwork is to be considered, and whether the counselor or the student maintains ownership of the finished product. Some theorists believe that art work placed in the student's record invades his or her right to privacy (Hammond & Gantt, 1998). However, since the counselor may need documentation in case of legal action, photographing the artwork and treating it as all students' records are handled is recommended. Issues of confidentiality, which include who will see the art, where it will be stored, and whether the work will be dismantled by the counselor or student, are also guidelines that need to be determined in advance (Hammond & Gantt; Kahn, 1999).
7. Specialized training in the use of these art forms is required for in-depth counseling.

SUMMARY

Counseling theory provides the foundation for the counseling process. Theoretical approaches guide the counseling process and provide counselors with the opportunity to think about personal assumptions and beliefs and about how one initiates change. Because most school counseling programs offer separate courses in theories, this chapter is not meant to substitute for this essential information. Instead, this chapter provides counselors who work with children and adolescents creative techniques for building rapport, assessing the child, and creating an atmosphere in which children feel comfortable expressing themselves without using words. The counseling process includes building a relationship, assessing the child or adolescent, providing intervention, and termination.

Several creative counseling techniques that have been successfully implemented in a school setting include play, including sand play: art modalities; imagery; movement and dance; music; bibliocounseling; and games. The school counselor, in using these techniques, works collaboratively with school personnel in explaining these strategies and creating procedures for dismissing students from class to see the counselor. Additionally, support, funding, ethical considerations, and specialized training are considerations when using these techniques with children.

REFERENCES

Baker, S. B. (2000). *School counseling for the twenty-first century* (3rd ed.). Upper Saddle River, NJ: Merrill.

Borders, S., & Paisley, P., O. (1992). Children's literature as a resource for classroom guidance. *Elementary School Guidance and Counseling, 27,* 131–139.

Bradley, L. J., & Gould, L. J. (1999). Individual counseling: Creative interventions. In A. Vernon (Ed.), *Counseling children and adolescents* (2nd ed., pp. 65–97). Denver: Love.

Carmichael, K. D. (1994). Sand play as an elementary school strategy. *Elementary School Guidance and Counseling, 28,* 302–307.

Coleman, V. D. (1998). Lifeline. In H. G. Rosenthal (Ed.), *Favorite counseling and therapy techniques* (pp. 51–53). Washington, DC: Accelerated Development.

DeShazer, S. (1985). *Keys to solution in brief therapy.* New York: W. W. Norton & Company.

Doyle, R. E. (1992). *Essential skills and strategies in the helping process.* Pacific Grove, CA: Brooks/Cole.

Erford, B. (2003). *Transforming the school counseling profession.* Upper Saddle River, NJ: Merrill Prentice-Hall.

Erk, R. R. (2004). *Counseling treatment for children and adolescents with* DSM-IV-TR *disorders.* Upper Saddle River, NJ: Pearson.

Gabarino, J., Stott, F. M., & Faculty of the Erikson Institute. (1992). *What children can tell us: Eliciting, interpreting, and evaluating critical information from children.* San Francisco: Jossey-Bass.

Gil, E. (1994). *Play in family therapy.* New York: Guilford Press.

Gladding, S. T. (1992). *Counseling as an art: The creative arts in counseling.* Alexandria, VA: American Association for Counseling and Development.

Hammond, L. C., & Gantt, L. (1998). Using art in counseling: Ethical considerations. *Journal of Counseling and Development, 76,* 271–276.

Hollis, J. W. (1998). The last five minutes technique. In H. G. Rosenthal (Ed.), *Favorite counseling and therapy techniques* (pp. 107–108). Washington, DC: Accelerated Press.

Johnson, L., McLeod, E. H., & Fall, M. (1997). Play therapy with labeled children in the schools. *Professional School Counseling, 1,* 31–34.

Kahn, B. B. (1999). Art therapy with adolescents: Making it work for school counselors. *Professional School Counseling, 2,* 291–297.

Korenblat-Hanin, M. T. (1998). Creative collection of therapeutic adventures: Feelings, fears, and worries. In H. G. Rosenthal (Ed.), *Favorite counseling and therapy techniques* (pp. 115–121). Washington, DC: Accelerated Press.

Kottman, T. (1999). Play therapy. In A. Vernon (Ed.), *Counseling children and adolescents* (2nd ed., pp. 97–120). Denver: Love.

Krumboltz, J. D., Blando, J. A., Kim, H., & Reikowski, D. J. (1994). Embedding work values in stories. *Journal of Counseling and Development, 73,* 57–62.

Moore, G. B., & Serby, T. (1988). *Becoming whole through games: Developing your child's brain power, motivation, and self-esteem.* Atlanta, GA: Tee Gee.

Muro, J. J., & Kottman, T. (1995). *Guidance and counseling in the elementary and middle schools: A practical approach.* Madison, WI: Brown & Benchmark.

Newsome, D. W., & Gladding, S. T. (2003). Counseling individuals and groups in school. In B. Erford (Ed), *Transforming the school counseling profession* (pp. 209–230). Upper Saddle River, NJ: Merrill Prentice-Hall.

Nickerson, E. T. Maas, J. M & O'Laughlin, K. S (1982). An introduction to the theory and practices of action-oriented therapies. In E. T. Nickerson & K. O'Laughlin (Eds.), *Helping through action: Action-oriented therapies* (pp. 1–8). Amherst, MA: Human Resource Development Press.

Rubin, J. A. (1988). *Art counseling: An alternative* (pp. 23–26). Moravia, NY: Chronical Guidance Publications.

Schmidt, J. J. (1999). *Counseling in schools: Essential services and comprehensive programs* (3rd ed.). Needham Heights, MA: Allyn & Bacon.

Wagner, W. G. (2003). *Counseling, psychology, and children: A multidimensional approach to intervention.* Upper Saddle River, NJ: Pearson Education Inc.

Warren, B. (1993). *Using the creative arts in therapy: A practical introduction* (2nd ed.). New York: Routledge.

Webb, N. B. (1991). *Play therapy with children in crisis: A casebook for practitioners.* New York: Guilford Press.

PART IV

Clinical Instruction

The clinical experience is considered as the final CACREP standard for school counseling programs. Although consultation is considered as section 3 under guidance knowledge and skill requirement for school counselors, it is included in this text under Part IV, clinical instruction. School counselors in training often serve as consultants for the first time during their clinical experience during the supervisory process. The final chapter in the text provides information on the supervision process, and how school counselors are key individuals to provide consultation on numerous topics to others in the school.

The chapter in this section is: The Supervision Process and the Professional School Counselor as a Consultant.

14

The Supervision Process and the Professional School Counselor as a Consultant

As I prepared to instruct my students enrolled in supervision, I asked them why they wanted to become school counselors. The answers ranged from,

"I had a very poor relationship with my high-school counselor and felt I made poor educational choices due to an inattentive counselor," to, "My school counselor helped me a lot; therefore, I would like to help other students with academic and personal concerns." When people outside of the counseling profession are asked the question, "What was your school counselor like?" Responses usually range from negative, "My high school counselor told me I'd never make it in college," to more positive answers such as, "My counselor really helped me out during a rough time in my life."

Attitudes are formed about this profession based on personal experiences and perceptions. Yet, common curricular experiences and knowledge obtained by students training for this profession are not always replicated in reality, leading to misconceptions about the duties, tasks, and role of the school counselor. Although supervisory experiences such as leading group and individual counseling are common among counselors, other activities performed under a supervisory experience differ from school to school and from program to program. Through supervision the school counseling student is able to engage in experiences that serve as a learning laboratory for the essential tasks performed by this vital school-based professional. The supervisory process is included in this chapter for two essential reasons: (a) the school counseling student often enters his or her clinical experiences with little understanding of what the process is all about, and (b) few supervisors in school settings have training in supervision. It is hoped that, when novice counselors become experienced counselors with the opportunity to guide others, the information in this chapter will assist with this role.

Consultation is a fundamental task of school counselors, yet little training is received in this crucial aspect of the profession. Information regarding the supervisory experience and consultation—a related, yet separate, component—are discussed in this chapter and includes anecdotes, examples, and activities, to provide a more thorough understanding.

SUPERVISION AND THE SCHOOL COUNSELOR IN TRAINING

After studying concepts, analyzing case studies, and scrutinizing individual beliefs and philosophy in relationship to counseling theories, the school counselor student is given the opportunity to put theory into practice through clinical experiences under supervision. *Supervision* is defined as an evaluative relationship that extends over a period of time with the purpose of enhancing the supervisee's professional functioning (Bernard & Goodyear, 1992).

Supervision is a relatively new concept that was first practiced in the 1950s when Carl Rogers trained individuals in the art of counseling through tapes and case reports. Interestingly, not until the 1980s was supervision considered as being distinct from the process of counseling (Holloway, 1995, as cited in Tyron, 2002).

Supervision is an intervention provided by a senior member of a profession (site supervisor and institution supervisor) to a junior member of that profession (supervisee or trainee) (Schectman & Wirzberger, 1999). The supervisory relationship is crucial to the growth of the supervisee as personal and professional goals are established (Tyron, 2002) and the institution's requirements are met (Ladany, Ellis, & Friedlander, 1999). The supervisor's role in the relationship is one of helping the supervisee with counseling skills, case conceptualization, professional identity, self-awareness, corrective feedback, and self-reflection (Getz, 1999). In exchange, the supervisee assists the already over-burdened supervisor (Goldberg, 2000). Interestingly, although the supervisor provides the opportunity to learn the culture, ethics, conventions, and customs that support the institutional decisions, it takes most individuals approximately 10 years of deliberate practice to perform as experts in the field (O'Byrne & Rosenberg, 1998).

Unfortunately, no two school counselors are trained alike, which creates further confusion of how a school counselor is to operate and function within the school system. Supervisors are faced with the issue of what quality experiences to provide to supervisees, while maintaining quality services for students (Ametrano & Stickel, 1999; Kahn, 1999). Supervisors report that supervisees need to have knowledge in computer scheduling, community resources, technical training, individual and group counseling, coordination, and consultation. Furthermore, supervisors report that student trainees with no teaching experience need additional guidance in understanding the school as a system, the learning process, and consultation with parents and teachers (Kahn). Supervisees report a need for strategies in implementing a developmental counseling program into an already existing traditional model.

Efforts have been made to regulate counselor preparation programs and to provide common experiences in clinical instruction. In 1981 the Council for Accreditation of Counseling and Related Educational Programs (CACREP) was created to "ensure that students develop a professional counselor identity and also master the knowledge and skills to practice effectively" (CACREP, 2001). Counselors throughout the United States began to recognize their "obligation to protect society, insofar as possible, from poorly prepared counselors . . . through accrediting of counselor education programs."

Although not all counselor preparation programs have adopted CACREP standards, they serve as a guide for program development and delivery and provide a foundation for curricula in counselor education programs. As described in the CACREP Manual, Section III (2001), "Clinical instruction includes supervised practica and internships completed within a student's program of study. Practicum and internship requirements are considered to be the most critical experience elements in the program" (p. 64). The guidelines specify requirements for institutional courses and criteria for site supervisors.

WHAT TO EXPECT DURING SUPERVISION

The school counseling student often enters this experience with a mixture of dread and anticipation. Supervisees are diverse in respect to their supervision expectations and their own professional background. The intent of the next section is to allay some of the fears many bring to this experience. In response to the instruction, "Describe one of your greatest fears about internship," the most common responses by students enrolled in internship include the following:

. . . not providing correct information to a student

. . . balancing my life between internship, school, work, family, friends, and health

. . . not being able to help students deal with their problems

Supervisees who have had little experience in a counseling setting initially prefer a teaching relationship in which counseling skills and techniques are highlighted, whereas others with more training and experience prefer a supervisor who focuses on self-reflection and conceptualization. The more advanced supervisees tend to prefer a supervisor who assumes a more collegial relationship (Schectman & Wirzberger, 1999).

Without a compass directing supervision expectations, the supervisory experience largely rests on the guidelines established by the counselor education institution, the site supervisor, and the supervisee. However, common experiences in supervision include: goal setting, skill training, self-reflection, case conceptualization, and role-playing.

Goal Setting

Supervisees are more likely to reach identifiable counseling goals if concretely defined action steps are designated and a strategy is outlined for assessment. In some instances the supervisee may already have identified personal and/or professional goals to accomplish during the process; and in other cases the supervisor may suggest areas that need improvement to serve as a foundation for goal setting. However the goals are determined, it is critical that the supervisors (site and program) and the supervisee make a plan that meets the needs of all identified parties (Neufeldt, 1999).

Skill Training

Student trainees report wanting greater opportunities to practice and refine their basic counseling skills. *Microtraining,* a method for obtaining skills developed by Ivey (Forsyth & Ivey, 1980, as cited in Borders & Leddick, 1987), consists of isolating and practicing skills through video and audiotapes, role plays, observation, and feedback. The supervisee has the opportunity to tape counseling sessions, self-evaluate, and seek feedback from the site and/or program supervisor.

Self-Assessment and Reflection

Critical self-analysis is a process in which trainees recreate counseling experiences by examining hypotheses, affect, and interventions (Card & House, 1998) to better understand the counseling experience. A good counselor needs to examine core values—those truths that guide, empower, and provide meaning. Too often trainees compromise their personal value system and agree to perform an activity that is contrary to their belief system. For example, familiar questions asked by the supervisee include: "If I perform this activity that is not counselor related, will it help me get a job?" or, "If I use the theoretical orientation to which my supervisor adheres, will I receive a better evaluation?" Through supervision, the supervisee discovers self-identity, ethical decision making, how the self fits into the profession (Palmer, 1998), and ways of handling conflict.

Case Conceptualization

One aspect of counseling supervision is developing an assumption about the student seeking counseling that includes a hypothesis of the student's past, feelings, thoughts, situation context, and/or a consideration of the student's environmental situation (Neufeldt, 1999). The supervisee may be encouraged to identify an intervention that has been successful in the past or select an option that has not yet been practiced, implement the strategy, and then evaluate it.

Role-Playing

Transfer of knowledge and application may occur when the supervisee assumes an identified K-12 student's role and situation, while the supervisor (role-playing a counselor) demonstrates a particular intervention. Role-playing can also assist in viewing a situation from a different perspective, practicing a new skill, and facilitating self-discovery.

THE SUPERVISION PROCESS

Supervisees often wonder what the supervisory experience will be like, what expectations are likely, and what types of tasks will be assigned. Perhaps the most vital element of a supervisory experience is the selection of a site supervisor, who serves as the role model for the future of the profession (Roberts & Morotti, 2001). Supervision takes a number of forms—in groups, individual, or both. How supervision is approached depends upon the motivation and needs of the supervisee. Generally, supervision is an opportunity to discuss difficult situations and to receive feedback on performance. It is also an opportunity to share successes and to develop confidence when gaining additional experience (Travers, 2002). It can also be thought of in developmental terms as the trainee progresses through a series of stages, from one in which there is a lot of anxiety to one in which there is more confidence and comfort in the position. These stages are not discrete steps but are linked as some skills are mastered while others remain novel and unique.

Stage 1

During the initial stage, the trainees are anxious but at the same time motivated to learn and to succeed. Therefore, the prudent supervisor will provide the trainee with an orientation of the supervision process by clarifying expectations, establishing a relationship, setting goals, and contracting counseling conditions. A written contract outlining the expectations and goals clarifies expectations and may alleviate some of the supervisee's anxiety. The supervisee's willingness to reflect on the counseling experiences and clinical demands is promoted when a positive learning relationship is developed and maintained (Card & House, 1998). The following questions answered prior to the initiation of supervision assist in developing clear expectations (Borders & Leddick, 1987):

1. What personal goals do you wish to accomplish during the supervisory process?
2. What professional goals do you wish to accomplish during the supervisory experience?
3. What strategies need to be selected to meet the identified goal(s)?
4. Frequency of meetings: How long? How often? Where?

5. Will sessions be audio- or videotaped? Who will hear/see the tapes? How will confidentiality be maintained? Will informed consent be required?
6. How will the supervision sessions be structured? What is expected of the supervisor/supervisee?
7. What are the procedures for emergency situations? Who needs to be contacted?
8. Does the supervisor have the appropriate scope of training?
9. What evaluative procedures will be used?
10. How are the practicum and internship hours to be organized? Group work? Guidance lessons? Parent consultations? Individual counseling?
11. How often will the counselor educator visit the field site?
12. What assessment tools will be used?
13. What number of absences will be accepted to successfully complete the supervisory contract?
14. What are the identified procedures for disputing evaluations in which there is disagreement?

A sample worksheet for goal setting is shown in Box 14.1. During this stage, supervisees often feel anxious and conflicted as they try to reconcile the gap between the classroom concepts and real-life experiences (Card & House, 1998).

Stage 2

When the goals and tasks of supervision established in the previous stage are clearly understood, the comfort level of the trainee is enhanced (Ladany, Ellis, & Friedlander, 1999). Since the trainee will display fluctuating levels of confidence and competence (Goldberg, 2000), the supervisor will need to challenge the supervisee regarding his or her selection of theoretical strategies utilized in certain situations (Stoltenberg, 1993). This supportive confrontation of attitudes, behaviors, and beliefs is a necessary part of the learning process. When the supervisee is faced with a unique situation, confusion and doubt may surface; but when the supervisee is encouraged to think through personal thoughts, feelings, and actions, growth occurs.

Self-assessment and personal reflection occur when the trainee asks him or herself the following questions (Borders & Leddick, 1987; Goldberg, 2000) following a counseling session:

1. What was I hearing the student counselee say?
2. What were my feelings toward the counselee?
3. How did my feelings influence the session?
4. What made me decide to use the interventions I chose?
5. What are my observations of the student counselee's reactions?

BOX 14.1 Goal-Setting Worksheet for Supervisees

1. What are some of your concerns about the internship experience?

   A.

   B.

   C.

2. What goals do you wish to accomplish during this experience?

Delivery System	Activities to Reach Goal	Time Frame	Evaluation
A. Guidance curriculum			
1. Structured groups			
2. Classroom presentations			
B. Individual planning			
1. Advisement			
2. Assessment			
3. Placement and follow-up			
C. Responsive services			
1. Individual counseling			
2. Small-group counseling			
3. Consultation			
4. Referral			
D. System support			
1. Management activities			
2. Consultation			
3. Community outreach			
4. Public relations			

Management System	Activities to Reach Goal	Time Frame	Evaluation
A. Student monitoring			
B. Action plans			
C. Calendar			
D. Other			
Accountability			
A. Data			
B. Assessment			
C. Advisory board			
D. Other			
Foundation			
A. Write personal philosophy statement.			
B. Evaluate competencies and strategies.			

Self-reflective activities are facilitated as the supervisee conducts classroom guidance sessions, learns school policies and procedures, and engages in other activities while interacting with students, parents, educators, and other constituents. Too often trainees are not provided with activities that provide experiences in a developmental, comprehensive school counseling model. A worksheet of sample supervisory activities with an evaluation based on the ASCA National Model is provided in Table 14.1.

Stage 3

During this stage, a wider variety of experiences are provided for the trainee to facilitate independent thinking and autonomy. Common activities at this stage include the creation of new programs or activities for K–12 students, consultation, continued self-supervision of performance, making judgments about actions, and adjusting counseling style (Nelson & Johnson, 1999).

All of these experiences provide supervisees with greater insight and professional self-awareness, which in turn facilitates an opportunity to problem-solve and to generate ideas in preparation for future situations. The supervisor's role will continue to be one of a teacher and a counselor, with a shift to one of a collegial consultant (Nelson & Johnson, 1999) that encourages and supports autonomy, sharing, and confrontation.

Stage 4

In this stage, the supervisee is encouraged to develop even greater autonomy in clinical self-assessment, case conceptualization (Card & House, 1998), program planning, and professional counseling-related activities (Bradley & Fiorini, 1999). The supervisor takes on an even greater consultant role and is now viewed more as a colleague.

As the supervisee engages in the various activities to more thoroughly understand and appreciate the role of the school counselor, performance is assessed for improvement in various areas. Too often supervisees are apprehensive about the evaluative process and view it from a negative viewpoint. Reframing this thinking more positively assists in looking at evaluation as an opportunity to improve and gain enhanced skills and to value the skills that have been mastered.

EVALUATION

One of the major roles of a supervisor is evaluation (Williams, 1995, as cited in Hanna & Smith, 1998). The purpose of this process is to improve learning, to assist in decision making, and to answer the questions, "How will we know when we have reached our expected outcome?" (Nelson & Johnson, 1999), and, "How well has the trainee performed in designated areas?" Traditionally, assessment has taken the form of checklists and/or narrative descriptions that are provided during meetings of all involved parties. An example of an evaluative checklist is shown in Box 14.2.

Table 14.1 Supervisory Activities Using the ASCA National Model

Delivery System

Guidance Curriculum— K–12 Students Will	**Intern Activities Intern Will**	**Rating Scale 1**	**2**	**3**	**4**
Use communication skills to ask for help when needed.	Teach a guidance lesson on assertiveness in grades 2–4–6				
Become self-directed learners.	Facilitate a group on study skills				
Individual Planning— K–12 Students Will	**Intern Activities Intern Will**				
Complete a 4-year plan of study.	Assist students with a 4-year curriculum of study.				
Complete a career interest inventory.	Orientate, administer, and interpret interest inventory results.				
Responsive Services— K–12 Students Will	**Intern Activities Intern Will**				
Apply decision-making skills to a problem situation.	Apply a theoretical model and appropriate techniques while providing individual counseling.				
Identify personal strengths and weaknesses.	Facilitate a group to enhance self-esteem.				
System Support— K–12 Students Will	**Intern Activities Intern Will**				
Identify community resources.	Direct students as to the types of agencies available in the community.				
Complete an evaluation of guidance services.	Design and administer a guidance evaluation form.				
Management System K–12 Students Will	**Intern Activities Intern Will**				
Complete an evaluation of the counseling process.	Design and administer an evaluation form to a student receiving counseling.				
Accountability K–12 Students Will	**Intern Activities Intern Will**				
Evaluate strategies implemented to reach goals.	Assess the evaluation results from student feedback.				
Foundation K–12 Students Will	**Intern Activities Intern Will**				
Select competencies they feel are important in each domain.	Identify one competency selected by students and present an intervention.				

Rating Scale

1 = Has not demonstrated competency

2 = Has minimally demonstrated competency but needs improvement

3 = Has satisfactorily demonstrated competency

4 = Has exceeded expectations

Because supervisees demonstrate multiple competencies and engage in different supervisory activities, identified measures selected in advance are considered good practice (Carney, Cobia, & Shannon, 1996, as cited in Hanna & Smith, 1998). Rubrics are proposed as a useful quantitative evaluation method since they provide a clear description of what is to be expected, an explicit definition of the performance standards, and a scoring scale (Hanna & Smith).

Evaluation is also beneficial to the supervisor. The supervisee has the opportunity to evaluate the designated experiences provided by the supervisor, the quality of instruction, advice, and feedback. A formal evaluation instrument, a university evaluation form, and a self-designed form are all tools for the supervisee to share how the experience was beneficial or could have been improved (Borders & Leddick, 1987).

CONSULTATION

Consultation is one aspect of supervision in which trainees report not receiving enough training. As school counselors conceptualize their role within the school and continue to collaborate with individuals within and outside of the environment, the consultative task remains significant because school counselors act as role models, provide coordination, and recruit individuals willing to assist students (Sink, 2002). The ASCA Position Statements continually reinforce and refer to the importance of consultation in working with at-risk students and support for parents and guardians, educators, and other constituents.

Consultation and supervision are similar in some ways, yet also different. For example, consultation is a voluntary process; supervision is not. Supervision requires an evaluation of the trainee's performance; consultation does not. Because of the importance of consultation in the role of the school counselor, a separate discussion of consultation is included in this chapter.

Although school counselors have been expected to provide consultation to program constituents (Gibson, Mitchell, & Basile, 1993), school counseling students receive little training in this process in comparison to the time spent on other counseling functions such as individual and group counseling experiences (Kahn, 1999). In particular, it is noted that students with little or no teaching experience need extra training in understanding the teaching process and school milieu. These individuals require this knowledge to appreciate the school as a system, the learning process, and the needs of parents and teachers (Kahn).

Consultation helps parents, teachers, and administrators to be more effective in problem-solving through the acquisition of knowledge and skills (Brown, 1993). School counselors, due to their education and training, are ideal candidates to lead this intervention through individual or group procedures, in-service activities, or parent education meetings (Campbell & Dahir, 1997; Vacc & Loesch, 1994).

Traditional definitions of consultation have too often been associated with "advice giving," when in reality consultation is much more complicated than

BOX 14.2 Evaluation Checklist for Student Intern

_____ Models professional skills
_____ Professional attitude in working with students, teachers, and parents
_____ Functions professionally on the job
_____ Receives feedback constructively
_____ Completes assignments and designated duties
_____ Ability to effectively lead groups
_____ Follows school policies and procedures
_____ Consults appropriately with teachers, parents, and administrators
_____ Appropriately self-evaluates activities
_____ Conceptualizes professional situations
_____ Identifies appropriate resources
_____ Effectively leads group guidance activities

Use the following scale to evaluate student:

1 Does not meet expectations
2 Improvement needed
3 Adequate, but more training needed
4 Performance exceeds expectations
5 Outstanding

Please discuss the student's strengths and the specific areas in which improvement is needed.

simply providing information (Brown, 1993). Numerous definitions for consultation exist; but, for the most part, consultation in the schools is a process that takes on different forms. Consultation varies based on the type of intervention, the setting in which it occurs, the identification of the student, and the responsibility for consultation outcome (Jackson & Hayes, 1993). Generally, but not always, the consultant (in this case the counselor) is contacted by a consultee (e.g., administrator, parent, teacher) to provide assistance to a student. Consultation is *not*

1. Supervision. Although supervisors as well as consultants give advice and provide support, the consultant is not in a position to direct or evaluate the consultee's work (Conoley & Conoley, 1992).
2. Program development. The consultant does not design a program for the consultee but, instead, teaches skills and provides information so that the consultee can design and implement programs (Conoley & Conoley) to best meet the needs of the school.
3. Counseling. Consultees seek assistance with professional concerns rather than personal concerns. The consultant assists in problem-solving but not with the intention of providing insight into a consultee's attitude, behaviors, and beliefs (Conoley & Conoley; Gibson et al., 1993).

Skills of the Consultant

The consultant needs to be aware of effective communication strategies including: *who* (the consultant) says *what* (the message) *to whom* (the audience) and *by what means* (channel of communication) (Myers, 1993). The effective consultant is one who is friendly, democratic, open, knowledgeable of group processes, empathic to consultees' concerns, supportive, flexible, and efficient and who exhibits prompt follow-up techniques (Bergan & Tombari, 1976, as cited in Zins, 1993).

Additionally, effective consultants can be viewed as experts and trustworthy as they convey concern and understanding through active listening skills and knowledge of nonverbal communication (Zins, 1993). For example, statistics from a credible source have a more lasting impact than frightening messages from less reliable sources (Myers, 1993). Although a dramatic, fear-arousing picture or message can be anxiety provoking, fear alone does not always make a message more salable. Frightening messages may be so disturbing that individuals may not know how to cope and therefore will not change destructive behaviors. However, if the disturbing message or picture is accompanied with advice on how to cope with an event, behavior may be altered. For example, around prom time, many schools stage dramatic scenes in which students view a simulated car accident caused by drinking and driving. Although this is impressionable, it is not enough. Concrete information on how to prevent drinking and driving such as a designated driver program, calling a friend, or using refusal strategies is informative with suggestions for handling a problem.

Consultants need to be cognizant of multicultural issues especially when consultants are culturally different from the consultee or student. Too often individuals from a minority group have historically felt disempowered by the mental health system (Lyles & Carter, 1982, as cited in Jackson & Hayes, 1993). Attention to such concepts as the perception of time can facilitate the consultation. In some cultures, a designated time is honored and respected, such as arriving at a meeting scheduled at 9:00 A.M. In other cultures, a specified meeting time means it "will happen when it happens" and a 9:00 A.M. meeting will occur at some point around this identified time. Also, some cultures value verbal contracts while others value written contracts. The consultant should honor these cultural differences for effective consultation (Jackson & Hayes, 1993).

Messages are even more influential when they are associated with positive feelings. In a study by Janis, Kaye, and Kirschner (1965, as cited in Myers, 1993), people who were given snacks as they read were more influenced by a message than those who were not given snacks while they read. Therefore, when planning a consultation, a comfortable room with a conducive atmosphere in which people can eat, drink, and feel satisfied are considerations.

THE SCHOOL COUNSELOR AS A CONSULTANT

School counselors are ideal consultants due to their training, skills, and expertise in human growth and development and interpersonal relationships. Oftentimes, a consultant who is employed outside of the system is more readily accepted than those employed within the system. These individuals are contacted not only because these peripheral individuals often have a different perspective of the problem but also because of the perception that external professionals have more information and training. Yet, there are several advantages to utilizing the services of individuals from the same setting. The internal consultant already has a clear understanding of the system and an established relationship with the consultee and students and may possess as much if not more knowledge, experience, and expertise as an external consultant (Conoley & Conoley, 1992). For example, a teacher was employed as the lead instructor of a marketing management program at a vocational high school. This individual was quite skilled in teaching strategies and possessed a vast amount of information and creativity surrounding this curricular area. Yet, when his school district determined that public support for the school was declining, the board of education voted to spend large amounts of money to bring in an outside marketing consultant to employ strategies to increase local support. The marketing instructor, quite knowledgeable of the system and public relations strategies, was overlooked as a consultant because of the erroneous belief that someone "from the outside" could provide them with better resources.

Knowing the precipitating events leading to the need for consultation is essential, and an internal consultant may have a greater understanding of the history leading to the present issue. The consultant needs to ask the questions, "Why now?" and "Why me?" A thorough understanding of personal skills, limitations, and the problem for which consultation is being sought will assist the consultant in determining whether he or she has the necessary skills to lead the intervention. Otherwise, performing this activity is considered unethical.

School counselors are often asked to resolve issues through a traditional, direct individual counseling model. However, when the school counselor teaches problem solving through consultation, more individuals can be reached, time is more effectively used, and skill application may be an end result. Teachers, administrators, parents, and/or outside agencies may benefit from consultation from the school counselor.

Consultation with Teachers

Mrs. Van Meter was concerned about the isolated, aloof behavior of Juanita, a student in her fifth-grade class. Ten-year-old Juanita used to be a conscientious student and concerned with her grades. Lately, this petite, dark-haired girl appeared disinterested in classroom activities and rarely handed in assignments. This behavior was extremely inconsistent with the outgoing behaviors Juanita exhibited earlier in the year. In addition, she seemed to actively avoid her friends and was more interested in computer games and deskwork that would not require any interaction with her classmates. Although Mrs. Van Meter tried talking to Juanita and made a special point to include her in group activities, nothing seemed to help. She contacted the school counselor for assistance.

Teachers are the key to the success of any program; and, without the support of these educators, counselors will be considered as remote, disengaged individuals with only vague connections to school academic success. Consultation with teachers is vital for improving teacher instructional methods and student learning effectiveness. The counselor can offer a fresh perspective with different methods that may include such interventions as contracting, journaling, tutor assistance, or leadership responsibilities (Gibson et al., 1993).

Consultation with Administrators

Mr. Nori is the assistant principal at a large, inner-city middle school with a student enrollment of 2,000 students in grades 5 through 8. Lately he has been concerned with the student absentee rate. Students are missing many more days of school than in previous years, and this behavior is accompanied by an increase in tardiness. Mr. Nori has tried numerous techniques to encourage the students to attend school and be in their classrooms on time, but nothing has seemed to make an impact on the students' attendance. Since Mr. Nori is aware that the school counselors have developed a positive rapport with students and have a good understanding of the developmental concerns of the students, he decides to consult with the school counselors for direction.

Because counselors are often the first individuals to know about issues and concerns that are impacting the educational process of the school, they are valuable to administrators. Counselors can educate administrators on such issues as class grouping that would best meet the needs of students; students who would achieve in a different classroom environment; needs of teachers, students, and parents; child abuse issues; and policies and procedures. More important, the counselor has an obligation to educate the administrator as to the role, function, and educational background of the school counselor so that the counselor can be utilized in a role that best meets the needs of students.

Consultation with Parents

> Mrs. Patterson and her husband have decided to divorce after 10 years of marriage. The Pattersons have three children, all under the age of 9. Although they have both tried to talk with their children about the change in the family, the oldest daughter, Susan, seems to be having a difficult time with her parents' decision. She is not eating, having difficulty sleeping, and refuses to talk about her feelings with her parents. Mrs. Patterson decided it was time to contact the school counselor for advice on how to help her daughter.

Parents often contact the school counselor about developmental and/or situational concerns of their children. School counselors need to remember that the parent is the expert on his or her own child and that the information parents provide is a valuable tool to better understand the child. Parents may also desire a meeting in which a specific topic can be addressed such as adolescent depression, eating disorders, or relationship issues. Group sessions with parents who share similar concerns may be desirable so that accurate, current information may be shared. Additional information on working with parents and families is found in Chapter 11.

Consultation with Community Agencies

> Spencer, a sophomore in high school, went to see his school counselor, Mr. Devlin, regarding his choice of classes for the following year. In talking with Spencer, the counselor learned that he was interested in becoming a child psychologist because he had been seeing a psychologist, Dr. Hime, for the past 2 years. Spencer also revealed that the medication he was given often made him lethargic and he was unable to concentrate on his school work. Mr. Devlin asked Spencer if he could contact Dr. Hime so that they could work together in assisting him. Spencer agreed to this request; and, upon receiving a signed parental permission form, Mr. Devlin contacted Spencer's psychologist and together they worked out strategies to assist Spencer.

Too often there is a sense of mistrust between community agencies and school counselors that often stems from role confusion, policy, philosophical discrepancies, and styles of counseling (Gibson et al., 1993). Consultation with outside agencies may involve communication, referral strategies, and service coordination. Even with the knowledge of how school counselors can assist others through consultation, there is still some confusion as to the "how" of consulting.

THE CONSULTATION PROCESS

Consultation models vary according to the interaction between the consultant and the individual(s) seeking assistance from the consultant (Keys, Green, Lockhart, & Luongo, 2003). These models are classified as triadic-dependent, collaborative-dependent, and collaborative-interdependent.

The Triadic-Dependent Model

Using the triadic-dependent model, consultation is a voluntary, nonsupervisory relationship that is usually characterized as a triadic process. The consultant shares knowledge, skills, or methods with a consultee for the purpose of assisting a third party (e.g., student, teacher, parent) (Gibson et al., 1993). Or, in other words, consulting is a professional service in which the consultee gains a "skill's transfer" and enhances the third party's well-being and performance (Kirby, 1985; Zins, 1993). In this case, the consultant (counselor) diagnoses the problem and makes recommendations to the consultee (e.g., teacher, parent, administrator, etc.), who is responsible for implementing the consultant's plan for 3rd party change (Keys, Bemak, Carpenter, & King-Sears, 1998; Keys et al., 2003). For example, a teacher may consult with the counselor about the inattentive behavior of a student. The counselor, using this model, will provide the teacher with a number of strategies that may be implemented. The teacher is then responsible for utilizing the strategy with the student and conducting an evaluation.

The Collaborative-Dependent Model

In the collaborative-dependent model, a partnership is created between the consultant and the consultee. The consultee shares information and knowledge with the consultant, and a plan is mutually created. This relationship may assist a specific student, the consultee, or the system, with the goal of student, consultee, or system change (Keys et al., 1998). The major difference between this model and the triadic-dependent model is that in this model all individuals are responsible for the outcome of the plan (Keys et al., 2003). For example, suppose the building principal feels that the students are being excused from class to see the counselor too often. The administrator (consultee) and the counselor (consultant) may devise a plan in which students are able to meet with the counselor without missing valuable classroom time.

The Collaborative-Interdependent Model

The collaborative-interdependent model is used when problems are more complex and many individuals and systems such as families, community agencies, educators, administrators, and others are involved. This model integrates the expertise of all group members through partnering and sharing of information to enable a comprehensive plan to evolve. In this model, each person is interdependent upon each other for problem identification, intervention, and evaluation (Keys et al., 1998; Keys et al., 2003). The school counselor, serving as the consultant, uses interpersonal counseling skills such as active listening, paraphrasing, questioning, and summarizing so that the skills of all team members are utilized. For example, a student with special needs may require a variety of services that the school alone cannot provide. Community individuals that have funding, expertise, and skills provide a wide range of options to assist this student.

The primary intervention for all these models focuses on overt, observable behaviors rather than strategies focusing on nonobservable thoughts and feelings (Vacc & Loesch, 1994; Zin, 1993). The school counselor as consultant can be quite effective if

1. Goals are established collaboratively.
2. A log of activities is maintained.
3. Easy-to-use checklists are supplied for providing data.
4. Formative evaluation is used to determine ongoing progress.
5. Summative evaluation is provided to assess the end result.
6. A follow-up evaluation to determine that the continuance of the consultation is executed (Conoley & Conoley, 1992).

Initially, many consultees and third-party participants are apprehensive about the purpose of the consultation, the qualifications of the consultant, expectations of participation, and consequences of the consultation. The consultant who is honest and "puts his or her cards on the table" will help alleviate any fears or concerns by asking him or herself the following questions prior to the initial meeting:

1. What is the issue that brought me here?
2. What are the anticipated results?
3. How did the problem come about?
4. Who is part of the problem?
5. Is the problem an issue for the student/parent/teacher?

The third-party participants may also prepare for consultation by asking and responding to the following questions:

1. Who will be involved in the consultation?
2. What happens if I don't participate?
3. Why am I here?
4. How will this benefit me? (Conoley & Conoley, 1992; Kirby, 1985)

An example of a consultation process follows for a better understanding of how this procedure works.

EXAMPLE OF A CONSULTATION PROCESS

Suppose a local school board is concerned about the social/personal problems confronting students. The traditional crisis approach to dealing with these concerns has not been effective, and the local educators believe that a preventive approach would more fully assist and benefit students. The consultee (administrator) calls upon district school counselors to serve in the consultant role. The counselors decide to use a collaborative-interdependent approach to bring about change using the following steps: define the problem, brainstorm solutions, choose a solution, implement a strategy, and evaluate its effectiveness.

Define the Problem

Counselors know that a solution cannot be implemented unless teachers and other individuals share in the process and are part of the solution.

Step 1: Consultants ask the teachers to randomly vocalize the problems they see influencing students in their classes. As the teachers declare their own perceptions of the problems, the counselors write the concerns on index cards (one concern per card) while another individual tapes them to a wall. The teachers continue to state their perceptions until the list of concerns is exhausted.

Drug and alcohol use	School attendance	Disrespectful attitude

Step 2: Each participant is given three stickers; he or she is to place a sticker on each of the concerns that he or she feels are the most significant factors influencing students. After the stickers have been placed, the consultants arrange the concerns in order from the concern with the most "votes" to the concern with the fewest "votes."

School attendance ******	Disrespectful attitude****	Drug and alcohol use **

⋆ = Number of teachers selecting the concern

Step 3: The consultants dismantle all of the concerns that were previously posted and leave only the top three concerns posted on the wall. Each teacher is now given one sticker to place on the index card to identify what he or she feels is the number one concern among the three problems still remaining. The concern that receives the most "votes" is the concern that will be the focus of the intervention. Once the problem is identified, brainstorming is used to generate high-quality ideas.

Brainstorm Solutions

Step 1: The consultants randomly place the participants in small groups. Each group designates a person to serve as a recorder and a member to serve as a reporter. The group recorder writes down solutions provided by the group members to address the identified problem. This session is to have an identified time limit with the following rules:

1. Generate as many ideas as possible.
2. Do not criticize or judge ideas.
3. Generate creative solutions by thinking "out of the box."
4. Keep brainstorming focused on the problem at hand.

Step 2: After the designated time limit, the group reporter reads the small-group-generated solutions to the larger group. Following the group reports, each small group is to choose a solution based on all the ideas that were created.

Choose a Solution

The consultee is ultimately responsible for the implementation of the plan with minimal guidance from the consultants. Therefore, it is essential that the consultants ask the small groups to consider a solution that can be implemented with the resources available within the institution. The consultants will ask the small groups to consider a solution based upon the following criteria:

1. Does it focus on prevention?
2. Will it reach all students?
3. Does the solution support the school mission?
4. Is this solution feasible?
5. Is it cost-effective?
6. Has this solution been successful elsewhere?
7. What political institutional policies and factors need to be considered?

The small groups report their solution to the larger group at which time several strategies may be determined. At this point, success is a result of accomplishing one step at a time. Therefore, it is important that the counselors suggest that no more than two identified strategies be implemented.

Implement a Strategy

The consultants need to remind participants that collaborative relationships should be established and the resources in the school and community identified to facilitate success. In addition, careful thought is given to the implementation of a timeline. In other words, decisions are made as to who will do what, when they will do it, and how it will be implemented. The counselors distribute an implementation worksheet to the groups to complete. An example is shown in Table 14.2.

Evaluate Effectiveness

Evaluation provides the opportunity to review, revise, and determine progress in reaching expected results. Two types of evaluation are to be considered. *Formative evaluation* is assessing the process and determining whether or not the plan is going as anticipated. *Summative evaluation* looks at the end product and determines whether or not the anticipated goal was reached. Some of the questions that need to be considered include:

1. What data are needed to determine whether or not the goal(s) have been reached?

Table 14.2 Implementation Worksheet

Problem	Solution Activities	When Implemented	Who Responsible	Expected Results/Evaluation	Anticipated Cost
School attendance	Provide tokens for attendance and students with 95% attendance will receive a prize.	Each grading period	Homeroom Teacher	80% increase in attendance	$100.00 with donations from community businesses
Disrespectful attitude	Put up signs in school emphasizing respect.	Each week students will design signs	Counselor	65% decrease in discipline problems	$200.00 for supplies

2. What benchmarks (or dates) are needed to assess progress?
3. Who will be responsible for monitoring and reporting results?

Evaluative tools that may be considered include:

- Baseline data
- Portfolios
- Data from teachers and/or administrators
- Checklists
- Journals
- Observations
- Anecdotal reports
- Tests/questionnaires/worksheets
- Grades

The worksheet shown in Table 14.3 may be implemented.

CONSULTATION TOPICS IN THE SCHOOL

Topics for in-service sessions or workshops that coincide with the training and education of school counselors may include the following:

Instructional methods for assisting students with different learning styles

Managing aggressive behaviors

Anger management

Crisis intervention

AD/HD

Test-taking skills

Decision making

Table 14.3 Evaluation Worksheet

Objective	Strategy	Benchmark	Expected Outcome	Evaluation Method

Careers within subject areas
Character building
Parenting education
Depression and suicide
Eating disorders
Gangs and cults
Conflict mediation
Peer facilitation
Self-mutilation
Suicidal ideation

WHO MAKES A TEAM A SUCCSXX??

Who makxs a team a succxss? Xvxn though my typxwritxr is an old modxl, it works quitx wxll xxcxpt for onx kxy. I havx wishxd many timxs that it workxd pxrfxctly. It is trux that thxrx arx 41 othxr kxys that do function wxll xnough, but just onx not working makxs all thx diffxrxncx.

Somextimxs it sxxms to mx that our team is somxwhat likx my typxwritxr . . . not all of thx mxmbxrs arx working propxrly.

You may say to yoursxlf, "Wxll, I am only onx pxrson. I won't makx or brxak our team." But, it doxs makx a diffxrxncx bxcausx a team to bx xffxctivx nxxds activx participation of xvxry singlx pxrson.

So thx nxxt timx you think you arx only onx pxrson, and that your xfforts arx not nxxdxd, rxmxmbxr my old typxwritxr and say to yoursxlf, "I am a kxy pxrson in that group, and I am nxxdxd vxry much!!"

SUMMARY

Supervision entails various aspects of learning, experiencing, growing, and reflecting on how attitudes, skills, and behaviors fit with the profession. The multiple experiences provided during internship are designed so that the trainee can function as an effective member of the profession. And, as in any profession, the more experience gained, the greater the comfort and confidence.

The school counselor is trained in human growth and development, interpersonal relationships, group dynamics, and communication—knowledge and skills that promote effective consultation. In addition, with the limited time and resources confronting school counselors, consultation can shift the focus from a direct counseling approach to one in which skills and knowledge are transferred to others.

REFERENCES

Ametrano, I. M., & Stickel, S. A. (1999). Restructuring the on-campus counselor education laboratory: Contemporary professional issues. *Counselor Education and Supervision, 38,* 280–292.

Bernard, J. M., & Goodyear, R. K. (1992). *Fundamentals of clinical supervision.* Boston: Allyn & Bacon.

Borders, L. D., & Leddick, G. R. (1987). *Handbook of counseling supervision.* Alexandria, VA: Association for Counselor Education and Supervision.

Bradley, C., & Fiorini, J. (1999). Evaluation of counseling practicum: National study of programs accredited by CACREP. *Counselor Education and Supervision, 39,* 110–119.

Brown, D. (1993). Training consultants: A call to action. *Journal of Counseling and Development, 72,* 139–143.

CACREP. (2001). *Council for Accreditation of Counseling and Related Educational Programs.* Alexandria, VA: Author.

Campbell, C. A., & Dahir, C. A. (1997). *Sharing the vision: The national standards for school counseling programs.* American School Counselor Association, 801 N. Fairfax Street, Suite 310, Alexandria, VA 22314.

Card, C., & House, R. M. (1998). Counseling supervision: A reflective model. *Counselor Education and Supervision, 38,* 23–33.

Conoley, J. C., & Conoley, C. W. (1992). *School consultation: Practice and training* (2nd ed.). Boston: Allyn and Bacon.

Getz, H. G. (1999). Assessment of clinical supervisor competencies. *Journal of Counseling and Development, 77,* 491–497.

Gibson, R. L., Mitchell, M. H., & Basile, S. K. (1993). *Counseling in the elementary school: A comprehensive approach.* Needham Heights, MA: Allyn and Bacon.

Goldberg, A. (2000, June). *Counselors as supervisors: Learning the craft.* Paper presented at the American School Conference Association International Conference, June 26, 2000, Cherry Hill, New Jersey.

Hanna, M. A., & Smith, J. (1998). Using rubrics for documentation of clinical work supervision. *Counselor Education and Supervision, 37,* 269–278.

Jackson, D. N., & Hayes, D. (1993). Multicultural issues in consultation. *Journal of Counseling and Development, 72,* 144–147.

Kahn, B. B. (1999). Priorities and practices in field supervision of school counseling students. *Professional School Counseling, 3,* 128–136.

Keys, S. G., Bemak, F., Carpenter, S. L., & King-Sears, M. E. (1998). Collaborative consultant: A new role for counselors serving at-risk youths. *Journal of Counseling and Development, 76,* 123–133.

Keys, S. G., Green, A., Lockhart, E., & Luongo, P. F. (2003). Consultation and collaboration. In B. T. Erford (Ed.), *Transforming the school counseling profession* (pp. 171–190). Upper Saddle River, NJ: Merrill Prentice-Hall.

Kirby, J. (1985). *Consultation: Practice and practitioner.* Muncie, IN: Accelerated Development Inc.

Ladany, N., Ellis, M. V., & Friedlander, M. L. (1999). The supervisory working alliance, trainee self-efficacy, and satisfaction. *Journal of Counseling and Development, 77,* 447–455.

Myers, D. G. (1993). *Social psychology* (4th ed.). New York: McGraw-Hill.

Nelson, M. D., & Johnson, P. (1999). School counselors are supervisors: An integrated approach for supervising school counseling interns. *Counselor Education and Supervision, 39,* 89–99.

Neufeldt, S. (1999). *Supervision strategies for the first practicum* (2nd ed.). Alexandria, VA: American Counseling Association.

O'Byrne, K., & Rosenberg, J. I. (1998). The practice of supervision: A sociocultural perspective. *Counselor Education and Supervision, 38,* 34–42.

Palmer, P. (1998). *The course to teach.* San Francisco: Jossey-Bass.

Roberts, W. B., & Morotti, A. A., (2001). Site supervisors of professional school counselor interns: Suggested guidelines. *Professional School Counselor Journal, 4,* 208–215.

Schectman, Z., & Wirzberger, A. (1999). Needs of preferred style of supervision among Israeli school counselors at different stages of professional development. *Journal of Counseling and Development, 77,* 457–464.

Sink, C. (2002). In search of the profession's finest hour: A critique of four views of 21st century school counseling. *Professional School Counseling, 5,* 156–163.

Stoltenberg, C. D. (1993). Supervising consultants in training: An application of a model of supervision. *Journal of Counseling and Development, 72,* 131–137.

Travers, P. (2002). *The counselor's help desk.* Pacific Grove, CA: Brooks/Cole.

Tyron, G. S. (2002). *Counseling based on process research: Applying what we know.* Boston: Allyn and Bacon.

Vacc, N. A., & Loesch, L. C. (1994). *A professional orientation to counseling* (2nd ed.). Levittown, PA: Accelerated Development.

Zins, J. E. (1993). Enhancing consultee problem-solving skills in consultative interactions. *Journal of Counseling and Development, 72,* 185–190.

Appendix A

Ethical Standards for School Counselors

American School Counselor Association

PREAMBLE

The American School Counselor Association (ASCA) is a professional organization whose members have a unique and distinctive preparation, grounded in the behavioral sciences, with training in clinical skills adapted to the school setting. The school counselor assists in the growth and development of each individual and uses his or her highly specialized skills to protect the interests of the counselee within the structure of the school system. School counselors subscribe to the following basic tenets of the counseling process from which professional responsibilities are derived:

- Each person has the right to respect and dignity as a human being and to counseling services without prejudice as to person, character, belief, or practice regardless of age, color, disability, ethnic group, gender, race, religion, sexual orientation, marital status, or socioeconomic status.
- Each person has the right to self-direction and self-development.
- Each person has the right of choice and the responsibility for goals reached.
- Each person has the right to privacy and thereby the right to expect the counselor–counselee relationship to comply with all laws, policies, and ethical standards pertaining to confidentiality.

Revised June 25, 1998

In this document, ASCA specifies the principles of ethical behavior necessary to regulate and maintain the high standards of integrity, leadership, and professionalism among its members. The Ethical Standards for School Counselors were developed to clarify the nature of ethical responsibilities held in common by school counseling professionals. The purposes of this document are to:

- Serve as a guide for the ethical practices of all professional school counselors regardless of level, area, population served, or membership in this professional Association;
- Provide benchmarks for both self-appraisal and peer evaluations regarding counselor responsibilities to counselees, parents, colleagues and professional associates, schools, and communities, as well as to one's self and the counseling profession; and
- Inform those served by the school counselor of acceptable counselor practices and expected professional behavior.

A.1. Responsibilities to Students

The professional school counselor:

a. Has a primary obligation to the counselee who is to be treated with respect as a unique individual.

b. Is concerned with the educational, career, emotional, and behavioral needs and encourages the maximum development of each counselee.

c. Refrains from consciously encouraging the counselee's acceptance of values, lifestyles, plans, decisions, and beliefs that represent the counselor's personal orientation.

d. Is responsible for keeping informed of laws, regulations, and policies relating to counselees and strives to ensure that the rights of counselees are adequately provided for and protected.

A.2. Confidentiality

The professional school counselor:

a. Informs the counselee of the purposes, goals, techniques, and rules of procedure under which she/he may receive counseling at or before the time when the counseling relationship is entered. Disclosure notice includes confidentiality issues such as the possible necessity for consulting with other professionals, privileged communication, and legal or authoritative restraints. The meaning and limits of confidentiality are clearly defined to counselees through a written and shared disclosure statement.

b. Keeps information confidential unless disclosure is required to prevent clear and imminent danger to the counselee or others or when legal requirements demand that confidential information be revealed. Counselors will consult with other professionals when in doubt as to the validity of an exception.

c. Discloses information to an identified third party who, by her or his relationship with the counselee, is at a high risk of contracting a disease that is commonly known to be communicable and fatal. Prior to disclosure, the counselor will ascertain that the counselee has not already informed the third party about his or her disease and he/she is not intending to inform the third party in the immediate future.

d. Requests of the court that disclosure not be required when the release of confidential information without a counselee's permission may lead to potential harm to the counselee.

e. Protects the confidentiality of counselee's records and releases personal data only according to prescribed laws and school policies. Student information maintained in computers is treated with the same care as traditional student records.

f. Protects the confidentiality of information received in the counseling relationship as specified by federal and state laws, written policies, and applicable ethical standards. Such information is only to be revealed to others with the informed consent of the counselee, consistent with the counselor's ethical obligation. In a group setting, the counselor sets a high norm of confidentiality and stresses its importance, yet clearly states that confidentiality in group counseling cannot be guaranteed.

A.3. Counseling Plans

The professional school counselor: works jointly with the counselee in developing integrated and effective counseling plans, consistent with both the abilities and circumstances of the counselee and counselor. Such plans will be regularly reviewed to ensure continued viability and effectiveness, respecting the counselee's freedom of choice.

A.4. Dual Relationships

The professional school counselor: avoids dual relationships which might impair her or his objectivity and increase the risk of harm to the client (e.g., counseling one's family members, close friends, or associates). If a dual relationship is unavoidable, the counselor is responsible for taking action to eliminate or reduce the potential for harm. Such safeguards might include informed consent, consultation, supervision, and documentation.

A.5. Appropriate Referrals

The professional school counselor: makes referrals when necessary or appropriate to outside resources. Appropriate referral necessitates knowledge of available resources and making proper plans for transitions with minimal interruption of services. Counselees retain the right to discontinue the counseling relationship at any time.

A.6. Group Work

The professional school counselor: screens prospective group members and maintains an awareness of participants' needs and goals in relation to the goals of the group. The counselor takes reasonable precautions to protect members from physical and psychological harm resulting from interaction within the group.

A.7. Danger to Self or Others

The professional school counselor: informs appropriate authorities when the counselee's condition indicates a clear and imminent danger to the counselee or others. This is to be done after careful deliberation and, where possible, after consultation with other counseling professionals. The counselor informs the counselee of actions to be taken so as to minimize his or her confusion and to clarify counselee and counselor expectations.

A.8. Student Records

The professional school counselor: maintains and secures records necessary for rendering professional services to the counselee as required by laws, regulations, institutional procedures, and confidentiality guidelines.

A.9. Evaluation, Assessment, and Interpretation

The professional school counselor:

a. Adheres to all professional standards regarding selecting, administering, and interpreting assessment measures. The counselor recognizes that computer-based testing programs require specific training in administration, scoring, and interpretation which may differ from that required in more traditional assessments.

b. Provides explanations of the nature, purposes, and results of assessment/evaluation measures in language the counselee(s) can understand.

c. Does not misuse assessment results and interpretations and takes reasonable steps to prevent others from misusing the information.

d. Uses caution when utilizing assessment techniques, making evaluations, and interpreting the performance of populations not represented in the norm group on which an instrument is standardized.

A.10. Computer Technology

The professional school counselor:

a. Promotes the benefits of appropriate computer applications and clarifies the limitations of computer technology. The counselor ensures that: (1) computer applications are appropriate for the individual needs of the counselee; (2) the counselee understands how to use the application; and (3) follow-up counseling assistance is provided. Members of under represented groups are assured equal access to computer technologies and are assured the absence of discriminatory information and values in computer applications.

b. Counselors who communicate with counselees via internet should follow the NBCC Standards for WebCounseling.

A.11. Peer Helper Programs

The professional school counselor: has unique responsibilities when working with peer helper programs. The school counselor is responsible for the welfare of counselees participating in peer programs under her or his direction. School counselors who function in training and supervisory capacities are referred to the preparation and supervision standards of professional counselor associations.

B. RESPONSIBILITIES TO PARENTS

B.1. Parent Rights and Responsibilities

The professional school counselor:

a. Respects the inherent rights and responsibilities of parents for their children and endeavors to establish, as appropriate, a collaborative relationship with parents to facilitate the counselee's maximum development.

b. Adheres to laws and local guidelines when assisting parents experiencing family difficulties that interfere with the counselee's effectiveness and welfare.

c. Is sensitive to cultural and social diversity among families and recognizes that all parents, custodial and noncustodial, are vested with certain rights and responsibilities for the welfare of their children by virtue of their role and according to law.

B.2. Parents and Confidentiality

The professional school Counselor:

a. Informs parents of the counselor's role with emphasis on the confidential nature of the counseling relationship between the counselor and counselee.

b. Provides parents with accurate, comprehensive, and relevant information in an objective and caring manner, as is appropriate and consistent with ethical responsibilities to the counselee.

c. Makes reasonable efforts to honor the wishes of parents and guardians concerning information that he/she may share regarding the counselee.

C. RESPONSIBILITIES TO COLLEAGUES AND PROFESSIONAL ASSOCIATES

C.1. Professional Relationships

The professional school counselor:

a. Establishes and maintains professional relationships with faculty, staff, and administration to facilitate the provision of optimal counseling services. The relationship is based on the counselor's definition and description of the parameter and levels of his or her professional roles.

b. Treats colleagues with professional respect, courtesy, and fairness. The qualifications, views, and findings of colleagues are represented to accurately reflect the image of competent professionals.

c. Is aware of and optimally utilizes related professions and organizations to whom the counselee may be referred.

C.2. Sharing Information with Other Professionals

The professional school counselor:

a. Promotes awareness and adherence to appropriate guidelines regarding confidentiality; the distinction between public and private information; and staff consultation.

b. Provides professional personnel with accurate, objective, concise, and meaningful data necessary to adequately evaluate, counsel, and assist the counselee.

c. If a counselee is receiving services from another counselor or other mental health professional, the counselor, with client consent, will inform the other professional and develop clear agreements to avoid confusion and conflict for the counselee.

D. RESPONSIBILITIES TO THE SCHOOL AND COMMUNITY

D.1. Responsibilities to the School

The professional school counselor:

a. Supports and protects the educational program against any infringement not in the best interest of counselees.

b. Informs appropriate officials of conditions that may be potentially disruptive or damaging to the school's mission, personnel, and property while honoring the confidentiality between the counselee and counselor.

c. Delineates and promotes the counselor's role and function in meeting the needs of those served. The counselor will notify appropriate officials of conditions which may limit or curtail her or his effectiveness in providing programs and services.

d. Accepts employment only for positions for which he/she is qualified by education, training, supervised experience, state and national professional credentials, and appropriate professional experience. Counselors recommend that administrators hire only qualified and competent individuals for professional counseling positions.

e. Assists in developing: (1) curricular and environmental conditions appropriate for the school and community; (2) educational procedures and programs to meet the counselee's developmental needs; and (3) a systematic evaluation process for comprehensive school counseling programs, services, and personnel. The counselor is guided by the findings of the evaluation data in planning programs and services.

D.2. Responsibility to the Community

The professional school counselor: collaborates with agencies, organizations, and individuals in the school and community in the best interest of counselees and without regard to personal reward or remuneration.

E. RESPONSIBILITIES TO SELF

E.1. Professional Competence

The professional school counselor:

a. Functions within the boundaries of individual professional competence and accepts responsibility for the consequences of his or her actions.

b. Monitors personal functioning and effectiveness and does not participate in any activity which may lead to inadequate professional services or harm to a client.

c. Strives through personal initiative to maintain professional competence and to keep abreast of professional information. Professional and personal growth are ongoing throughout the counselor's career.

E.2. Multicultural Skills

The professional school counselor: understands the diverse cultural backgrounds of the counselees with whom he/she works. This includes, but is not limited to, learning how the school counselor's own cultural/ethnic/racial identity impacts her or his values and beliefs about the counseling process.

F. RESPONSIBILITIES TO THE PROFESSION

F.1. Professionalism

The professional school counselor:

a. Accepts the policies and processes for handling ethical violations as a result of maintaining membership in the American School Counselor Association.

b. Conducts herself/himself in such a manner as to advance individual ethical practice and the profession.

c. Conducts appropriate research and reports findings in a manner consistent with acceptable educational and psychological research practices. When using client data for research or for statistical or program planning purposes, the counselor ensures protection of the individual counselee's identity.

d. Adheres to ethical standards of the profession, other official policy statements pertaining to counseling, and relevant statutes established by federal, state, and local governments.

e. Clearly distinguishes between statements and actions made as a private individual and those made as a representative of the school counseling profession.

f. Does not use his or her professional position to recruit or gain clients, consultees for her or his private practice, seek and receive unjustified personal gains, unfair advantage, sexual favors, or unearned goods or services.

F.2. Contribution to the Profession

The professional school counselor:

a. Actively participates in local, state, and national associations which foster the development and improvement of school counseling.

b. Contributes to the development of the profession through sharing skills, ideas, and expertise with colleagues.

G. MAINTENANCE OF STANDARDS

Ethical behavior among professional school counselors, Association members and nonmembers, is expected at all times. When there exists serious doubt as to the ethical behavior of colleagues, or if counselors are forced to work in situations or abide by policies which do not reflect the standards as outlined in these Ethical Standards for School Counselors, the counselor is obligated to take appropriate action to rectify the condition. The following procedure may serve as a guide:

1. The counselor should consult confidentially with a professional colleague to discuss the nature of a complaint to see if she/he views the situation as an ethical violation.

2. When feasible, the counselor should directly approach the colleague whose behavior is in question to discuss the complaint and seek resolution.

3. If resolution is not forthcoming at the personal level, the counselor shall utilize the channels established within the school, school district, the state SCA, and ASCA Ethics Committee.

4. If the matter still remains unresolved, referral for review and appropriate action should be made to the Ethics Committees in the following sequence:
—state school counselor association
—American School Counselor Association

5. The ASCA Ethics Committee is responsible for educating—and consulting with—the membership regarding ethical standards. The Committee periodically reviews an recommends changes in code. The Committee will also receive and process questions to clarify the application of such standards. Questions must be submitted in writing to the ASCA Ethics Chair. Finally, the Committee will handle complaints of alleged violations of our ethical standards. Therefore, at the national level, complaints should be submitted in writing to the ASCA Ethics Committee, c/o the Executive Director, American School Counselor Association, 801 North Fairfax, Suite 310, Alexandria, VA 22314.

H. RESOURCES

School counselors are responsible for being aware of, and acting in accord with, standards and positions of the counseling profession as represented in official documents such as those listed below:

American Counseling Association. (1995). Code of ethics and standards of practice. Alexandria, VA. (5999 Stevenson Ave., Alexandria, VA 22034) 1 800 347 6647 www.counseling.org.

American School Counselor Association. (1997). The national standards for school counseling programs. Alexandria, VA. (801 North Fairfax Street, Suite 310, Alexandria, VA 22314) 1 800 306 4722 www.schoolcounselor. org.

American School Counselor Association. (1998). Position Statements. Alexandria, VA.

American School Counselor Association. (1998). Professional liability insurance program. (Brochure). Alexandria, VA.

Arrendondo, Toperek, Brown, Jones, Locke, Sanchez, and Stadler. (1996). Multicultural counseling competencies and standards. Journal of Multicultural Counseling and Development. Vol. 24, No. 1. See American Counseling Association.

Arthur, G. L. and Swanson, C. D. (1993). Confidentiality and privileged communication. (1993). See American Counseling Association.

Association for Specialists in Group Work. (1989). Ethical Guidelines for group counselors. (1989). Alexandria, VA. See American Counseling Association.

Corey, G., Corey, M. S. and Callanan. (1998). Issues and Ethics in the Helping Professions. Pacific Grove, CA: Brooks/Cole. (Brooks/Cole, 511 Forest Lodge Rd., Pacific Grove, CA 93950) www.thomson.com.

Crawford, R. (1994). Avoiding counselor malpractice. Alexandria, VA. See American Counseling Association.

Forrester-Miller, H. and Davis, T. E. (1996). A practitioner's guide to ethical decision making. Alexandria, VA. See American Counseling Association.

Herlihy, B. and Corey, G. (1996). ACA ethical standards casebook. Fifth ed. Alexandria, VA. See American Counseling Association.

Herlihy, B. and Corey, G. (1992). Dual relationships in counseling. Alexandria, VA. See American Counseling Association.

Huey, W. C. and Remley, T. P. (1988). Ethical and legal issues in school counseling. Alexandria, VA. See American School Counselor Association.

Joint Committee on Testing Practices. (1988). Code of fair testing practices in education. Washington, DC: American Psychological Association. (1200 17th Street, NW, Washington, DC 20036) 202 336 5500

Mitchell, R. W. (1991). Documentation in counseling records. Alexandria, VA. See American Counseling Association.

National Board for Certified Counselors. (1998). National board for certified counselors: code of ethics. Greensboro, NC. (3 Terrace Way, Suite D, Greensboro, NC 27403-3660) 336 547 0607 www.nbcc.org.

National Board for Certified Counselors. (1997). Standards for the ethical practice of webcounseling. Greensboro, NC.

National Peer Helpers Association. (1989). Code of ethics for peer helping professionals. Greenville, NC. PO Box 2684, Greenville, NC 27836. 919 522 3959. nphaorg@aol.com.

Salo, M. and Schumate, S. (1993). Counseling minor clients. Alexandria, VA. See American School Counselor Association.

Stevens-Smith, P. and Hughes, M. (1993). Legal issues in marriage and family counseling. Alexandria, VA. See American School Counselor Association.

Wheeler, N. and Bertram, B. (1994). Legal aspects of counseling: avoiding lawsuits and legal problems. (Videotape). Alexandria, VA. See American School Counselor Association.

Ethical Standards for School Counselors was adopted by the ASCA Delegate Assembly, March 19, 1984. The first revision was approved by the ASCA Delegate Assembly, March 27, 1992. The second revision was approved by the ASCA Governing Board on March 30, 1998 and adopted on June 25, 1998.

Index